MUSIC AND TRANSCENDENCE

For Daniel

Music and Transcendence

Edited by
FÉRDIA J. STONE-DAVIS
University of Göttingen, Germany

ASHGATE

Published by
Ashgate Publishing Limited
Wey Court East
Union Road
Farnham
Surrey, GU9 7PT
England

Ashgate Publishing Company
110 Cherry Street
Suite 3-1
Burlington, VT 05401-3818
USA

www.ashgate.com

British Library Cataloguing in Publication Data
A catalogue record for this book is available from the British Library

The Library of Congress has cataloged the printed edition as follows:
Music and transcendence / edited by Férdia J. Stone-Davis.
        pages ; cm
    Includes bibliographical references and index.
    ISBN 978-1-4724-1595-0 (hardcover) – ISBN 978-1-4724-1596-7 (ebook) –
    ISBN 978-1-4724-1597-4 (epub) 1. Music and philosophy. 2. Music–Religious
aspects. 3. Transcendence (Philosophy) I. Stone-Davis, Férdia J., editor.

    ML3921.M87 2015
    781.1–dc23

2014045784

ISBN 9781472415950 (hbk)
ISBN 9781472415967 (ebk – PDF)
ISBN 9781472415974 (ebk – ePUB)

Printed in the United Kingdom by Henry Ling Limited, at the Dorset Press, Dorchester, DT1 1HD

Contents

PART II: MUSIC AND IMMANENT TRANSCENDENCE

List of Music Examples

Notes on Contributors

Jeremy S. Begbie is the Thomas A. Langford Research Professor in Theology at Duke Divinity School, North Carolina. He teaches systematic theology and specialises in the interface between theology and the arts. His particular research interest is the interplay between music and theology. He is also senior member of Wolfson College, Cambridge and an affiliated lecturer in the faculties of Divinity and Music at the University of Cambridge. He is author of a number of books, including *Theology, Music and Time* (Cambridge University Press, 2000), *Resounding Truth: Christian Wisdom in the World of Music* (Baker/SPCK, 2007) and *Music, Modernity, and God* (Oxford University Press, 2013). He is a professionally trained and active musician. He has taught widely in the UK and North America and has delivered multimedia performance-lectures across the world, from Israel to Australia and Hong Kong.

Bruce Ellis Benson is Professor of Philosophy at Wheaton College, Illinois. He is the author or editor of 11 books, including *The Improvisation of Musical Dialogue: A Phenomenology of Music* (Cambridge University Press, 2003) and *Liturgy as a Way of Life: Embodying the Arts in Christian Worship* (Baker/SPCK, 2013).

Andrew Bowie is Professor of Philosophy and German at Royal Holloway, University of London. He is concerned with core issues in modern philosophy, particularly those explored by the German tradition from Kant to the present. He has written extensively about music and literature as well as philosophy. His many books include *Music, Philosophy, and Modernity* (Cambridge University Press, 2009) and most recently *Adorno and the Ends of Philosophy* (Polity, 2013).

John Habron is Senior Lecturer at Coventry University and Senior Research Fellow in the MASARA (Musical Arts in Southern Africa: Resources and Applications) research group (North-West University, South Africa). A transdisciplinary researcher, his publications focus on music and wellbeing, music education and spirituality in music. He convenes the International Conference of Dalcroze Studies (Coventry 2013, Vienna 2015) and in 2015–2016 is guest editor of the journal *Approaches: Music Therapy & Special Music Education*. He is regularly invited to teach abroad, most recently in Austria, Colombia, Ireland, Poland and South Africa. As a music therapist he works mainly with people with dementia.

Jonas Lundblad pursues a dual career in research and musical performance, primarily as an organ recitalist. He has previously carried out research in theological aesthetics, specifically the aesthetics of Friedrich Schleiermacher, at Lund University, Sweden. He is currently engaged in an artistic study of the interplay between musical time, subjectivity and performance practice in Olivier Messiaen's organ works (Swedish Research Council/Uppsala University). He is a Visiting Research Fellow at Glasgow University and recently spent two years as a visiting researcher at the Humboldt University and the Berlin-Brandenburg Academy of Sciences and Humanities.

Thomas J. Mulherin is an Adjunct Lecturer in Philosophy at Georgetown University, Washington DC. His research interests include post-Kantian German philosophy (particularly Romanticism and the Frankfurt School), the philosophy of music and Continental social and political thought. Currently, he is working on Adorno's philosophy of musical performance and the relationship between early nineteenth-century German thought about music and Romantic *Naturphilosophie*.

Christopher Norris is Distinguished Research Professor in Philosophy at the University of Cardiff and has taught and lectured at many universities around the world. He has written more than 30 books on aspects of philosophy and literary theory, among them *Platonism, Music and the Listener's Share* (Continuum, 2006), *Badiou's* Being and Event: *A Reader's Guide* (Continuum, 2009), *Re-Thinking the Cogito: Naturalism, Reason and the Venture of Thought* (Continuum, 2010) and *Derrida, Badiou and the Formal Imperative* (Continuum, 2012). His latest book is *Philosophy Outside-In: A Critique of Academic Reason* (Continuum, 2013). A volume of verse-essays, *The Cardinal's Dog and Other Poems*, was published earlier this year.

Christopher Page is Professor of Medieval Music and Literature at the University of Cambridge and a fellow of the British Academy, the Society of Antiquaries and Sidney Sussex College, Cambridge. His most recent book is *The Christian West and Its Singers: The First Thousand Years* (Yale University Press, 2010). His next, *The Guitar in Tudor England: A Social and Musical History* has just gone to press. He is currently working on a major project, *The Guitar in Romantic England*, due for delivery in 2016.

Russell Re Manning is Senior Lecturer in Philosophy and Ethics at Bath Spa University and Visiting Fellow at St Edmund's College, Cambridge. From 2011 to 2014 he held the Lord Gifford Fellowship at the University of Aberdeen. His work centres on questions in the philosophy of religion concerning the interrelations of religion and culture. Recent publications include *The Oxford Handbook of Natural Theology* (Oxford University Press, 2013), *Science and Religion in the Twenty-First Century* (SCM, 2013) and *The Cambridge Companion to Paul Tillich* (Cambridge University Press, 2011).

Oane Reitsma has taught theological aesthetics at VU University, Amsterdam. The public defence of his doctoral dissertation, 'Music as a Religious Sound Phenomenon', was held in 2014. He is a Fellow of the Amsterdam Centre for Cultural and Religious Diversity (ACCORD) at VU University, Amsterdam, and an ordained minister of the Protestant Church in the Netherlands.

Sukanya Sarbadhikary is an anthropologist of southern Asia. She is interested in questions of affect and sanctity as interacting modes of southern Asian cosmological representations. She has worked among a Hindu sect in eastern India, theorizing various practices involving the mind, body and senses, to think about how religion inscribes itself in and continues through corporeal capacities. She completed her doctoral dissertation in social anthropology at the University of Cambridge and is now Assistant Professor in Sociology at Presidency University, Kolkata. She also has a longstanding interest in southern Asian musical traditions, especially religious musical practices, and is herself a trained Indian classical singer. Her book, *The Place of Devotion: Siting and Experiencing Divinity in Bengal-Vaishnavism* will be published in 2015 (University of California Press).

Roger Scruton is currently a Senior Research Fellow of Blackfriars Hall, Oxford and Senior Fellow at the Ethics and Public Policy Center, Washington DC. He was for a while employed by Birkbeck College at the University of London, but since 1990 has been self-employed. He is author of over 30 books, including works of criticism, political theory and aesthetics, as well as novels and short stories. His writings include *The Aesthetics of Music* (Oxford University Press, 1997), *Death-Devoted Heart: Sex and the Sacred in Wagner's* Tristan und Isolde (Oxford University Press, 2003) and *Understanding Music* (Continuum, 2009). He is a fellow of the Royal Society of Literature, the European Academy of Arts and Sciences and the British Academy. He lives with his wife and two children in Malmesbury, England.

Diane V. Silverthorne is an art historian with research interests in fin-de-siècle Vienna, as well as music, modernism and the visual arts from the 1850s onwards. She holds a post at Central St Martin's, University of the Arts. Her doctoral thesis examined the aesthetics of Alfred Roller, a founder of the Vienna Secession and later stage design director at the Vienna Court Opera during the Mahler years. She has contributed to several anthologies, most recently, *The Routledge Companion to Music and Visual Culture* (2013) on Wagner's *Gesamtkunstwerk*.

Férdia J. Stone-Davis is an interdisciplinary academic working at the intersection of music, philosophy and theology as well as a musician. Publications include a monograph *Musical Beauty: Negotiating the Boundary between Subject and Object* (Cascade, Wipf & Stock, 2011) and a co-edited volume titled *The Soundtrack of Conflict: The Role of Music in Radio Broadcasting in Wartime and* *in Conflict Situations* (Georg Olms Verlag, 2013). She is currently working as a research assistant in the Musicology Department of the University of Göttingen.

Joshua A. Waggener is an Assistant Professor of Music and Christian Worship at Southeastern Baptist Theological Seminary in Wake Forest, North Carolina, where he teaches courses in music history, theology and worship studies. He also directs music ensembles and co-ordinates degree programmes in music and worship leadership. He holds undergraduate and graduate degrees in music and church music from Trinity University (Texas), the University of Georgia, and Southeastern. His doctorate is from the University of Durham, where he studied music, theology and aesthetics, with a thesis titled 'Mendelssohn and the Musical Sublime'.

Acknowledgements

I would like to acknowledge the support lent to the 'Music and Transcendence' conference by Anglia Ruskin University, particularly Alison Ainley and Paul Jackson, and by the British Society of Aesthetics. I would also like to express gratitude to Jason Dixon, whose help was indispensable to its organisation and running, and to Heidi Bishop for accepting this project. I am thankful to contributing authors, to Charissa Granger and Simon Waters for their time and support in the process of preparing the volume, to Andrew Bowie and Roger Scruton, and particularly to Jeremy Begbie for his endless encouragement. Finally, I would like to thank Daniel Healy, Veronica Stone and Ralph Davis for making so many things possible.

Introduction

Férdia J. Stone-Davis

To transcend is to go beyond. Understood as such, the term has a wide application to a variety of phenomena and across a range of disciplines. However, within the domains of theology and philosophy (and discussions between the two) the idea of transcendence has acquired particular relevance. Here, two understandings tend to prevail: transcendence is either conceived in vertical terms, situated in relation to an 'absolute' that lies *beyond* the material, or it is unpacked in horizontal terms, remaining situated *within* the 'immanent', within the material realm and its evanescence.[1]

The conceptual separation of these two understandings has been located in a historical shift that sees a move away from a worldview that is anchored metaphysically and is vertically oriented (one often termed pre-modern) towards one that is grounded in and arises from the world and is horizontally oriented (one frequently associated with the modern).[2] Within the vertical, or absolute, worldview, the cosmos and everything contained within it is given and ordered by an ultimate, external and otherworldly source: knowledge is bound up with the discovery of a certain contiguity between this absolute and its immanent manifestation. Hence the importance of the *quadrivium* (arithmetic, music, geometry and astronomy) within the classical education system, and Anicius

---

[1] Mark Johnson conceptualises the vertical and horizontal forms of transcendence thus: vertical transcendence is the 'alleged capacity to rise above and shed our finite human form and to "plug into the infinite"'. Horizontal transcendence 'recognises the inescapability of human finitude and is compatible with the embodiment of meaning, mind, and personal identity. From this human perspective, transcendence consists in our happy ability to sometimes "go beyond" our present situation in transformative acts that change both our world and ourselves' (*The Meaning of the Body: Aesthetics of Human Understanding* (Chicago, 2007), p. 281).

[2] Charles Taylor sees this move from vertical or transcendent world structures to those that are horizontal and closed as constitutive of modernity ('Closed World Structures', in Mark A. Wrathall (ed.), *Religion after Metaphysics* (Cambridge, 2003), pp. 47–68). This is worked out more substantially in Charles Taylor, *A Secular Age* (Cambridge, Mass. and London, 2007). For an overview of some of the features contributing to a disappearance of the 'transcendentally oriented cosmic vision', see Férdia J. Stone-Davis, *Musical Beauty: Negotiating the Boundary between Subject and Object* (Eugene, Oreg., 2011), pp. 179–82 (p. 181).

Boethius's claim that arithmetic is the most significant amongst its disciplines due to its reliance upon number:[3]

> From the beginning, all things whatever which have been created may be seen by the nature of things to be formed by reason of numbers. Number was the principal exemplar in the mind of the creator. From it were derived the multiplicity of the four elements, from it were derived the changes of the seasons, from it the movement of the stars and the turning of the heavens.[4]

Within the horizontal, or immanent, worldview, the cosmic whole and its ultimate foundation no longer stand in view, and the locus of knowledge shifts to the subject. Immanuel Kant is indicative of such a move to the immanent realm, since within his account (theoretical) reason cannot attain absolute and unconditional knowledge but encounters boundaries beyond which it cannot proceed without contradiction. In its legitimate use it leads to knowledge but only when circumscribed by the constraint of 'possible experience'. When used to transcend experience, reason leads into a realm of illusion. Kant therefore proposes a 'Copernican revolution' for philosophy:

> Previously it has been assumed that *all of our cognition must conform itself to objects*; but under this assumption all attempts to decide something about objects *a priori* through concepts, and by which our cognition would be extended, have come to nothing. Let us now, therefore, test whether we do not make better progress on the problems of metaphysics by assuming that *objects must conform themselves to our cognition.*[5]

In the process of this historical and conceptual shift from absolute to immanent transcendence, a set of dualisms is put in place, opposing universal and particular, eternal and temporal, immaterial and material. Moreover, the two planes of

---

[3]   Boethius was concerned to transmit ancient Greek knowledge to the Latin-speaking world. He is said to have coined the term *quadrivium* and whilst there were two extant orderings of its disciplines (one by Boethius, the other by Martianus Capella), it was the Boethian one that was studied in schools and universities throughout the Middle Ages (see Stone-Davis, *Musical Beauty*, pp. 2–3).

[4]   Anicius Boethius, *De Institutione Musica* [Fundamentals of Music], 1.2, trans. C.M. Bower, ed. C.V. Palisca (New Haven, Conn., 1989).

[5]   Immanuel Kant, *Critique of Pure Reason*, Preface to the Second Edition, b xvi, in *Prolegomena to Any Future Metaphysics that will be able to Come Forward as Science with Selections from the Critique of Pure Reason*, trans. and ed. Gary Hatfield, revd edn (Cambridge, 2004): italics added. Kant continues: 'Matters stand here just as they did for the first thoughts of Copernicus, who, when things did not go well for explaining the celestial motions if he assumed that the entire host of stars rotates about the observer, sought to find whether things might not go better if he had the observer rotate, and by contrast left the stars at rest' (ibid., xvii).

transcendence are very often disconnected, such that either one plane is reduced to the other,[6] or transcendence is altogether negated.[7] Such an oppositional logic is not the only option however. It is in recognition of this that Calvin Schrag posits the term 'transversality' in relation to religion. According to Schrag, transversality acknowledges the formative role of the vertical and horizontal conceptions of transcendence whilst pressing forward non-dualistically, splitting the difference between 'the metaphysical postulates of vertically elevated transcendence and horizontally demarcated immanence'.[8] How so? Alterity, a sense of 'otherness', is integral to the idea of transcendence, since in going beyond I am brought into contact with that which is 'other'. This otherness is conceived differently in conceptions of absolute and immanent transcendence. In the former, according to Schrag, alterity is 'vertically super-imposed, hierarchically over-arching, hegemonic and heteronomous'.[9] This framework is reflected in Boethius's writings. This contrasts with the latter, where alterity is fleeting, resulting from 'a random juxtaposition and serial succession on a horizontal plane of pure immanence'.[10] Thus, for Deleuze, whom Schrag draws attention to, immanence 'is not in something, *to* something; it does not depend on an object or belong to a subject'.[11] Rather, absolute immanence

---

[6]   As an example of the reduction of horizontal to vertical transcendence, Schrag directs attention to Emmanuel Levinas, who posits the 'preeminence of transcendence over immanence' (Calvin O. Schrag, 'Transcendence and Transversality', in John D. Caputo and Michael J. Scanlon (eds), *Transcendence and Beyond: A Postmodern Enquiry* (Bloomington and Indianapolis, 2007), pp. 204–18 (p. 208)). This understanding is supported by Caputo and Scanlon who cast Levinas's work as an articulation of 'hypertranscendence', that is, 'an even more transcendent transcendence' (John D. Caputo and Michael J. Scanlon, 'Introduction: Do We Need to Transcend Transcendence?', in Caputo and Scanlon (eds), *Transcendence and Beyond*, pp. 1–14 (p. 2)). Illustrating the converse, Schrag cites Gilles Deleuze's espousal of 'pure immanence' ('Transcendence and Transversality', p. 207). Caputo and Scanlon select Gianni Vattimo as indicative of the move towards 'post-transcendence', where transcendence is accomplished 'within the horizon of the world' ('Introduction', p. 4). More recently, Mark Johnston provides noteworthy attempts to re-conceptualise issues formerly associated with 'absolute' transcendence within a naturalised (that is, 'immanent') frame (see *Saving God: Religion after Idolatry* (Princeton, NJ, 2009); *Surviving Death* (Princeton, NJ, 2010)).

[7]   Extreme forms of the immanent tendency are tangible within some circles of contemporary thought, especially in recent forms of rational fundamentalism, including 'scientism' (see Richard Dawkins, *The God Delusion* (London, 2006); for a response to Dawkins, see Alister McGrath, *The Dawkins Delusion? Atheist Fundamentalism and the Denial of the Divine* (London, 2007)). For an outline of scientism in relation to the non-existence of 'self', as well as a refutation of this position, see Mary Midgley, *Are You an Illusion?* (Durham, 2014).

[8]   Schrag, 'Transcendence and Transversality', p. 211.

[9]   Ibid.

[10]   Ibid.

[11]   Gilles Deleuze, *Pure Immanence: Essays on A Life*, trans. A. Boyman (New York, 2001), p. 26. Deleuze continues: 'immanence is not related to Some Thing as a unity

is 'a life', a series of 'singularities' and 'events' that unfolds, is never complete and is constantly becoming other.[12]

Transversality is neither entirely absolute nor wholly immanent. It is 'a convergence without coincidence, a congruence without identity, an interaction without assimilation'.[13] Giving an example of how transcendence conceived transversally might work in the sphere of religion, Schrag turns to the command to love one's neighbour as oneself.[14] Such love, he maintains, exhibits a transversal dynamic: it exhibits an alterity that is 'always other and prior to our discourse and action',[15] since it is 'truly a love that exceeds and surpasses, transcendence in a quite robust sense, an *other* that is truly other than all the others within the circulation of distribution and exchange that stimulates the economies of the mundane culture-spheres'.[16] Within this context, and conceived as transversal, love interrupts the vertical-horizontal axis: its invocation allows elements to interconnect on the horizontal plane in relation to a source that lies beyond and issues a call to them.

If the vertical and horizontal senses of transcendence have developed particularly in relation to theology and philosophy, why a collection on music and transcendence? Moreover, how is a transversally conceived transcendence to be situated in relation to music? Two answers present themselves immediately. First, music is enmeshed in the historical and conceptual shift outlined above and the conceptions of absolute and immanent transcendence, both in terms of its practice and the ways in which it is theorised. Thus, in broad terms, the spatial translation from absolute to immanent marks a shift away from understanding music as part of the fabric of the cosmos towards understanding it in relation to the material realm conceived immanently. It also involves a re-conception of the connection between music, self-understanding and self-expression. Second, although music has become entangled with the dualisms accompanying the dichotomisation of the absolute and the immanent, it pursues a course that is transversal, since it unsettles any simple divisions. The music event[17] relies upon

---

superior to all things or to a Subject as an act that brings about a synthesis of things' (ibid., p. 27; quoted in Schrag, 'Transcendence and Transversality', p. 207).

[12] 'A life has quite different features than those Locke associated with the self – consciousness, memory, and personal identity. It unfolds according to another logic: a logic of impersonal individuation rather than personal individualisation, of singularities rather than particularities. It can never be completely specified. It is always indefinite – *a life*' (John Rajchman, 'Introduction', in Deleuze, *Pure Immanence*, pp. 7–23 (p. 8)).

[13] Schrag, 'Transcendence and Transversality', p. 217.

[14] Ibid., p. 216.

[15] Ibid., p. 217.

[16] Ibid., pp. 216–17.

[17] Elsewhere, I elaborate my preference for speaking of the music event, since it recognises that music is not a singular entity but a temporally performed practice that is manifold in occurrence and in each instantiation performs its own logic, its own way of contemplating (see Férdia J. Stone-Davis, 'Music and Liminality: Becoming Sensitized',

the destabilisation of inside and outside, involving the commingling of sound and the human body. Not only is the aural threshold easily trespassed, so is that of the entire body, which internalises external sounds:

> The human experience of sound involves, in addition to the sympathetic vibration of the ear-drums, the sympathetic vibration of the resonators of the body. Sound, shaped and resonating with the properties of the internal and external configurations, textures and movements of the objects of the external world, can thus be felt in addition to being heard.[18]

The music event is also simultaneously universal and particular (in some sense eternal and temporal), since it occurs in time but has its own time. Indeed, appearing at different points in time, musical iterations can be homologous and yet distinct. Moreover, the music event is immaterial and material: it is produced through physical means and yet when heard as music is not simply an event in physical space. It is a movement within a space of its own.

This transversal dynamic is further exemplified within the music event by virtue of the dynamic of call and response which it exhibits. Although performed, music is not reducible to the physical actions that give rise to it. In fact, music issues its own call to and exerts its own demand on those who experience it, since the sounds produced exhibit a resistance to the gestures that give rise to them and this resistance shapes subsequent actions. Thus, although 'lengths of channels of air and pieces of string are altered through the impression of the human body', the interaction is not one-way, since 'the sound yielded in turn has an impact on the player, who responds to it'.[19] It is on this basis that the musician's practice session functions and that musical contours emerge. This call and response extends further: music always eschews singular ascriptions of meaning, remaining at all times polysemic. It resists unidirectional cause-and-effect models of communication and instead evokes a variety of responses. In this way, music is not dissimilar from love. Music issues a call to which responses are made, forming a point of orientation and offering interconnection on the horizontal plane whilst remaining resistant to appropriation (the requisition of music is never wholly successful).[20] Music remains beyond the circulation of distribution and exchange through the strength of its alterity.

---

in Birgit Abels (ed.), *Embracing Restlessness: Cultural Musicology* (Hildesheim, forthcoming)).

[18]   John Shepherd and Peter Wicke, *Music and Cultural Theory* (Cambridge, 1997), p. 127.

[19]   Stone-Davis, *Musical Beauty*, p. 162.

[20]   For specific examples of how this so, see M.J. Grant and Férdia J. Stone-Davis (eds), *The Soundtrack of Conflict: The Role of Radio Broadcasting in Wartime and Conflict Situations* (Hildesheim, 2013).

In sum, music is not only bound up with the notions of absolute and immanent transcendence as they have developed both historically and conceptually; but, by virtue of its mode of being, which enacts a transversal dynamic and remains poised between the two, is able to elucidate the limitations of such a development and its accompanying dualisms. This makes sense in (at least) two ways: (1) if transcendence refers to going beyond, then it is unreasonable to delimit a priori how, in what way and to what extent it does so; (2) acknowledging the limitations of the division between absolute and immanent transcendence and the advantages of a transversal conception (which remains open to the two) facilitates discussions about the notion of transcendence across disciplines. As Schrag notes in relation to rationality: 'one can give reasons for the truth of propositions, right actions, and good art without having the criteria of judgement in each of the spheres becoming coincident with one to the other'.[21] Thus, one can embrace the fact, as Albrecht Wellmer suggests elsewhere, that different 'language games' correspond to 'different perspectives from which we "look at" empirical reality'.[22]

Drawing upon a one-day international interdisciplinary conference held at the Cambridge Union with the support of Anglia Ruskin University and the British Society of Aesthetics, this collection offers musicological, theological and philosophical explorations of music and transcendence. The organisation of the volume enacts in some measure the issues central to the discussion above and the importance of music. The contributions are gathered into two sections: 'Music and Absolute Transcendence' and 'Music and Immanent Transcendence'. Each section begins with contributions that take specific musical instances as their focus (pieces, practices, figures and events) and moves towards contributions that have theoretical issues as their main concern. As will become clear, the notion of transcendence is built into the structure of music through its refusal of oppositions. It is here, through its transversal dynamic, that meaning accrues. Thus, although contributions are situated primarily in relation to either the notion of absolute or the notion of immanent transcendence, they very often gesture outwards to, and very often integrate aspects of, the other.

Music and Absolute Transcendence

Beginning the section 'Music and Absolute Transcendence', Christopher Page elucidates how the development and practice of Gregorian chant, which arises within the pre-modern worldview, is bound up with absolute transcendence. Most markedly, chant interlaces with events that mark the punctuation of the natural by the supernatural, acting transformatively in the process. Importantly,

---

[21]   Calvin O. Schrag, *God as Otherwise than Being: Towards a Semantics of the Gift* (Evanston, Ill., 2002), p. 41.

[22]   Albrecht Wellmer, 'On Spirit as Part of Nature', *Constellations*, 16/2 (2009): 213–26 (p. 217).

however, such events are embedded within and facilitated by more earthly modes of transcendence: music's capacity to include and exclude, to consolidate and separate, draws together the bodies and minds of those of holy orders who sing the chants. Through the evolution of liturgical repertory, music and text create a sense of Christian identity that traverses Europe but not in a way that eradicates difference. On the contrary, local identities are reinforced and rendered meaningful through the difference of individual chants from the 'norm' provided by repertory. Another earthly and wholly practical development is notation. Although it, in a certain sense, renders the intangibility of music tangible by capturing and fixing it in visible form, it does so in order that clergy might increase the hours they dedicate to pious works, thereby transcending the desires of the body. Thus, the universality granted by earthly, immanent developments in the dissemination of Frankish-Roman chant allows a vertical, absolute extension: heaven and earth become intimately associated such that the contingent is held within the embrace of eternity.

The intermingling of the absolute and the immanent finds different articulation in Sukanya Sarbadhikary's contribution, which focuses on accounts of participants and musicians involved in *kirtan*. Exploring its phenomenology, Sarbadhikary shows how this devotional practice of the Bengal Vaishnavas prompts a 'sonic sensuality' that at once manifests the erotic interplay between the Hindu deity consort Radha-Krishna whilst enveloping participants within the transcendental place in which it occurs. The bodies of participants as well as the bodies of instruments are integral to this process: the repetitive and heightening chant that participants aspirate invoke the erotics of Krishna and Radha, as do the acoustics of the instruments, rendering their bodies and sounds sacred, and drawing them into close proximity with the bodies of the musicians who play them. The desire for corporeal oneness is invoked at every level of *kirtan*, entwining those involved with the pastimes of Radha-Krishna.

Exploring the traces that remain of a cosmic perspective of music within a modern purview, John Habron considers the thought and compositional practice of Ferruccio Busoni and the importance of the 'realm of music', which stands beyond time and space, framing earthly instances of music. Here, dualities are held in tension such that past and present are contained within an eternal flux, and all manner of melodies and tonalities co-exist. These provide the material for music composition and performance, and Habron shows how Busoni attempts not only to explore the implications of the other-worldly character of music within his compositional practice but also strives to retain something of this even whilst bounding it within particular instances.

Bruce Ellis Benson shows how transcendence, conceived in absolute terms, manifests in conceptions of artistic practice, demonstrating how the notion of divine *creatio ex nihilo* and the concomitant notions of absolute power and freedom which ensure God's otherness, are mirrored in conceptions of the artist that emphasise genius. The artistic genius is innovative, working inexplicably and producing results that are exemplary in character. Benson makes a case for considering both divine and artistic creation as improvisatory, structured by a 'call' that always precedes the 'response' that follows. The response is never a solitary one but emerges from and on behalf of others, so that notions of quotation and originality, old and new, and even you and me, unravel.

If Habron's and Benson's contributions show how a top-down way of thinking about transcendence finds articulation in understandings of music, Russell Re Manning and Roger Scruton are more bottom-up, thinking through how that which is absolute might be gestured towards by musical experience. Russell Re Manning makes a case for a natural theology of music, where music points beyond itself to a transcendent (and divine) reality. Here, the transcendent can be understood apart from either any preceding sense of divine revelation or any commitment to an established religious tradition. Through the notion of iconic distance, Re Manning suggests that music opens onto transcendence and sustains its depth, balanced between the tangible and the intangible, revealing the presence of transcendence without worked-out knowledge of it.

Roger Scruton asks whether it is possible to reach beyond to that which transcends the empirical world and, arguing that there are different ways of knowing, suggests that knowledge of the transcendent is not unrealisable. Rather, it is built into human experience, most notably interpersonal encounters, wherein I seek out the 'I' in you. This overreaching, where I am brought to the brink of the empirical world, lies at the core of attentive listening. Here, I am directed towards, and by, the acousmatic space of music and the virtual causality it exhibits, moved by an intentionality that is beyond my own.

Attending to the intertwining of absolute and immanent conceptions of transcendence, Jonas Lundblad elucidates the basis upon which music and religion stand in close proximity in the thought of Friedrich Schleiermacher. For Schleiermacher, both art and religion are mediations of 'feeling' or 'immediacy'. His aesthetically inclined conception of human transcendence attempts to circumvent propositional language's distinction between subject and object and thereby modernity's tendency towards a purposive and objectifying stance in relation to external reality. The medium of music, as Lundblad demonstrates, is paradigmatic within Schleiermacher's vision.

Jeremy Begbie draws 'Music and Absolute Transcendence' to a close and in doing so pushes beyond the points made by the other contributions, situating them theologically. Aware that theological conceptions of transcendence are all too easily dismissed and that philosophical and theological accounts often proceed according to frameworks grounded in a priori notions of human limits, he asks for a closer examination of particular conceptions of transcendence within theological traditions. Such examinations, he suggests, will challenge the idea that transcendence is something that simply stands at the edge of human capacities. They will also question the idea that in relation to music and language one must endorse an either/or approach. Furthermore, such examinations will lead us to consider how music presents a foretaste of what the world is to become, rather than drawing us out of this world into one that lies beyond.

Music and Immanent Transcendence

The section 'Music and Immanent Transcendence' starts with Joshua Waggener's positioning of Rudolf Otto's notion of the 'holy' as the 'non-rational core of religion' in relation to C.P.E. Bach's *Heilig*. Otto suggests that certain sublime pieces of music give articulation to the *mysterium tremendum*. Since Bach's *Heilig* was praised in the eighteenth century as sublime, Waggener uses it to examine to what extent it simulates an encounter with transcendence, using the elements comprising the *mysterium tremendum fascinans et augustum* as the structuring principle of analysis.

In my contribution to the volume, I explore the ways in which transcendence is built into the structure of the music event: music is a border (or liminal) practice that relies upon a process that entails going beyond since it is always 'in between'. Detailing the sensory, processual and relational thresholds that music invokes, I suggest that, in a process analogous to autobiography, music provides a significant means of situating the subject, enabling her to assemble meaning and inhabit both real and virtual (imaginative) places. The last movement of Haydn's String Quartet in E-flat major is used to elucidate this process.

Taking a different tack, one that explores the literal concretion of the musical artist as genius, Diane Silverthorne immerses us in the artistic world of Vienna and in the shift towards veneration of the composer as God. With Beethoven revered there as a genius and his music hailed as sublime, Silverthorne leads us through the philosophical, musical and artistic dynamics that shaped the staging of the 'Klinger: Beethoven Exhibition'. More than this, she guides us through the exhibition itself which, inspired by the principle that all art should aspire to the condition of music, manoeuvres the exhibition visitor ritualistically through passages that lead to and prepare them for an encounter with Klinger's *Beethoven* statue.

Thomas Mulherin re-examines the assumption that E.T.A. Hoffmann's writings advocate absolute music as metaphysical, revealing a realm that transcends this world. Focusing on 'Beethoven's Instrumentalmusik' and *Kreisleriana*, Mulherin maintains that the object of musical revelation is more immanent than absolute, since, through musical form, it represents nature rather than heaven. Such a solution, he suggests, challenges those who would claim that absolute music is devoid of meaning, on the one hand; and disrupts a narrative of aesthetic development that traces a simple historical movement from art as representational to art as expressive, on the other.

Oane Reitsma takes instrumental music as his point of focus, asking on what basis it might be understood as 'religious'. Reitsma argues that musical form instigates 'play' in Gadamerian terms and that it is in this that the performer and listener participate. Within this process, individual horizons fuse with the music encountered, although the music always remains somewhat resistant, unfamiliar and unassimilated. It is on the basis of this dynamic that a particular piece of music can be said to be religious: when musical form fuses in a particular way with the horizon of an interpreter such that religious ascriptions are assigned, a 'transcendent player' enters the scene.

Christopher Norris explicitly considers how transcendence works on an immanent level. He argues that an adequate ontology of music must account for the fact that musical works transcend themselves in their iteration within different times and contexts. In doing so, Norris presses towards an account of the potential for personal, political and societal transformation that such works permit. Thus, arguing that in order for any kind of ontology of musical works to have explanatory force, limit cases need to be taken account of, Norris reflects on political song and reconsiders the notion of the 'classic'. Political song calls into question assumptions that often shadow, if not shape, philosophical ontologies and challenges the idea of classic as that which is timeless, transcendent, ahistorical, apolitical and disinterested. Using the thought of Badiou to provide momentum and taking political song as the litmus test, Norris makes a case for the classic as that which renews its inspirational force over a range of historical, geographical and socio-political situations.

Concluding the section 'Music and Immanent Transcendence', Andrew Bowie prefers not to offer philosophical arguments for the use of transcendence in relation to music, since doing so overlooks the fact that it is because music is non-conceptual that it is philosophically significant. Bowie argues for the importance of understanding music as a sense-making practice. In doing so, he makes a case for understanding transcendence immanently: located within the bounds of human existence, music enables a means of understanding freedom, since it permits moments of liberation and transformation in relation to the constraints of human finitude.

As the contributions to the volume demonstrate, transcendence is integral to every aspect of music: it enables its production, is fundamental to the experience of it and is evident in responses to and reflections upon it. In an important way, music arises from and feeds the human desire to go beyond. It is thus that it acts transformatively and becomes a powerful means of locating oneself within the world and so making sense of it.

PART I
Music and Absolute Transcendence

Chapter 1

Music and the Beyond in the Later Middle Ages

Christopher Page

In a great many pages, and with almost as many transcendental events to report, the Frankish historian and hagiographer Gregory of Tours (d. 594) rarely offers anything to suggest that the chant of Mass or Office might provoke a vision, a miraculous cure or a flood of divine inspiration. Although he accepts that the supernatural constantly breaks through the surface of life, especially the life of monks, his sense that chanting might be some form of conjuration or that human singers share a repertoire of vocal praise in words and music with their angelic counterparts seems intermittent at best. At no point in Gregory's writing, for example, does any pious man or woman see and hear a saint or angel singing a text and associated melody with the kind of stabilised identity or fixed place in the liturgy that might encourage Gregory to give the incipit of the text and identify the feast(s) where the chant was used.

By the later Middle Ages, however, the situation was rather different. Many texts from the twelfth century onwards contain detailed accounts of events in which the performance of a chant from the liturgy precipitates a supernatural happening. One of the earliest is reported to have taken place soon after 900, when a female recluse named Wiborada, dwelling near the abbey of St Gall, had a vision (and audition) of the abbey's patron, St Gall himself, singing the Gregorian Introit *Ne timeas Zacharia* for the Nativity of John the Baptist 'with a company of radiant souls'.[1] The question of why medieval writing from the tenth century onwards contains so many stories of this kind, often involving specific chants that the author is careful to cite by incipit, while earlier narratives, like those of Gregory of Tours, contain so few, has rarely been broached. In raising that question here, I do not wish to overdraw the contrast: some of the chants associated with miraculous events in the later Middle Ages, such as the *Te deum*, were very ancient, so whatever powers they possessed in the thirteenth century, for example, cannot have been so very new. Yet there is something to be explained, nonetheless, and it will not be enough to remember what is easily forgotten, namely that a large proportion of literate men and women in the later medieval west spent much of their lives standing shoulder to shoulder,

---

[1] *Ekkehard I: Vita Sanctae Wiboradae*, trans. and ed. Walter Berschin (St Gallen, 1983), pp. 56, 58.

engaged in what we would now call ensemble singing. That was also true in the early Middle Ages when far fewer stories of this kind were generated. Nor can we maintain that we are asking a question about some entity we might call 'medieval music' with an internal history. Once medieval singers assumed the various forms of life they chose for themselves, they were neither musicians, as we might immediately understand the term, nor an audience. This does not have to mean that their singing was always self-effacing. There was ample scope in the liturgy for a soloist to display a fine voice, and some believed there was a great deal too much; even then, however, plainsong was not exactly music in any immediately familiar sense. The singers heard, but did not exactly listen; they sang but did not exactly perform.

And yet the explanation for this marked increase in the number of stories where a chant is reported to have produced a transcendent experience probably does lie, in large measure, with the history of medieval music, or rather with music and text together as they evolved in one particular and eventually trans-European liturgical repertory: Gregorian chant. It is now generally agreed that Gregorian (or better 'Frankish-Roman') chant arose between about 750 and 825 in monastic and cathedral communities located in the political core of the Frankish kingdom, approximately between the Seine and the Rhine. This is the territory that is marked out, with considerable precision, by two of the earliest centres for the development of the music, Rouen and Aachen. Gregorian plainsong seems to have emerged during a protracted attempt to reform the liturgy of the Frankish Church on the model of Roman custom, a process that certainly did involve the importation of the Roman liturgical calendar and a large amount of textual material for the Mass Propers of the entire liturgical year, adapted in some respects to suit Frankish usages and customs. The Carolingian kings and emperors did much to sponsor this liturgical reform in a process that began with the first of their line, Pippin (d. 768), and gathered strength under his much more famous son, Charlemagne.[2]

When Frankish-Roman chant begins to appear in consolidated and decipherable notations, the melodies prove to be astonishingly stable from one source to another, even when the books in question were compiled many hundreds of miles apart and show no genetic link. These chants were indeed sacred melodies: each one was a sequence of pitches, perhaps with durations assigned to them, deemed fitter for the ritual purpose in hand than anything

---

[2]   David Hiley offers a superb introduction and guide (*Western Plainchant: A Handbook* (Oxford, 1993)). There is a large specialist literature on Frankish-Roman chant (see Kenneth Levy, *Gregorian Chant and the Carolingians* (Princeton, NJ, 1998); James McKinnon, *The Advent Project: The Later Seventh-Century Creation of the Roman Mass Proper* (Berkeley, 2000); Leo Treitler, *With Voice and Pen: Coming to Know Medieval Song and How It was Made* (Oxford, 2003)). For the social and political context, see Christopher Page, *The Christian West and Its Singers: The First Thousand Years* (New Haven, Conn., 2010), pp. 281–328.

likely to be achieved by making major adjustments in performance or by extemporising something new. They resemble finds of coins, discovered in many different regions but showing a remarkable consistency of weight and composition. Sustaining the metaphor, we might say many of them suggest a series of interrelated and regulated mints at work.

Like much else given the stamp of Charlemagne's royal and eventually imperial authority, Gregorian chant spread wide, which invites us to ponder music and transcendence in a rather different sense to anything we have encountered up to now. As applied to an experience, the term 'transcendence' is commonly taken to mean a potentially transformative contact with something that cannot be reduced to nature, often the divine. Yet I would like to consider a terrestrial, indeed political, meaning of the term in which a body of shared music may be said to transcend narrow political or ethnic allegiances. Music has an extraordinary power to do this: to consolidate human groups in relation to others deemed 'primitive' and perhaps threatening because their music is different. An example from the later Middle Ages will serve to make the point.[3] There are Flemish paintings of the fifteenth century that show the Virgin sitting in a chair placed upon a fine Turkish carpet. Such things were clearly admired, but what of Turkish music? In the 1480s, a Fleming named Johannes Tinctoris heard Turkish captives in Naples playing the long-necked lute, or *saz*, that is still played in Ankara today: he reacted sharply, believing that the music expressed only the barbarity of the players who made it. Tinctoris was a trained musician whose ears were saturated with the idioms of Gregorian chant and with the great compositions of Franco-Flemish masters such as Dufay, Ockeghem and Busnois.[4] As he listened to the Turks, he assumed the role for which many years of training had prepared him: he appointed himself the representative of a Latin-Christian sound-world whose musical landscape had suddenly experienced a sharp intrusion.

By the 1200s, Gregorian chant did indeed transcend the cellular jurisdictions of kingdom, bishopric, principality and county in much of Latin Europe to create a soundscape. From Cadiz in Western Spain to Esztergom in Hungary, from Trondheim in Norway to the verge of the kingdom of Granada, monks, nuns, clergy, canons and friars by 1300 were gathering in churches, several times a day, to sing plainsong, with its historical core of Frankish-Roman chant or

---

[3]   For a Persian treatise of the tenth century AD which records that 'one tribe may find airs and melodies to their taste which others do not appreciate or take pleasure in, as witness the singing of the Turks, the Arabs and the Armenians', see Werner Bachmann, *The Origins of Bowing and the Development of Bowed Instruments up to the Thirteenth Century*, trans. N. Deane (Oxford, 1969), pp. 18, 42; see also Georgina Born and David Hesmondhalgh (eds), *Western Music and Its Others: Difference, Representation and Appropriation in Music* (Berkeley, 2000).

[4]   Anthony Baines, 'Fifteenth-Century Instruments in Tinctoris's *De Inventione et Usu Musicae*', *Galpin Society Journal*, 3 (1950): 19–26 (p. 23).

relatively new chants such as the *Salve Regina*. The singers breathed as one and resumed, after each pause, as one, for that is how plainsong works: it helped the singers transcend the varied and disorganised breathing that marks any gathering of individuals, with as yet scattered minds. Illuminated initials in Psalters, from the twelfth century onwards, show singers standing close to one other, often maintaining a light physical contact as if to ensure that the circuit of energy flowing between them remains unbroken.[5] As the community worked its way through the liturgical calendar of their house, familiar items of chant came and went with the lengthening and shortening of days, and with the arrival of seasonal fruits on the common table.

The internationalism (as we might call it) of this chant made the localism of other plainsongs, notably those in honour of local saints, all the more conspicuous, entrenched and (in local terms) meaningful. What is more, regional or even national differences in the manner of singing had become a subject of pointed and sometimes intemperate comment by the thirteenth century. But the idea of a common repertory throughout the Latin church existed and helped to establish a comprehensive allegiance in a place that was increasingly called 'the Latin world', or *Latinitas*, after 1100. This was a new development, for to authors of late antiquity the term *latinitas* had meant the Latin language and the resources of vocabulary and grammar in Latin that variously allowed, impeded or prohibited exact translations to be made of scriptures and commentaries written in Greek. The word carries a different but related sense, however, when Lanfranc of Bec (d. 1089) refers to the fame of a particular churchman and declares that 'all *Latinitas* knows this'. *Latinitas* is now a community and one partly defined by its own repertoire of chant.[6] When, in the next generation, St Malachy (d. 1148) first studied the core of Latin chant for the Mass and Office, his contemporary biographer judged that he was learning to sing 'according to the manner of the entire world', which meant singing 'after the usage of the Holy Roman Church'. Malachy was moving away from the localism (and 'primitivism') of his Irish background or so his biographer (none other than St Bernard of Clairvaux) plainly believed.

By the time of Bernard, Gregorian plainsongs could be used to fix the day when something occurred or was planned to take place. The chants at issue are almost invariably Introit antiphons, the chants that begin the service of the Mass. One of the earliest examples shows St Anselm referring to his consecration as archbishop of Canterbury (1093) 'on the Sunday when the Introit *Populus Syon* is sung'. After 1100, however, it becomes increasingly common for chroniclers and others to place an event 'on the Sunday of *Laetare Jerusalem*'

---

⁵ For examples, see Christopher Page, 'An English Motet of the 14th Century in Performance: Two Contemporary Images', *Early Music*, 25 (1997): 7–32.

⁶ Lanfranc of Bec, *De corpore et sanguine Domini adversus Berengarium Turonensem liber*, Patrologiae cursus completes: Series Latina 150, ed. J.P. Migne (Paris, 1844–45), col. 410.

(the Fourth Sunday in Lent) or in relation to other Introits that include *Oculi mei* (Third Sunday in Lent), *Dum sanctificatus* (Pentecost Sunday), *Esto mihi* (Sixth Sunday after Pentecost) and *Dicit dominus: Ego cogito* (Thirty-Third Sunday after Pentecost). In 1131, the Introit *Laetare Jerusalem* identifies an appointed day in a letter of Innocent II, showing that this method to define the day of some past or future event was already so universally understood that it could be used in a document issued by the patriarch of the Latin West. The repertory of liturgical singers had by now joined the movement of celestial bodies as a cycle that defined the passage of time in a yearly cycle.[7]

The sense of Christian universalism that the possession of such music could induce, with contingent events on earth seeming to replay the mystery of the incarnation and passion of Christ, related in texts whose forms of expression acknowledged no frontier of either time or place, emerges clearly from the work of chroniclers entrusted to relate the major events in the life of a pious magnate or churchman. In 1202, Abbot William of Eskill in Zeeland died on the eve of Easter Sunday, and one of his disciples traced his last hours through the liturgical services in which the saint barely had the strength to engage. On the Thursday, William tried to perform the *Mandatum* ceremony but was too weak to wash the brothers' feet. Led to his chamber, he eventually asked for his bed to be carried into the choir so that he could take part in the Easter Day liturgy. At Matins, the choir had just begun the third Responsory, *Dum transisset sabbatum*, when a sign was given that Abbot William was now at the point of death. He began to cross over into the next life as the community traversed the midnight of the Sabbath and passed into the next day. Dawn broke, and after singing the Responsory *Ut venientes ungerent Jesum*, describing the anointing of Christ's body, the Prior and some of the brothers left the choir to anoint William with holy oil. William was then dressed in penitential clothes and laid on a bed of cinders. He died soon afterward, rising to a new life on the Day of the Resurrection as the choir tearfully but triumphantly sang the appointed chant to end the service before the beginning of Lauds, *Te deum laudamus*. William passed the last years of his life in one of the most remote abbeys of Latin Christendom, yet, by the time of his death in 1202, there were many hundreds of churches and monasteries where this account would be intelligible, in its fullest and most moving spiritual depth, because the Office antiphoners and ordinals in those houses prescribed essentially the same sequence of chants for these same hours. The compiler perceives the meaning of what happened, and indeed the facts of what happened, in terms of the appointed readings and chants. His account transcends the distinction between events in the life of Christ foretold by the prophets, occurring now and always in the Easter Mass, and the life of William in the sharply contingent and temporal context of a remote Scandinavian bishopric.[8]

---

[7]   Page, *The Christian West*, p. 514.

[8]   Martin C. Gertz (ed.), *Vitae Sanctorum Danorum*, vol. 2 (Copenhagen, 1910), pp. 287–386.

The dissemination of a common repertoire of Gregorian chant, in an authoritative form, was immeasurably strengthened by important developments in musical notation, during the eleventh and twelfth centuries, which were distinctive to Western Europe. With the emergence of practical notations in the ninth century (to judge by what survives), the slow process of creating visual analogues of vocal sound began, detaching plainsong from particular modes of existence sustained by the kinds of collegiality that kept individuals together for long periods, as in a monastery, college of priests or canons. In such a context, the question of what might make musical notation useful to any particular individual has no simple answer, for it touched upon different ways of living some form of common life and balancing its demands. A singer's need for notation, if he had one, might vary considerably according to the office he held, the books it was his business to consult, the general scrupulosity of the church in which he served, the time that accomplished singers could spare to train him and much else besides. Any form of musical notation therefore implicitly set out a scheme for using the gift of time to better advantage and profit of the spirit.

It has long been recognised that the crucial invention in this domain was made by the Italian monk Guido, often called Guido of Arezzo (d. *c*.1060), whose writings have almost invariably been studied as a musician's work. But that approach imposes some unexpected limitations and has even made some seminal aspects of Guido's writing invisible. Among the five authentic works of Guido, two of his musical treatises describe a notational system that he emphatically presents as his own new solution to an old problem: to find a means of reducing a melody to a written record that is so complete and accurate that a singer can use it to perform an unknown chant at sight without the aid of a teacher. The lines and spaces of Guido's systems, and of all subsequent staves in mainstream practice down to the present, correspond to a musical scale whose degrees are assigned a letter of the alphabet, residually present in the various clefs that are still in use but much more actively present in many forms of Guido's method. His point of departure was therefore an alphabetic method of recording pitch. Guido accordingly placed a rack of letters on the left-hand side of the page, where writing began, so that each letter needed only to be written once and was now in force, prolonged across the page in its own 'rank' or *ordo*. The next step was to mark these ranks to the eye with a line that could be traced in ink but did not have to be, for it might only be ruled in dry point (with results that do not yield well to photography). The great innovation of the system is that both the lines and the spaces between them mark a rank. This is the ancestor of the five-line stave that is still in use.

In the *Epistola ad Michahelem*, a letter to his brother Michael, Guido says that his system will help novices to learn their plainsong more quickly, contracting a lifetime's work into just two years. This is the Guido one expects to meet from nearly a thousand years of the reception of his works. Yet Guido is not content to say only that his new method will allow a lifetime of study to be accomplished in 24 months, although that is already saying a great deal; he also maintains that monks and clergy will now have more time for 'works of piety': prayer, recitation of psalms, denial of the body's desire for food, sleep and sexual gratification by fasting, vigils and other duties that he calls *opera pietatis*, the works of devotion. Referring to the nocturnal vigils that represent one of the more ascetic devotions he has in mind, Guido envisages that monks and clergy will be able to keep them *cum puritate*, 'with purity'.[9]

The purity of monks, and especially of clergy, meaning freedom from the contagion of money or sexual contact, among other things, was a matter of intense concern in the eleventh-century west. The clergy were required to transcend the grossness of the body that desired food, sleep and coitus. There is a wealth of material at hand in sermons, monastic rules and works of theology to interpret what Guido means by expecting monks and clergy to attend their vigils *cum puritate* now that they will be able to complete their training in plainsong so much more quickly. His new notation will give them more time to enhance and deepen the quality of their spiritual life; they will have the means, if they are prepared to make the effort, to be cleansed from any temptation to simony and have more time to pray for freedom from the troubling dreams and phantasmata that sully the body in the hours of nocturnal prayer and have effects that are worse still in sleep. Guido, long remembered by his patrons as an ascetic, has restored to monks and clergy the time they need to live Christian lives to a high standard of observance and rectitude.

The sense of a repertory shared throughout *Latinitas*, and which could be securely recorded in notated service books, profoundly modified transactions between heaven and earth. It was no longer any surprise to a monk, canon or nun if a saint or an angelic being visited the earth singing exactly the same words and music they had sung themselves that day. That is one reason, perhaps the principal one, why St Gall may sing the Gregorian Introit *Ne timeas Zacharia* for the Feast of the Nativity of John the Baptist or a company of radiant souls the *Salve Regina* in a way that heavenly beings could not do so readily, or could not do at all, in the sixth-century of Gregory of Tours. Many other such tales are preserved in collections where they appear as documents of the Church Militant, perhaps alluding to a specific place or to the church of a particular order but otherwise imprecise.

The evidence gradually becomes abundant, beginning about 925–50 and mounting thereafter. A contemporary of Wiborada, the chronicler Thietmar of Merseburg (d. 1018), reports a dream in which he saw two boys coming out of the old treasury at Magdeburg singing the Responsory *Martinus Abrahe sinu*.[10]

---

[9] Guido of Arezzo, *Regule Rithmice, Prologus in Antiphonarium and Epistola ad Michahelem: A Critical Text and Translation*, trans. and ed. Dolores Pesce, Institute of Mediaeval Music Musicological Studies 73 (Ottawa, 1999), pp. 410–11.

[10] Thietmar of Merseburg, *Die Chronik des Bischofs Thietmar von Merseburg und ihre Korveier Überarbeitung*, ed. Robert Holtzmann, Monumenta Germaniae historica: Scriptores rerum Germanicarum, NS 9 (Berlin, 1955), p. 9.

Considerably more spectacular was the vision granted to Gerard of Sauve-Majeure (d. 1095) as he lay prostrate near the door of his abbey church alone in prayer. Gerard saw Christ with angels and archangels enter the monastery to prepare for the celebration of Mass. As Christ approached the altar, the question was duly asked whether everyone required for the service were present. Christ himself replied that one person was missing: the individual who was occupied in prayer by the door. Gerard was brought forward and placed in the choir, whereupon the heavenly company began to sing the Introit *Gaudeamus omnes in Domino.*[11]

The Marian emphasis in much of this material is clear, and the Cistercians, whose monastic churches were dedicated to the Virgin, generated many such stories. The following example is characteristic and concerns the antiphon with which the white monks appear to have had an especially close connection, the *Salve Regina.* While a great storm rages with thunder and lightening, the members of a Cistercian community hasten to their conventual church and begin to sing the *Salve Regina*; when they reach the words 'therefore, our advocate, turn those merciful eyes of yours towards us' there is a massive clap of thunder and all the glass in the church shatters. Terrified, the monks kneel and sing the words that come next: 'and show us, in this exile, Jesus the blessed fruit of thy womb'. Now the text of the chant becomes a conjuration: the cross hanging between the choir of the monks and the choir of the lay brothers turns, of its own accord, to face the monastic choir as the monks sing the words 'turn those eyes towards us'. The image of Christ crucified comes to life as they sing *Jesum ... ostende*, 'show ... Jesus'. Then the storm abates.[12]

Other conjurations were considerably less benign. Behind the service books of the medieval church, with their bright staves ruled in red and often meticulous square notation, stood a vast tribe of spirits, revenants and apparitions: some of them radiant, but some terrifying and diabolical, covered with the fur and filth of farmyard beasts. There also stood the spectres of hunger and disease. The cult of saints and relics in the Middle Ages was to a large extent driven by sickness, by the malformation of limbs through malnutrition and inbreeding, blindness caused by infection and by many kinds of chronic pain. When monks and clergy compiled their accounts of transcendent events at the shrines in their custody or wrote the lives of their local saints, they often reported how twisted limbs were straightened, misted eyes made clear and malodorous sores healed. Some of these accounts leave no doubt that it was music and text together that precipitated the moment where divine power became manifest to all. Examples are legion. Soon after 1095 and the preaching of the First Crusade at Clermont,

---

[11]   Gerard of Sauve-Majeure, in *Acta Sanctorum*, ed. J. Bolland et al. (Brussels and Antwerp, 1643–1940), *Aprilis* I, 418 (Vita I: Gerard standing at the door), 425 (Vita II: Gerard prostrated).

[12]   Christopher Page, *The Owl and the Nightingale: Musical Life and Ideas in France 1100–1300* (London, 1989), pp. 168–9.

a crippled woman from Picardy took the cross with her son and made her way to Venice. In the abbey of St Nicholas of the Lido she was cured of her malady as the monks sang the processional antiphon *O Christi pietas* from the liturgy of the patron saint. Those standing by 'were astonished to hear her bones crack, as if they would shatter, and her sinews stretch, as if they would break. ... Afterwards she felt nothing and woke as if from a sweet sleep'.[13] This is plainsong as conjuration, exorcism and miraculous cure.

---

[13] 'Historia de translatione sanctorum magni Nicolai terra marique miraculis gloriosi, ejusdem avunculi, alterius Nicolai, Theodorique, martyris pretiosi de civitate Mirea in monasterium S. Nicolai de Littore Venetiarum', in *Recueil des Historiens des Croisades: Historiens Occidentaux*, vol. 5 (Paris, 1866), p. 290.

Chapter 2

Hearing the Transcendental Place: Sound, Spirituality and Sensuality in the Musical Practices of an Indian Devotional Order

Sukanya Sarbadhikary

Sound, Place and Emotion

In this chapter, I analyse the sensory experiences felt during the performance of *kirtan*, an Indian devotional musical practice which involves the repetitive chanting of the names of the Hindu deity Krishna and his consort Radha. Worshippers of Radha-Krishna are known as Vaishnavas, and they constitute one of the largest Hindu sects.[1] My research is based on 15 months of intensive fieldwork among the Vaishnavas of Bengal.[2] Chanting is believed by Bengal Vaishnavas to manifest the transcendental place of the deities' erotic sport in the very site of musical utterance. In other words, the chants are underpinned theologically such that they are speech-acts or performative utterances which 'body forth' and unveil the transcendental-erotic place through the re-sounding of the names. The instruments used in *kirtan* manifest the erotic place within the corporeal interior of the musically insightful devotee.

The sound theology of *kirtan* borrows from Indic philosophical assertions about the indistinguishability of the phonological and the divine, of the name and named. As the names of the deities are uttered, the deities make themselves and their presence in the transcendental place, Vrindavan, apparent to the singers at the site of sonic utterance.[3] I argue, however, that this unveiling also follows from innate phenomenological relations between sound experiences and place experiences.

While it is relatively easy to appreciate that places have their own sounds, it is not immediately obvious how sound in turn intrinsically emplaces selves. Western philosophical reflections on sound minutely demonstrate how 'locality',

---

[1] 'Radha-Krishna' is the composite name most used by the Vaishnavas of Bengal.

[2] The Vaishnavism that developed in Bengal is practised all over India and even internationally.

[3] The term 'singer' incorporates many different aspects which are reflected throughout the chapter: 'devotee-singer', 'listener-singer', 'hearer-singer', 'lover-singer'.

or placeness, has its seat in the 'nature of sound'.[4] Most theorizing about sound experiences tries to situate the sources, objects and/or directionality of sound.[5] In other words, they try to place sound. Robert Pasnau says that 'we should insist on putting sound back where it belongs'.[6] The purpose of these studies is to locate an undeniable presence through the auditory sense, its capacity to evoke a 'nowness', a sense of being-in-place. This is most easily understood through the fact that sound can have a common source and recipient – it is uttered by us and returns to us.[7] Thus we can hear ourselves speaking, singing or whispering, as the case may be.[8] This sonic enveloping gives us the rounded sense of being emplaced as both sounding subjects (sources) and objects (recipients). In the Vaishnava context this translates as the listeners', or the choral collective's, intuited experience of feeling the presence of (and being emplaced in) Vrindavan, through the concentrated, passionate musical utterance of the names of Krishna and his eternal lover Radha.

That sound experiences also have affective dimensions in general and erotic possibilities in particular is hinted at in studies that have shown, for instance, that hearing is the most insistent sense, invading our interiors even while we are asleep.[9] Because of its total penetrative effect and inward potential, sound is characterised as the most passionate sense.[10] Indeed, there is a Vaishnava proverb: 'In chanting itself will eros be found.' Vrindavan, devotees assert, is the affective spatial concentrate of the sublime erotics of the divine couple. This chapter will demonstrate that the phenomenology of the *kirtan* 'acoustemology',[11] through which musical subjects apprehend the cosmic sensual place, is itself

---

[4]   Brian O'Shaughnessy, 'The Location of Sound', *Mind*, NS 66/264 (1957): 471–90 (p. 483).

[5]   See Thomas Clifton and Alfred Pike, 'A Phenomenological Analysis of Musical Experience and Other Related Essays', *Journal of Musical Theory*, 14/2 (1970): 237–46; Claude Schryer, 'Sound Ecology', *Leonardo*, 25/2 (1992): 219–20 (p. 219); Steven Connor, 'Edison's Teeth: Touching Hearing', in Veit Erlmann (ed.), *Hearing Cultures: Essays on Sound, Listening and Modernity* (Oxford and New York, 2004), pp. 153–72.

[6]   Robert Pasnau, 'What is Sound', *Philosophical Quarterly*, 49/196 (1999): 309–24 (p. 324).

[7]   See Joseph Margolis, 'Nothing Can Be Heard But Sound', *Analysis*, 20/4 (1960): 82–7 (p. 82).

[8]   Ibid.

[9]   See Steven Feld and Donald Brenneis, 'Doing Anthropology in Sound', *American Ethnologist*, 31/4 (2004): 461–74 (p. 468).

[10] See Paul Rodaway, *Sensuous Geographies: Body, Sense and Place* (London and New York, 1994), p. 95.

[11] See, Steven Feld, 'Waterfalls of Song: An Acoustemology of Place Resounding in Bosavi, Papua New Guinea', in Steven Feld and Keith H. Basso (eds), *Senses of Place* (Santa Fe, N.Mex., 1997), pp. 91–136 (p. 91); Feld and Brenneis, 'Doing Anthropology in Sound', p. 462.

effectuated by an intrinsic 'aural eros',[12] a fundamental overlap between musical ecstasy and heightened sexuality.

Based on an ethnographic philosophy foregrounding the nuances of 'participant-hearing', participants' and musicians' accounts of their experiences of a hearing which mediates intense emotion and devotion, and auto-ethnographic introspection, I demonstrate three ways in which the transcendental place is intuited through this particular genre of devotional music. First, the repeated chanting and escalating rhythm contribute to an auditory sensuous envelope that impacts corporeally and transports the listener-singer to the place of the deities' erotic pastimes. Second, the material acoustics of the *kirtan* instruments recreate the sonics of the divine embrace. Third, body-theological practices integrate iterative chants into the breathing interior of the individual musician's corporeal space, such that the interiorised sensory capacities are also believed to echo the aural aesthetics of Vrindavan.

The relationship between music and transcendence in this chapter, therefore, is addressed through the lens of an intrinsic sonic sensuality. Here, the moment of the erotic-musical experience in this world is also the moment of transcendence. Theological assertions about *kirtan* music manifesting the transcendental erotic place to devotee-singers can also be deduced from philosophical systems of thought about relations between sound and place, on the one hand, and sound and emotions, on the other. The boundaries between theological and philosophical understandings of music are thus blurred by experiences that arise within this genre of sonic participation.

My ethnographic research confirms Tim Ingold's opinion that sounds engender the possibility of being felt as much by the hearer's bodily interior as by the external sense.[13] In this case, however, it is the divine erotics of Radha-Krishna which is experienced musically either/both in the intersubjective domain, along with other hearer-singers, or/and within the inner sensory recesses of the individual musician's body. Thus, insofar as devotees assert the structure of alterity and their subservience to Radha-Krishna in their understandings of sacred music, these experiences are religious and transcendental.[14]

Music as *Eros*: The Pleasures of Repetitive Chanting

Bengal Vaishnavas repeat the chant 'Hare Krishna Hare Krishna Krishna Krishna Hare Hare Hare Rama Hare Rama Rama Rama Hare Hare'. Many Vaishnavas

---

[12]   Judith A. Peraino, 'Listening to the Sirens: Music as Queer Ethical Practice', *Journal of Lesbian and Gay Studies*, 9/4 (2003): 433–70 (p. 440).

[13]   Tim Ingold, *The Perception of the Environment: Essays on Livelihood, Dwelling and Skill* (London and New York, 2000), pp. 155–6, 268.

[14]   See Thomas J. Csordas, 'Asymptote of the Ineffable: Embodiment, Alterity, and the Theory of Religion', *Current Anthropology*, 45/2 (2004): 163–85.

agree that Hare (the one who steals the heart) is Krishna's eternally repeated call to Radha, and the terms Krishna (the all attractor) and Rama (the pleasure giver) are uttered in reciprocation by her. The sonic universe is imagined as a perpetual chant, constituted by the constant cries of separation and union between Krishna and his pleasure principle, Radha. All Vaishnavas thus seek eventual subservience to the names, such that the ideal is to chant all the time, consciously or unconsciously, under the breath, thereby feeling the deities' love, continuously.

Kirtan singing, to sum up, is like a synesthetic bath. The aroma of incense creates an atmosphere within which the echoes of *kirtan* resound. The *khol* (drums with a deep sound) and *kartaal* (cymbals) are the main instrumental accompaniments. The auditory space resonates synchronously with the beat of the heart. The tactile sensibilities are equally in operation as people sit close together singing.[15] Boundaries dissolve as the skin of individuals touches and their discrete voices merge in unison. The intense emotion and devotion that results creates an altered perception and an indomitable community spirit. In such settings, the embodiedness of each listener 'carries an anticipation of others' bodies'.[16] Thus, Norvin Hein, in his analysis of Radha worship predominant Vaishnava communities, argues that a 'bond of erotic imagination' may develop in devotional congregations.[17]

The reverberatory potentials of sound are especially effective in creating genuine occasions of intersubjective, participatory communion.[18] Such acoustemologies thus give a sense of de-individuation, of affective and corporeal oneness with others.[19] Roger Dean and Freya Bailes also argue that music helps stimulate empathic sensibilities and 'social coalitions'.[20]

The seating arrangement of the participants in a circular structure is considered to be the spherical stage for Krishna's appearance before his lover-singers. The roundness corresponds to the ceaseless, cyclical name-repetitions. What is enchanting about *kirtan*, therefore, is that, 'in identifying the sung *name* of God with divinity itself, *kirtan* singers in the same moment, *create* that which they propitiate'.[21] The spirit of *kirtan* lies in its entrancing iterative zeal: the constant repetition is

---

[15]   See Sudhir Kakar, 'Psychoanalysis and Religious Healing: Siblings or Strangers?', *Journal of the American Academy of Religion*, 53/4 (1985): 841–53 (p. 844).

[16]   Greg Downey, 'Listening to Capoeira: Phenomenology, Embodiment and the Materiality of Music', *Ethnomusicology*, 46/3 (2002): 487–509 (p. 504).

[17]   Norvin Hein, 'Comments: Radha and Erotic Community', in John Stratton Hawley and Donna Marie Wulff (eds), *The Divine Consort: Radha and the Goddesses of India* (Berkeley, Calif., 1982), pp. 116–24 (p. 121).

[18]   See David Burrows, 'On Hearing Things: Music, The World and Ourselves', *Musical Quarterly*, 66/2 (1980): 180–91 (pp. 188–9).

[19]   See Sara Cohen, 'Sounding Out the City: Music and the Sensuous Production of Place', *Transactions of the Institute of British Geographers*, 20/4 (1995): 434–46 (p. 444).

[20]   Roger T. Dean and Freya Bailes, 'Toward a Sociobiology of Music', *Music Perception: An Interdisciplinary Journal*, 24/1 (2006): 83–5.

[21]   Stephen M. Slawek, 'Popular Kirtan in Benaras: Some "Great" Aspects of a Little Tradition', *Ethnomusicology*, 32/2 (1988): 77–92 (p. 90).

addictive, yet it also creates a restless anticipation in the listener. Thus constraint and freedom together create tensions in the body which, as we shall see, becomes 'tuned'. While the repetitious routine generates an inescapable sense of habitual pleasure, the certitudes of security, one also feels the urge to break through the same, to wander off beat. This sort of perceptual experience points to 'a genre of being with respect to which the subject is not sovereign, but without his being imprisoned in it'.[22] Metaphorically, it is this tension that can be heard between the mismatched and almost tussling, somber and hollow sounds of the drums, on the one hand, and the cacophonous impatient sounds of the cymbals, on the other. It is also this tension that invokes a sense of the sexual impatience that resonates within the perpetual call between Krishna and Radha, asserted by the Vaishnavas in the continuous naming.

The sense of acoustic anxiety manifests itself especially with the progressively ascending *kirtan* rhythm. The continuously escalating rhythmic pattern is an immediate phenomenological correlate of the erotic act.[23] The rhythm automatically involves a sense of passage, sensory arousal and most pleasurable climax. This is also when devotees, with raised hands ululate together and shout the different names of Radha-Krishna. While some have said that music replaces sexual arousal, calling it a 'misattribution of effervescence',[24] and others maintain that the eros in Indian devotion finds transformed and indirect expression in symbolisms of music and dance,[25] I would argue that such a distinction between music and sexuality is misplaced. The structure of music does not merely replace or express but generates a sexual aura.

The participants swaying their bodies to the *kirtan* melodies, quivering to the sonic vibrations and the accompanying tranced dances of some devotees, are only a few markers of the intense bodily reactions to the music which spread over the entire epidermal surface. The collective rigorous clapping articulates a euphoric climactic anticipation. This anticipation, which involves the entire 'body as an auditory instrument',[26] however, carries with it the 'incorporated', satisfying aural memory of earlier participations. The pleasure is never in the quick realisation of the climax, however. The end is incessantly postponed through continuously rising rhythms, a process which I call 'devotional long-ing', which intentionally prolongs the singing process, so that the sonic pleasures may be experienced

---

[22]   Maurice Merleau-Ponty, *Resumes de cours* (Paris, 1945), p. 66, cited in David Farrell Krell, 'Phenomenology of Memory from Husserl to Merleau Ponty', *Philosophy and Phenomenological Research*, 42/4 (1982): 492–505 (p. 503).

[23]   See Jonathan H. Shannon, 'The Aesthetics of Spiritual Practice and the Creation of Moral and Musical Subjectivities in Aleppo, Syria', *Ethnology*, 43/4 (2004): 381–91.

[24]   Douglas A. Marshall, 'Behavior, Belonging and Belief: A Theory of Ritual Practice', *Sociological Theory*, 20/3 (2002): 360–80 (p. 366).

[25]   See Gananath Obeyeskere, 'The Fire Walkers of Kataragama: The Rise of Bhakti Religiosity in Buddhist Sri Lanka', *Journal of Asian Studies*, 37/3 (1978): 457–76 (p. 472).

[26]   Charles Hirschkind, *The Ethical Soundscape: Cassette Sermons and Islamic Counterpublics* (New York, 2006), p. 78.

over and again. Repetition and anticipation thus inhabit a confused body where postponement becomes a telos in itself. The end is simultaneously also craved for. For without it, no musical experience is possible. However, with the completion of one *kirtan* cycle, another begins immediately.

Where is sonic desire located then? Is it in the exhausting, cathartic end when participants cry? Or is it in the erotic and nervous expressions of the music to which the tears refer in nostalgia? 'The body asserts itself as a primary field for the play of phenomenological presence and absence and the endlessly deferred moment of self-coincidence.'[27] It is most common to find devotees crying profusely during and after the musical sessions. These climactic tears approximate Elliot R. Wolfson's analysis of tears in Jewish mysticism, about which he says, 'weeping of the eye symbolically displaces the seminal discharge of the phallus'.[28] The obvious associations of trance-like music and sexuality also led Jaak Panksepp to call 'chills' felt during musical gatherings, 'skin orgasms'.[29]

Embodied Instruments and Audible Bodies

The chief instruments used during *kirtan*, the *khol* and *kartaal*, are held to be sacred objects themselves, and before beginning any *kirtan* performance the drummer first offers mantras to the *khol*. Following a complex phenomenology of listening practices, musicians and instrumentalists state that careful audition of the materiality of *khol* and *kartaal* sounds can manifest Vrindavan pastimes. Paul Stoller, a pioneer in the anthropology of senses, pointed out two decades ago that the sound of musical instruments has not been subject to much scrutiny.[30] The situation has not improved since. However, I analyse devotees' claims that the instruments' sounds are themselves sonic secrets of Vrindavan, attention to which helps unravel a conception of transcendental erotics.

Most local theorisations about *khol* sounds come down as oral lore, through generations of trained instrumentalists, and I will summarise the views expressed by practising musicians, especially *khol* players from Bengal. Among those musicians with whom I spent time, my intimacy with GP, one of the most

---

[27]   Stanton B. Garner Jr., 'Still Living Flesh: Beckett, Merleau Ponty, and the Phenomenological Body', *Theatre Journal*, 65/4 (1993): 443–60 (pp. 452–3).

[28]   Elliot R. Wolfson, 'Weeping, Death and Spiritual Ascent in Sixteenth-Century Jewish Mysticism', in John Corrigan (ed.), *Religion and Emotion: Approaches and Interpretations* (New York, 2004), 271–304 (p. 281).

[29]   Jaak Panksepp, 'The Emotional Sources of "Chills" Induced by Music', *Music Perception: An Interdisciplinary Journal*, 13/2 (1995): 171–207 (p. 203), cited in Judith Becker, *Deep Listeners: Music, Emotion and Trancing* (Bloomington and Indianapolis, 2004), p. 63.

[30]   Paul Stoller, *The Taste of Ethnographic Things: The Senses in Anthropology* (Philadelphia, 1989), p. 108.

renowned drummers of Bengal, proved to be most productive in honing both my own listening acumen and musical imagination.

The classical name for *khol* is *mridangam*, which literally means, 'body of mud'. *Khols* are asymmetrical, conical drums, about 24 inches in length and 45 inches in breadth. The body is made of mud and covered with cowskin – considered sacred by Hindus – held in place by 32 strings stretched from top to bottom. The tension produced by these strings tunes the instrument. A small air hole is punched through one of the instrument's edges to release the sound. Cymbals are of different sizes. The smallest (*mandira/manjari*) make a 'tung tung' sound, the middle ones (*kartaal*) make a similar sound with more resonance and the big ones (*jhompo*), together weighing about a kilo, make a loud 'jh(n)a jh(n)a' sound.

The *khol* and *kartaal* make the ideal combination to accompany *kirtan*, as their tunings suit any scale of singing. This suitability is attributed by devotees not only to the instruments' musical properties, but also to their innate sacredness. Eben Graves says that the *khol* has an 'affecting presence' in the Vaishnava world and that this is intrinsically connected to the instrument's materiality, such that it is treated more as an embodied person than a thing.[31] The sonic ontology of Vaishnavism is thus situated at the junction of the religious imagination and the phenomenological efficacy of instrument sounds.

Related to the idea of the sacrality of instrumental sounds, however, is a parallel discourse about the sounds that comprise the spiritually perfected body. Musicians assert that the *khol* is the perfect correlate of the human body and that the ultimate spiritual purpose of all musicians and advanced practitioners is to be able to hear the instrument's sounds arising from one's own corporeal interior, even when the physical instrument stops playing. Since the *khol* and *kartaal* sounds are imagined as recreating the music of divine sensuality, it is thought that when the sounds are heard within one's own body, Vrindavan is manifest, with all of its erotic charge, in the interiors of the skin.

A *kirtan* singer, SD, asked me what I feel when I listen attentively to the *khol* and *kartaal*. I told her: 'I cannot concentrate on them for too long, as the repetitive *khol* sound bangs intensely in the middle of my naval and chest, and the shrill sounds of *kartaal* are deafening.' She explained:

> Precisely. The middle of the naval, chest and so on are the energy centres of the body, whose intrinsic, hidden sounds are then in tune with the *khol* sounds outside. And the deafening sounds of the *kartaal* are the embodiments of Radha's anklets. ... If you keep chanting well, your breath-chant will resound the body-*khol* one day.[32]

---

[31] Eben Graves, 'Chaitanya Vaishnava Perspectives on the Bengali Khol', *Journal of Vaishnava Studies*, 17/2 (2009): 103–26 (p. 105).

[32] All interviews were conducted in Bengali. The English translations are my own.

I was hardly able to understand what she meant, until GP, much later, told me about Vaishnava musicians' beliefs.

The Body as a Tuned Instrument

According to mythology, when Radha-Krishna decided to be reborn together in this age in the body of a Vaishnava saint, their indispensable belongings, Krishna's flute and Radha's anklets, also wanted to come along. Since the flute and anklets sound together during the deities' love encounters, Radha-Krishna desired that the flute and anklets be incarnated as drums and cymbals for chanting-music. Passion, in other words, was incarnate as music.[33] Thus, during one of my conversations with a musician couple, the man said:

> When Krishna lovers run to meet him, they giggle, and their anklets dance in pleasure. ... Those are the same tinkling sounds that the *kartaals* make. ... Also you will see that the *kartaals* play in the same rhythm in which the *kirtan* participants clap. As if Radharani's ornaments are clapping in rhythm in the devotee's heart temple.

Krishna's flute is often a metaphor for erotic irresistibility: its seductive sound is claimed to be like a direct, penetrative eros, entering the body through the interstices of the ear.[34] The poetics of the flute are described in a similar vein in Vaishnava poetry, which devotees know and recite by heart. For instance, one poem describes how, as Krishna exhales his moist breath into the flute, distinct tunes emerge, carrying his lip-nectar, filling the air in Vrindavan and attracting his various lovers.

The passionate flute sounds are conceptualised as being in tune with the breathing body. A 92-year-old Muslim villager with a keen interest in Vaishnava aesthetics elaborated: 'One of Krishna's flutes has nine openings, and so have our body (ears, nose, eyes, mouth, anus and genitals). When through spiritual practice we draw breath/air upwards and shut these nine doors, we trap breath/ sound inside us ... and the body/flute plays.' Others say that one of Krishna's flutes has five holes, through which he attracts the five senses.

The flute and the *khol* are both hollow, so that air can pass without hindrance. Devotees see this as emblematic of the feminine heart's subservience to the lover Krishna, which is without any obstruction or ego. With the spiritually perfected breath passing through the energy centres in the hollow of the practitioner's body as well as the *khol* or flute, the musically honed body and instruments

---

[33] See Barbara A. Holdrege, 'From Nama-Avatara to Nama-Samkirtana: Gaudiya Perspectives on the Name', *Journal of Vaisnava Studies*, 17/2 (2009): 3–36 (p. 24).

[34] See Glen A. Hayes, 'The Vaishnava Sahajiya Traditions of Medieval Bengal', in Donald S. Lopez Jr. (ed.), *Religions of India in Practice* (Princeton, NJ, 1995), pp. 333–52 (p. 348).

can echo Vrindavan's passions. Luce Irigaray similarly argues that yogic religious practices sensitive to breathing apprehend the subterranean, feminine, subservient and erotic aspects of the self.[35] Similar to the phenomenology of the flute, she says that we are breathed as much as we breathe.[36]

The nature of the sounds heard in the practitioner's body is deeply in tune with the sounds of the *khol* and *kartaal*. The timbre of instruments, as Laura-Lee Balkwill and William Forde Thompson remind us, often determines the emotional moods accompanying them.[37] Thus, when, during a *kirtan* performance, the rhythm reaches its climax, the musical/orgasmic pleasure bursts forth both in the collective shouts as well as in the space of the individual listener's body. The hearer and heard are within the same body.[38] GP's student, who has been playing the *khol* for 16 years, provided a wonderfully explicit explanation:

> The right hand part of the *khol* has a treble, sharp sound (*tang tang*). … Its echo resonates for a long time after striking it. There are large, round bangles around the edges of the *khol*, which are like Radha's ornaments. When we strike the *khol*, the bangle also sounds (*chn chn*). The sounds of the *kartaal*, which are also like different ornaments of Radha, echo almost for 30 seconds after striking it. As the sharp rebounds resonate, our minds travel on the echo of the instruments' sounds to Vrindavan, and we can hear and see Radha dancing, her ornaments sounding in rhythm with Krishna's flute. … The left hand side of the *khol* has a deep, hollow, base sound. As its repeated *dhakdhakdhak* or *gurgurgurgur* sound strikes, the heartbeats also pounce, as if, in the excitement of seeing the deities together.

In a particular yogic position called *bhramar asana* (honey-bee posture), one is supposed to pull in the breath and shut the eyes, ears, mouth and nose and create the repeated reverberation of the sound 'M' inside. At a certain point, the timbre echoes in the cavity of the chest.[39] In the Vaishnava discourse, drawing in the

---

[35] Luce Irigaray, *Between East and West: From Singularity to Community* (New York, 2002), pp. 84–100, discussed in Cleo McNelly Kearns, 'Irigaray's *Between East and West*: Breath, Pranayama, and the Phenomenology of Prayer', in Bruce Ellis Benson and Norman Wirzba (eds), *The Phenomenology of Prayer* (New York, 2005), pp. 103–18 (p. 110).

[36] Ibid., p. 113.

[37] Laura-Lee Balkwill and William Forde Thompson, 'A Cross-Cultural Investigation of the Perception of Emotion in Music: Psychophysical and Cultural Cues', *Music Perception: An Interdisciplinary Journal*, 17/1 (1999): 43–64 (p. 50).

[38] See Christopher Tilley, *Body and Image: Explorations in Landscape Phenomenology 2* (Walnut Creek, Calif., 2008), p. 40; James Morley, 'Inspiration and Expiration: Yoga Practice through Merleau-Ponty's Phenomenology of the Body', *Philosophy East and West*, 51/1 (2001): 73–82 (p. 78).

[39] See Gian Giuseppe Fillippi and Thomas Dahnhardt, 'Ananda Yoga: A Contemporary Crossing Between Sufism and Hinduism', in Vasudha Dalmia, Angelika Malinar and Martin Christof (eds), *Charisma and Canon: Essays on the Religious History of the Indian Subcontinent* (Oxford and New York, 2001), pp. 350–59 (p. 355).

breath signifies shutting the doors of the body, so that the sonic/emotional upsurge is introjected, rather than let out.[40] GP makes the connection clear:

> In our sonic philosophy, the sound of 'M' apprehends the sense of dreamless sleep. When the honey bee hums, this is the same nagging sound. Krishna, as the honey bee comes to savour the interior space of the body-lotus. ... This is possible through constant chanting. Krishna then breathes into the body and it sounds the *khol*. ... She hears the buzzing bee right in the middle of the chest.

The sensory vibration of the bee's buzzing is monotonous and insistent. Its clear, grain-like sensation is similar to the vibrating resonance of stringed instruments. Indeed, in tantric traditions and *nada* yoga (sonic meditation), 'the word nada signifies the reverberating tone of vocal sound, especially the buzzing nasal sound with which the word AUM fades away'.[41] The nasal sound of the body is replicated in a number of names for *khol* rhythms (for instance, *jhna, jhni, najhi, nako, jhini*, etc.) which are also suggestive of heavy anklet sounds. Musicians often complain of a lazy hand, when playing the *khol* for a long time. The sensation of the lazy hand, once again, has a sensory similitude with the nagging, grainy feeling of the 'M' and has a nasal name itself – *jh(n)i jh(n)i*. Thus, musician gurus tell their students not to stop playing the *khol* even when encumbered by the tired, lazy sensation of the hands, as it is considered to be a yogic blessing.

Nasal sounds in general are said to echo in the body when a practitioner, with a straight spine, pulls up the breath through the central yogic nerve.[42] When drawing up the breath, the energy centres are also pulled up. In the yogic imagination, the area from the anus up to the middle of the chest represents the journey from silence to sounds. However, when finally the sound moves up from the middle of the eyebrow to the head, Vrindavan is said to manifest with all of its passion acoustics in the 'touch-hearing geography'.[43]

The Body in the Drum and the Drum in the Body

The *khol* is imagined to be the exact corporeal counterpart of the practitioner's body. According to GP, 'like the *khol*, we have a small opening for breathing in the

---

[40]   See June McDaniel, 'Emotion in Bengali Religious Thought: Substance and Metaphor', in Joel Marks and Roger T. Ames (eds), *Emotions in Asian Thought: A Dialogue in Comparative Philosophy* (Albany, NY, 1995), pp. 39–64 (pp. 50–51).

[41]   Guy L. Beck, *Sonic Theology* (Columbia, SC, 1993), p. 82.

[42]   See Paul Williams, 'Some Mahayana Buddhist Perspectives on the Body', in Sarah Coakley (ed.), *Religion and the Body* (Cambridge, 1997), pp. 205–31 (p. 223); Ann Grodzins Gold and Daniel Gold, 'Fate of the Householder Nath', *History of Religions*, 24/2 (1984): 113–32 (p. 120).

[43]   Rodaway, *Sensuous Geographies*, p. 100.

nose, and like our naval maintains the balance of the body, the middle portion of the *khol* is most essential for sonic balance.'

The small black patch on the right-side of the *khol*, musicians say, is the embodiment of Krishna, and the white patch on the left-side, of Radha. This is because Krishna is imagined as the dark lord and Radha as the fair maiden. As the two are struck together, when Radha-Krishna are in erotic vibration, sounds overflow from the affective body-space of the instrument. As a *khol* player put it, 'friction makes sound, and friction gives pleasure. As the edges of the *khol* shiver in sound, the couple vibrates in love.' Similarly, in yogic discourse, the body, naval downwards, is the embodiment of feminine vitality, and upwards, of masculine energy. When breathing and chanting connect the two, it sounds out the desired love.[44]

In the 'intuitive imagery' of the 'inner senses',[45] the different energy centres of the body are imagined as lotuses and known as *cakras*. Each of these, practitioners assert, has its own distinctive sound and are thus assigned letters with phonetic resemblance to those sounds.[46] Which letters reside in which energy centre is a practitioner's secret and remains undisclosed. However, when the practitioner pulls up the breath and the breath traverses the different *cakras* of the body, the petals of the lotuses are supposed to blossom, and the sounds within reverberate.[47]

The *khol* is similarly imagined as divided into corresponding *cakras*, some below the middle portion (the naval of the body) and some above. The same alphabet combinations that pertain to the *cakras* can be played on the *khol* as rhythms. When a sensitive *khol* player thus plays and hears the repetitive *khol* rhythms, he is able to hear the same sounds within the body. When the *khol* player plays, the instrument is hung with a string from the shoulders, and the player shuts his eyes and tilts his ears towards the instrument in concentration. Here, the kinesthesia involved in striking the *khol* and shaking the body proves that his *khol* in the body and *khol* on the body are entirely in sync. There are many more sounds about which the practitioners are unwilling to talk, remaining secret from the non-initiated and non-musical.

Stefan Helmreich's anthropology of sound has been very useful in thinking about the phenomenology of instrumental music, in sensitising my ethnographic ear to the tactile in the sonic, to the bodily interior as the reverberator of sonic

---

[44]   See Beck, *Sonic Theology*, p. 101.

[45]   Thomas J. Csordas, *The Sacred Self: A Cultural Phenomenology of Charismatic Healing* (Berkeley, Los Angeles, and London, 1994), p. 89.

[46]   See Beck, *Sonic Theology*, p. 94.

[47]   See Daniel Gold, 'Nath Yogis as Established Alternatives: Householders and Ascetics Today', in Karigoudar Ishwaran (ed.), *Ascetic Culture: Renunciation and Worldly Engagement*, International studies in Sociology and Social Anthropology 73 (Leiden, Boston, Mass. and Cologne, 1999), pp. 68–88 (p. 73); Carol Salomon, 'Baul Songs', in Lopez (ed.), *Religions of India in Practice*, pp. 187–208 (p. 190); Carl W. Ernst, 'Situating Sufism and Yoga', *Journal of the Royal Asiatic Society*, 3rd ser., 15/1 (2005): 15–43 (p. 26).

transcendence, to the blurring of boundaries between external and internal soundscapes,[48] and to conceptualisations of the 'esoteric physiology of sound'.[49] In this case, however, the intimate 'immersion'[50] has been in the deep oceanic recesses of the transcendental music in the body.

---

[48]   See Stefan Helmreich, 'An Anthropologist Underwater: Immersive Soundscapes, Submarine Cyborgs, and Transductive Ethnography', *American Ethnologist*, 34/4 (2007): 621–41.
[49]   Beck, *Sonic Theology*, pp. 91–7.
[50]   Helmreich, 'An Anthropologist Underwater'.

Chapter 3

'Sonorous Air': The Transcendent in Ferruccio Busoni's Aesthetics of Music

John Habron[1]

The Realm of Music

In 'The Realm of Music' (1910), composer and virtuoso pianist Ferruccio Busoni (1866–1924) described a transcendent space in which 'all melodies heard before or never heard, resound completely and simultaneously'.[2] It is from this infinite storehouse of melodies that Busoni, or any other composer with access to the realm, is able to draw materials for composition. The realm of music appears as the free-floating amalgam of all possible musical worlds, which offers the 'poetic raw material' of music.[3] Busoni's description of the realm of music thus gives us a picture of absolute transcendence, another world, beyond time and space. His 1910 text is in fact an epilogue to 'Sketch of a New Esthetic of Music' (1907; English translation, 1911), the ideas of which begin to point to the realm of music.[4] This chapter will explore these writings with regard to the transcendent and will discuss how Busoni's aesthetics relate to notions of creation, temporality, language and improvisation. In particular, it shows how Busoni's emphasis on the fluidity of performance and the collapsing of time, alongside the idea of the realm of music as an ahistorical and dialogical space, result in a phenomenology of music that has a proto-postmodernist character.

The realm of music has obvious historical resonances with medieval cosmology, in particular *musica mundana*, but it is distinct. The music of the spheres is generated by the mathematical proportions of the natural world, emerging as a

---

[1]   My thanks to those who attended my paper at the 2011 'Music and Transcendence' conference and offered searching questions and helpful suggestions, in particular Anthony Gritten, Matthew Ward and Bennett Zon. Also, my gratitude to Antonio Cascelli, Michael Finnissy, Erinn Knyt and Liesl van Der Merwe for their comments on an earlier draft of this chapter.

[2]   Ferruccio Busoni, 'The Realm of Music: An Epilogue to the New Esthetic', in *The Essence of Music and Other Papers*, trans. R. Ley (London, 1957), pp. 188–9 (p. 189).

[3]   George Steiner, *Grammars of Creation* (London, 2002), p. 99.

[4]   Ferruccio Busoni, 'Sketch of a New Esthetic of Music', in *Three Classics in the Aesthetic of Music* (New York, 1962), pp. 75–102. 'The Realm of Music' is a letter Busoni penned to his wife on 3 March 1910. It was published, with added material, and translated by R. Ley, in *The Essence of Music and Other Papers*.

result of a celestial harmony that is inaudible to human ears but is rendered as such by voices and instruments (*musica instrumentalis*). Busoni's realm of music, by contrast, is teeming with sound, with bits and pieces of music – of all pieces written and not yet written. Although he mentions stars and planets, the picture he conjures up is more akin to the colourful and noisy profusion of Italian futurist painting than it is to the other-worldly music of planets fixed in their orbits: 'innumerable are its voices; compared with them the murmuring of the harp is a din; the blare of a thousand trombones a chirrup'.[5]

Busoni describes the realm of music as being beyond an iron fence, which separates the material from the eternal. To enter it, one must undo and throw away the 'fetters' of earthly existence.[6] Only then will one be able to apprehend the immeasurable and endless nature of the realm 'down to unfathomable depths and up to the vaulted roof of heaven'.[7] Busoni is no stranger to paradox, and it is through this rhetorical mechanism that he expresses the incomprehensible yet wondrous nature of the realm. We hear nothing 'because everything resounds'; that is, it appears that there is no ground against which to perceive musical figures, because everything is music.[8] The realm of music is both astonishing and yet 'from the beginning we feel it is homelike'.[9] The hearts that beat on each of the stars 'agree and are separate and yet are whole'.[10] All beings are 'illimitably great and illimitably small: the greatest expansion is like a point', and 'unthought-of scales extend like bands from one world to another, *stationary and yet eternally in motion*'.[11]

These paradoxes are in keeping with the transcendent orientation shared by many religious and mystical traditions. They are also typical of pre-Socratic philosophy, in particular that of Heraclitus, who wrote of the unity of opposites and the essence of the world as process.[12] Two of Heraclitus's most famous paradoxes are 'everything is one' and 'everything is in flux'. Both of these resonate strongly with Busoni's account of the realm of music. Indeed, Busoni may have been aware of Heraclitus through Hölderlin, since he had Hölderlin's

---

[5]   Busoni, 'The Realm of Music', p. 189. In this sense I would disagree with Erinn E. Knyt, who suggests that the music of the realm is 'an inaudible primordial source of all music' ('Ferruccio Busoni and the Absolute in Music: Form, Nature and *Idee*', *Journal of Royal Musical Association*, 137/1 (2012): 35–69 (p. 50)). Any reading is personal and the experience of reading Busoni's text brings to my mind an abundance of sound. The cross-fertilisation between Busoni and Italian futurism has been discussed by Daniele Lombardi (*Il suono veloce: Futurismo e futurismi in musica* (Milan, 1996)) and Luciano Chessa (*Luigi Russolo, Futurist: Noise, Visual Arts and the Occult* (Berkeley and Los Angeles, 2012)).

[6]   Busoni, 'The Realm of Music', p. 189.

[7]   Ibid.

[8]   Ibid.

[9]   Ibid.

[10]   Ibid.

[11]   Ibid.: italics original.

[12]   See Jonathan Barnes (trans. and ed.), *Early Greek Philosophy* (London, 1987).

work in his personal library.[13] Whatever the source of Busoni's propensity for paradoxical constructions, however, the presence of duality is fundamental to his aesthetics.[14]

In 'Sketch of a New Esthetic of Music', Busoni uses the word 'realm' only once, but the context clearly presages the vision he would go on to express in his 1910 text:

> If Nirvana be the realm 'beyond the Good and the Bad', *one* way leading thither is here pointed out. A way to the very portal. To the bars that divide Man from Eternity – or that open to admit that which was temporal. Beyond that portal sounds *music*. Not the strains of 'musical art.' – It may be, that we must leave Earth to find that music. But only to the pilgrim who has succeeded on the way in freeing himself from earthly shackles, shall the bars open.[15]

The same features appear in the two texts: a dividing structure (a portal with bars) between humankind/earth and eternity and one that can only be approached by leaving earthly shackles behind. Busoni sees himself in spiritual terms as a pilgrim who seeks an 'upward path'.[16] He also claims that a work of art itself has a spirit, which outlasts its form or manner of expression. This takes a similar form to the Platonic duality of soul and body, in which the soul is eternal and the body temporal.[17]

To distinguish the realm of music from 'musical art' – pieces of music fashioned in earthly terms – Busoni introduces the term *Ur-Musik*, a formulation that emphasises the timeless, primordial and transcendent.[18] *Ur-Musik* is the music that approaches nearest to that of the realm. He singles out Bach's organ fantasias as an example, as well as introductory or transitional passages in Beethoven, Brahms and Schumann.[19] However, the term *Ur-Musik* not only refers to the

---

[13] Erinn E. Knyt, 'Ferruccio Busoni and the Ontology of the Musical Work: Permutations and Possibilities' (PhD thesis: Stanford University, 2010), p. 60.

[14] It is equally possible that any knowledge Busoni may have had of Heraclitus came through his interest in esotericism and the occult.

[15] Busoni, 'Sketch of a New Esthetic of Music', p. 97.

[16] Ibid., p. 75.

[17] Here, Busoni appeals to Platonism (the world of perfect immaterial objects), whilst elsewhere Heraclitan flux (the world of becoming) predominates. Similarly, he claims, for example, that 'the musical art-work exists, before its tones resound and after they die away, *complete and intact*' (ibid., p. 86: italics original). This type of transcendence has an affinity with Plato's Forms, which transcend time, space and any particular instantiation in matter. Yet, here Busoni appears to contradict the philosophical grounds for his own assertions about the realm of music being a resounding space that is in eternal motion. The dialectical tension between these two positions may itself be another version of Heraclitan paradox, which he seemingly prefers to inhabit.

[18] Ibid., p. 79.

[19] Ibid., pp. 79–80.

'boundlessness of this pan-art' that is the 'true nature of music',[20] it also hints at the somehow originating and timeless nature of this music, the fact of its always having been there. George Steiner, referring to 'the untranslatable monosyllable of the primal, *Ur*', notes that 'German mentality is fascinated ... by the turbulent dark of inception and instauration. ... A thirst for legitimacy of foundation, of empowering ancestry inspires German thought and politics'.[21] The extent to which Busoni's nationality and background formed his thinking on this matter is arguable (he was born in Italy, but spent significant portions of his life in Germany and identified strongly with German culture). Nevertheless his writings evince a fascination with music's very origins, the genealogy of music.[22]

Music as a Child

Tied up with the realm of music, as implied in 'Sketch of a New Esthetic of Music', is the extended metaphor of music as a child:

> Music ... is a child that has learned to walk, but must still be led. It is a virgin art, without experience in life or suffering. It is all unconscious as yet of what garb is becoming. ... Music as an art ... is hardly four hundred years old; its state is one of development. ... We apply laws made for maturity to a child that knows nothing of responsibility! Young as it is, this child ... it *floats on air*! It touches not the earth with its feet. It knows no law of gravitation. It is wellnigh incorporeal. Its material is transparent. It is sonorous air. It is almost Nature herself. It is – free.[23]

Here we have confirmation of music as free, processual and something akin to nature, as well as of its phenomenal nature as sound waves. This latter fact is for Busoni a hallmark of music's uniqueness amongst the arts and seals for him its spiritual and ideal nature.[24] The figure of the child, however, also allows Busoni to impart to music innocence, a need for careful handling, and a profound sense of its potential.[25] Perhaps anticipating Busoni's metaphor, Wackenroder presents the child as being preternaturally sensitive to musical experiences:

---

[20]   Ibid., p. 79.

[21]   Steiner, *Grammars of Creation*, pp. 93–4: italics original.

[22]   For Busoni's fascination with genealogy, see Knyt, 'Ferruccio Busoni and the Ontology of the Musical Work', pp. 43–6.

[23]   Busoni, 'Sketch of a New Esthetic of Music', pp. 76–7.

[24]   Knyt argues that this is also related to recent theories of acoustics with which Busoni had become acquainted ('Ferruccio Busoni and the Absolute', p. 50).

[25]   Wackenroder was another presence in Busoni's library (Knyt, 'Ferruccio Busoni and the Ontology of the Musical Work', p. 63). In addition to the presentation of the figure of the child, the *Phantasien über die Kunst* (Fantasies on Art for Friends of Art, 1799)

Truly, it is an innocent, touching pleasure to rejoice over sounds, over pure sounds! A childlike joy! While others deafen themselves with restless activity and, buzzed by confused thoughts as by an army of strange night birds and evil insects, finally fall to the ground unconscious; – O, then I submerge my head in the holy, cooling wellspring of sounds and the healing goddess instils the innocence of childhood in me again, so that I regard the world with fresh eyes and melt into universal, joyous reconciliation.[26]

Busoni is keenly aware of music's need for liberation and intuits that there lurks the possibility of weightiness and restriction, of the fall that the floating child is precariously avoiding:

[People] disavow the mission of this child; they hang weights upon it. This buoyant creature must walk decently, like anybody else. It may scarcely be allowed to leap – when it were its joy to follow the line of the rainbow, and to break sunbeams with the clouds. Music was born free; and to win freedom is its destiny.[27]

The desire to escape gravity pervaded historical developments contemporary with 'Sketch of a New Esthetic of Music', such as the advent of air flight itself as well as the growth of body culture, especially the fascination with leaping and jumping. With regard to the latter, Michael Cowan states that photography had allowed the jumping body to replace the angel 'as a visualization of the soul's

---

may offer precursors of other aspects of Busoni's aesthetics. For example, Wackenroder writes that the sonorous nature of music 'floats gently on the breezes, and then silently sinks down to earth again' (Wilhelm Heinrich Wackenroder, 'Fantasies on Art for Friends of Art', in *Confessions and Fantasies*, trans. M. H. Schubert (University Park, Pa., 1971), pp. 161–97 (p. 178)). In terms of its youthfulness, he claims: 'In its present perfection it is the youngest of all the arts' (ibid., p. 188). In words that bear a strong resemblance to Busoni's description of the realm of music itself, Wackenroder continues: 'Furthermore, no other art but music has a raw material which is, in and of itself, already impregnated with such divine spirit. Its vibrating material ... comes to meet the creating hands halfway and expresses beautiful emotions. ... Thus it is that many musical pieces ... speak a magnificent, emotionally rich poetry when they are performed on instruments, although the composer may have little imagined that, in his scholarly work, the enchanted spirit in the realm of music would beat its wings so magnificently for initiated senses' (ibid., p. 189). Schubert notes that 'Wackenroder's search for the "kernel" of the creative process is simultaneously a search for a higher metaphysical reality' ('Introduction', to Wackenroder, *Confessions and Fantasies*, pp. 3–72 (p. 72)). In as much as Busoni's search is similar, the influence of Wackenroder on Busoni's aesthetics would bear further study.

26 Wackenroder, 'Fantasies on Art for Friends of Art', pp. 178–9.
27 Busoni, 'Sketch of a New Esthetic of Music', p. 76.

liberation from the prison house of materiality'.[28] In Busoni's text, a sense of loss shadows the child, which may lose divine insight as it matures and becomes worldlier. Busoni wishes the child – perhaps a personification of *Ur-Musik* due to its essence as a moving, free agent – to remain precisely other-worldly. He wishes it to maintain its spiritual essence, to remain in – or at least in communion with – the realm of music.[29]

If Busoni's music-child is born free and needs to remain free ('its destiny'), then the fetters and shackles that threaten to bring it down to earth are musical traditions and beliefs about musical composition and performance. Indeed, Busoni eventually rejected any attempt to make use, wholesale, of past formal models, believing that they were the ineluctable constraints brought about by the very facts of materialisation or representation, by the capturing in earthly terms of what the transcendental realm of music offers.

Strivings for the Beyond: Musical Materials and Notation

The music of Busoni's realm is materialised in instrumental and vocal media and in musical notation. These are the ways in which it is made manifest on the earth. In both areas, however, Busoni's thought cleaves to the transcendent, and he struggles with the implications of making bound that which is unbounded. We will look at musical materials and notation in turn.

Busoni is well known for having theorised several aspects of musical material. Pitch features prominently in 'Sketch of a New Esthetic of Music', where he records his wish to transcend the duality of consonance and dissonance, as well as the 'meagreness' of the diatonic system. In so doing, he appeals once more to the infinity of the realm of music: 'our whole system of tone, key, and tonality … is only a part of a fraction of one diffracted ray from that Sun, "Music", in the empyrean of the "eternal harmony"'.[30] Instead of the diatonic system, he puts forward 113 seven-note scales, which repeat at the octave. Busoni also notes that the pitch spectrum itself is infinite and develops a notation for sixth tones: 'Nature created an infinite gradation – infinite!'[31] Therefore, not only does the realm of

---

[28] Michael Cowan, *Cult of the Will: Nervousness and German Modernity* (University Park, Pa., 2008), p. 136. Antony Beaumont notes that Busoni wanted to be able to fly, a psychological fact that may inform this aspect of Busoni's writing (*Busoni the Composer* (London, 1985), p. 30). Busoni writes: 'Who has not dreamt that he could float on air? and firmly believed his dream to be a reality?' ('Sketch of a New Esthetic of Music', p. 95).

[29] Busoni's vision here would go on to be echoed, in part, by the figure of the child rising from the ground and walking confidently towards the future that appears in the final tableau of *Doktor Faust*. In Busoni's magnum opus, composed between 1916 and 1923, but left unfinished at his death, the plot contrasts this figure with the inert, straw effigy of a child born to the Duchess of Parma.

[30] Busoni, 'Sketch of a New Esthetic of Music', pp. 92–3.

[31] Ibid., p. 89.

music contain all melodies heard and not heard, we must presume that it also comprises all possible microtonalities and their instantiation in melody.

Busoni does not put forward any proposals regarding duration or rhythm in 'Sketch of a New Esthetic of Music'. Yet, there is one area in which the related but broader issue of temporality does figure. When talking about *Ur-Musik*, Busoni points to introductory and transitional material as that in which the true nature of music is revealed:

> All composers have drawn nearest the true nature of music in preparatory and intermediary passages (preludes and transitions), where they felt at liberty to disregard symmetrical proportions, and unconsciously drew free breath. ... But the moment they cross the threshold of the *Principal Subject*, their attitude becomes stiff and conventional, like that of a man entering some high bureau of officialdom.[32]

Raymond Monelle's distinction between 'lyric' and 'progressive' time maps neatly onto Busoni's opposition and helps to clarify it.[33] According to Monelle, lyric time is that of seamless melodic unfolding, an unceasing 'now' in which the melody is perceived as a oneness as it happens, not as a series of disconnected individual pitches or moments. Furthermore, lyric time tends to be based on a cyclical pattern of stresses deriving ultimately from dance metres; its phrases lean to the harmonically stable and syntactically symmetrical. In contrast, progressive time gives a sense of forward movement towards, or away from, lyric time. This is heard in transitional and modulatory sequences, which tend towards the harmonically unstable and syntactically asymmetrical. Monelle traces an increase in the prominence of progressive time in musical composition from the late sixteenth to the twentieth century. It would seem, then, that progressive time – which emphasises flux and transcends the lyric moment – is for Busoni the temporality that most closely approaches *Ur-Musik*. This speculation finds support in 'The Realm of Music', when Busoni describes the 'unthought-of-scales ... *eternally in motion*'.[34] Music as an art of becoming, of movement forwards, seems to be what Busoni is espousing.

Busoni's comments on notation are perhaps the most frequently quoted part of the 'Sketch of a New Esthetic of Music': 'Every notation is, in itself, the transcription of an abstract idea. The instant the pen seizes it, the idea loses its original form.'[35] Here, Busoni displays a keen awareness of what is at stake for the composer. He perceives an irreconcilable tension between how to keep music afloat ('this child, it floats on air!') whilst using notation (*'the rigidity of*

---

[32] Ibid., p. 79.

[33] Raymond Monelle, *The Sense of Music: Semiotic Essays* (Princeton, NJ, 2000), esp. pp. 81–114.

[34] Busoni, 'The Realm of Music', p. 189.

[35] Busoni, 'Sketch of a New Esthetic of Music', p. 85.

the signs').[36] To borrow Jeanne Bamberger's terminology, we can say that for Busoni the melodies of the realm of music are 'events' which notation threatens to turn into 'objects'.[37] The sense of eternal becoming in the realm of music is made, through musical notation, into something static. Fixity replaces flux.

In its language-like nature, musical notation is amenable to consideration in terms of the philosophy of language. It shares with language the essence of abstraction. In both language and musical notation, there is a disjunction between the signifier and signified. In terms of language, this fact was recognised by Busoni's contemporaries. Just five years before 'Sketch of a New Esthetic of Music' was published, Hugo von Hofmanstahl wrote the 'Lord Chandos Letter' which Busoni would go on to quote in his 1907 tract. In a text with several echoes of Busoni's writings, Hofmanstahl shares his scepticism about the possibilities of language as a means of thought and expression. He tells of 'a kind of feverish thinking, but thinking in a medium more direct, fluid, and passionate than words' as well as his desire to write a book in 'a language of which I know not one word, a language in which mute things speak to me and in which I will perhaps have something to say for myself someday when I am dead and standing before an unknown judge'.[38] Thus we have an expression of what became known as the *Sprachkrise*, a crisis of language that would encompass the work of many significant figures in the first part of the twentieth century, including Ludwig Wittgenstein, whose *Tractatus Logico-Philosophicus* (1921) gives perhaps the most famous expression of the limits of language: 'Whereof we cannot speak, thereof we must remain silent.'[39]

Whilst for Busoni the slippage in the process of translation from the realm into notation entails a loss, his aesthetics maintain an idealistic stance, and he does not think himself into a corner of quietism or a 'mysticism of silence'.[40]

---

[36]   Ibid., pp. 77, 84.

[37]   Jeanne Bamberger, 'How the Conventions of Music Notation Shape Musical Perception and Performance', in Dorothy Miell, Raymond MacDonald and David J. Hargreaves (eds), *Musical Communication* (Oxford, 2005), pp. 143–70 (p. 143).

[38]   Hugo von Hofmanstahl, 'The Lord Chandos Letter', in *The Lord Chandos Letter and Other Writings*, ed. Joel Rotenberg (New York, 2005), pp. 117–28 (pp. 127–8). The quote appears at the end of Busoni's 'Sketch of a New Esthetic of Music' (p. 102). In the introduction to Rotenberg's edition, John Banville notes that, for Hofmanstahl, poetry mediates 'between life of the spirit and life in the world' and the lyric 'brings us to a realization of universal unity' ('Introduction', to Hofmanstahl, *The Lord Chandos Letter*, pp. vii–xii (p. viii)). The transposition of these sentiments to the realm of music is obvious in Busoni's texts.

[39]   Ludwig Wittgenstein, *Tractatus Logico-Philosophicus* (London, 1974), p. 74. For a specific discussion of the dissolution of duality in language in terms of the *Sprachkrise*, see Sami Sjöberg, 'Mysticism of Immanence: Lettrism, Sprachkritik, and the Immediate Message', *Partial Answers: Journal of Literature and the History of Ideas*, 11/1 (2013): 53–69.

[40]   Sjöberg, 'Mysticism of Immanence', p. 54.

For him, any loss that the instability of musical notation brings about is not irrevocable: 'What the composer's inspiration *necessarily loses* through notation, his interpreter should restore by his own. ... Great artists play their own works ... according to the given conditions of that "eternal harmony".'[41] This allows for the tradition of performance to be an organic one, but places an ethical responsibility on the performer to fathom the spirit of the work. Similarly, although Hofmanstahl writes: 'I felt an inexplicable uneasiness in even pronouncing the words "spirit", "soul", or "body"', Busoni has no such qualms.[42] Whilst he acknowledges the absence of absolute truth in notational or performative terms, he nevertheless seems to maintain a certain confidence in language itself, using it to describe aspects of the realm of music. Busoni's constant resort to certain rhetorical figures does suggest that he is working at the limits of language: hyperbole, repetition and above all paradox each play their part in expressing the immensity of the 'realm of music'. The hope placed in the role of the interpreter and in what is possible provides Busoni with the impetus to continue in his musical and spiritual quest. Idealism appears to win out. As Erinn Knyt puts it, 'Busoni considered it impossible actually to attain the "absolute" in tangible works. But this did not mean that it was not a very real concept for him – it was certainly worth striving for and influenced how he composed.'[43]

Returning to the possible influence of Hölderlin on Busoni, we can enlist Steiner, who puts in a nutshell what is at stake for the creative artist in the act of giving form to what is protean. Although Busoni is not mentioned by name, his aesthetic constellation of the infinite, the universality of the child, the inescapability of abstraction and paradox, and the notion of perpetual motion are all present:

> Hölderlin defines the function and aim of art as '*die Vergegenwärtung des Unendlichen*' ('the making present, the making contemporary of the unbounded'). How, he asks, can that which is in incessant motion ... be made 'punctual'. ... The poet, the artist, chooses freely to set himself or herself in opposition to the claims of the non-finite. He seeks mediation between a child's indiscriminate identification with the wholeness of the world ... and the willed abstraction which, ineluctably, chooses expressive but bounded form. Thus there

---

[41] Busoni, 'Sketch of a New Esthetic of Music', pp. 84–5.

[42] Hofmanstahl, 'The Lord Chandos Letter', p. 121.

[43] Knyt, 'Ferruccio Busoni and the Ontology of the Musical Work', p. 63. Tamara Levitz also shows how Busoni's idealism shone through in his teaching and notes that idealism informed much of 'musical life in general in Berlin in the 1920s' (*Teaching New Classicality: Ferruccio Busoni's Master Class in Composition* (Frankfurt am Main, 1996), p. 289).

is in mature poetics an understanding ... of irreconcilable contradiction. Motion
is at rest, communicating the paradox of the 'momentarily lasting'.[44]

Improvisation and Dialogue

Just as the early years of the twentieth century saw a crisis in language, they
also witnessed a paradigm shift in the way that time was understood. Einstein's
theories of special and general relativity were published in 1905 and 1916
respectively. During which period Busoni espoused the idea of the omnipresence
of time, according to which it did not move linearly but in all directions.[45] His
view on this matter explains in part why Busoni felt so near to the music of the
past and why he intuited future developments so enthusiastically, even if he
himself did not realise many of his visions. Busoni strove for the dissolution of
the duality of past and present, in a way similar to his quest for the dissolution
of signifier and signified.

The overcoming of opposites is fundamental to Busoni's emphasis on oneness
in the production and reception of music: 'The time has come to recognise the
whole phenomenon of music as a "oneness" and no longer to split it up according
to its purpose, form and sound-medium.'[46] Busoni's concern is to divine the
essence of music and in so doing to transcend the barriers of language, which sets
up generic labels that obfuscate music's nature. This divination entails a sort of
phenomenological 'bracketing off', whose appeal, as Wayne Bowman puts it, lies
in its promise 'to help people set aside their tendencies to hear types and classes,
in order to experience [music's] essentially sonorous nature'.[47] This in turn echoes
Busoni's assertion that music is 'sonorous air'.[48] To this extent, and along with
his ideas about notation, performance and the realm of music, we can therefore

---

[44]   Steiner, *Grammars of Creation*, p. 102.

[45]   Busoni, letter to his wife Gerda, 30 March 1911, cited in Beaumont, *Busoni the
Composer*, p. 29. Della Couling notes that the relativity of time was also central to *Die
Serapionsbrüder*, E.T.A. Hoffmann's collection of stories, which predated Einstein's
theories by a century and would give Busoni the inspiration for his opera *Die Brautwahl*
(1908) (Della Couling, *Ferruccio Busoni: A Musical Ishmael* (Oxford, 2005), p. 247).

[46]   Ferruccio Busoni, 'The Essence and Oneness of Music', in *The Essence of Music
and Other Papers*, pp. 1–16 (p. 1). Busoni's focus on oneness may also be traced through
his background and is probably, in part, a result of his cosmopolitanism and relative
rootlessness (Beaumont, *Busoni the Composer*, p. 23) as well as his striving for 'a spiritual
plane above the level of conflicting opposites' (Geiser, quoted in Levitz, *Teaching New
Classicality*, p. 226).

[47]   Wayne C. Bowman, *Philosophical Perspectives on Music* (Oxford, 1998), p. 259.

[48]   Busoni, 'Sketch of a New Esthetic of Music', p. 77.

understand Busoni's writings as an expression of a particular, if unsystematic, phenomenology of music.[49]

Within such a phenomenology, Busoni considered himself able to draw together and work with the 'stuff of music', which filled the realm. In a bid to foster what he termed a 'Young' or 'New Classicality', Busoni encouraged his students to do the same, to compose in a synthetic and transformative way: 'I mean the mastery, the sifting and the turning to account of all the gains of previous experiments and their inclusion in strong and beautiful forms.'[50] This is exemplified in Busoni's own music, in the large number of pieces that are based on existing motives, textures, themes and pieces, for instance his piano transcription of the chaconne from Bach's *Partita No. 2* for solo violin. In taking another's music and reworking it in quite remarkable ways Busoni swam against the tide of prevailing aesthetic values, which prized 'original' works above all other musical expressions. However, if, as Busoni maintains, all the strains of music exist already in the realm of music, we might well ask how anything can be original. Busoni put it succinctly: 'There is no new or old. Only known and not yet known.'[51]

Busoni saw the activity of the composer as one of synthesis and transformation, not 'creation' per se. In this way, Busoni prefigures by almost 100 years the insights of Bruce Ellis Benson:

> Composers never create *ex nihilo*, but instead 'improvise': sometimes on tunes that already exist, but more frequently and importantly on the tradition in which they work. ... The problem here is that neither creation nor discovery seems quite adequate to describe the process of composing. ... But *improvisation* very nicely captures both of these aspects. To improvise is to rework something that already exists ... and thus to transform it into something that both has connections to what it once was but now has a new identity. ... By replacing the 'creation model' with an *improvisational model*, I think we have a more phenomenologically accurate picture of what actually takes place in making music.[52]

There is no better articulation of Busoni's compositional practice than this: improvisation over diverse traditions. In this way, Busoni can be read as being

---

[49] Paul Fleet, more than any other, discusses how Busoni's aesthetics complement and align with phenomenology (*Ferruccio Busoni: A Phenomenological Approach to his Music and Aesthetics* (Saarbrücken, 2009)).

[50] Ferruccio Busoni, 'Young Classicism', in *The Essence of Music and Other Papers*, pp. 19–23 (p. 20). For a comprehensive discussion of Busoni's teaching of the Young or New Classicality, see Levitz, *Teaching New Classicality*.

[51] Ferruccio Busoni, 'Self-Criticism', in *The Essence of Music and Other Papers*, pp. 46–50 (p. 47).

[52] Bruce Ellis Benson, *The Improvisation of Musical Dialogue: A Phenomenology of Music* (Oxford, 2003), pp. 25, 45, 52.

in dialogue with those whom he paraphrases and quotes. His writings and music make a virtue of the fact that the artist's work is always 'phenomenologically social'.[53] The realm of music is directly accessible to him and once entered puts him in contact with many other musicians and musics. It is this, besides an ongoing tradition of quotation and paraphrase, which gives Busoni the freedom to play with and rework existing music in his arrangements and transcriptions.

Thus, we can now add that, besides being a transcendent space, the realm of music is also an improvisational and dialogical space, which permits Busoni to converse artistically with past and future music. In this way, Busoni's peregrinations in the realm of music mirror the explorations of hell, purgatory and paradise in the work of Dante Alighieri. Dante was one of Busoni's favourite authors during his teenage years and exerted a fascination on him throughout his life.[54] In *La divina commedia*, many personages, who lived at different times, co-exist and communicate with one another. Even though their respective degrees of dialogism may be different, the imaginaries of Dante and Busoni both transcend historical boundaries and allow their respective authors to interact creatively with consciousnesses from other epochs.

Polyphony, the Work Concept and Proto-Postmodernism

Above all the elements of music, Busoni prioritised melody. Levitz states that for Busoni, 'the melodic germ expressed an eternal spiritual truth'.[55] This led naturally to a passion for polyphony, which, in the hands of Busoni, meant simultaneous melodic lines of increasing independence. The fact that the melodic voices of the realm of music are innumerable and 'resound completely and simultaneously' gives us a picture of the realm as a thoroughly polyphonic space.[56] This vast intertwining polyphony is made manifest in earthly terms not only in the organ music of Bach (which Busoni praises above all else), but is also realised to some extent through his own contrapuntal skill, for example in the *Fantasia contrappuntistica* (1912), and also in his poly-stylism. This plurality, which bears out his striving for musical oneness, is heard both within single pieces that explore different musical styles and registers, such as *Doktor Faust* (begun in 1916 but left unfinished at his death) and between diverse pieces that reference sources such as Native American, middle Eastern and oriental folk traditions (*Indianisches Tagebuch*, 1916; *Turandot*, 1917), opera (*Kammerfantasie über Carmen*, 1920)

---

[53]   Steiner, *Grammars of Creation*, p. 180.

[54]   The work of Dante also features prominently in Busoni's theatre piece *Arlecchino* (1916), and Busoni for many years considered Dante as a choice of hero for his final opera, an honour that would eventually go to Doktor Faustus.

[55]   Levitz, *Teaching New Classicality*, p. 203.

[56]   Busoni, 'The Realm of Music', p. 189.

and the work of Bach, Mozart and Rossini, amongst others.[57] In all cases, the intertextuality of musical composition comes to the fore.

This became uncomfortable for some of Busoni's contemporaries, especially when their music was the subject of his transcriptions or arrangements. As Edward Dent wrote, Busoni 'refused to see anything sacred and unalterable in the written notes of a piece of music, or in the sounds produced by any one particular instrument'.[58] This attitude led Busoni famously to make free with Schoenberg's *Klavierstück* op. 11 no. 2, much to the Viennese composer's alarm.[59] For Busoni, this new piece was just another instance of unknown music having been made known. Due to his access to the realm of music, it was as available to him for reworking as was Bach's chaconne. Theoretically speaking, one could claim that the realm of music contained all the versions of the *Klavierstück* that Schoenberg did not write. For Busoni, perhaps, it is simply one of these that he transcribed.

This affair pointed up one of the fundamental differences between the two composers. Whereas Schoenberg's view of musical progress was teleological and tended towards historical inevitability, Busoni's perspective was ahistorical, allowing – theoretically at least – for an infinite number of possible solutions to the problems of artistic creativity. Schoenberg, more than Busoni, was wedded to nineteenth-century notions of the ownership of original musical material, clearly demarcated authorship and the work concept. In contrast to this, Busoni's attitude prefigured a range of later twentieth-century musical practices that promoted distributed authorship and emphasised music as process rather than product, such as free jazz, experimental improvisation and Fluxus, to name but three. In these practices there is also an element of transcendence, at least in the fact that they move beyond the neat boundaries of composer-performer or performer-score relationships that rely on a hypostasised division of labour. Busoni himself ensured that performers of his music had choices not allowed by his contemporaries; some of his compositions provide diverse options for performance, such as the *Paganini–Liszt Etüde no. 6* (1914), which contains not only Busoni's versions, but the 'originals' as well.[60] The idea that the performer's art is fundamentally one of making choices, and not following slavishly '*the rigidity of the signs*', is made explicit.[61] However, in Busoni's aesthetics there remains at root a tension between what is in flux and what is bounded. As John

---

[57] For Busoni's poly-stylism, see Knyt, 'Ferruccio Busoni and the Ontology of the Musical Work'.

[58] Edward J. Dent, *Ferruccio Busoni: A Biography* (Oxford, 1933), p. 111.

[59] For a detailed analysis of Busoni's reworking of Schoenberg's piece, see Erinn E. Knyt, '"How I Compose": Ferruccio Busoni's Views about Invention, Quotation, and the Compositional Process', *Journal of Musicology*, 27/2 (2011): 224–64 (esp. pp. 228–32).

[60] For a detailed exegesis of this piece, see ibid.

[61] Busoni, 'Sketch of a New Esthetic of Music', p. 84.

Williamson states, 'Busoni verged on a performance-led musical culture, while seeming to subscribe implicitly to ... the sanctity of the work'.[62]

Busoni's emphasis on the fluidity of performance and the collapsing of time, alongside the idea of the realm of music as an ahistorical and dialogical space, result in a phenomenology of music that has a proto-postmodernist character. The realm can be read as a picture of the inevitable intertextuality of creative work and the way in which one text implicates every other. As Busoni himself expressed it, 'if you focus your attention on one of them [all the melodies heard before or never heard] you perceive how it is connected with all the others'.[63] Thus, Jacques Derrida's 'there is nothing outside of the text' can easily be applied to Busoni's vision of the realm of music, which in this light figures as a musical meta-text, with no outside, no limits, historical or otherwise.[64] A decade previous to Derrida's formulation, Jorge Luis Borges wrote his well-known fable of the infinite library, which shares a similar vision. Borges conceived the library as a sphere that is total and whose 'shelves register ... all that it is given to express, in all languages'.[65] Whereas this would seem to be a literary analogue to Busoni's musical realm, there is a darker side to Borges's imaginary: 'The certitude that everything has been written negates us.'[66] For Busoni, on the other hand, the realm of music is one of transcendental plenitude, of infinite promise, which, rather than negating the composer or performer, demands engagement from them, even if it is not given to them to manifest its abundance fully.

---

[62]   John Williamson, 'The Musical Artwork and Its Materials in the Music and Aesthetics of Busoni', in Michael Talbot (ed.), *The Musical Work: Reality or Invention?* (Liverpool, 2000), pp. 187–204 (p. 200).

[63]   Busoni, 'The Realm of Music', p. 189.

[64]   Jacques Derrida, *Of Grammatology*, trans. Gayatri Chakravorty Spivak (Baltimore, 1997), p. 158. In the realm of music, not only are historical boundaries of time and space transcended, but earthly legal ones are also called into question. It comes as no surprise, therefore, that in his last years Busoni made notes about copyright and plagiarism (Levitz, *Teaching New Classicality*, pp. 204–5).

[65]   Jorge Luis Borges, *Labyrinths* (London, 1970), p. 81.

[66]   Ibid., p. 85.

Chapter 4

Creatio ex improvisatione: Chrétien on the Call

Bruce Ellis Benson

Ex nihilo nihil fit. From nothing comes nothing. That would seem to be the collective wisdom of the ancients, whether Babylonian, Greek or Hebrew. Thus, the creation accounts found in various ancient Mesopotamian texts are always 'from something'. And yet this is not the orthodox Christian version of creation, despite what some consider to be biblical evidence in favour of it. Early Christian theologians generally supported the 'from something' account and probably would have considered the 'from nothing' account to be nonsense. Of course, as one might guess, things are somewhat more complicated than this. But one thing is sure, the German theologian Gerhard May is certainly right when he states: 'church theology wants through the proposition *creatio ex nihilo* to express and safeguard the omnipotence and freedom of God acting in history'.[1] At issue, then, are the notions of 'power' and 'freedom'. The God who can create *ex nihilo* is simply more powerful and free than the God who merely creates from that which already exists.

Not surprisingly, power and freedom are very much part of our conception of the creations wrought by human beings. Our views of the genesis of art have been heavily shaped by our views of the nature of divine creation. Just as we can distinguish between a 'strong creator' and a 'weak creator' of the cosmos, so we can differentiate between strong and weak creators of arts. In what follows, I seek to accomplish three tasks. First, I briefly consider the Christian doctrine of *creatio ex nihilo* and bring that consideration to bear on how we think about artistic creation. Second, I return to the biblical text to provide an alternative conception of artistic creation, one that moves from the idea of 'creation' to that of 'improvisation'. In so doing, the artist is seen in a significantly different light. Third, I relate this idea of improvisation to the call and response structure put forth by Jean-Louis Chrétien.

Creatio ex nihilo

The writer of Genesis opens by saying:

---

[1]   Gerhard May, *Creatio Ex Nihilo: The Doctrine of 'Creation out of Nothing' in Early Christian Thought*, trans. A.S. Worrall (Edinburgh, 1994), p. 180.

In the beginning when God created the heavens and the earth, the earth was a formless void and darkness covered the face of the deep, while a wind from God swept over the face of the waters. Then God said, 'Let there be light'; and there was light.[2]

What exactly is God doing here? Further, what is this 'beginning' (*re'sit*) and where does it begin? These are the basic questions regarding any kind of genesis, which boils down to: at what point can we say that something begins? It is significant that the *Oxford English Dictionary* defines 'genesis' as 'the action of building up from simple or basic elements to more complex ones', for something like that seems to be described here. The earth is described as 'a formless void' and 'darkness covered the face of the deep [*tohu vabohu* or "the depth in the dark"]'. And then God creates (*bara*). On this account, things are already *in medias res*, 'in the middle of affairs'. That is, there is already something going on and then God enters the picture.

Yet, even though Ian Barbour claims that 'creation "out of nothing" is not a biblical concept', there exists evidence to the contrary.[3] In 2 Maccabees 7:28, a mother implores her son to 'recognize that God did not make them out of things that existed' (NRSV); we could translate this phrase simply as 'realize that God made them [the world] out of nothing'. Gerhard von Rad claims quite simply that 'the conceptional formulation creatio ex nihilo is first found' in this passage.[4] Further, one can point to New Testament passages in which God or Christ is claimed by Paul to be the creator of all things: Romans 11:36 tells us that 'from him … are all things'; Colossians 1:16 says that 'in him [or by him, i.e. Christ] all things in heaven and on earth were created, things visible and invisible'. Paul is very clearly attempting to establish Christ as a very powerful figure.

Let us leave aside the theological case for the moment and ask a different, though very closely related question. What would a strong artistic account of creation look like? Here it is helpful to turn to the philosopher Immanuel Kant (1724–1804). A phrase we can use to unpack his account is his claim that 'fine art is the art of genius'.[5] But, first, a couple of points of comparison in relation to the notion of 'genius'. In 1746, the French theorist Charles Batteux (1713–80) had argued that art was all about 'imitating' nature and that the genius was the one who was a superb imitator.[6] This conception of genius is easy enough to understand, for such a genius is essentially someone who has learned the techniques of a given type of art form and has become a highly developed craftsman. Johann Sebastian Bach (1685–1750) would seem to have held such a view, given his reported

2   Gen. 1:1–3 (NRSV).
3   Ian Barbour, *Issues in Science and Religion* (Englewood Cliffs, NJ, 1966), p. 384.
4   Gerhard von Rad, *Old Testament Theology*, trans. D.M.G. Stalker, vol. 1 (New York, 1962), p. 142.
5   Immanuel Kant, *Critique of Judgment*, trans. W.S. Pluhar (Indianapolis, 1987), §46.
6   Charles Batteux, *Les Beaux Arts réduits à un même principe* (Paris, 1746).

comment: 'I worked hard. Anyone who works as hard as I did can achieve the same results.'[7] Yet consider how different the following description of the genius is, given by William Duff (1732–1815) in 1770:

> A man of genius is really a kind of different being from the rest of the species. The bent of his disposition, the complexion of his temper, the general turn of his character, his passions and his pursuits are for the most part very dissimilar from those of the bulk of mankind. Hence partly it happens that his manners appear ridiculous to some and disagreeable to others.[8]

Someone like Vincent van Gogh comes to mind.

To sum up Kant's account of genius in *Critique of Judgement*: (1) true geniuses are original, (2) what they create is exemplary for everyone else and (3) they are unable to explain how they created their masterpieces. Accordingly, artistic creations are both original and exemplary and the art of the genius is innovative. No more influential expression of this idea of creation exists than that from a famous letter attributed to Wolfgang Amadeus Mozart (1756–91):

> Concerning my way of composing ... I can really say no more on this subject than the following; for I myself know no more about it, and cannot account for it. When I am, as it were, completely myself, entirely alone, and of good cheer – say, travelling in a carriage, or walking after a good meal, or during the night when I cannot sleep; it is on such occasions that my ideas flow best and most abundantly. *Whence* and *how* they come, I know not; nor can I force them. ... When I proceed to write down my ideas, I take out of the bag of my memory ... what has previously been collected into it. ... For this reason the committing to paper is done quickly enough, for everything is, as I said before, already finished; and it rarely differs on paper from what it was in my imagination.[9]

There is something so gloriously 'romantic' about this account that it is almost painful to discover that it is a pure fabrication by Friedrich Rochlitz, who was both a fan of Mozart and had been influenced by Kant's notion of the genius. Rochlitz's account of Mozart's composition process is how Rochlitz envisioned it to be. It is as if we want our artists to be capable of something like magical power. The contemporary philosopher of music Jerrold Levinson goes so far as to say:

> The whole tradition of art assumes art is creative in the strict sense, that it is a godlike activity in which the artist brings into being what did not exist

---

[7] This quotation is commonly attributed to Bach.

[8] William Duff, *Critical Observations on the Writings of the Most Celebrated Original Geniuses in Poetry* (London, 1770), p. 339.

[9] Quoted in Maynard Solomon, 'Beethoven's Creative Process: A Two-Part Invention', in *Beethoven Essays* (Cambridge, Mass., 1988), pp. 126–38 (p. 129).

beforehand – much as a demiurge forms a world out of inchoate matter. ... There is a special aura that envelops composers, as well as other artists, because we think of them as true creators.[10]

While one cannot universalise this view to 'the *whole* tradition of art', it has clearly held sway for more or less the last couple of centuries, that is, during the modern, or Romantic, period.

Seeing the true artist as genius has consequences, quite problematic ones. First, the genius myth has promoted the myth of the artist as some sort of 'lone creator' who neither needs nor wants the influence of, or interaction with, others – the artist alone in a garret. Second, whereas artists had generally been seen as craftsmen (Bach's view was a predominant one in western history up until that point), now they become 'godlike'. For instance, the German writers Wilhelm Heinrich Wackenroder (1773–98) and Ludwig Tieck (1773–1853) speak of artists as 'a few chosen men whom [God] has anointed as His favorites'.[11] Johann Nikolaus Forkel (1749–1818), in his biography of Bach, suggests that some of Bach's works could be mentioned 'only with a kind of holy worship' (a claim that Bach – who wrote S.D.G. for *Soli Deo gloria* (for God's glory alone) on his scores – could never have imagined making).[12] George Bizet (1838–75) goes so far as to say that 'Beethoven is not a human, he is a god.'[13] And Carl Maria von Weber demands that the composer become 'free as a god'.[14] So artists become either special agents of God or else gods themselves. It is one thing to say that God is the giver of talents that allows us to make art; it is quite another thing to say that the artist is thereby somehow like or equal to God.

As should be clear from the account I have given so far, the rise in status of the artist was all about power and freedom. In this respect, it strongly mirrors the conception of God as creator *ex nihilo*. Further, whilst I realise that I am painting with a rather broad brush and that all points are contestable, I think that the general contours of my argument are correct, even if exceptions can be found.

Yet what if we were to return to the creation account and mould a very different conception of artistic activity?

---

[10]   Jerrold Levinson, 'What a Musical Work Is', in *Music, Art, and Metaphysics: Essays in Philosophical Aesthetics* (Ithaca, NY, 1990), pp. 63–88 (pp. 66–7).

[11]   Wilhelm Heinrich Wackenroder and Ludwig Tieck, *Outpourings of an Art-Loving Friar*, trans. E. Mornin (New York, 1975), p. 59.

[12]   Johann Nikolaus Forkel, *Über Johann Sebastian Bachs Leben, Kunst und Kunstwerke*, ed. W. Vetter (Kassel, 1970), p. 12.

[13]   Walter Salmen, 'Social Obligations of the Emancipated Musician in the 19th Century', trans. H. Kaufman and B. Reisner, in W. Salmen, H. Kaufman and B. Reisner (eds), *The Social Status of the Professional Musician from the Middle Ages to the 19th Century* (New York, 1983), pp. 265–81 (p. 269).

[14]   Friedrich Blume, *Classic and Romantic Music: A Comprehensive Survey*, trans. M.D. Herter Horton (New York: 1970), p. 91.

Creatio ex improvisatione

Theologian Catherine Keller speaks of 'the mystery of the missing chaos'.[15] How, she asks, have theologians simply forgotten about chaos? The goal of her book *Face of the Deep: A Theology of Becoming* is to deconstruct *ex nihilo* theology and return to the forgotten chaos. Writing as a feminist theologian, she claims that the *ex nihilo* account is a highly masculine one. As we have seen, it belongs to a discourse of power. In its place, Keller suggests a theology of becoming in which we rethink the very notion of beginning. In this respect, she is indebted to Edward Said, who distinguishes between 'beginning' and 'origin'. Whereas beginnings are 'secular, humanly produced and ceaselessly re-examined', origins are 'divine, mythical and privileged'.[16] In effect, the problem with origin is that it erases the deep and the past. It speaks only of a moment, and it passes over the chaos out of which creation takes place. Yet, to quote Keller, 'what if we begin instead to read the Word from the vantage point of its own fecund multiplicity, its flux into flesh, its overflow?'[17]

Keller reminds us that we begin amidst chaos and flux. In this respect, the verb 'to begin' means something other than at least one definition that the *OED* provides – 'take the first step'. One never truly begins, for there is always a step that has already been made. Keller wants to make this point not merely for human beings but also for God. She quotes theologian William P. Brown approvingly: 'by and large God does not work *de novo* or *ex nihilo*, but *ex voce* and *per collaborationi*'.[18] To understand what Brown means by this statement, we must return to the Genesis account and note that God works with the earth and the waters in a collaborative way so as to produce animals and sea monsters. God says: 'Be fruitful and multiply and fill the waters in the seas' and 'Let the earth bring forth living creatures of every kind.'[19]

The second-century Church Father Justin Martyr wrote that 'in the beginning [God] of His goodness, for people's sakes, formed all things out of unformed matter'.[20] On this account, God orders that which already exists. And that is precisely the problem for the third-century Church Father Athanasius:

> If this be so, God will be on their theory a Mechanic only, and not a Creator out of nothing; if, that is, He works at existing material, but is not Himself the cause

---

[15] Catherine Keller, *Face of the Deep: A Theology of Becoming* (London, 2003), ch. 1.

[16] Edward Said, *Beginnings: Intention and Method* (New York, 1985), pp. xii–xiii.

[17] Keller, *Face of the Deep*, p. 19.

[18] William P. Brown, *The Ethos of the Cosmos: The Genesis of Moral Imagination in the Bible* (Grand Rapids, Mich., 1999), p. 41.

[19] Gen. 1:22, 24.

[20] Justin Martyr, *The First Apology*, 10, in *St Justin Martyr: The First and Second Apologies*, trans. L.W. Barnard (Mahwah, NJ, 1997), p. 28.

of the material. For He could not in any sense be called Creator unless He is Creator of the material of which the things created have in their turn been made.[21]

Yet Athanasius gives us what is surely a false dilemma: we must choose between a God who acts as a mechanic and a God who is a creator *ex nihilo*. Is there no middle ground? While working on this chapter, I was delighted to discover that a colleague of mine – an Old Testament scholar named John Walton – has provided what I consider to be a very helpful interpretation. He insists that we must consider the question 'What is the text asserting that God did in this context?' His answer is that God brings heaven and earth, or the cosmos, into existence 'by assigning roles and functions'.[22] In other words, the text is not about 'Where does the cosmos come from?' but 'Why does the cosmos have the order and structure that it has?' Of course, it also gives us a different idea of creation – even God works with material that is already there. And Walton makes the point that this is exactly what is meant by the Hebrew word *bara* that we translate as '[God] created'. So the issue is not existence versus non-existence but order.

On either view, God is an improviser. For creation – however we define it – is precisely God setting in motion a reality of 'ceaseless alterations' (to cite John Milbank).[23] Thus, the very being of life is improvisatory – by which I mean that it is a mixture of both structure and contingency, of regularity and unpredictability, of constraint and possibility. Further, if God is indeed still at work in the world, then God is likewise part of that improvisatory movement, and creatures, embedded in multiple and ever-changing historical and cultural milieus, with existences that arise from our relations to others and the world inhabited, also take part in that improvisatory movement.[24]

So how would this view of God translate into an account of artistic creation? On my view, we end up with *creatio ex improvisatione* (a Latin term that only rarely occurs and only after the fifteenth century). Artistic genesis, then, always begins somewhere. Some ideas come in a moment, but many aspects have to be worked out over days, weeks, months – even years. And those ideas do not usually arise in isolation but by being connected: with other artists, the history of art, inspiring friends, and the world of everyday life.

---

[21]   Athanasius, *On the Incarnation of the Word* II.3.4, in *Selected Works and Letters*, ed. A. Robinson, Nicene and Post-Nicene Fathers, ser. 2: 4 (Buffalo, NY, 1892).

[22]   John H. Walton, *The Lost World of Genesis One: Ancient Cosmology and the Origins Debate* (Downers Grove, Ill., 2009), p. 62; id., *Genesis*, NIV Application Commentary (Grand Rapids, Mich., 2001), p. 71.

[23]   John Milbank, '"Postmodern Critical Augustinianism": A Short Summa in Forty-Two Responses to Unasked Questions', *Modern Theology*, 7/3 (1991): 225–37 (p. 227).

[24]   Hegel may be the first to show how inter-subjectivity – the interconnected nature of human persons – is constitutive of human subjectivity, though he is certainly not the last (see Georg Wilhelm Friedrich Hegel, *Phenomenology of Spirit*, trans. A.V. Miller (Oxford, 1977), pp. 178–96).

Romantic music celebrates the original innovative artist. In contrast, Baroque music does virtually the opposite. Baroque music is much more of a community affair, something not done alone but with others. This was true of both how composers and performers worked, in true improvisatory fashion. The musicologist David Fuller describes the situation as follows: 'A large part of the music of the whole era was sketched rather than fully realised, and the performer had something of the responsibility of a child with a colouring book, to turn these sketches into rounded art-works.' Fuller compares the 'scores' of Baroque music to the 'charts' or 'fake books' one finds in jazz.[25] The composer provided some idea of how the piece was to go, but a substantial portion of the heard musical shape was up to the performer.

Yet it was not merely the performer who was improvising; it was likewise the composer. Here it is helpful to juxtapose the notion of creation with that of improvisation. By using the term 'improvisation' instead of 'creation', I mean to stress that artists 'fabricate out of what is conveniently on hand' rather than create in the sense of 'to produce where nothing was before'.[26] In making art, we always start with something. The extreme side of such borrowing would today come under the rubric of plagiarism. It may come as rather a surprise that Bach was in the habit of starting with a melody appropriated from either himself or someone else. A well-known example of his creative borrowing is how the popular song 'Innsbruch, ich muß dich lassen' (Innsbruch, I must leave you) morphed into 'O Welt, ich muß dich lassen' (Oh World, I must leave you), becoming part of his *St Matthew Passion*. Of course, this was standard practice at the time – a time when the idea of ownership of intellectual property did not really exist.

Such a conception of artistic creation is strikingly at odds with that of the modern/Romantic paradigm. Now, I admit that many modern artists both have been and are currently committed to 'pushing the envelope'. What I am questioning is just how original even the most supposed original pieces of art actually are. I fully admit that, say, Pablo Picasso's painting *Les Desmoiselles d'Avignon* (1907) and the Beatles's album *Sgt Pepper's Lonely Hearts Club Band* (1967) are landmark – even in ways original – artistic contributions. Yet it strikes me that these examples are nothing like a complete departure from their respective genres but instead are a significant advance within them. That is to say that they are still part of a recognizable genre and not something entirely new, representing ways of reworking what already existed in semi-new ways. Thus, I am contending that the old wisdom of Ecclesiastes still holds: 'There is nothing new under the sun.'[27] Without doubt, there is reworking, revision, rethinking and renewal – but

---

[25] David Fuller, 'The Performer as Composer', in H.M. Brown and S. Sadie (eds), *Performance Practice*, vol. 2 (Houndmills, UK, 1989), pp. 117–18. A 'fake book' provides the performer with chords and melody, with the expectation that the performer 'fake' the rest.

[26] See *Merriam-Webster's Collegiate Dictionary*, s.v. 'improvise'; *OED*, s.v. 'create'.

[27] Eccles. 1:9.

there is no true revolution. Here I side with the philosopher Hans-Georg Gadamer who writes: 'Even where life changes violently, as in ages of revolution, far more of the old is preserved in the supposed transformation of everything than anyone knows, and it combines with the new to create a new value.'[28] Rock 'n' roll may be a new genre, but it could never have come into existence without heavy borrowing from the blues.

Gadamer's concept of *Spiel* (play) also goes a long way toward helping us think about how artistic improvisation takes place. Play might seem to be merely something we do as recreation, but Gadamer suggests that it gives us a clue to human activity in general. Note that the German term *Spiel* can be translated into English as either 'play' or 'game'. If we take the latter meaning into account, we can say that 'to play' is to take part in an activity that exists apart from the single player. Gadamer thinks of the making of art as beginning in the to and fro of play but ending in what he calls '*transformation into structure*'.[29] The beginning of a musical phrase turns into a full melody. Some lines hastily sketched on a canvas become more defined as other lines are drawn. A piece of stone is transformed from a square block to an increasingly defined shape. But how does all of this happen? Here there can be no simple answer, for pieces of art come into existence in different ways over varying lengths of time. Gustav Mahler's (1860–1911) *First Symphony* is interesting in this respect. While Mahler wrote the bulk of it in 1888, parts of its material date back to the 1870s, and he revised it more than once. The final version dates to 1906.

Slowly, not infrequently with painstaking decision-making and trial and error, something is transformed into a kind of structure and starts to have its own identity. Kay Ryan, a former US Poet Laureate, claims that although she writes her poetry in one sitting, the ideas have been swirling around in her head for months. Of course, sometimes the whole thing arrives at once.

It was Friedrich Nietzsche (1844–1900) who (in)famously insisted that 'life itself is *essentially* a process of appropriating … "Exploitation" does not belong to a corrupted or imperfect, primitive society: it belongs to the *essence* of being alive'.[30] Certainly all art making is essentially appropriation. The *OED* defines 'appropriation' as 'taking as one's own or to one's own use'. A simple example of this lies in the fact that poetry and novels rely upon the appropriation of words from language. Since language is owned by no one in particular, one is quite free to do so. Go right ahead. But improvising art requires more than just borrowing from language. It requires appropriating from life, from the world of ideas and from the 'language' of painting or film or sculpture or music. Indeed, it is so basic to artistic improvisation that the novelist Margaret Drabble (1939–) boldly admits

---

[28]   Hans.Georg Gadamer, *Truth and Method*, trans. J. Weinsheimer and D.G. Marshall, 2nd revd edn (New York, 1989), p. 281.

[29]   Ibid., p. 110.

[30]   Friedrich Nietzsche, *Beyond Good and Evil*, trans. J. Norman (Cambridge, 2002), §259.

that 'appropriation is what novelists do. Whatever we write is, knowingly or unknowingly, a borrowing. Nothing comes from nowhere.'[31]

The question, then, is simply: how much does any given piece of art depend upon another? The answer is: it all depends. For appropriation and dependency represent a rather wide spectrum. Even if one tries to come up with examples that are truly original, one inevitably finds influences and sources upon which they draw. A typical example of an original piece of art is Igor Stravinsky's (1882–1971) *The Rite of Spring*, which first premiered in 1913. Consider the following description of it from 1927: 'Harmonic tradition collapsed; everything became permissible and it was but necessary to find one's bearings in these riches obtained by this unexpected "license". … Stravinsky broke down everything at one blow.'[32] The musicologist and Stravinsky scholar Richard Taruskin quotes these words and then says:

> Minus the rampant animus, this is more or less how *The Rite of Spring* is still viewed today. The usual account of the work places almost exclusive emphasis on its putative rupture with tradition; and despite all his subsequent disclaimers, that is the view the composer chose to abet, increasingly alienated as he was from the cultural milieu in which the ballet was conceived. It was, however, precisely because *The Rite* was so profoundly *traditional*, both as to cultural outlook and as to musical technique, that Stravinsky was able to find through it a voice that would serve him through the next difficult phase of his career. Precisely because *The Rite* was neither rupture nor upheaval but a magnificent extension, it revealed to Stravinsky a path that would sustain him through a decade of unimaginable ruptures and upheavals brought on by events far beyond his control.[33]

Taruskin's point is that what sounds so new and different is actually very strongly grounded in the tradition of Russian music that Stravinsky inherits. *The Rite of Spring* is thus marked by its fusion of traditional and modern elements. Taruskin points out that Stravinsky generally chose to promote the revolutionary interpretation of the piece, since that made *The Rite of Spring* (and thus Stravinsky himself) seem all the more remarkable. Yet this kind of rhetoric is just that: ways of talking that make pieces of art seem more extraordinary than they really are by overemphasising the new aspects and downplaying the more traditional ones. However innovative a piece of art might be, it is always very

---

[31]   Margaret Drabble, 'Introduction', to *The Red Queen: A Transcultural Tragicomedy* (Orlando, 2004), p. x.

[32]   Leonid Sabaneyeff, *Modern Russian Composers*, trans. J.A. Joffe (1927; repr., New York, 1975), pp. 78–9; quoted in Richard Taruskin, *Stravinsky and the Russian Traditions: A Biography of the Works Through Mavra*, vol. 1 (Berkeley, Calif., 1996), p. 847.

[33]   Taruskin, *Stravinsky and the Russian Traditions*, p. 847.

strongly dependent upon tradition. The avant-garde composer Pierre Boulez (1925–) captures this nicely:

> The composer is exactly like you, constantly on the horns of the same dilemma, caught in the same dialectic – the great models and an unknown future. He cannot take off into the unknown. When people tell me, 'I am taking off into the unknown and ignoring the past', it is complete nonsense.[34]

Indeed, what could 'taking off into the unknown' possibly look (or sound) like?

Folk music relies on borrowing and 'remixing' strands from other pieces of music that can result in either something that is very close to an existing song or something quite different from anything that already exists. Folk music is so strongly inter-textual that, if such borrowing ceased, so would the genre. According to the musicologist Charles Seeger (1886–1979), 'the attempt to make sense out of copyright law reaches its limit in folk song. For here is the illustration par excellence of the Law of Plagiarism. The folk song is, by definition and, as far as we can tell, by reality, entirely a product of plagiarism.'[35] As mentioned earlier, rock music would be unthinkable without the very direct influence of the blues. It was not just that rock musicians were listening to blues musicians and getting ideas; it was that they were actually ripping them off. For example, Led Zeppelin's eponymous debut album is heavily indebted to Willie Dixon's songs 'You Shook Me', 'I Can't Quit You Baby' and 'You Need Love'. Of course, once such pieces of art start to generate huge revenues, creative borrowing becomes highly problematic. Thus, Dixon sued Led Zeppelin and the family of African composer Solomon Linda, who wrote the song 'The Lion Sleeps Tonight' that was used by Disney in *The Lion King*, filed suit again Abilene Music. However, Picasso and others appropriated from African art back when such borrowing seemed perfectly acceptable and, more recently, Bob Dylan borrowed from the Confederate poet Henry Timrod. Dylan's 'When the Deal Goes Down' has the line 'more frailer than the flowers, these precious hours', whereas Timrod's 'Rhapsody of a Southern Winter Night' goes: 'A round of precious hours ... And strove, with logic frailer than the flowers'.

Perhaps we need to be more honest and simply recognise that borrowing is what makes art possible. Back in 1876, Ralph Waldo Emerson (1803–82) had already noted:

> Our debt to tradition through reading and conversation is so massive, our protest or private addition so rare and insignificant, – and this commonly on the ground

---

[34] Pierre Boulez, *Orientations*, trans. M. Cooper (Cambridge, Mass., 1986), p. 454.
[35] Charles Seeger, 'Who Owns Folklore? A Rejoinder', *Western Folklore*, 21/2 (1962): 93–101 (p. 97).

of other reading or hearing, – that, in a large sense, one would say there is no pure originality. All minds quote.[36]

Of course, there has long been something like a consensus on what kind of borrowing is permissible. The poet John Milton (1608–74) gives us the formula in brief: 'If it be not bettered by the borrower, among good authors it is counted Plagiaré.'[37] Johann Mattheson (1681–1784) expands on this idea: 'Borrowing is permissible; but one must return the thing borrowed with interest, i.e. one must so construct and develop imitations that they are prettier and better than the pieces from which they are derived.'[38]

It should not be difficult to see that defining the role of artists in terms of improvisation changes matters substantially. If artists are indebted to one another, there can be no lone genius, disconnected from the community. Instead, we are all improvisers together, quoting one another, saying the same thing in numerous ways and taking different perspectives on the same things. There is an ever-shifting balance between quotation and originality, between old and new, between you and me. Some of what I say is more 'mine'; some is more 'yours'; some is more 'traditional'. Ascertaining the exact nature of the ownership may only be possible to a certain extent.

Responding to the Call

How might one think about this kind of improvisatory movement? What sort of structure does it take? And how might we rethink the idea of genesis? As the subtitle of my paper suggests, we are 'responding to the call'. But what call is this? Certainly, there is nothing like 'one call'. Instead, the call and response structure is basic to existence. If you have never read the Hebrew Bible and the New Testament in terms of the call and response structure, you may never have noticed just how frequently it occurs. It is virtually everywhere. We have already seen how the world comes into existence by God's call 'let there be light'. God calls to Adam and Eve in the Garden. Then, God calls Abraham to go to a foreign land where he will make Abraham's descendents into a new nation.[39] But it is in Exodus, when God calls to Moses from the burning bush, that we get both the call and the classic form of the response. God says: 'Moses, Moses!' To that call,

---

[36] Ralph Waldo Emerson, 'Quotation and Originality', in *The Collected Works of Ralph Waldo Emerson*, vol. 8: *Letters and Social Aims*, ed. R.A. Bosco, G.M. Johnson and J. Myerson (Cambridge, Mass., 2010), p. 91.

[37] John Milton, *Eikonoklastes*, in Complete Prose Works of John Milton, vol. 3, *1648–1649*, ed. M.Y. Hughes (New Haven, Conn., 1962), p. 547.

[38] Johann Mattheson, *Der vollkommene Capellmeister*, trans. E.C. Harris (Ann Arbor, Mich., 1981), p. 298.

[39] Gen. 12.

Moses gives the standard biblical reply: 'Here I am.'[40] Similarly, God calls to Samuel and he responds: 'Speak, for your servant is listening.'[41] The ultimate call in the Hebrew Bible is: 'Hear, O Israel: The Lord is our God, the Lord alone.'[42] We are constantly being called by God to give the reply 'Here I am', which means 'I am at your disposal.'

Even though this pattern of call and response goes back at least as far as creation, there is no one call, even in the creation narrative. Instead, there are multiple calls – calls upon calls – and thus responses upon responses, an intricate web that is ever being improvised and thus a ceaseless reverberation of call and response. Yet what structures this relation of call and response? Here I follow Jean-Louis Chrétien's account as laid out in his book *The Call and the Response*.[43] Chrétien reminds us just how central this structure of call and response is to creaturely existence and how intimately connected to goodness and beauty it is. Chrétien says that 'things and forms do not beckon us because they are beautiful in themselves, *for their own sake*, as it were. Rather, we call them beautiful precisely because they call us and recall us.'[44]

Here we have a surprising reversal. Chrétien is clear regarding the relation of call, beauty and goodness. But it is the order of them that he puts into question: 'Beautiful, *kalon*, is what comes from a call, *kalein*.'[45] So the call is what constitutes the beautiful, rather than the other way around. Things are beautiful precisely because they call out to us. Or, we might put this the other way around: God's call precedes the pronouncement of beauty. 'Let there be light', says God, and only after calling it into being does he then reflect on its goodness.[46] In this sense, *kaleō* (to call) is more primordial than *kalon*. Or, as Chrétien puts it, 'the word "beautiful" is not primary, but responds and corresponds to the first call, which is the call sent by thought construed as a power to call and to name.'[47]

Yet the creation of light lacks the dimension of a human call. Light may respond by illuminating, but a person called by God responds both by a readiness to hear and a readiness to act. Earlier, we noted the similarity of the calls and responses in the Old Testament. What takes place in these exchanges is a crucial reversal. Emmanuel Levinas puts it as follows: 'here I am (*me voici*)! The accusative here is remarkable: here I am, under your eyes, at your service, your obedient servant.'[48]

---

[40]   Exod. 3:4.

[41]   1 Sam. 3:9.

[42]   Deut. 6:4.

[43]   Jean-Louis Chrétien, *The Call and the Response*, trans. A.A. Davenport (New York, 2004).

[44]   Ibid., p. 3: italics added.

[45]   Ibid., p. 7.

[46]   Gen. 1:3–4.

[47]   Chrétien, *The Call and the Response*, p. 7.

[48]   Emmanuel Levinas, 'God and Philosophy', in *Basic Philosophical Writings*, eds A.T. Peperzak, S. Critchley and R. Bernasconi (Bloomington, 1996), pp. 129–48 (p. 146).

In other words, the subject is now truly *subject* to the Other, the one who calls and so stands in the accusative case.

Yet how does beauty call and what is its attraction? While the Hebraic priority of the voice has often been contrasted with the Hellenic priority of sight, the call can come in either form or another form altogether. Relating his enlightenment from Diotima in the *Symposium*, Socrates speaks of moving from an *eros* for the body to an *eros* for the soul to an *eros* for beauty itself.[49] Ultimately, this *eros* for – or, we might well say, call to – beauty is disconnected from both sight and sound. So it would seem that the call may be delivered through sight or sound or even something else. However, Chrétien points out that, even in the Socratic dialogue *Symposium*, 'vision, at every step, produces speech in response [the very speech that Socrates is making at the banquet]' and so concludes that 'visible beauty calls for spoken beauty'.[50] What exactly, though, is beauty's allure? In commenting on Plato, the neo-Platonist philosopher Proclus makes the insightful etymological observation that beauty calls (*kalein*) 'because it enchants and charms [*kelein*]'.[51] Chrétien concludes that the charm beauty exerts results in 'voice, speech, and music'.[52] Of course, Chrétien is overstating his case. No doubt beauty often results in speech and music, but it can likewise move us to paint or sculpt. Further, Chrétien may sound like he is guilty of putting forth a conception of beauty that is too sweet and precious. Yet his essay on Jacob's wrestling with the stranger/angel/ God entitled 'How to Wrestle with the Irresistible' in his book *Hand to Hand: Listening to the Work of Art* gives a subtle, nuanced account of beauty that is violent and unsettling.[53] Whatever beauty is – and beauty is not really the subject of this chapter – it is, at least in this world, often broken and flawed. At times, it is more like Kant's sublime – raw and unnerving. It may be soothing, but it may just as well be biting and uncomfortable. So the call may be aggressive and even violent.

In any case, Proclus does more than define beauty in terms of enchantment and charm, for he likewise connects this enchantment with God. In *Platonic Theology*, he writes: 'beauty converts all things to itself, sets them in motion, causes them to be possessed by the divine, and *recalls them to itself through the intermediary of love*'.[54] We find this same connection of beauty and God in Pseudo-Dionysius's *The Divine Names*, again by way of the call: 'Beauty "calls" all things to itself

---

[49] Plato, *Symposium*, 210a–e, in *The Collected Dialogues*, ed. E. Hamilton and H. Cairns (Princeton, N.J. 1961).

[50] Chrétien, *The Call and the Response*, p. 11.

[51] Proclus, *Commentary on the First Alcibiades* (cited ibid., p. 12).

[52] Chrétien, *The Call and the Response*, p. 12.

[53] Jean-Louis Chrétien, *Hand to Hand: Listening to the Work of Art*, trans. S.E. Lewis (New York, 2003).

[54] Proclus, *The Platonic Theology* (cited in Chrétien, *The Call and the Response*, pp. 9–10: italics added).

(whence it is called "beauty")', he writes, making it clear that 'Beauty' here is another name for God.[55]

So beauty enchants and this enchantment ultimately comes from God. But how do we participate in the call? In one sense, participation is possible because God both transcends the world and yet is reflected by it. One can – on this point – agree with John Milbank, who writes that 'participation can be extended also to language, history and culture: the whole realm of human culture' precisely because 'human making participates in a God who is infinite poetic utterance'.[56] While it seems to me that Milbank here unduly limits participation to *poiesis* (the ancient Greek term for artistic making) – and I would want to broaden it to include *phronesis* (the ancient Greek term for practical wisdom) – the context for these reflections certainly makes *poiesis* an appropriate way in which to participate in the divine beauty. Of course, there are different ways of thinking *poiesis*. Let me develop that notion here in terms of jazz.

Jazz illuminates what takes place in the call and the response: (1) the call always *precedes* me; (2) in responding, I do not speak entirely on my own behalf but on my behalf and the behalf of others; and (3) the improvised response is always a repetition and an improvisation. The first characteristic, then, is that the call always precedes me. It is not just that the response is a response to a prior call, it is that the call itself echoes a prior call. That call pertains to previous performances of songs and pieces, but it can likewise be traced back to earlier calls. This is why Chrétien speaks of it being 'always too late for there to be an origin',[57] for the origin of the present call far precedes it. Thus, responding to the call is both a responding to a present call – one here and now – and to the calls that have preceded it. We do not *first* call; rather, we call because we have already been called. To improvise in jazz, then, is to respond to a call, to join in something that is always already in progress. One becomes an improviser by becoming part of the discourse of jazz.

While it would take a considerably deeper analysis than we have time for here to explain what is involved in becoming a jazz musician and learning how to improvise, the process can be briefly summarised as follows. Speaking with Pierre Bourdieu, we might say that one must cultivate a *habitus*, a way of being that is both nurtured by and results in what Bourdieu terms 'regulated improvisations'.[58] They are 'regulated' precisely by the constraints that make jazz 'jazz' and not something else. One becomes habituated into this *habitus* by listening, and learning

---

[55] Pseudo-Dionysius, *The Divine Names*, 701c–d, in *The Complete Works*, trans. C. Luibheid and P. Rorem (New York, 1987). The English translation uses 'bids' in place of 'calls'. But, since the verb is *kaloun* in the Greek text, 'calls' seems a more accurate translation.

[56] John Milbank, *Being Reconciled: Ontology and Pardon* (London, 2003), p. ix.

[57] Chrétien, *The Call and the Response*, p. 5.

[58] Pierre Bourdieu, *Outline of a Theory of Practice*, trans. R. Nice (Cambridge, 1977), p. 78.

to listen is the precondition for all future improvisations – especially when one improvises with others. So we can say that each improvisation is a response to improvisations of the past. To become an improviser, one must have an intimate knowledge of past improvisations and the conditions for those improvisations (the conventions of improvising). To be able to improvise means one is steeped in the tradition and knows how to respond to the call of other improvisers. Although we tend to think of jazz improvisation in terms of spontaneity, that quality of improvisation – while undoubtedly present – is usually greatly exaggerated. It is also remarkably paradoxical. Not only are many improvisations often heavily 'scripted' but spontaneity is only possible when one is well prepared. It takes a great deal of work to be spontaneous.

Being spontaneous is not something one simply wills, since one wills not to will. Keith Johnstone notes that it is the 'decision not to try and control the future' that allows for spontaneity.[59] The implication here is that one opens oneself up to the future to allow something to happen. But, of course, opening oneself up to the future is only possible by being fully prepared and that requires a thorough grounding in the tradition. In jazz, knowing the past is what makes the future possible. Of course, in realising the debt to and dependency upon the past, the jazz musician is aware that any response to the call is made possible by a 'gift'. The call is a gift to me, something that comes – like life itself – ultimately unbidden and simply disseminated. There is, of course, a long tradition (both inside and outside of the Christian tradition) in which the ability to paint or sculpt or improvise has been seen as a gift, something bestowed upon one that calls for responsibility on the part of the receiver to cultivate, nurture and exercise.[60] In this sense, both the ability and the products that arise from that ability are gifts. If one takes their gift character seriously, then one senses a kind of responsibility in exercising artistic gifts. Although it is theatrical rather than jazz improvisers who speak in these terms, the call is like an 'offer' that can be either 'accepted' or 'blocked'.[61] To accept the call is to respond in kind, to say 'yes' to what is being offered and thus to develop the call.

The second characteristic of the call and response structure signalled by jazz is that my response is never mine alone. To be sure, I speak for myself, yet also for others and in their name. To improvise is always to speak to others, with others (even when one improvises alone) and in the name of others. Given that the call precedes me, I do not begin the discourse nor do I bring it to a conclusion. For

---

[59] Keith Johnstone, *Impro: Improvisation and the Theatre* (New York, 1979), p. 32.

[60] For example, '[the famed jazz guitarist] Les Paul says his greatest God-given gifts are perfect pitch, a love for music with the ability to learn it quickly, and the curiosity and persistence of an inventor who wants to know "how things tick"' (<http://www.pioneertroubadours.com/les_paul.htm> (accessed 7 Mar. 2015)).

[61] 'I call anything that an actor does an "offer." Each offer can either be accepted, or blocked. … A block is anything that prevents the action from developing' (Johnstone, *Impro*, p. 97).

instance, if I am playing one of the perennial standards of jazz, I do so along with many others – whether those playing alongside me, those playing the tune in some other corner of the world, or those who have played it before. Moreover, when I play a tune, I am never simply improvising on that tune alone. I am improvising on the tradition formed by the improvisations upon that tune – what literary theorists call its 'reception history'. Whereas in regard to literature, Harold Bloom has spoken of 'the *anxiety* of influence' – which is the desire to be new, fresh, and original – jazz musicians would rather speak of 'the *joy* of influence'.[62] Bloom's talk of anxiety stems from the idea of genesis found within the Romantic paradigm of art, which drives towards originality. But, as we have already seen, jazz provides a very different model for the artist.

This question of identity naturally leads to the third characteristic, which is that my response is always both a repetition and an innovation. Chrétien writes of the strange logic of improvisation (even though he is hardly thinking explicitly of improvisation, let alone jazz): 'Our response can only repeat. It starts by repeating. Yet it does not repeat by restating.'[63] Chrétien goes on to explain this enigmatic claim by saying that there is a kind of space that is opened up *in ourselves* that gives us a voice so that we are able to pass on the call without mere repetition. We hear the call and we translate it into an idiom of our own.

Thus, to return to Said, we can say that artistic improvisation has no origin, even if it has a beginning, for a beginning in this sense is one that has always already begun. Artistic genesis happens within the flux and the chaos. When God says 'Let there be light', to whom or what is God speaking? On the *ex nihilo* account, it would seem that there is no one there. Yet, on an improvisatory account, it makes perfect sense that God is asking that the light, which already exists, separate itself from the darkness. It likewise makes sense that the call is always an echo of a previous call. And it is only in being called that we respond.

---

[62]   Harold Bloom, *The Anxiety of Influence* (Oxford, 1973); John P. Murphy, 'Jazz Improvisation: The Joy of Influence', *Black Perspective in Music*, 18/1–2 (1990): 7–19.

[63]   Chrétien, *The Call and the Response*, p. 25.

Chapter 5

Unwritten Theology: Notes Towards a Natural Theology of Music

Russell Re Manning

Prelude

This chapter engages with Paul Tillich's theology of culture and George Steiner's powerfully suggestive characterisation of music as 'unwritten theology' to suggest ways in which the possibility of a natural theology of music might be theorised.[1]

Steiner's claim exposes a central dilemma for work that seeks to explore the ways in which music relates to transcendence. On the one hand, for those such as Jeremy Begbie, 'music can serve to enrich and advance theology' in its ongoing quest, in his words, 'to extend our wisdom about God, God's relation to us, and to the world at large'.[2] Music, in this case, serves as an aid to reflection, further equipping the theologian in her inescapably writerly enterprise. On the other hand, as Frank Burch Brown asks: what if the theologian of art allows that art not only assist theology but further 'reshape, somehow, the image and sound, the look and feel, of the substance of faith'?[3] For such an approach, music itself becomes theology and hence the theologian's task is radically transformed. No longer able to make use of music to enrich her writing, the theologian is thus re-positioned and the linguistic hegemony of theo*logy* is challenged in favour of a 'theology without writing'.

This chapter explores the possibilities for theorising a 'theology after writing' capable of 'reshaping, somehow' not simply the form but also the substance of faith by drawing on resources from Tillich's cultural-theological analyses of what he characterises as art with 'religious style, but non-religious content', as well as Jean-Luc Marion's notion of iconic distance (particularly as developed by James Herbert). Taking seriously the challenge of thinking of music as 'unwritten theology', the chapter suggests that a framework of a natural theology of

---

[1]   George Steiner, *Real Presences: Is There Anything in What We Say?* (Chicago, 1989), p. 218.

[2]   Jeremy S. Begbie, *Theology, Music and Time* (Cambridge, 2000), p. 3.

[3]   Frank Burch Brown, 'Aesthetics and the Arts in Relation to Natural Theology', in Russell Re Manning (ed.), *The Oxford Handbook of Natural Theology* (Oxford, 2013), pp. 523–38 (p. 535).

music, that is to say a theology of music that does not presuppose revelation or a commitment to an established religious tradition, might provide the necessary openness to discovery that Steiner's description requires.[4]

Towards a Natural Theology of Culture

In his 1989 work *Real Presences*, subtitled *Is there Anything in What We Say?*, Steiner recognised the centrality of the question of the meaning of music to his general argument against the cultural *misère* of what he called 'the secondary city'. Such a situation is characterised by Steiner as a culture without criticism, dominated by 'the secondary and the parasitic' and ignorant of hermeneutics as 'the enactment of answerable understanding, of active apprehension'.[5] In awe to the idolatry of the informational, such a culture elevates what Steiner bitingly characterises as the 'academic-journalistic' talk about the aesthetic that mistakes pragmatic and anonymous 'philology' for 'the life of the creative imagination'.[6] By contrast, the burden of Steiner's work is to argue for, or perhaps better to show forth, the possibility of another, 'primary', city, in which hermeneutics is restored to its status as, in effect, a continuation or repetition of the art that it interprets. Such interpretation, then, is no longer limited to the passive cataloguing of cultural productions characteristic of so much 'art history' but rather aims to pass judgements of aesthetic quality. At the same time, Steiner rails against a (perhaps distorted or at least exaggerated) view of deconstruction as a similar avoidance of any normative stance towards works of art. For Steiner, both the catalogue compiler and the deconstructionist abdicate the critic's responsibility – an ethical and spiritual responsibility – to the work's truth, its meaning. This, Steiner acknowledges, entails a wager, a wager on meaning, which is itself a wager on the passage from meaning to meaningfulness. Yet such a wager is, for Steiner, a necessary one and unavoidably a theological one:

> The wager on the meaning of meaning, on the potential of insight, when we come face to face with the text and work of art or music, which is to say when we encounter the *other* in its condition of freedom, is a wager on transcendence.[7]

In rejecting the Feuerbachian–Nietzschean diagnosis of the God who 'clings to our culture' as 'a phantom of grammar, a fossil embedded in the childhood of rational speech', Steiner unambiguously declares his thesis:

> That any coherent understanding of what language is and how language performs,
> that any coherent account of the capacity of human speech to communicate

---

4   Re Manning (ed.), *The Oxford Handbook of Natural Theology*.
5   Steiner, *Real Presences*, p. 7.
6   Ibid., pp. 6–7.
7   Ibid., p. 4.

meaning and feeling, is, in the final analysis, underwritten by the assumption of God's presence. I will put forward the argument that the experience of aesthetic meaning in particular, that of literature, of the arts, of musical form, infers the necessary possibility of this 'real presence'.[8]

Strikingly, Steiner's argument, whilst it stands against the empiricising tendencies said to characterise modern scientific forms of natural theology is nonetheless itself clearly a sort of natural theology.[9] It is, as it were, a 'cultural-natural theology' that, in Graham Ward's words, 'locates the theological postulate ... in the ordinariness of human communication and the nature of man himself'.[10] Ward locates Steiner's argument with reference to David Tracey and Paul Ricoeur, but surely a better parallel can be drawn to Tillich's project of a theonomous theology of culture (or cultural theology), in which the meaning of culture is identified with its religious dimension of depth.[11] Just as for Steiner, so for Tillich, the cultural and the theological effectively coincide. Drawing an explicit contrast between nature and culture Tillich, in an unpublished 1926 essay, defines culture in terms of the unconditional demand of meaning:

> Culture is not simply the process of life, but obligation, an unconditional obligation. For behind it is the meaning-bearing idea of truth and society. Its realisation is culture, as the cultured forms and not as the unmediated life-process. It is not nature, but a demand placed upon nature.[12]

Hence, for Tillich, the cultural theologian, as much as Steiner's critic, must recognise her own participation within culture and the responsibility that this places on her as 'participat[ing] in the positing of the objects [she] seeks to know'.[13] Such a natural theology of culture is, for Tillich, not only 're-creative' but also 'co-creative, or productive'.[14]

---

[8]   Ibid., p. 3.

[9]   Re Manning, *The Oxford Handbook of Natural Theology*.

[10]   Graham Ward, 'Review Article: George Steiner's Real Presences', *Journal of Literature and Theology*, 4/2 (1990): 226–38 (p. 237).

[11]   Russell Re Manning, 'Tillich's Theology of Art', in id. (ed.), *The Cambridge Companion to Paul Tillich* (Cambridge, 2009), pp. 152–72 (pp. 157–61); id., 'The Religious Meaning of Culture. Paul Tillich and Beyond', *International Journal of Systematic Theology*, 15/4 (2013): 437–52.

[12]   Paul Tillich, 'Das Wesen der Bildung und das Bildungsideal (1926)', in *Ergänzungs- und Nachlassbände zu den Gesammelten Werken von Paul Tillich*, vol. 11: *Religion, Kultur, Gesellschaft. Unveröffentliche Texte aus der deutschen Zeit (1908–1933)*, ed. Erdmann Sturm, Pt 2 (Berlin, 1999), pp. 28–32 (p. 30): my trans.

[13]   Paul Tillich, *The System of the Sciences: According to Objects and Methods*, trans. P. Wiebe (East Brunswick, NJ, 1981), p. 146.

[14]   Ibid.

Interestingly, both seem to give the central role of theological discernment not to the artists themselves but rather to the theorist – the critic or the theologian of culture. In a sense, this is unsurprising: both are after all primarily 'secondary', in that they are the interpreters and not the producers of culture. And yet, of course, both aim to blur the lines between producer and interpreter, Steiner with his ideal of the primary city and Tillich with his ideal of theonomy. Here, then, the non-aesthetic discourse of a natural theology of culture seeks to mimic the culture that it seeks to re-present. Hence the importance for both Steiner and Tillich of the ethical and spiritual disposition of the cultural theorist – not, of course, according to the bourgeois mores and creedal pieties of established or positive ethics or religion, but in response to what Steiner calls 'the presence of a realness, of a "substantiation" (the theological reach of this word is obvious) within language and form' or to what Tillich designates as 'the experience of the unconditioned' as 'an actuality of meaning that convulses everything and builds everything anew'.[15]

Here I suggest it may be helpful to bring a third (and perhaps surprising) voice into this attempt to theorise a natural theology of culture: that of Jean-Luc Marion. In his phenomenology of givenness, of the Heideggerian *es gibt*, Marion, in contradistinction to Derrida, defends a philosophy of revelation that seeks to recognise the saturation of the present by the infinite.[16] For Marion, theological presence is iconic when the finite cultural form resists the temptation to present itself as sufficient to its representation and instead enacts in its presenting its distance from that which it represents. Referring to Christ's iconicity, Marion writes that 'God withdraws in the distance, unthinkable, unconditioned, and therefore infinitely closer'.[17] In contrast to the idol – the attempt to collapse the distance between God and the object – Marion writes of the icon's quality:

> It reveals and conceals that upon which it rests: the separation in it between the divine and its face. Visibility of the invisible, a visibility where the invisible gives itself to be seen as such, the icon reinforces the one through the other. ... The icon [offers] a sort of negative theophany: the figure remains authentically insurpassable (norm, self-reference) only in that it opens in its depth upon an invisibility whose distance it does not abolish but reveals.[18]

Whilst Marion famously restricts such iconic exposure to the icon of Christ (a revelation repeated in the Eucharist), James Herbert has recently applied Marion's

---

[15]   Steiner, *Real Presences*, p. 4; Victor Nuovo, *Visionary Science: A Translation of Tillich's 'On the Idea of a Theology of Culture' with Interpretive Essay* (Detroit, 1987), pp. 24–5.

[16]   Jean-Luc Marion, 'The Final Appeal of the Subject', in John D. Caputo (ed.), *The Religious* (Oxford, 2002), pp. 131–44.

[17]   Jean-Luc Marion, *The Idol and the Distance: Five Studies*, trans. T.A. Carlson (New York, 2001), p. 215.

[18]   Ibid., pp. 8–9.

notion of iconic distance to suggest what he calls a 'theology of art' that explores various cultural manifestations by venturing into 'the strange expanse between God and humanity [once] rid of the metaphysical miasma of presupposed Being and non-Being'.[19] In other words, Herbert aims to derive from Marion's concept of iconic distance a tool to enable him to explore the presence of theological concerns in works of art that have no explicitly religious content and to make sense of the surprising ways in which art with explicit religious content can subvert that content. The key is interpretation: 'the divine emerges more often as the subject of sight and sound than as their object'.[20] Here, once more, we find a form of a natural theology of culture. Marion's concept of iconic distance, as much as Steiner's notion of real presence and Tillich's of theonomy enable the discernment in culture of what we might call 'non-religious' or 'non-heteronomous' natural revelation and with that the attempt to respond appropriately in the form of a cultural theology.

One final consideration is required before turning explicitly to music and the potential for a natural theology of music. The framework that I am developing here of a cultural theology not only invites the theologian to engage with the wager of transcendence in cultural productions (and thus frees theology from a confinement to the religious), it also requires that same theologian, as theologian of culture, to be a participatory cultural critic, to be a member of Steiner's primary city. As such, any theology of music must be so much more than simply a commentary upon the repetitions or analogues in musical form of privileged primarily linguistic theology. A theology of art as a theology remains words about God, in the same way that Steiner's art criticism remains a written or spoken response to a work of art and does not take the form of art itself. And yet, as co-creative with the art to which it responds, it must equally work against itself to show forth the theological meaning of the work of art in its very autonomous particularity. In short, for the theologian of culture, what is at stake in her theological engagement with culture is as much the nature of theology itself as the religious meaning of culture: cultural theology is not just theology applied to culture, but theology transformed by culture. Potentially even a cultural theology might be a theology without *logos*, a theology unwritten by the real presence of the transcendence that gives iconic culture its ultimate concern.

Music as Unwritten Theology

In the second section of this chapter, I want to sketch out the contours of a natural theology of music in light of the above theoretical considerations and Steiner's

---

[19]   James Herbert, *Our Distance from God: Studies of the Divine and the Mundane in Western Art and Music* (Berkeley, Calif. and London, 2008), p. 7.

[20]   Ibid., p. 3.

explicit and suggestive comments about the centrality of music to his argument
and its potential to 'un-write' creedal/religious theology.

Steiner writes:

> The question of whether anything meaningful can be *said* (or written) about the
> nature and sense of music lies at the heart of this essay. … More than any other
> act of intelligibility and executive form, music entails differentiations between
> that which can be understood, this is to say, paraphrased, and that which can be
> thought and lived in categories which are, rigorously considered, transcendent
> to such understanding. … The truths, the necessities of ordered feeling in the
> musical experience are not irrational; but they are irreducible to reason or
> pragmatic reckoning.[21]

This much may be familiar and mainstream to much philosophy of music (especially
that influenced by the Romantic tradition), but in what follows next Steiner gives
this affirmation of the irreducibility of music to spoken or written language a new
twist that propels him beyond the Romantic elevation of the autonomy of 'pure' or
'absolute' music and towards a natural theology of music. He continues:

> This irreducibility is the spring of my argument. It may well be that man is man,
> and that man 'borders on' limitations of a peculiar and open 'otherness', because
> he can produce and be possessed by music.[22]

Steiner returns to this suggestion as he concludes his essay. He quotes Leibniz that
'music is a secret arithmetic of the soul unknowing of the fact that it is counting'
and explains:

> This is why music has been at the centre of my argument throughout. What
> every human being whom music moves, to whom it is a life-giving agency, can
> say of it is platitudinous. Music means. It is brimful with meanings which will
> not translate into logical structures or verbal expression.[23]

But this is no mere emotivism of the power of music to move the heart; it is the
archetypal instance of culture as theology:

> Music makes utterly substantive what I have sought to suggest of the real presence
> in meaning where that presence cannot be analytically shown or paraphrased. …
> Music has celebrated the mystery of intuitions of transcendence from the songs
> of Orpheus, counter-creative to death, to the *Missa Solemnis*, from Schubert's
> late piano sonatas to Schoenberg's *Moses and Aron* and Messiaen's *Quatuor*

---

[21]   Steiner, *Real Presences*, pp. 18–19.
[22]   Ibid., p. 19.
[23]   Ibid., p. 217.

pour la fin du temps. Countless times, this celebration has had manifest relations
to religion. But the core-relation far exceeds any specific religious motive or
occasion. In ways so obvious as to make any statement a tired cliché, yet of an
undefinable and tremendous nature, music puts our being as men and women in
touch with that which transcends the sayable, which outstrips the analysable. ...
The meanings of the meaning of music transcend. It has long been, it continues
to be, the unwritten theology of those who lack or reject any formal creed.[24]

Far from illustrating or serving religion, as a positivist theological analysis of the
religious meaning of music might contend, here music comes before religion. It is
the unwritten theology that first articulates the real presence of transcendence to
humanity. Steiner, in effect, reverses the usual relation between religion and music,
in which music more or less inadequately expresses religious truths as a vehicle
for a primarily religious meaning. Instead, for Steiner, it is religion that expresses
the theological truth of music. As he puts it, 'for many human beings, religion has
been the music which they believe in'.[25] Here, then, is a clear example of Frank
Burch Brown's suggestion that art cannot only assist religion in re-expressing
what it already knows, but further can 'reshape, somehow, the image and sound,
the look and feel, of the substance of faith'.[26]

Just as for Tillich in his famous affirmation that 'it is not an exaggeration to
ascribe more of the quality of sacredness to a still life by Cézanne or a tree by van
Gogh than to a picture of Jesus by Uhde', so for Steiner the religious meaning of
culture stands apart from a determinative relation to explicitly religious content.[27]
In the case of music this is radically so, given the difficulties inherent in defining
the idea of the content of music, religious or otherwise. It is perhaps strange
that Tillich wrote so very little about music in his theology of culture, given the
obvious overlap of Steiner's argument with Tillich's analysis of the significance
for the theology of culture of the depth dimension or substance (*Gehalt*, sometimes
translated as 'import') of culture that comes to expression in specific form (*Form*)
and explicit content (*Inhalt*), sometimes explicitly religious, sometimes not.
For Tillich, the greater the predominance of substance over content, the clearer
the theological meaning of a cultural production. Arguably it is with music, the
area of culture least circumscribed by content, that such a cultural-theological
expressiveness can be most clearly manifest. Music may offer, in this way, an
exemplary opportunity for a Tillichian theology of culture, in which what it is
that a work of art is apparently about (its explicit content) is most completely
subordinated to what it is really about (its substance). Perhaps, however, Tillich's
theology of culture remains too wedded to the determinate, even as he rails against
the religious positivism characteristic of his age. After all, Tillich's theology is,

---

24   Ibid., p. 218.
25   Ibid.
26   Brown, 'Aesthetics and the Arts in Relation to Natural Theology', p. 535.
27   Paul Tillich, *What is Religion?*, ed. J.L. Adams (New York, 1969), pp. 88–9.

in essence, symbolic; and symbols whilst they break through to that in which they participate, nonetheless remain tied to some form of content, even when that content evacuates itself in favour of substance.[28] Perhaps, then, Tillich cannot quite fully un-write his theology, even as he re-writes it as a theology of culture, such that he cannot produce a co-creative natural theology of music?

In conclusion, I refer once again to Marion's notion of iconic distance as a way, perhaps, of shaking the foundations of Tillich's symbolism to enable a cultural theological response to Steiner's invitation to theorise music as unwritten theology. In this I aim to understand Steiner's characterisation of music as unwritten theology not as a description of some kind of pre-theological character to music that needs to be 'spelt out' as it were with the verbal and written resources of *logos*, but as 'a logic of sense other than that of reason' that is 'the truest name we have for the logic at work in the springs of being that generate vital forms'.[29] Music as unwritten theology is not simply a theology-in-waiting, but it is a theology without writing. But, of course, a theology without writing is a paradox in which the tension between the unwritten and the *logos* threatens to collapse into the pole of inarticulate, silent emoting, on the one hand, and over-particular analysis, on the other. Steiner recognises this when he writes:

> Music is at once cerebral in the highest degree – I repeat that the energies and form-relations in the playing of a quartet, in the interactions of voice and instrument are among the most complex events known to man – and it is at the same time somatic, carnal and a searching out of resonances in our bodies at deeper levels of will or consciousness. These are banalities.[30]

Herbert's use of iconic distance can be helpful here. For Marion, in Herbert's words, 'the icon, rather than representing an essence, represents a relation'.[31] The icon's insistence on distance in effect suspends it between the visible and the invisible, the figured and the unfigurable. This, then, is an image of the unwritten theology of music – between substance and content, between emotive silence and rational logic – whose meaning is precisely to mean. According to such a natural theology of music, music does not reveal particular religious content, but nor does it show forth nothing – it does not simply speak itself. Rather music as unwritten theology is the possibility of non-heteronomous revelation of the real presence of transcendence, protected against idolatrous distortion by its incorporation of iconic distance. It is, to invoke another of Tillich's notions, the *Grundoffenbarung*,

---

28   For a fuller account of Tillich's analysis of the constitutive elements of culture, see Russell Re Manning, *Theology at the End of Culture: Paul Tillich's Theology of Culture and Art* (Leuven, 2005).

29   Steiner, *Real Presences*, p. 218.

30   Ibid., p. 217.

31   Herbert, *Our Distance from God*, p. 7.

or the foundational revelation, by which the birth of religion itself is enabled. Tillich writes:

> The moment of the breakthrough of *Grundoffenbarung* is altogether indifferent with regard to its content. Man has no knowledge, no content to show. The divine is the ground and the abyss of meaning, the beginning and the end of every possible content. ... This is the hour of the birth of religion in every man.[32]

For Tillich, *Grundoffenbarung* 'reveals the presence of God prior to any knowledge of God'. It is perhaps, the closest Tillich gets to an unwritten theology, even if for Tillich it is more closely associated not with music, but with the existential howl of angst.[33] Steiner's, perhaps, is a more melodious *Grundoffenbarung* and it is with his words of a co-creative critical theology of music that I conclude:

> Music and the metaphysical, in the root sense of that term, music and religious feeling, have been virtually inseparable. It is in and through music that we are more immediately in the presence of the logically, of the verbally inexpressible but wholly palpable energy in being that communicates to our senses and to our reflection of what little we can grasp of the naked wonder of life. I take music to be the naming of the naming of life.[34]

---

[32] Paul Tillich, 'Rechtfertigung und Zweifel (1924)', in *Gesammelte Werke*, vol. 8: *Offenbarung und Glaube. Schriften zur Theologie II*, ed. Renate Albrecht (Stuttgart, 1970), pp. 85–100 (p. 92): my trans.

[33] Werner Schüßler, 'Where Does Religion Come From? Paul Tillich's Concept of *Grundoffenbarung*', in Michel Despland, Jean-Claude Petit and Jean Richard (eds), *Religion et Culture* (Laval, 1987), pp. 159–71 (p. 161).

[34] Steiner, *Real Presences*, pp. 216–17.

Chapter 6

Music and the Transcendental

Roger Scruton

When the question of the meaning of music was debated by the German Romantics, the idea began to emerge that there is an especially pure kind of music that would encapsulate what music really and truly means, without the 'adulteration' of words, dance or theatre. At a certain point critics and philosophers began to refer to *absolute Tonkunst*, the absolute art of sound, in order to distinguish the purely instrumental music of the concert hall, designed to be listened to in silence and presented in an atmosphere of reverential attention, from the applications of music in opera and song, in dance and *Gebrauchmusik*. The phrase probably first appears in E.T.A. Hoffmann's celebrated review of Beethoven's Fifth Symphony, in 1810. By then the claim had already been made – by Tieck, Wackenroder and others – that music offers access to the 'transcendental', its significance lying largely in its power to accomplish this.[1]

Before considering what this reference to the transcendental might mean, we must acknowledge the enormous cultural chasm that separates us from the world of the German Romantics. Their musical culture was a listening culture; ours is a culture of hearing as well as listening. Much music is heard; not much now is listened to. And among the music that is heard, far more is overheard than directly heard in the centre of attention. A new kind of music has emerged precisely to occupy the background, rather than the foreground, of our attention. You hear this music in bars and restaurants all across the world, and people habituated to it can be encouraged to hear music only if the music is pushed rudely through the barrier of background noise – say by a loud beat or a sexy voice or both. To suggest that music has a special relation to the transcendental, when the primary experience of music is merely that of an unceasing murmur on the auditory horizon, is to strain credibility. But if music is to be appreciated through an act of reverential attention, which isolates it from the surrounding noise and frames it in a sound world of its own, then the suggestion does not seem so absurd.

Even in the listening culture, however, listening is only one way of relating to music and always depends on another and more intimate engagement with sound. As Férdia Stone-Davis has emphasised in her contribution to this volume, music is first and foremost something that we do – it is brought into being by human actions, and those actions do not occur in a cultural void. Performances come to

---

[1] See Linda Siegel, 'Wackenroder's Musical Essays in "Phantasien über die Kunst"', *Journal of Aesthetics and Art Criticism*, 30/3 (1972): 351–8.

us marked with the intentions and bodily movements of their participants. Music does not leak onto the airwaves from some transcendental source. It arises from the activities of real and present individuals, for whom, as Stone-Davis puts it, music is a process in which performers negotiate thresholds between one action and its sequel or between self and other.

Music requires us to divide and measure time, to understand movement in time and to link actions to each other in terms of their temporal relations. In which case the claim that music has some special and intimate connection to the transcendental begins to look decidedly odd. Music ought to be more bound than any other art form to temporal, transient and empirical happenings, since that is what it essentially is: an event in time, produced by the strenuous activity of ordinary mortals. So how is it that we are tempted to think of music in another way, as a window onto the transcendental, a place in the order of time where the eternal shines through? It is not only the German Romantics who saw music in this way. The ancient theory of the 'music of the spheres' was based on a similar idea, and the many attempts to give a mathematical foundation to the theory of harmony have prompted the thought that music expounds, in time, relations and realities that are in themselves timeless. And when this idea was taken up by the German Romantics, it was in the context of a kind of theological anxiety – the anxiety that humankind was losing its religious anchor and needed another way of reaching and holding on to the transcendental than that provided by religion. The Romantics had the question of God: music was part of their answer.

The terms 'transcendent' and 'transcendental' have many applications, three of which particularly concern us. There is the theological idea, according to which God is said to transcend the world of creation and also to transcend our attempts to define or describe him. There is the philosophical idea, typified by Kant, according to which certain objects of thought transcend the conditions laid down by the understanding and can therefore be thought only negatively, as lying beyond thought, so to speak. And there is what we might call the aesthetic idea, in which we speak of transcendent versions of empirical phenomena. Thus we might refer to Tristan's passion for Isolde as transcending the bounds of ordinary erotic love, while nevertheless being an example of it; or Iago's hatred of Othello as transcending the bounds of ordinary hatred, while yet being hatred. As to whether this third use of the language of transcendence has any bearing on musical meaning, this is an issue to which I return below.

Theologians are often prepared to allow knowledge of God, even though he transcends our cognitive powers, while Kant did not allow positive knowledge of the transcendental. There is, in the literature, a lot of having cake and eating it, and it is rare to find philosophers or theologians who take seriously their own conclusion that this or that is really transcendental, since if it is so, how can they know that it is so? The whole concept only makes sense on the assumption that we can in some way reach beyond the ordinary empirical world, to the something we know not what that transcends it. Can we or can't we? This is the dilemma that Kant bequeathed to his immediate successors, and they did not resolve the dilemma but tried to have things both ways – espousing a kind of idealism that both denied access to the transcendental and then allowed it through the dialectic of reason – as in Hegel's *Logic*. But in that case, of course, it is no longer transcendental. Hegel called it 'absolute' instead, and the word entered philosophy in this way, just about the same time as it entered the study of music in the writings of Hoffmann and Hanslick.

Now I have a lot of time for Hegel. Nevertheless, I do not think that the path of absolute idealism is the one that we should take out of this dilemma. The assumption in Hegel is that whenever we encounter a limit in thought, feeling or conduct we can, as it were, rise above it and thereby see to the other side. To say that is both to affirm and to deny that there are limits. It is not to advance beyond the limits but simply to muddle them, so that we do not know where they are.

I take it that those who have turned to music in this dilemma have done so precisely because approaching the transcendental through music does not require the belief that we can approach it through language or through our ordinary conceptual powers. In this way we can maintain the belief that the transcendental is incapable of being defined or described while surreptitiously offering a back route to it, so to speak. We offer a way of effing the ineffable. Just such a move was made by Schopenhauer, in 'The Metaphysics of Music' included in the second volume of *The World as Will and Representation*. According to Schopenhauer music is a non-conceptual medium which, for that very reason, is able to 'get behind' the world of representations, so as to present the underlying reality, which is Will. Music presents the Will directly, without the intervening veil of concepts. Is this a coherent response to our dilemma? Does it not invite Frank Ramsey's remark to Wittgenstein, that 'What we can't say we can't say, and we can't whistle it either'?

The first step in confronting that response is to recognise that there is more than one kind of knowledge. Philosophers are used to the distinction between knowing that and knowing how and to the wider distinction between theoretical and practical knowledge. Someone who knows what to do in some difficult situation certainly has a cognitive possession that the merely bewildered lack: but it is not a possession that could be stated as a collection of truths. He could know what to do even if he had no words to express it. And his knowledge exists not as a prediction of some future state of affairs but as a readiness to act, spread over intentions and perceptions that lie below the horizon of language.

Kant was inclined to say that the only way to understand the transcendental is to flip from theoretical to practical reason, to recognise that we are wrong to think that we can have knowledge about the transcendental, but right to think that, when we reach the limit of empirical knowledge, there is still somewhere to go. We should step sideways, as it were, recognise that reason does not merely describe the world but also commands us to change it. And really the invocation of the transcendental is a reminder that reason knows the world in another way – as a sphere of action, in which we can freely change the way things are.

Whatever we think of Kant's way out of the dilemma, it is clearly not what people have had in mind in invoking music as a channel to the transcendental. Music is an action, and in certain circumstances it is also an invitation to action on the part of its listeners – for instance, dancing. But this invitation can be resisted, and it is precisely when resisting, so as to contemplate the musical movement as something objective, outside us, occurring in a space of its own, that we feel its transcendental gravity. It is in these circumstances that music seems to lift us free from our ordinary preoccupations. It works on us then like the Hindu and Buddhist meditation techniques, detaching our thoughts and emotions from the things of this world, and directing them to a realm in which temporal things find their eternal counterparts.

However, what would be the difference, on this view, between contemplating the transcendental by means of the music and just contemplating the music? Granted that fixing your attention on the music conveys a sense of sublime peacefulness or release from this world, why is that not simply an effect of the music, rather than of something transcendental that we perceive through the music? The very transcendental nature of the alleged object implies that we could not make the difference in practice between the two accounts and that therefore the invocation of the transcendental is, so to speak, doing no work of its own. It is just something we say, without grounds and without knowing what we mean by it.

It is not only the transcendental that is ineffable: many of our experiences are like this, containing some core content that we cannot put into words, since all words fall short of it. A nameless fear, an indefinable joy, a *je ne sais quoi*, an inexpressible longing and so on. There is an interesting example of music filling in the gap left by words in Beethoven's setting of 'O Namenlöse Freude', 'nameless joy' in *Fidelio*. Here we really do feel that the music has supplied what words could never express – a joy that is not of this world and which unites Florestan and Leonora in a space of their own, visitors from some angelic realm that you and I could never attain to. Is this an example of music opening a path to the transcendental? Not exactly. After all, the words go some way to identifying the feeling that the characters are trying to express. We are dealing here with the aesthetic, rather than the metaphysical, idea of the transcendental. Beethoven is presenting an empirical experience that points beyond its own limit, so to speak. He is not taking us into a transcendental realm. His music works in the way operatic music works in general: by taking a defined situation and filling it with a movement of its own.

We can draw a few lessons from the example nevertheless. First, the music is presenting us with something. It does not describe the 'nameless joy' of the protagonists and is therefore not a vehicle of 'knowledge that'. But it makes us acquainted with their feelings: in other words, it conveys a kind of 'knowledge by acquaintance'. And perhaps this is a useful paradigm in art. Susanne Langer wrote of art as a system of 'presentational symbols' (in *Feeling and Form* and elsewhere). I am not sure what she meant exactly, but there is certainly a cognitively significant process that involves presenting something for attention, without describing it. The original of this idea is Croce's theory, in his *Aesthetic*, that art expresses the 'intuition' rather than the concept of its subject matter. And something of that idea survives, too, in Nelson Goodman's theory of expression as metaphorical exemplification.[2] It is as though art draws our attention to things, without reducing them to examples of some general category. Art shows, presents, the individual, standing forth from the integument of our concepts in a naked completeness. The implication is that it takes art to achieve this presentation and that individual things, experiences, people and situations do not do this on their own. It is as though we can reach, through art, to a perfect version of our imperfect states of mind: a version that transcends the ordinary limitations of the human psyche.

Knowledge by acquaintance is not replaceable by knowledge by description and contains a component that could reasonably be described as 'ineffable' – the critical 'what it is like', which we might attempt to capture in metaphors but which can be properly known only through acquaintance, as feelings are known. It is a plausible claim that this kind of knowledge is conveyed by works of art. And maybe there is a sense in which the ineffable heart of our more elusive experiences can be 'effed' by a work of music, even though it cannot be put into words. The Schubert songs seem so often to work in this way, taking a simple situation and conveying a 'quite peculiar' emotion towards it, an emotion which comes immediately to mind in the music, but which we struggle in vain to describe. (Think of the way in which Schubert captures the sentiment of Rückert's 'Du bist die Ruh', for instance).

This observation connects with what Collingwood says about the 'particular' emotion conveyed by Brahms's 'Feldeinsamkeit', in *Principles of Art*, and Wittgenstein's remarks in *The Brown Book*, contrasting the transitive and intransitive senses of 'particular'.[3] When you say that a piece of music expresses a quite particular or peculiar feeling, you are using the words 'particular' or 'peculiar' intransitively, so as to refuse any further description of the feeling than the one you have given. You are referring to just this particular feeling, the feeling conveyed by 'Feldeinsamkeit', which is the full and sufficient identification of what you have in mind. And you are implying that the feeling could be fully and sufficiently identified only in this way. In the language of literary theory, you are saying that here form and content are inseparable.

When we speak of the way in which a work of music captures or presents some state of mind we are not speaking neutrally, as though recording some conventional or external connection. We are referring to the achieved content of the work. In general, works of art have meaning only to the extent that they are meaningful, and meaningful only to the extent that they are successful acts of communication with

---

[2]   Susanne Langer, *Feeling and Form: A Theory of Art Developed from Philosophy in a New Key* (New York, 1953); Nelson Goodman, *Languages of Art: An Approach to a Theory of Symbols* (Oxford, 1969).

[3]   Ludwig Wittgenstein, *The Blue and Brown Books* (Oxford, 1958) pp. 158–9; Robin G. Collingwood, *The Principles of Art* (Oxford, 1938), ch. 6.

the audience. A work of music that succeeds in effing some ineffable emotion is, to that extent, a successful work of music, one that has crossed the barrier from artistic nothingness into the realm of aesthetic value. Only a minority of works do this.

Thus if someone were to say that music in general acquaints us with the transcendental, then, even if we can make sense of that, it would not amount to very much. 'So what?' is the response. If all music does this, even the trite and the meaningless, then this gives us no reason for thinking that music tells us anything that we wanted to know. The only interesting thesis would be that there are pieces of meaningful music, in which the meaningfulness resides in presenting, in some way, the transcendental and thereby effing the ineffable.

You can appreciate what I have in mind by turning again to the case of meditation. People use many different props and catalysts in order to meditate. Some burn joss sticks, some play soft music, some listen to Indian ragas, some sit by still waters and dream. But clearly none of those things bears within it the essential reference to the transcendental that the meditating person hopes to recuperate. If there is a case of music actually putting us in touch with the transcendental then this must be an achievement of the same order as that of Schubert's 'Der Doppelgänger', as it presents us with the dreadful experience recounted in Heine's poem and so leads us, cynical postmoderns though we are, to know by acquaintance the corrosive jealousy of unrequited romantic love, in those days when you could not get on your bicycle and check out the girls across the valley.

If we are to make headway with our quest for a relation between music and the transcendental then we should think of some particular piece of music, which is both meaningful as music, and points, through its meaning, towards the transcendental, in such a way as to make the transcendental present to our minds. I suspect that many people want to say some such thing of the late Beethoven quartets, which so often have the air of an inner communing with God, or of sacred polyphony set to simple words, like the *Ave verum corpus* of Mozart or that of Byrd. But it is seldom clear that we could distinguish, in such cases, between a piece of music that presents us with the transcendental and a piece that presents us with feelings towards the transcendental. There is much religious music, and the great examples, Victoria, Palestrina, Bach, Rachmaninov and similar, acquaint us with profound religious feelings. It would be normal for religious people to describe their feelings on hearing such music as directed towards, or about, the transcendental. But that does not mean that the music expressing those feelings is about the transcendental. In all musical communication sentiment is passed by sympathy from the music to the listener, but it is sentiment that is passed not the thing it is about. And when this thing is described as transcendental – in other words, as lying in some way beyond the reach of human knowledge – the natural conclusion to draw is that music cannot reach that far.

We seem to have come up against an impassable barrier, therefore. We can assign a role to music in effing the ineffable, when the ineffable is the non-propositional content of our states of mind – a content that can be presented to the imagination but not described in words. But it cannot eff what lies beyond human acquaintance entirely. Is that, then, the end of the story? Not quite.

Consider our knowledge of each other. When I react to your words and behaviour, to your facial expression, to the many signs that you give of your awareness of me, I am reacting to a human being. My emotions and thoughts are focused on you, as revealed to me in the flesh. But that is not how I see you. I see you as a subject like me, another in whose point of view I too appear as another. My feelings and responses reach across to you, but overshoot their target, so to speak, not latching on to the visible embodiment of you but seeking out the 'I' in you. I address my words and looks to the thing that addresses me from your words and looks, and that thing I see as an individual centre of consciousness, located nowhere visible, but standing as though on the horizon of our shared world. I suspect that this is a primary experience of the transcendental – of that which is somehow beyond the limit of the empirical world. My emotions and responses towards the other reach out beyond the observable other, as though to make contact with this thing on the horizon, this pure perspective which I cannot reach because to reach it I would have to be you.

In other words, there seems to be, contained within our ordinary inter-personal attitudes, an element of overreach, a direction on the world that looks through the world to that which cannot be contained in it. There is, in our outlook on the world, a kind of hunger for the transcendent – a reaching beyond what is given to the subjectivity that is revealed in it.[4] This hunger is satisfied only when we can sense ourselves to be in the 'real presence', the *shekhinah*, by which what is transcendent makes itself manifest in the here and now. Religion lays great store by this experience, which of its nature cannot be given an a priori guarantee but which is recorded by all the great mystics and divines as the core of their faith. It is the *mysterium tremendum et fascinans* referred to by Rudolf Otto in his *Das Heilige* (1917).[5] And it is an experience whose ineffability is part of what is valued: for it is a visitation from a sphere that cannot be reached by any merely human effort and cannot be known except in this way. It is a kind of gift, for which we cannot ask since we lack words to summon it. Hence, in usual religious parlance, it is identified as one manifestation of the grace of God.

Could it be that music can capture this experience and make it imaginatively available to us ordinary mortals? I think this is what people have had in mind when they have defended the view that music can reach the transcendental. Music can put us in the presence of something that has no place in this world and which moves in a world of its own. And it can do this in a way that seems both orderly and personal, moving with a complete necessity that is also a kind of freedom. Two features of music contribute to this effect. First, the space of music, in a listening

---

[4]   I have developed this point in Roger Scruton, *The Soul of the World* (Princeton, NJ, 2014).

[5]   Rudolf Otto, *The Idea of the Holy: An Inquiry into the Non-Rational Factor in the Idea of the Divine and Its Relation to the Rational*, trans. J.W. Harvey (London and New York, 1923).

culture, is what I call an 'acousmatic space': it is a space full of movement and fields of force in which nothing actually moves and of which we ourselves could never be a part. In a mysterious way the order of music transforms sequences of sounds into melodies that begin and end, chords that occupy whole areas and gravitational fields that push and pull in ways of their own. I have elaborated on this in *The Aesthetics of Music*, and I think one conclusion to be drawn is that musical space is a space in which things move with a singular freedom, precisely because it contains no obstacles – no part of it is occupied, in the way physical space is occupied, but all of it is open.[6]

Secondly, the virtual causality that operates in musical space is, or aims to be, a causality of reason. In successful works of music there is a reason for each note, though not necessarily a reason that could be put into words. Each note is a response to the one preceding it and an invitation to its successor. Of course, sequences in music may sound facile, mechanical or arbitrary, so that the listener has no sense of a reasoned progression. But when that happens we are apt to dismiss the music as trivial or meaningless. Real music is not a sequence of mechanical movements but a continuous action, to which the 'Why?' of inter-personal understanding applies. The important works exhibit both the freedom and the necessity to which our self-sufficient actions always aspire – each detail must be as it is and where it is, and yet each detail must also be freely chosen. It is as though the space of music were awaiting visitation, and whatever appears in it is called upon to live the life of reason, just as we do.

This returns me to the observations made earlier. Stone-Davis is right that music is an action which takes place in physical space and which creates relations, differences, proximities and thresholds in the world of human communities. She is also correct that music is a physical action of a special kind, one that creates a virtual action in a space of its own. For just as the painter applying pigments in one space creates a world of imaginary beings in another, so does the musician making sounds in our space create virtual actions and movements in the acousmatic space of music. I have tried elsewhere to say just why this is important and why it is a mistake to argue, as Andy Hamilton argues, for example, that the physical activity and its attributes deliver the real essence of music, with the acousmatic experience as just one, historically transient, way of hearing it.[7] On the contrary,

---

[6]   See Roger Scruton, *The Aesthetics of Music* (Oxford, 1997), chs 1, 2. The musical space that I describe there is a phenomenological space whose places are identifiable without strain by ordinary listeners. In my view this space has nothing to do with the geometrical representation of musical relations given by Dmitri Tymoczko, who shows how to collate common practice voice-leading with transformations of points on a Möbius strip (*The Geometry of Music and Counterpoint in the Extended Common Practice* (Oxford, 2011); see also Roger Scruton 'The Space of Music: Review Essay of Dmitri Tymoczko's *A Geometry of Music*', *Reason Papers*, 34/2 (2012): 167–83).

[7]   Andy Hamilton, *Aesthetics and Music* (London, 2007); see Roger Scruton, 'Review: Aesthetics and Music, by Andy Hamilton', *Mind*, 117/467 (2008): 702–5.

the acousmatic experience of the listener is the source of what we most value in music, and if it disappeared what remains would not be the artform that has been so central to our civilisation since ancient times. In listening to music we enter another space from the one occupied by the performer, and in that space a kind of free causality opens to our perception – a causality in which gestures achieve completion from their own inner urgency, unimpeded by the obstacles that clutter the physical world. This, it seems to me, is what the Romantics noticed, when they singled out music as leading us out of this world, into a transcendental reality that we otherwise would not encounter.

Thanks to the two features I mentioned we hear music as imbued with an intentionality, an 'aboutness' of its own. It is as though it is reacting in its own way to something that we cannot know or observe, since this thing is buried in that space that we cannot enter, audible, so to speak, on its far horizon, but heard only by the music and not by us. Yet we move with the music's sympathetic movement, and it is this, I think, which gives us the impression that we have been put in touch, in some way, with the transcendental. I suggest that this experience is familiar from the world of chamber music and from the instrumental works of Bach, as well as from much sacred music. The polyphony of Palestrina, the plangent *Tenebrae responsories* of Victoria, the solo violin Partitas of Bach, and the latter's *The Art of Fugue* and *Goldberg Variations* all seem to move in sympathy to some source beyond the limits of this world but which finds an echo in the 'sacred' space of music.

Of course, the best we can conclude from this is that the music helps us to imagine some kind of contact with the transcendental. It certainly offers no proof that such contact is possible. Perhaps our hunger for the transcendental is a primitive fact about us which corresponds to nothing real. But about that there is nothing to be said in any case. Of course, the desire to find comfort in the unknowable is always with us, the knowable being so devastatingly devoid of it. But we are led always into contradiction by the pursuit of this desire. Consider St Paul's and the Prayer Book's reference to the 'peace which passeth understanding': is this not already a contradiction – for if it really passes understanding, how do we know it is peace? It would not offer comfort to think of this thing, if we did not think of it as bringing the peace and reconciliation that we long for. And the same goes for the transcendental realm that we glimpse in the 'sacred' space of music. We feel that music is putting us in touch with another world, beyond the reach of our human knowledge, the very world that appears in the epiphanies referred to by Rudolf Otto, in *Das Heilige*. But we also want that world to be good to us, to contain a solace and a vindication, and to ease us as it were onto its breast. What would be the point otherwise? And yet music can do this only as the Prayer Book does it, by helping us to see that unattainable world in human terms – providing us like Beethoven's *Heilige Dankgesang* with an image of healing or like Bach's 'Erbarme Dich' with a supreme act of penitence into which we are drawn and which comforts us with the sense that, if there is forgiveness, then it will be granted in return for this. These experiences transcend our ordinary ability to articulate them and do so thanks to the music. But to say that they reach beyond the empirical to the transcendental is to misrepresent their way of working.

This returns me in conclusion to the aesthetic idea of the transcendental. Human beings find significance in many things and attempt to convey that significance in works of art. But works of art also alter and embellish the things that they convey – make the beautiful more beautiful, the moving more moving and the profound more profound. They do this by pushing the empirical phenomenon to its limit, so to speak, to the point where it seems to break free of itself and to cast a shadow in the beyond. That is what Beethoven does in 'O Namenlöse Freude' and Bach in 'Erbarme Dich'. It is not that there is a transcendent reality which is made present by these sublime expressions of emotion, but rather that they endow empirical emotions with a completeness and purity that, in everyday life, they could never attain. Always our feelings are mixed, contaminated by other concerns, by needs and distractions. Never in everyday life can we give ourselves completely to love, joy, forgiveness, grief or worship. But these emotions nevertheless conjure a pure world of sympathy, in which they exist in their completed form, unsullied by self-interest, objects of contemplation which bear their meaning entirely within themselves. Music can take us into that world, presenting us with transcendent versions of emotions that we know only in their bounded and empirical form. But, in saying this, we are not endorsing the view that music gives us access to the transcendental. On the contrary, we are saying that it presents us with the empirical, the here and now, by showing it in its purified and completed form. And maybe that is the best that we can ask for.

Chapter 7
Theomusical Subjectivity: Schleiermacher and the Transcendence of Immediacy

Jonas Lundblad[1]

> What the music I love expresses to me, is not thought too indefinite to put into words, but on the contrary, too definite.[2]

Studying the significance of music in interplay with the notion of 'transcendence' opens up wide cultural and intellectual vistas. It is even tempting to say that such a standpoint facilitates a gleaming framework of almost limitless potential for the keen sighted. The term 'gleaming' might suggest some general characteristics of transcendence as a dimension of human experience: it fascinates as evocative, existentially pregnant and yet is evasive enough to call foreclosed conceptions of the commonplace into question. The structure of this volume hospitably provides space for music studies to engage with the notion of transcendence through two main categorical frameworks: as posited within an immanent frame or relating to an absolute otherness. However, the concept of transcendence might even be allowed to destabilise any mutual exclusivity between secularist and theological frameworks. In both cases, the idea of transcendence necessarily entails some form of demarcation from a prior framework of immanence; a domain that is to some degree self-contained, but whose boundaries can nevertheless still be transgressed, allowing a fundamental, wider horizon to shine forth. The evolution of occidental culture (and its music) can hardly be fully comprehended without attending to historically variable differentiations between a finite (desacralised) sphere and its counterpart in a realm of moral and religious transcendence. It is only natural that philosophical, theological and indeed political implications of this distinction are constantly contested and renegotiated, intermingled as they are with our conceptions of reality, human freedom and the legitimacy of government and legislation. Considerably less noticed is the historicity of cultural conditions in which the human ability to discern reality with the categories of immanence and transcendence has its original genesis.

In one of modernity's most significant theories of transcendence, the so-called 'axial age thesis', Karl Jaspers describes a specific 'age of transcendence'[3] in

---

[1]   This chapter has been written with financial support from the Helge Ax:son Johnson Foundation, Stockholm.

[2]   Felix Mendelssohn Bartholdy to Marc-André Souchay (15 Oct. 1841), in Felix Mendelssohn Bartholdy, *Letters of Felix Mendelssohn Bartholdy from 1833–1847*, eds P. Mendelssohn Bartholdy and C. Mendelssohn Bartholdy (London, 1864), p. 276.

[3]   See Benjamin I. Schwartz, 'The Age of Transcendence', *Daedalus*, 104/2 (1975): 1–7.

which humanity first attained the reflexive tools necessary to develop the multi-layered worldviews required to instil an awareness of transcendence. According to his theory, the idea of a transcendent realm was dependent on scribal and aesthetic medias and could only emerge within innovative modes of reflexivity, themselves conditioned by the creative formation of core scriptures in 'high civilizations', among them prophetic Judaism, Zoroastrianism, Buddhism, Confucianism and Greek antiquity.[4]

The aesthetics of Friedrich Schleiermacher (1768–1834) transfers us to the milieu of German Romanticism, an age when music came to be regarded as a paradigmatic means of attaining transcendence. His theories of aesthetics and religion are intimately interwoven, hinging upon the pivotal and kindred notions of feeling (*Gefühl*) and immediacy (*Unmittelbarkeit*). Both concepts function as pillars in Schleiermacher's theory of human subjectivity, which itself provides a framework for the staging of a critical interplay between the modern conditions of epistemology and morality, theology and art. Ever a mediating figure, Schleiermacher attempted an 'eternal covenant' between the theological concerns of Christianity and the critical enquiries of modern society, an endeavour which included one of modernity's most striking affirmations of an inherent reciprocity between art and religion.[5] Music emerges as a crucial medium of communication in Schleiermacher's attempt to envision human subjectivity as constantly unfolding in and reciprocally conditioned by nature and culture. Articulating his theory within the gradual rise of aesthetic autonomy, Schleiermacher simultaneously champions and yet disavows modernity's elevation of music as either the consummation or substitution of traditional religion.[6] After almost 200 years, his attention to the formative potentials of both language and art remains challenging, and his mediating framework can prove viable to interpreting the transcendence of music in an age which, like his own, witnesses less palpably discernible boundaries between art and religion, secular 'immanence' and theological 'ultimacy'.

---

[4]   Jaspers's classic articulation of this historiography appeared in his 1949 book *Vom Ursprung und Ziel der Geschichte*. In his opinion these cultural transformations can be located between 800 and 200 BCE. Although certainly susceptible to detailed historical criticism, the axial age thesis continues to attract scholarly attention (see Robert N. Bellah and Hans Joas (eds), *The Axial Age and Its Consequences* (Cambridge, Mass., 2012), esp. Hans Joas, 'The Axial Age Debate as Religious Discourse', pp. 9–29).

[5]   For an introduction to Schleiermacher, see Terrence N. Tice, *Schleiermacher* (Nashville, Tenn., 2006), or more substantially, Kurt Nowak, *Schleiermacher: Leben, Werk und Wirkung* (Göttingen, 2002).

[6]   On Schleiermacher's aesthetics of music, see Gunter Scholtz, *Schleiermachers Musikphilosophie* (Göttingen, 1981); id., 'Schleiermacher', trans. S.H. Gillespie, in Stefan Lorenz Sorgner and Oliver Fürbeth (eds), *Music in German Philosophy* (Chicago, 2010), pp. 47–68; Andrew Bowie, *Music, Philosophy, and Modernity* (Cambridge, 2007), pp. 152–65.

Immediacy as Transcendence in *On Religion*

Schleiermacher's most famous work, the 1799 version of *On Religion: Speeches to its Cultured Despisers*, is an epochal text which inaugurates vital traditions of theorising religion and theology within the conditions of modern society. Generations of scholars associate the work with famous formulas such as: 'religion's essence is neither thinking nor action, but intuition and feeling' and 'religion is the sensibility and taste for the infinite'.[7] Both phrases belong to Schleiermacher's novel attempt to find an overarching conceptual definition of religion, apt to mediate between a cultural theory of religion as a non-reducible dimension of human world-making and a theological conviction of its ultimate origin in divine immanence and self-communication. Having described religion as 'immediate experiences of the existence and action of the universe'[8] and as a longing 'to be grasped and filled by the universe's immediate influences',[9] Schleiermacher finally gives a description, both elaborate and exuberant, of how an act of ordinary sense perception becomes transformed into an experience of 'immediacy' – a holistic unity with external reality:

> That first mysterious moment that occurs in every sensory perception, before intuition and feeling have separated, where sense and its objects have, as it were, flowed into one another and become one, before both turn back to their original position – I know how indescribable it is and how quickly it passes away. But I wish that you were able to hold on to it and also to recognize it again in the higher and divine religious activity of the mind. Would that I could and might express it, at least indicate it, without having to desecrate it! It is as fleeting and transparent as the first scent with which the dew gently caresses the waking flowers, as modest and delicate as a maiden's kiss, as holy and fruitful as a nuptial embrace; indeed, not like these, but it is itself all of these. A manifestation, an event develops quickly and magically into an image of the universe. Even as the beloved and ever-sought-for form fashions itself, my soul flees toward it; I embrace it, not as a shadow, but as the holy essence itself. I lie on the bosom of the infinite world. At this moment I am its soul, for I feel all its powers and its infinite life as my own; at this moment it is my body, for I penetrate its muscles and its limbs as my own, and its innermost nerves move according to my sense and my presentiments as my own. With the slightest trembling the holy embrace is dispersed, and now for the first time the intuition stands before me as a separate form; I survey it, and it mirrors itself in my open soul like the image of the vanishing beloved in the awakened eye of a youth; now for the first time the

---

[7]   Friedrich Schleiermacher, *On Religion: Speeches to Its Cultured Despisers*, trans. and ed. R. Crouter, (Cambridge, 1996), pp. 22–3.

[8]   Ibid., p. 26.

[9]   Ibid., p. 22.

feeling works its way up from inside and diffuses itself like the blush of shame
and desire on his cheek. This moment is the highest flowering of religion.[10]

This metaphorical narrative is paradigmatic of Schleiermacher's notion of
immediacy but remains both provocative and enigmatic in its claim to have
rendered an experience which both constitutes the living presence of religion in
the subject (as such being 'the natal hour' of religion[11]) and simultaneously marks
the consummation or most characteristic fulfilment of what religion strives to
become ('the highest flowering of religion'). Striking in its contradictory attempt
to communicate a 'fleeting' moment which has been declared indescribable,
the narration also relates several temporal stages of activity within a single
moment. Depicting sense perception through imagery of consumed erotic
desire results in a relational account where the 'lovers', the given content of
perception and the perceiving subject, mutually seek to attain a perfect degree of
physical and spiritual interpenetration. Thus sense perception forms a mode of
dissolving transcendence: in its immediacy the sensible and intellectual realms
of the self become insolubly intermingled as finite humanity merges with an
infinite reality.[12] However, the image of a union logically requires two distinct
agents, and the course of events within the 'immediate' experience ultimately
results in a renewed differentiation between intuition (*Anschauung*) and feeling.
In *On Religion*, a work thoroughly rooted in post-Kantian philosophy, the
concept of intuition refers to the objective dimension of sense or the 'content'
of the experience as presented to the mind. Feeling is not intended to imply
any specifically emotional quality but rather serves as a technical term for
the amalgamating activity in which the subject receives and processes the
information provided by the sense organs.[13] Thus the immediacy described by

---

[10]   Ibid., pp. 31–2.

[11]   Ibid., p. 32. Taking the final remark literally, Christian Albrecht attempted to
abstract *On Religion*'s integral understanding of religion from this passage. In his view
it describes a constitutive religious primordial affectation, an *Uraffektion* (see Christian
Albrecht, *Schleiermachers Theorie der Frömmigkeit: Ihr wissenschaftlicher Ort und ihr
systematischer Gehalt in den Reden, in der Glaubenslehre und in der Dialektik* (Berlin and
New York, 1994)).

[12]   Crouter rightly brings attention to the corresponding Socratic myth of intellectual
desire in *Phaedrus* and indicates the thorough influence of an 'aesthetic' Platonism in
Schleiermacher's thinking (Schleiermacher, *On Religion*, p. 31), natural in the light of
Schleiermacher's endeavour to translate the entire Platonic corpus.

[13]   The English translation of *Anschauung* as 'intuition' can occlude the connotations it
would have had for Schleiermacher in the aftermath of Kant and Fichte. Intuition is here not
primarily a question of non-conceptual or instinctive experience but the objective side of
experience or the presence of the object in the subject. This difference and its (inadequate)
reception in anglophone research is brought out in Theodore Vial, 'Anschauung and
Intuition, Again (Or, "We Remain Bound to the Earth")', in Brent W. Sockness and
Wilhelm Gräb (eds), *Schleiermacher, the Study of Religion, and the Future of Theology: A*

Schleiermacher both seeks to heal the rift between object and subject and yet affirms that its own vision of transcendence is fleeting: as soon as the subject becomes aware of an object, the state of transcendence has passed and a fence between subject and object has been raised. In his narrative, Schleiermacher seeks to safeguard the integrity of both subject and object through metaphors which underscore how both counterparts actively strive towards the boundless union of transcendence. Although the subject consciously turns towards the perception and wants to incorporate it into its own organism, it does not violate the integrity of the object; on the contrary, it respects the autonomy of the perception and wants to allow for its ability to constitute its own form (*Gestalt*).

At this juncture, the desire to safeguard the autonomy of form, arguably the most pivotal concept in the development of nineteenth-century musical aesthetics, begins to illuminate how Schleiermacher's effort to situate religion within the epistemological debates of transcendental philosophy also has far-reaching implications for the role of music in modern culture. In polemics with influential philosophies of his day, Schleiermacher argues that the characteristic mark of religion's dealings with reality is its respect for the integrity of individuality and plurality.[14] This lofty ideal is developed within his own dichotomy between understanding (as human activity outwards) and sense (as human receptivity inwards) in which both art and religion are situated within the category of 'sense'; thus supposedly eschewing a self-centred 'Promethean' reductionist and purposive attitude towards exteriority. Although the subject longs for immediacy, as a holistic intermingling of human subjectivity and sensible form, Schleiermacher's narrative seeks to steer clear of injurious dimensions within competing philosophical standpoints. On the one hand, it states that knowledge and experience presuppose an active openness to transcendence beyond the narrow confines of the self, thus affirming the need for a prior immediate union with the world and others. This attitude simultaneously entails a conviction that subjects never have access to objects outside of themselves apart from the individual feeling that marks the activity through which perceptions are received and made presentable to thought. On the other hand, such transcendence must be balanced with a respect for the specific form of different perceptions, thereby avoiding a purposive stance where perceptions and reality become the arena for an unbridled subjectivity

---

Transatlantic Dialogue (New York and Berlin, 2010), pp. 39–50. Schleiermacher himself repeatedly lamented the insufficient precision of 'feeling' as a philosophical term and was later to bring many of its connotations into his usage of the notion 'immediate self-consciousness'.

[14] For Schleiermacher, 'the universe and the relationship of humanity to it' is the common subject matter of both religion, theoretical ('metaphysics') and practical philosophy ('morals'). Religion's irreducible contribution does not lie with its specific content but is summed up by its attitude towards reality: 'Religion must treat this subject matter completely differently, express or work out another relationship of humanity to it' (*On Religion*, p. 19).

which ultimately takes an interest in objects only to the extent that they can be processed and used for individual self-expression.[15]

It is certainly no coincidence that Schleiermacher's narration of immediacy-as-transcendence appears in the cast of a consumed erotic scene. On the contrary, its idealised depiction of sense perception is fully congruent with an early Romantic vision of physical love, seeking to resolve the interplay between mind and body, desire and respect for the integrity of the other.[16] The musical relevance of this discussion is that Schleiermacher throughout his subsequent aesthetic reflection will present ever new articulations of how the experience of music is a paradigmatic instance of such an erotic immediacy. In light of his narrative, modernity's theme of respecting music's autonomous form can be understood as part of a wider safeguarding of perceptions' integrity. Whereas the immediate experience of music represents the transcending and primordial unity of subject and object, reflection upon musical form allows for music's freedom to constitute and manifest its own specific image.

Subjectivity, Freedom and Art Religion

Schleiermacher's *On Religion* is famous for its theory of religion, developed out of the paradigm of post-Kantian transcendentalism. The lasting relevance of the theory depends on its situation within a specific diagnosis of modernity and a corresponding programme to remedy its shortcomings.[17] Schleiermacher's general dichotomy between understanding and sense questions what he considers

---

[15] It is certainly possible to read Schleiermacher's narrative of immediacy and the integrity of the given form as a transcendentalist re-articulation of a traditional Protestant doctrine of revelation. Doing so serves to safeguard the individual's ability to enter into unity with the content of divine self-communication and be formed by it.

[16] Schleiermacher scholarship has repeatedly tried to set him apart from his Romantic companion Friedrich Schlegel on the subject of physical love, thereby making the young Schleiermacher appear less affirmative. Andreas Arndt has rightly questioned the textual validity of such a reading in the interpretation of Hans Dierkes (see Hans Dierkes, 'Die problematische Poesie: Schleiermachers Beitrag zur Frühromantik', in K.-V. Selge (ed.), *Internationaler Schleiermacher-Kongreß Berlin 1984* (Berlin, 1985), pp. 61–98; Andreas Arndt, '"Bedenke, daß alle Poesie schlechthin als Werk der Liebe anzusehen ist": Ethik und Ästhetik bei Schleiermacher', in *Friedrich Schleiermacher als Philosoph* (Berlin, 2013), pp. 336–47).

[17] Recent research has highlighted how *On Religion* can be said to integrate three levels: a socio-cultural diagnosis of modernity, a theory of religion and a call for a renewal of aesthetic-religious communication (see Ulrich Barth, 'Die Religionstheorie der "Reden": Schleiermachers theologisches Modernisierungsprogramm', in *Aufgeklärter Protestantismus* (Tübingen, 2004), pp. 259–90; Folkart Wittekind, 'Die Vision der Gesellschaft und die Bedeutung religiöser Kommunikation: Schleiermachers Kritik am Atheismusstreit als Leitmotiv der "Reden"', in Ulrich Barth and Claus-Dieter Osthövener

to be an impeding narrowness of bourgeois utility where knowledge, morality and human dignity are reduced to practical purposes and objectifying designs. In his analysis, the legacy of the Enlightenment contains one-sided ideals of understanding and knowledge whose predominance have come to hamper the wider cultivation of human individuality, sensibility and imagination: qualities he finds vital to the development of the human capacity for both art and religion. Situated at the heart of early German Romanticism and sharing its emphasis upon the role of the arts in societal transformation, Schleiermacher attaches the renewal of both society and religion to contemporary pursuits for a general and emancipatory aesthetic education of humanity. ('Everything, therefore, must begin by putting an end to the bondage in which human sense is held for the purpose of ... understanding.'[18])

It is within his own elucidation of such education that Schleiermacher coins the famous notion of *Kunstreligion*, thus (unintentionally) inscribing himself into the history of modern aesthetics as a theorist, and even, 'the theologian of art religion'.[19] According to Carl Dahlhaus, Schleiermacher legitimised the idea 'that the art religion of the nineteenth century was truly a religion and not just a travesty of one'.[20] However, in *On Religion*, the existence of such a thorough

---

(eds), *200 Jahre 'Reden über die Religion': Akten des 1. Internationalen Kongresses der Schleiermacher Gesellschaft, Halle, 14.–17. März 1999* (Berlin, 2000), pp. 397–415).

[18]   Schleiermacher, *On Religion*, p. 66. In the aftermath of Schiller's *Über die ästetische Erziehung des Menschen* (1795), without doubt the most famous programme for aesthetic *Bildung*, Schleiermacher was one of the Romantics who renounced Kant's way of accomplishing the ideal of transcendental freedom. Like other thinkers of his generation, he deplored how Kantian thought seemed to diminish the significance of art and ascribed a more radical formative potential to aesthetic expressions. Although misrepresenting Schleiermacher's understanding of religion, Frederick C. Beiser provides a helpful introduction to the German educational ideal of art (see *The Romantic Imperative: The Concept of Early German Romanticism* (Cambridge, Mass., 2003), pp. 88–105).

[19]   Carl Dahlhaus, *The Idea of Absolute Music*, trans. R. Lustig (Chicago, 1991), p. 86.

[20]   For Dahlhaus, Schleiermacher is the theologian who provided the theory behind the aesthetic contemplation of music as a kind of religious devotion: 'music expresses the feeling of infinity that is the substance of religion' (ibid., p. 86). A positive evaluation of art religion remains theologically controversial, and it remains wise to remember that the notion, as a derived concept, relies upon a logical and empirical primacy of religion from which art is differentiated and yet related. However, to speak of art religion does not per se claim any internal precedence of authenticity or legitimacy, although in modernity art, and not least music, is ascribed an access to the sacred which equals or replaces traditional religion. See Heinrich Detering, 'Was ist Kunstreligion? Systematische und historische Bemerkungen', in Albert Meier et al. (eds), *Kunstreligion: Ein ästhetisches Konzept der moderne in seiner historischen Entfaltung*, vol. 1: *Der Ursprung des Konzepts um 1800* (Berlin and New York, 2011), pp. 11–27. The individuality of Schleiermacher's position is developed in Folkart Wittekind, '"... die Musik meiner Religion": Schleiermachers ethische Funktionalisierung der Musik bis zur "Weihnachtsfeier" und seine Kritik der frühromantischen Kunstreligion', in Ulrich Barth, Andreas Arndt and Wilhelm Gräb (eds),

confluence of art and religion is as yet an unrealised ideal; religion and art are yet 'friendly souls whose inner affinity ... is nevertheless still unknown to them'. 'To bring them together and to unite them in one bed is the only thing that can bring religion to completion'.[21]

Schleiermacher's desire to emancipate 'sense' stems from perceived shortcomings within transcendental philosophy. He was worried about the wider societal effects of a paradigm wherein the interaction between human subjectivity and external reality is understood primarily as conditioned by a self-caused rationality. While seeking to defend moral freedom, Schleiermacher finds such paradigms to have failed both theoretically, in their quest for a highest unifying principle, as well as practically, in a purposeful subjugation of nature and humankind.[22] In Schleiermacher's view, true freedom presupposes a fundamental unity between nature and spirit, and the trajectory towards it necessitates an inverted epistemology where thinking and action are regarded as primarily receptive to sense perception. Both his terminology of feeling and immediacy, as well as the situation of religion within an aesthetic paradigm, can thus be understood as critical contributions within a post-Kantian tradition.

In Kant's system, knowledge famously requires a synthesis of a given perception with the given concepts of the spontaneously thinking self. As unconstrained by the causality of nature, thinking is transcendental and therefore capable of validating empirical knowledge as well as human freedom to act according to moral reason. The lasting awkwardness within this system was Kant's inability to attain knowledge of this free self-consciousness, the highest principle of his thought: if the freedom of self-consciousness is to be preserved, the self can neither be given by perception (in an intuition) nor can it subsume itself under a general concept. The enduring consequence of Kant's problem was to deny the 'I' the status of knowledge, in the end leaving self-awareness to 'nothing more than the feeling of an existence without the least concept and only a representation of that to which all thinking relates'.[23]

Conceiving self-consciousness as primarily non-conceptual and non-objectifying is pivotal to appreciating the prehistory of Schleiermacher's aesthetics

---

Christentum – Staat – Kultur: Akten des Kongresses der Internationalen Schleiermacher gesellschaft, Berlin, März 2006 (Berlin, 2008), pp. 271–300.

[21]   Schleiermacher, *On Religion*, pp. 69–70.

[22]   Schleiermacher's diagnosis of his age is given in broad, yet suggestive, brush strokes. He portrays the turbulent aftermath of the French Revolution, a purposeful ethics of utility and the predominance of technology over art as symptoms of a common cultural malaise: the desire to reduce reality to the measures and gains of the self, thereby ensnaring humanity in purposeful attitudes towards nature, others and (not least) God. The most incisive study of Schleiermacher's cultural critique is still Kurt Nowak, *Schleiermacher und die Frühromantik: Eine literaturgeschichtliche Studie zum romantischen Religionsverständnis und Menschenbild am Ende des 18. Jahrhunderts in Deutschland* (Göttingen, 1986).

[23]   Kant, *Prolegomena to Any Future Metaphysics*, cited in Andrew Bowie, *Aesthetics and Subjectivity: From Kant to Nietzsche* (Manchester, 2003), p. 23, see pp. 16–24.

and theology. At the time of *On Religion*, the most prominent solution to Kant's aporia was J.G. Fichte's philosophy, erected upon the assertion of an immediate certainty of the 'I'. For Fichte, the 'I' is not mirrored as an object in self-awareness but induces its own self-consciousness and thus both grounds and constitutes itself autonomously. Self-consciousness forestalls the object-subject distinction and knows itself in a non-sensible immediate self-consciousness, externally indemonstrable and contrasted with the conceptual or reflexive consciousness which it underlies.[24]

In *On Religion*, Schleiermacher rejects a secluded unity of the human mind and opposes Fichte's non-sensible intellectual intuition as a solution to the problem of the missing 'highest principle'. Although thoroughly immersed in Fichte's theoretical development of transcendentalism, Schleiermacher cheekily dismisses both him and British utilitarianism in his own preference for the receptivity of sense over against modern subject-centred 'understanding'. The polemical nature of Schleiermacher's argumentation arguably overstates its differentiation between these orientations, but, in common with a great number of subsequent aesthetic theories, he is deeply concerned with the consequences of utilising and egotistic attitudes in both theoretical and social realms. Thus, there is a certain irony in how several of his influential interpreters, from Hegel to Karl Barth to 'Wittgensteinian' postmodernists, have critiqued his notion of sensible immediacy as overly subjectivist, logically vacuous or lacking in attention to the formative mediation of language.[25] In contrast to his critics, Schleiermacher's main contribution in this area is to indicate an alternative epistemology that supplies one of modernity's most ardent assertions of the formative role of aesthetic means of communication, thus forcefully challenging the understanding that a non-conceptual mediation equals an unmediated immediacy.

---

[24]   For a qualified discussion of Fichte and Schleiermacher's reception of him, see Peter Grove, *Deutungen des Subjekts: Schleiermachers Philosophie der Religion* (Berlin, 2004), pp. 170–231.

[25]   Hegel's most developed criticism was to appear in his 1824 *Lectures on the Philosophy of Religion* and relates directly to Schleiermacher's 1822 *The Christian Faith*. In an ironic evaluation of Schleiermacher's *Christmas Eve Celebration*, Karl Barth opposed its musical 'indeterminacy' with the proper determinations of theological language (see Karl Barth, 'Schleiermachers "Weihnachtsfeier"', in *Gesamtausgabe*, vol. 3: *Vorträge und kleinere Arbeiten 1922–1925*, ed. Holger Finze (Zurich, 1990), pp. 467–8). In the 1980s, George A. Lindbeck and Wayne Proudfoot delivered influential criticisms of Schleiermacher's immediacy as a postdated liberal attempt which had withdrawn human subjectivity from the influence of language, either in traditional theological notions or critical scientific explanations of religion (George A. Lindbeck, *The Nature of Doctrine; Religion and Theology in a Postliberal Age* (London, 1984); Wayne Proudfoot, *Religious Experience* (Berkeley, Calif. 1985)).

Immediacy in Intermedial Religious Communication

Schleiermacher's previously mentioned call to align religion with aesthetic education implies a social and historical situation of human immediacy, thereby articulating a conviction that a renewal of religion requires cultivation of a heightened sensitivity through which sensible intuitions can be apprehended and grasped. For Schleiermacher a lack of such sensitivity resembles an incapability to become seized by a work of art before an explanatory commentary is provided.[26] The possibility to intuit is not only dependent on the givenness of objective intuitions but also requires an education of sensibility, a prior participation in social structures where previously given intuitions are communicated. In no sense does Schleiermacher match up to caricatures of liberal theology where religious experience occurs unmediated; on the contrary, he is quite convinced that experiences of transcending immediacy are received and interpreted with the aid of socially and cultural-linguistically attained ideas. At the same time, the sensible nature of this immediacy does not reduce transcendence to mere sensuous experience as it always requires a unification of tangible sensations and a thinking, interpretative subject. Nor does an immediate presence of infinity through intuition entail an undifferentiated equality of sensation and God. Although the experience of immediacy involves distinct temporal moments, it is vital to see that its form of transcendence describes an integral aspect of sense perception per se and thus amounts to a continuous dimension of human experience.

Immediacy, as transcendence, is generally described as a seamless unification of subject and object, but in order to be distinguishable as religious transcendence it crucially entails further interpretation where the received form is taken to be 'an image of the universe'. Schleiermacher calls for a 'higher realism', an attitude where ordinary physical sensations and finite actions are interpreted as caused by a vitalising and sustaining infinitude. Schleiermacher's description of religious 'immediate' perception finally upholds that a sensible intuition (*sinnliche Anschauung*) is received and interpreted as a symbolic representation of the totality of existence: infinitude inheres within a concretely tangible finitude.[27]

---

[26]   Schleiermacher, *On Religion*, p. 58.

[27]   The concept of 'higher realism' is linked with Schleiermacher's avowal of Spinozism. 'The chief tenet of this "realism" is that the highest principle of reality, which alone is divine, is inexpressible in thought and that the infinite is knowable only as mediated through the finite' (Crouter, in Schleiermacher, *On Religion*, p. 24). The most substantial study of Spinozan streaks in *On Religions*'s theory of religion is Christof Ellsiepen, *Anschauung des Universums und Scientia Intuitiva: Die spinozistische Grundlagen von Schleiermachers frühe Religionstheorie* (Berlin, 2006). Ellsiepen clearly shows how Schleiermacher's conception of religious intuition presupposes that the universe (or God) actively communicates its inherence in every finite thing, an understanding which for the pious strengthens the imperative to safeguard the integrity of all perceived forms.

While at first seemingly uncritical, Schleiermacher's description of immediacy, as transcendence, turns out to be a complex and multi-layered experience, requiring both a prior conception of transcendental wholeness and the sensibility to receive and interpret sense perceptions as symbolic manifestations of this transcendental infinitude.[28]

The fourth chapter of *On Religion* presents an idealised theory of how a religious community can facilitate both of these requirements through its own specific hallmark: free and rhetorical communication. Religious communication must be free from design and purpose and therefore needs to be decisively rhetorical, or 'aesthetic', thus freely renouncing claims to be metaphysically and conceptually grounded.[29] The immediacy of religious experience is for Schleiermacher a strictly individual experience but simultaneously the fortunate fruit of a community and its symbolic forms of interaction. While Schleiermacher believes that such experiences in themselves are fleeting and fundamentally incommunicable, the community nevertheless employs different symbolic media in their attempts to reciprocally share and evoke transcendence. When unhampered, this communication manages to be both expressive and formative of individuals' experiences and serves to mediate between individuals without constraint, bringing them into a shared vision of humanity and a common fundamental intuition of the universe.

Schleiermacher's theory of religious communities is aesthetically far sighted not only because of its attention to communication as a pivotal category of human interaction but also more specifically for its insight into the potential of different aesthetic forms. In a quite revolutionary way he indicates how different media have singular abilities to represent and evoke the imprint of immediacy, thus ascribing them world-making capacities through which they facilitate experiences which would otherwise remain unattainable. From this insight stems an urgency to renew the religious repertoire of aesthetic expressive forms. Schleiermacher draws a *tableau vivant* of religious communication which stresses that language is the most adequate medium to communicate the definite nature and quality of religious intuitions: 'It is impossible to express and communicate religion other than verbally with all the effort and artistry of

---

[28] Grove describes Schleiermacher's term 'intuition of the universe' as an abbreviation, for 'a religious intuition is an intuition of the finite as representation of the infinite or the universe, or of the individual as part of the whole. The religious intuition then has an apophantic, indicating structure: Something is seen as something' (*Deutungen des Subjekts*, p. 344: my trans.).

[29] With a later aesthetic term, Schleiermacher can be said to propose a 'performative' religious aesthetics: that is, the opinion that any presence of the infinite remains conditioned by the constant performance of a religious tradition. The immediate transcendence which forms the basis of religion is evoked and expressed by the aesthetic symbols of the community and must never be conceived as linguistically stipulated in abstraction from the individuals who partake in religious 'performance'.

language'.[30] However, such definiteness can at the same time be detrimental to the range of sensibility if abstracted concepts and doctrines come to function as replacements of living religion. Therefore, the ideal of religious language, signifying the objective or definite content of religion, is an elevation towards music:

> For just as such a speech is music even without song and tone, so is there also a music ... that becomes speech without words, the most definite, most understandable expression of what is innermost. ... In holy hymns and choruses, to which the words of the poet cling only loosely and lightly, that is exhaled which definite speech can no longer comprehend.[31]

In this rather striking passage, the boundaries between language and music are dissolved, and music is posited as the prime medium of religious communication with a more intensive degree of intimacy and comprehension than language.[32]

Concomitant with this evaluation, Schleiermacher frequently uses music as a primary metaphor to describe the subject in a state of religious immediacy. Religion should ideally be neither accidental nor temporary but ought to remain a constant horizon accompanying all individual impressions, thoughts and actions occurring in the human mind. As such, religion is fundamentally located at the level of feeling, the amalgamating and unifying self-consciousness which underlies ordinary representational consciousness. In resounding metaphors, Schleiermacher claims that religion should 'accompany every human deed as a holy music'[33] and laments those who will not allow their individual 'chords' and 'melodies' to transcend into the richer polyphonic web of a greater 'harmony'.[34] However, it should be kept

---

[30]   Schleiermacher, *On Religion*, p. 74.

[31]   Ibid., p. 75. The most direct impact of Schleiermacher's aesthetics of a mutual interplay between language and music might be found in his Berlin companion Felix Mendelssohn, most strikingly in the *Lieder ohne Worte* but also in a widely religious conception of music (see Thomas Erne, 'Schleiermacher on Music and Religion: The "Sound" of Schleiermacher in Felix Mendelssohn-Bartholdy's Music', in Dietrich Korsch and Amber L. Griffioen (eds), *Interpreting Religion* (Tübingen, 2011), pp. 113–21).

[32]   Schleiermacher, together with Novalis and Friedrich Schlegel, primarily conceived of music in terms of 'musicality' – an aesthetic quality of poetic language. As such his (early) musical aesthetics arguably reflects poetic and philosophical ideals rather than a wide experience of actual music. The historical relevance of early Romantic aesthetics is tied to its influence on composers who later transformed its poetic vision into genuine musical creativity (Robert Schumann might be the prime instance of this intermedial exchange of aesthetic ideals). See Barbara Naumann, *Musikalisches Ideen-Instrument: Das Musikalische in Poetik und Sprachtheorie der Frühromantik* (Stuttgart, 1990).

[33]   Schleiermacher, *On Religion*, p. 30.

[34]   'A person's virtuosity is ... merely the melody of his life; and it remains individual tones if he does not add religion to it. The latter accompanies the former in ever-richer variation ... and thus transforms the simple song of life into a full-voiced and

in mind that Schleiermacher's religious aesthetics of music, in analogy with the transcendence of immediacy, presupposes a shared cultural-linguistic framework. Schleiermacher's aesthetic ideal here is not any autonomous music. Rather, the musically evoked subjectivity of immediacy is seen as the ideal fulfilment of, and thus subsequent to, the definite character of linguistic mediation. In his early works, the seamless and mutual integration of music and religion is both an ideal and an imperative: 'Christianity and music must adhere closely together, because they elevate and give radiance to each other.'[35] Thus music can be described as a definite form of intimate communication in a community where the meaning of music is interwoven with other common intuitions and ideas.

Music as Expression and Mediation of Immediacy: the *Aesthetics*

Throughout the gradual development of his mature and comprehensive system of thought, Schleiermacher continued to assert the mutual kinship of music and religion as expressions of feeling (or immediate self-consciousness). Both his *Aesthetics*[36] and theology remain significant articulations of a general Romantic aesthetic paradigm where art is described as expressive of human subjectivity (or, more precisely, feeling). In contrast to many popular presuppositions, Schleiermacher's works suggest that the lasting profoundness of this paradigm lies in its dialectical nature, thus, in an emphasis that subjectivity and art are reciprocally transformative.[37] An analogy to this view is Schleiermacher's

---

magnificent harmony' (ibid., p. 48). Schleiermacher's early aesthetics is deeply resonant with Pythagorean images of a *harmonia mundi*, a fact that simultaneously establishes a musical preference for harmony over against melody. However, this harmony is no longer pre-critically established through mathematical and rational procedures but through the immediate relations between the self and the world, intuition and feeling, mind and body. See Scholtz, *Schleiermachers Musikphilosophie*, pp. 21–3.

[35] Friedrich Schleiermacher, *Christmas Eve Celebration: A Dialogue*, trans. and ed. T.N. Tice (Eugene, Oreg., 2010), p. 31; see also: 'What the word has declared the tones of music must make alive, in harmony conveying it to one's whole inner being and holding it fast there' (ibid., p. 29).

[36] A wider reception of Schleiermacher's *Aesthetics* is still impeded by the lack of a critical edition and an English translation. It is available in editions by Carl Lommatzsch (Berlin, 1842), Rudolf Odebrecht (Berlin and Leipzig, 1931) and Thomas Lehnerer (Hamburg, 1984). The most important monograph on the *Aesthetics* remains Thomas Lehnerer, *Die Kunsttheorie Friedrich Schleiermachers* (Stuttgart: 1987); see also Bowie, *Aesthetics*, pp. 183–220.

[37] Carl Dahlhaus and Norbert Miller have rightfully used the designation 'dialectic' to describe the early Romantic aesthetic paradigm of feeling (primarily relating to the thought of Schleiermacher's Berlin colleague K.W.F. Solger) (*Europäische Romantik in der Musik*, vol. 2: *Oper und symphonischer Stil 1800–1850: Von E.T.A. Hoffmann zu Richard Wagner* (Stuttgart, 2007), pp. 236–40).

'linguistic turn *avant la lettre*',[38] his attention to the interdependency of language – which he calls an open system of signs or symbols of consciousness – and the process of acquiring knowledge. Whereas the concepts of knowledge are used to express a high degree of objectivity, artistic forms are equivalent signs or symbols interdependent with the expression of subjective experience. Although artistic expression entails a direction of subjectivity outwards, the dialectical nature of Schleiermacher's thought simultaneously implies that art is formative in processes of moulding human subjectivity.[39]

The *Aesthetics* is situated within the wider scope of the *Lectures on Philosophical Ethics*, Schleiermacher's highly original attempt to expound selfhood and individual action in an evolving correlation with human society and history.[40] From a presupposition that maintains a fundamental reciprocity of reason and nature within humankind, society is theorised through the contrasting notions of communal generality and individual particularity and is conceived in terms of organising (as externally directed) and cognitive (as internally receptive) actions. While these four poles remain ideal archetypes, concrete human actions can be posited as oscillations and mediations within this schema: thus, on one axis, different forms of action are located in a continuum between generality and particularity and, on the other, as directed primarily outwards or inwards. This theory entails that both humankind and the individual self are constantly being transformed in a gradual interplay between individuality and communality, as well as expressive and formative uses of communication. The boundaries between the individual and the community are constantly renegotiated and the expressions of individual subjectivity are simultaneously a means of inter-subjective communication and formation. In this sense Schleiermacher's *Lectures on Philosophical Ethics* develops the implicit idea of *On Religion* that subjective experiences of immediacy stand in dialectically conditioning relations with a mediated communal generality. A further vital consequence of this circumstance is a gradual transition between the objectivity of knowledge and individual subjectivity, between language and art.

The hallmark of Schleiermacher's *Aesthetics* stems not least from the presupposed reciprocity between human reason and nature. Whereas *On Religion* departed from a general dichotomy between understanding and sense, the *Lectures on Philosophical Ethics* posit a continuous transition where sense perception,

---

[38]   Manfred Frank has recurrently made this claim. For details see his introduction to Friedrich Schleiermacher, *Dialektik*, ed. Manfred Frank (Frankfurt, 2001), p. 22.

[39]   However, both in *Aesthetics* and the introduction to *The Christian Faith* Schleiermacher arguably gives insufficient attention to the formative role of both art and theology. In both cases this can be interpreted in line with his general commitment to the free nature of these expressions, a freedom which is vital to their potential for surpassing the designs and purposes of a reducing and narrow ethical conception of communication.

[40]   See Friedrich Schleiermacher, *Lectures on Philosophical Ethics*, ed. Robert B. Louden (Cambridge, 2002).

as primarily physical and receptive, is only gradually differentiated from the self-caused activities of reason and its expressions. This leads Schleiermacher to the conclusion that even 'receiving' acts of sense perception have a creative dimension, which is fulfilled in artistic expression. Whereas *On Religion* stands in a general Enlightenment tradition of constructing epistemology (and thereby aesthetic theory) from what is externally given (perception), Schleiermacher's *Aesthetics* is innovatively structured in analogy with the process of artistic productivity. Therefore, not impressions from outside but feeling (or immediate self-consciousness) is portrayed as the initial activity and common origin of art, which is its semiotic and symbolic form of expression.

Although the *Aesthetics* itself is vital to interpret the notion of feeling, at this point it is wise to consult Schleiermacher's *Dialectics*, the fundamental epistemological discipline within his thought. It contains his mature solution to the Kantian and Fichtean concern for a resolution of the relation between knowledge and the unity of the self. Schleiermacher describes immediate self-consciousness as the general and primordial mode of relating to oneself (*Sich-selbst-habens*). It underlies the objectifying consciousness, where an individual attains consciousness of herself, her thoughts, emotions and actions through linguistic meditation. Schleiermacher underscores that he is not referring to an unconscious state but to an immediacy which accompanies all the contents of reflection but which does not offer the (logical) possibility of attaining objective consciousness of the 'I'. In a striking change in understanding the ideal of an autonomous self-consciousness, Schleiermacher's theory of the immediate self-consciousness intends to provide the epistemologically necessary unification of thought and empirical being which can ground the correspondence between concepts and empirical reality.[41] Human thinking and freedom is thus conclusively situated within natural, social and cultural history. In this way the unification of moral action and knowledge transcends the reflexive self-consciousness and is ultimately rendered possible only through immediate self-consciousness.[42]

---

[41] The epistemology of Schleiermacher's intricate theory of subjectivity must here be compressed to present some of the conclusions vital to grasp the implied significance of music. For an excellent overview, see David Klemm, 'Schleiermacher on the Self: Immediate Self-Consciousness as Feeling and as Thinking', in David Klemm and Günter Zöller (eds), *Figuring the Self: Subject, Absolute and Others in Classical German Philosophy* (Albany, NY, 1997), pp. 169–92. The crucial original arguments can be found in Friedrich Schleiermacher, *Vorlesungen über die Dialektik*, ed. Andreas Arndt (Berlin, 2002), pp. 560–75.

[42] 'No author has stressed the objectlessness and the non-reflexive character of immediate self-consciousness as much as Schleiermacher. He is unique in relating immediate self-consciousness to the insight that self-consciousness does not arise in virtue of its own being, but is absolutely dependent on Being' (Manfred Frank, 'Metaphysical Foundations: A Look at Schleiermacher's *Dialectic*', in Jacqueline Mariña (ed.), *The Cambridge Companion to Friedrich Schleiermacher* (Cambridge, 2005), pp. 15–34 (p. 26)).

Schleiermacher's theory of immediate self-consciousness brings together an epistemological critique of a self-contained reflexive consciousness and stresses art as the social and historical mediation of individual immediacy. As such it indicates a theory of human subjectivity which intends to meet the critical standards of theoretical philosophy and theology whilst also proposing trajectories for the necessary unfolding of individual subjectivities within social aesthetic and religious practices. Immediacy, as the 'general form of relating to oneself', can positively be described as our often unthematised awareness of living as human beings within the world. The *Aesthetics* calls it a mode of cognition (*Erkennen*) and a self-willed action where individuals respond creatively to the continual manifold of influences and perceptions.[43] Whereas the activity of thought mediates human experience with the aid of conceptual language, the equivalent activity of feeling becomes immediately visible in unconscious expressions such as natural facial and bodily movements, cries and sounds. Schleiermacher acknowledges that even these to some degree are culturally conditioned and strives to bridge the gap between such primary signs of feeling and artistic musical forms, which, in Schleiermacher's time, had been developed to a new level of complexity and autonomy. He wants to show that modern fine art is a fitting development of 'original' human abilities and yet at the same time stresses a dividing line which distinguishes a higher dimension of artistic creativity: namely a unifying action in which the artist assembles and transcends the diverse affectations and manifold of feelings which appear in a continuous stream. Thus Schleiermacher, no less than Hanslick later, repudiates any theory of distinct musical affects (*Affektenlehre*) and the notion that the contents of music are expressions of individual, fleeting emotions. Rather, he claims that all art stems from a more complex and extended mood (*Stimmung*), also describable as a specific modification of feeling.[44] Here the temporal character of affected subjectivity is grasped and set with a greater degree of permanence, an archetypal image (*Urbild*) or primary level of objectification which, with the aid of human fantasy and processes of skilful technical representation, can ultimately be communicated to others in artistic forms. Processes of musical productivity are complex and require that affect, reflection and technical skill conjoin to produce a musical structure which can be interpreted speculatively as a sounding exteriorisation and representation of the immediate self (*Selbstdarstellung*). The ideal of musical immediacy is thus not intended to neglect mediation within elaborate composition. Rather, Schleiermacher's holistic account of the entire creative process permits the theoretical elucidation of the unity and mutual interrelatedness of communicative subjectivity and sounding musical form.[45]

---

[43]   Friedrich Schleiermacher, *Ästhetik*, ed. Rudolf Odebrecht (Berlin and Leipzig, 1931), pp. 28–34, 44–8.

[44]   Ibid., pp. 38–9, 48–57. This amalgamating activity can thus be seen as a more theoretical account of the process which in *On Religion* was described metaphorically as the collection of individual tones into one full harmony.

[45]   The rationale behind Schleiermacher's Romantic aesthetics does not limit art to individual expression as such but opens a trajectory to understand the rising formalism

Schleiermacher's categorisation of individual art forms contrasts the 'immediate' arts of music and dance with the 'mediated' expressions of architecture, visual arts and poetry (a term which in Schleiermacher's early Romantic context incorporates all literary forms). In an age prior to abstract arts, it was still natural for him to presuppose that both visual and literary arts represent a particular image of the world and thus maintain a high degree of mimetic representation. Both dance and music are supposed to remain at some level independent of external means of expressions and are less conditioned by particular intuitions of the world. In musical creativity, the archetypal image, or the primordial idea of the expression, does not resemble an external intuition but develops through an 'inner voice' and an 'inner ear' which directly mediates inner dispositions into representations of musical sound and structure. However, already in these first representations of sound and music's elements, the individual moves within existing traditions of musical form, the landscape of music in which the artist seeks to articulate her own contribution. In the end Schleiermacher ascribes music (and dance) the potential to provide 'symbols [*Sinnbilder*] of the particular inner world', the most intimate manifestations and determinations of immediate self-consciousness.[46] In acts of listening, physical, emotional and intellectual dimensions of subjectivity join in a desiring attention towards the objectivity of musical form as immediately perceived within the body.[47] When the receptivity of sense has been developed, the immediate self-consciousness is influenced and transfigured through the experience of musical form, thus encountering and learning from a manifold repertoire of possible subjective determinations. To evoke such symbols of human subjectivities, as immediately and tangibly penetrated by external reality, might indeed be one of music's paradigmatic contributions to the cultural history of modernity.[48] Schleiermacher's *Aesthetics* remains a striking manifestation of how

---

within nineteeth-century aesthetics. Thus Philip Stoltzfus's interesting attempt to contrast Schleiermacher's 'Orpheic' aesthetics with Karl Barth's and Hanslick's formalism in theology and music fails to recognise the intimate affinity between Schleiermacher's and Hanslick's aesthetic paradigms (Philip Stoltzfus, *Theology as Performance: Music, Aesthetics, and God in Western Thought* (New York and London, 2006), pp. 49–106).

[46] Schleiermacher, *Ästhetik*, ed. Odebrecht, p. 57. On the 'inner ear' as the musical equivalent of a general drive towards artistic depiction, see ibid., p. 147.

[47] Cf. 'The physical character of musical experience discloses a first-order mode of being, one that involves a suspension of the distinction between subject and object ... or, rather, a retrieval of the pre-reflective moment before this distinction asserts itself' (Férdia J. Stone-Davis, *Musical Beauty: Negotiating the Boundary between Subject and Object* (Eugene, Oreg., 2011), pp. 158–9).

[48] 'Die Geschichte von Religion und Musik [hat] an der Geschichte der Subjektivität Anteil, wie sie sich in der weiteren Geschichte der Moderne darstellt. Je weniger das selbstverständliche Korrelat von Innen und Außen, Selbstempfindung und Universum gegeben ist, um so intensiver muß diese riskante Entsprechung dargestellt werden – mit den Mitteln der Subjektivität selbst, die dadurch an ihrem eigenen Problem arbeitet' (Dietrich Korsch, 'Das Universum im Ohr: Umrisse einer theologischen Musikästhetik', in Dietrich

the experience of music invokes the intermingling and receptive immediacy which in *On Religion* is called the 'highest flowering of religion'.

For Schleiermacher, the designation of immediate arts simultaneously indicates an accompanying role, since musical expressions call for the interpretation of words, thereby ultimately seeking to accomplish a reconciliation of subjectivity and objectivity.[49] This is a hazardous point around which Schleiermacher revolves in the development of his musical aesthetics. In lectures from 1831/2 he grants a greater amount of autonomy to music and declares its natural trajectory to be a quest for a self-contained organic form, liberated from words.[50] On the one hand, the principle of an autonomous musical form serves a specific cosmological ideal crucial to his theology. On the other hand, such autonomy indicates that music is finally being emancipated from the theological tradition and interpretative linguistic framework in which he for decades sought to integrate it.

Musical Form, God and the Determination of Subjectivity

Schleiermacher's aesthetics of music remains a fascinating attempt to champion, albeit critically, the emancipation of music towards the ideal of autonomous form as conclusive aesthetic norm. Rather than promoting a specific conception of beauty he posits two kinds of perfection (*Vollkommenheit*) as the ideal of art: elementary perfection entails the capacity to employ the natural and acoustic properties of musical rhythm, melody and harmony; organic perfection indicates the creation of a well-ordered independent form wherein the single elements stand in immanent harmony and balance with the work as a whole.[51] A similar ideal of an 'aesthetic' organic integration structures his ethical anthropology and the societal reciprocity between individuality and communality. Concomitant with this ideal is an emphasis on rhythm as the constitutive element of music, yielding temporal measure and determination and thereby transcendence amidst fleeting temporality.[52] At this point it becomes possible to grasp the degree to

---

Korsch, Klaus Röhring and Joachim Herten (eds), *Das Universum im Ohr: Variationen zu einer theologischen Musikästhetik* (Leipzig, 2011), pp. 15–24 (p. 21)).

[49]   Schleiermacher, *Ästhetik*, ed. Odebrecht, p. 57.

[50]   'Auch wo er [der Tonkünstler] dem Dichter folgt, ringt der beste nach Unabhängigkeit ... sein höchster Triumph ist, wo er der Sprache ganz Lebewohl sagt und alle Lebensschaure, welche die Seele durchziehen können, verkörpert in dieser unendlich abwechselnden Fülle von Tonfolgen und Zusammenklängen' (Friedrich Schleiermacher, *Ästhetik (1819/25): Über den Begriff der Kunst*, ed. Thomas Lehnerer (Hamburg, 1984), p. 179.

[51]   Schleiermacher, *Ästhetik*, ed. Odebrecht, pp. 91–116.

[52]   'Der Rhythmus ist das differente, aber streng gemessene Verhältnis des Tones zur Zeit. Das bestimmte Maas ist hier wieder der eigentliche Charakter der Kunst ... Ohne Rhythmus geht die Kunst, selbst bei Vorhandensein von Melodie, verloren. So ist der Rhythmus das erste und vollkommen unentbehrlich' (ibid., p. 179).

which Schleiermacher integrated modern aesthetic theories of an organic and self-contained whole as pillars in his philosophical and theological reflection.[53] He repeatedly rejected theological critiques of his thought as inherently pantheistic and highlights the difference between two possible intentionalities of human transcendence: the totality of existence can be interpreted in relation to two different transcendental presuppositions: the notion of the world or the more encompassing notion of God. In the world of art, Schleiermacher believes that these distinct notions condition how the artist negotiates between the more mundane freedom of individual elements and the overarching unity of the work. Schleiermacher erects a theory in which social (*gesellige Kunst*) and religious artistic styles form two general branches of art, developed in accordance with the two presuppositions of transcendental unity. Though far from neglecting the worth of the first kind, Schleiermacher undoubtedly evaluates speculative religious forms of art as superior.[54] His remaining imperative to musicians is thus not to create absolutely autonomous art but art in which the unity of the work seeks to represent an absolute totality of being. The theological rationale for endorsing musical autonomy is ultimately conditioned by the integrating unity of the work as a formative representation of immediate self-consciousness as situated in a world where every individual element shares in a cosmic organic form.

For the theologian Schleiermacher, the final truth behind Kant's missing transcendental unity of self-consciousness is not only a need to embed human subjectivity within the web of natural causality. For, although such an open-ended structure of subjectivity makes the subject interdependent with the totality of nature and culture, Schleiermacher's further theological conclusion is that even the totality of causal finitude, or the world as an integral work of art, cannot finally be interpreted as independently sovereign. Rather, analogous to how the immediate unification of human thought and action is transcendent to reflexive self-consciousness, the whole of being shares in its equal dependence on God as the transcendental and absolute unity of thought and action. Among the amalgamating human moods which form the basis of artistic expression, Schleiermacher famously highlights the 'feeling of absolute dependence', a determination of immediate self-consciousness in terms of the conviction that the self is dependent on the surrounding world and that the totality of this world is equally dependent on the absolute God.[55] Thus in Schleiermacher's thought, religious piety is the highest, or most harmoniously integrating, form of self-consciousness and entails an awareness of the self as one of many elements in God's artistic creation of the world. Musical form not only represents and communicates an immanent immediate transcendence but, finally,

---

[53]   The aesthetically inclined notion of organic wholeness serves as an underlying structure both in his theology of creation, sin (as the impossibility to grasp this unity) and Christology (where Christ serves as the *Urbild* of Christian consciousness).

[54]   Schleiermacher, *Ästhetik*, ed. Odebrecht, pp. 66–78.

[55]   See Friedrich Schleiermacher, *The Christian Faith* (London and New York, 1999), §4.

discloses a subjectivity whose underlying unity is transcendent to itself and can be uncovered only within an absolute infinitude.

With historical hindsight it is obvious that Schleiermacher championed an integration of art and religion in which the common religious framework was to become less tangible and prominent. Schleiermacher could, as a theologian, unproblematically embrace the modern evolution of musical complexity in a conviction that its meaning could still be comprehended within the shared linguistic framework of a common Christian western culture. He promoted musical modernity for its revelatory potential to uncover and communicate symbolic representations of human subjectivity in unique and non-objectifying forms. However, within modernity's further evolution, the aesthetic expressions of the Christian church would generally cease to evolve within the paradigms of contemporary art and Schleiermacher's seamless mediation between art music and religion became increasingly utopian.

His final theological interpretation of human immediate transcendence as a revelation of the self's participation in a living divine presence obviously remains a point of difference. On the one hand, modern music can be interpreted as 'the unwritten theology of those who lack or reject any formal creed'; on the other, there are theological voices who argue that a 'rethinking of the gospel can enable a richer description and deeper understanding of music'.[56] Whether musically evoked transcendence today is posited on the basis of a theological ontology or not, Schleiermacher remains a vital theoretical proponent of a Romantic ideal where music and philosophy unite to uncover and explore a dimension of consciousness which is not exclusively tied to a discursive mode.[57] In this tradition, Schleiermacher stands united with the artistic experience of Mendelssohn and many other musicians who are convinced of music's potential to articulate subtle but yet exceedingly precise determinations. Thus art and specifically music, which borrows its expression from 'immediacy of feeling',[58] challenges an epistemology that reduces inter-subjective determinacy to linguistic or conceptual semiotics. Such ideals may entail reductive and potentially perilous detractions from music's cognitive, transformative and socially mediating capacities. From the perspective of Schleiermacher's *Aesthetics*, rather, the generalised forms of conceptual language can be found wanting in determinacy through their inability to express and mould the infinite variety and particularity of individual human subjectivities.

---

[56]   George Steiner, *Real Presences* (Chicago, 1989), p. 218; Jeremy S. Begbie and Steven R. Guthrie (eds), *Resonant Witness: Conversations between Music and Theology* (Grand Rapids, Mich., 2011), p. 9. It should be stated that Schleiermacher himself scrutinised the credibility of a non-religious interpretation of the grounds of immediate self-consciousness but in his theology rejected an explanation within a framework of finitude.

[57]   See Lawrence Kramer, *Music and Poetry: The Nineteenth Century and After* (Berkeley, Calif., 1984), pp. 4–23; Michael P. Steinberg, *Listening to Reason: Culture, Subjectivity, and Nineteenth-Century Music* (Princeton, NJ, 2006).

[58]   Schleiermacher, *Ästhetik*, ed. Lehnerer, p. 17.

Chapter 8

Negotiating Musical Transcendence

Jeremy S. Begbie

The chapters in this section of the book represent a huge array of perspectives, and traverse a very wide musical and philosophical-theological terrain. The aim here is neither to attempt any kind of synthesis nor to respond to all the principal points made by each writer. Rather, it is to press forward the discussion by examining some of the larger and further-reaching issues raised by these provocative pieces.

We can begin by highlighting two features of many present-day discussions of music and transcendence, evident in at least some of these chapters (even if only as a background). First, it is commonly noted that there is an ineradicable, perhaps even essential, link between music and transcendence. As Christopher Page eloquently reminds us, the association has had a long and distinguished history. And many have remarked on the way in which the language of 'transcendence', the 'transcendent', the 'spiritual', the 'sacred' and so forth is widely and readily used today to describe the experience of music, certainly far beyond the church. Second, many who point to this link will also contend that in the contemporary cultural and philosophical climate, transcendence has become a profoundly problematic concept. Especially significant here is a suspicion of full-blooded theological accounts of transcendence (classically involving the transcendence of a deity or deities) or, indeed, of any notion of transcendence that involves invoking realities that are not in principle accessible to our sense perception, rational knowledge or speech. Few need reminding of the horrors perpetrated by those who have claimed direct and unquestionable access to a truth or authority that in some way subsists 'above' all peoples and all ages, to principles or ideals supposedly applicable to all times and places. Transcendence has often assumed dark and destructive colours, especially in the hands of religious tyrants. Hence the frequent recourse over the last few decades to 'immanent' or 'inner-worldly' notions of transcendence: those which, for example, locate it in the ethical demand presented by other persons or in the type of dynamic involved in reconciliation or even in the trans-personal dimensions of social practices.

In the modern and late modern philosophical arena, then, we are presented with an intriguing situation in which, on the one hand, there is a concern to retain some sense or senses in which music can be said to afford transcendent experience and perhaps to preserve some form of 'God-talk' and, on the other, a reluctance to understand this in what are perceived to be traditional theological terms and a keenness to find chastened, 'post-theological' conceptions of transcendence which might still throw light on the powerful effects of music.

As a theologian, I am very sympathetic to the suspicion of at least some theological concepts of transcendence and the ways they have been yoked to music and thus to some of the current attempts to find alternative construals. Nonetheless, I also believe that the currently burgeoning discussion of music and transcendence cannot make very much progress without examining rather more closely what has or has not been claimed with regard to transcendence in particular theological traditions. If at least some theological or quasi-theological arguments are to be rejected – and some, I believe, deserve to be rejected – it is important not to operate with half-remembered and dubious impressions of the way transcendence has actually been conceived theologically. To that end, I would like to highlight just two broad areas where more attention to classic theological notions of transcendence might call into question several of the assumptions behind some contemporary treatments of music and transcendence, assumptions that appear in at least some of the preceding chapters.

Transcendence and Limits

The first concerns a widespread tendency to philosophise (or theologise) within frameworks determined by a priori conceptions of human limits. I do not find this questioned or challenged in any of these chapters (though, to be fair, this may not be so relevant to Sukanya Sarbadhikary's). As Roger Scruton demonstrates very clearly, as long as one remains within a broadly Kantian stream, transcendence will be theorised in ways that are fundamentally shaped by an awareness of the limits of our powers of representation, an intense sense of the inadequacy of the capacities of human language and thought, the stubborn resistance of certain realities to linguistic and conceptual seizure. When this is given a theological reading, God's transcendence is naturally aligned to the same scheme – God is essentially beyond the knowable, the speakable. And in this broad context, as Scruton observes, music, being irreducibly distinct from language, is appealed to as providing a measure of access, unique access, to the transcendent (whether this is conceived theistically or not).

To be a little more specific historically, music is frequently linked to something akin to the eighteenth-century concept of the sublime – to a sense of the untamable, formless, indeterminate and uncontrollable. Some have argued that the purported modern denial of transcendence is in fact a re-writing of transcendence as sublimity:

> One might easily suppose that modernity is characterized by a simple rejection of transcendence in favour of immanence, meaning the pure self-sufficiency of the finite world to itself. Yet although the shift to immanentism was certainly crucial, *the re-conceptualization of transcendence as sublimity* was of equal importance: either in tension with, or else as a complement to this shift … modernity and postmodernity tend strictly to *substitute* sublimity for transcendence. Exaltation

of the unrepresentable, gestured towards wherever representation is ruptured, its limits manifest. This means that all that persists of transcendence is sheer unknowability or its quality of non-representability and non-depictability.[1]

Understandably, Scruton points to the propensity of Kantians 'to have it both ways' – denying epistemological access to the transcendental, on the one hand, but nonetheless apparently being able to say a great deal about it, on the other. Scruton's comment that 'it is rare to find a philosopher or theologian who takes seriously his own conclusion that this or that is really transcendental' is surely apt.

Needless to say, it is notoriously hard to align an utterly unknowable transcendence of this sort with, for example, the God of Judaism or Christianity or to pretend that the former is not substantially altered or re-configured by the latter – however much one may appeal to apophatic traditions. (Although I warm very much to Russell Re Manning's desire to find a way of appropriating music in a theological engagement with culture, I am less enthusiastic than him about George Steiner: for all the latter's eloquence and fecundity, the deity that haunts Steiner's *Real Presences* would seem to be far too empty of content to justify the enthusiasm with which this book was greeted by some theologians). In any case, what I want to highlight here is the supposition that transcendence can (and must?) be theorised from a basic perspective located in an awareness of our own limits. A lively stream within postmodern philosophical theology has become acutely aware of the problems of such an approach. For almost inevitably, it will be assumed that God transcends the world in the same way as finite objects in the world transcend each other, consequently trapping God in a spatial logic of 'sameness', where by default (even if not by intention) God is treated in a way that is analogous to an item in the world's furniture, only now in a sphere above rather than in the world.[2] Ironically, this is essentially the same logic that can be found in those who attack supposedly traditional theological concepts of transcendence and invites all too quickly the Feuerbachian charge that the theologian's language about God is merely the outward projection of human, creaturely categories.

Of course, at this point, one could jettison even the possibility of a theological (and metaphysical) transcendence. But it is at least worth registering that in a classically mainstream Christian account, divine transcendence is not conceived in terms of the transcendence of finite objects over each other – indeed, this is strenuously rejected, for just the kind of reasons contemporary opponents of theological transcendence adduce. Conceptualising transcendence in this tradition

---

[1] John Milbank, 'Sublimity: The Modern Transcendent', in Regina M. Schwartz (ed.), *Transcendence: Philosophy, Literature, and Theology Approach the Beyond* (New York, 2004), pp. 211–34 (pp. 211, 213): italics added.

[2] As Walter Lowe puts it, 'the qualifier "infinite" does not assure exemption from the hegemony of "the Same"' ('Postmodern Theology', in J.B. Webster, Kathryn Tanner and Iain R. Torrance [eds], *The Oxford Handbook of Systematic Theology* [Oxford, 2007], pp. 617–33 [p. 618]).

takes its cue not first of all by attending to human limits, but to God's own self-presentation, which discloses a type of transcendence that cannot be designed or mapped out a priori. Transcendence will not be sought primarily at the limits or edges of human capacities, where our powers of perception are felt to have been exhausted, but rather where transcendence decisively occurs, where it has decisively reached us, so to speak: and that means supremely in a fully embodied, spatially located human being, in the midst of human history. It is here, so the tradition affirms, in this union of divine and human in Jesus Christ, that the true differentiation of creator and creation has been made manifest, the nature of human limits disclosed, and the real 'crisis of representation' not only revealed but also healed.

What might all this have to do with music? Much could be said at this point, but at the very least, a noticeably more positive and dynamic conception of transcendence is opened up than that associated with the somewhat pale and inert quasi-divinity of the sublime. And here music has indeed much to offer. Bruce Ellis Benson's chapter, for example, evokes in effect a musical vision of divine transcendence far removed from the negatively driven philosophies that have come to be so popular of late: the transcendence of a creator committed to the transformation of the world, active within space and time, involved in a to-and-fro of call and response, engaged in an interplay of 'structure and contingency, of regularity and unpredictability, of constraint and possibility'. In this scenario, space and time, human physicality, our bodies, desires and material actions, are not to be escaped, denigrated or left behind, but are taken into a transforming movement of the transcendent. Scruton's comments about music pulling us into a particular temporal dynamic in which 'we move with music's sympathetic movement' would seem especially pertinent in this connection.

Music and God-Talk

Closely related to this is a second area of concern – the vexed question of the relation of music to language. Faced with the immense struggle to speak and write effectively about God, few will not have been attracted to music, with its legendary capacity to transcend language, to say the unsayable. In modern times, this received perhaps its most powerful articulation in the music-saturated philosophising of the early German Romantics, for whom music's (relative) freedom from language and concepts was thought to give it huge metaphysical reach and theological promise. (Schleiermacher's warm estimation of music, ably expounded by Jonas Lundblad, in some respects draws on this tradition). Music's potential in the midst of language's inadequacies has found a number of advocates in postmodern academia. We find a fierce insistence on a radical and unbridgeable incommensurability between language and world: it is urged that all language and concepts inevitably do violence to the 'Other' through a lust for mastery, the drive to enclose, delimit and dominate and – not surprisingly – that theological language is especially vulnerable to such coercive ploys. Music holds out huge hope here, it will be said, for of all art forms it is the least reducible to words and concepts and thus not only a paradigmatic model of what communion with God entails but a superlative vehicle for it. The fascination of some current scholarship with the notion of 'ineffability' is of a piece with this.

There is of course a critically important stress here on the 'unenclosability' of the divine, and on the irreducibility of music, its distinctive non-linguistic powers. But what I find more questionable is the way in which these emphases are quickly allied to fixed yet mistaken assumptions about the role of language in religious faith, especially in the Abrahamic traditions. In Judaism and Christianity, for example, there is a core conviction that language has been directly assumed into divine purposes, that human speech is part of what God has acted to heal and redeem. To hold this need not entail a capitulation to crude fundamentalisms which suggest the divine can in some way be contained or circumscribed by words: hence the strong theological traditions which underline with great intensity the limits of language vis-à-vis the divine. Nor need it mean ignoring the human propensity for destructive uses of language. But it does entail a commitment to the direct engagement with language by an active transcendence and thus the normativity of at least some given language forms.

This is where I find myself parting company with Re Manning in his quest to enlist music in the project of 'theology without writing' – and I am presuming he does not wish to exclude, for example, Christian theology in this connection. The question naturally arises: why should we want to be released from language per se? Rowan Williams's warning about some forms of negative theology is apposite here:

> The risk of a negative theology in abstraction, the identification of the sacred with the void, is the purchase it gives to a depoliticized – or even anti-political – aesthetic, in which there is a subtle but unmistakable suggestion that social and linguistic order (as opposed to this or that questionable order) is what we need to be delivered from, and that a particular kind of artistic praxis can so deliver.[3]

Re Manning is justifiably eager not to allow language to become (as he puts it) 'hegemonic' in theology and is quite properly keen to allow music an irreducible role in the exploration and articulation of faith. But how can claims about 'the real presence of transcendence' ever be evaluated or distinguished from mere wish fulfilment, without an appeal (at some stage) to at least some language deemed to be authoritative? In the Christian tradition, what he calls 'privileging linguistic theology' is not an arbitrary decision taken by those with a fetish for words, but simply the outworking of the content of Jewish-Christian belief about the action of God. Such a privileging need not negate or render trivial the potential of music to

---

[3]   Rowan Williams and Mike Higton (eds), *Wrestling with Angels: Conversations in Modern Theology* (Grand Rapids, Mich., 2007), p. 31.

enrich theology. To hold to the normativity of certain texts (something aspired to by millions of the world's inhabitants) need not in any way lessen the distinctive contribution music can make in opening up, in its own way, the realities to which those texts bear witness and in which they are caught up.

To bring this to a head: I want to challenge what I believe is a false 'either/or', rather too common when the music-language relation is discussed in relation to theological transcendence: either we allow music a central and methodologically decisive role in revising the content of theology or music is to be treated as mere gloss, commentary, repetition. That these are not the only options is well illustrated by a striking phenomenon brought to light in Christopher Page's chapter. He points to a strand of early Christian theology according to which singing was regarded as an anticipation, a bodily foretaste of the resurrected life of the world to come: the 'use of the [singing] voice was [seen as] one of the principal continuities between the states of bodily life on either side of the grave'. Vocal praise in worship was believed to enact the life of the resurrection body to come, a form of existence the apostle Paul struggles to articulate in his First Letter to the Corinthians. Here, I submit, we see theology being enriched by music. Is music here merely a commentary or repetition? Clearly not, it is providing something which the scriptural words on their own are incapable of providing, and in this sense, it 'effs the ineffable', transcends what language can offer. Indeed, music acts as a potent reminder of the fact that words will always fall short of extra-linguistic reality. But does this encourage us to pursue 'theology without writing'? Hardly, for this musical experience is being interpreted in the light of, and regarded as a faithful enactment of, the realities to which particular biblical texts bear testimony.

In closing, it is worth underlining that this last example opens up a type of transcendence which is mentioned in passing in these chapters but one which I think is worth exploring much more thoroughly: where music is believed to prefigure in the present a richer, fuller future. Page's example has nothing to do with music pulling us out of this world into another, superior one, but everything to do with music offering, in the life of this world, a foretaste of what the world is yet to become. The present is transcended, certainly, but not in such a way as to leave it or this earth behind. Music is believed to provide a concrete promise here and now of a final transformation of our present condition. To pick up Page's words, 'music was truly universal, and truly transcendental if, with the human body, it crossed the boundary between this life and the next'.

PART II
Music and Immanent Transcendence

Chapter 9

C.P.E. Bach's *Heilig* and 'the Holy' of Rudolf Otto: An Eighteenth-Century Experience of the *Mysterium Tremendum*

Joshua A. Waggener

In 1776, C.P.E. Bach's double-choir *Heilig* (H. 778, Wq. 217) premiered in Hamburg. Bach based this grand work partially on the text of Isaiah 6, which depicts the prophet's vision of Yahweh at which the angels declare, 'Holy, holy, holy is the Lord of hosts; the whole earth is full of His glory!' In 1785, the *Hamburgischer unpartheyischer Correspondent* praised Bach's *Heilig* as 'one of the most perfect and most sublime pieces of music ever composed'. Bach considered the composition his swan song, and indeed, it was mentioned in a laudatory obituary after his death in 1788.[1]

Over 130 years later, another German would compose a work focused on the word *heilig*. In 1917, Rudolf Otto (1869–1937), theologian and pioneer of studies in the philosophy of religion, published *Das Heilige*, which would soon be translated into many languages, becoming possibly the most widely read German theological work of the twentieth century.[2] In this work, Otto identifies 'the holy' as 'the real innermost core' of religion, coining the term 'numinous' to consider the holy without regard to moral or rational factors.[3] Furthermore, he explicates an experience with the holy through his Latin phrase: *mysterium tremendum fascinans et augustum*.[4] As an avid music lover, Otto also mentions several works

---

[1] See Annette Richards, 'An Enduring Moment: C.P.E. Bach and the Musical Sublime', in ead. (ed.), *C.P.E. Bach Studies* (Cambridge and New York, 2006), pp. 150–51.

[2] For an account of the impact and reception of Otto's work, see Todd A. Gooch, *The Numinous and Modernity: An Interpretation of Rudolf Otto's Philosophy of Religion*, Beihefte zur Zeitschrift für die Alttestamentliche Wissenschaft (Berlin and New York, 2000), pp. 1–8.

[3] Rudolf Otto, *The Idea of the Holy: An Inquiry into the Non-Rational Factor in the Idea of the Divine and Its Relation to the Rational*, trans. and ed. J.W. Harvey, 2nd edn (London and New York, 1950), pp. 6–7.

[4] Otto's use of Latin terminology to describe the experience of the holy comes about as he seeks to 'consider the deepest and most fundamental element in all strong and sincerely felt religious emotion' (ibid., p. 12). He begins simply with the words *mysterium tremendum*, but later adds qualifiers to further clarify the expression. To do justice to the complexity of Otto's thought, no direct translation will be offered here. Instead, Otto's phrase will be explained term by term below.

of 'sublime' music, commenting briefly on their ability to express the *mysterium tremendum* experience.

The present chapter begins with a summary of Otto's comments on aesthetic sublimity, looking to the function of sublime music as an expression of the numinous. It then briefly considers sublime aspects of Bach's *Heilig* with respect to eighteenth-century aesthetic views before exploring more fully the connection between *Heilig* and Otto's description of an experience of the holy through conceptual comparison and musical analysis. Finally, the chapter evaluates the correspondence between Bach's *Heilig* and Otto's *mysterium tremendum* and uses this to consider the relationship between music and transcendence, the natural and the numinous. It argues that, although there is much in common between Bach's work and Otto's description, there is a limit to the correspondence, a limit that resembles Otto's own reservations about the extent to which music can simulate an encounter with transcendence.

Sublime Music as an Expression of the Holy

Like German Idealists of earlier generations, Otto recognised aesthetic experience, including music listening, as a valid expression of religious experience. In particular, aesthetic sublimity was seen by Otto as exhibiting 'the same peculiar dual character as the numinous; it is at once daunting, and yet again singularly attracting'.[5] Otto goes so far as to describe particular pieces of music which express, in a 'sublime' way, an encounter with the holy. First, Otto praises the subdued approach, heavenly counterpoint, and harmonic 'eccentricities' of J.S. Bach's '[Et] Incarnatus' from the B Minor Mass (BWV 232) which 'render so well the sense of awe-struck wonder ... [of the] *mysterium*'.[6] Second, Otto compliments the 'restrained and repressed' aspects of Felix Mendelssohn's setting of Psalm 2 (Op. 78), especially v. 11, 'Dienet dem Herrn mit Furcht!' (Serve the Lord with fear!), which clearly expresses the *tremendum*.[7] Third, Otto describes the 'muffled tremor' and textural contrasts of Tomás Luis de Victoria's 'Populus meus', which (in Otto's words) 'gets as near to the heart of the matter as any music can'.[8]

As Otto states, making use of Kantian terminology, music becomes an 'authentic schema of the holy'.[9] Otto further describes this as an 'indirect means'

---

[5]   Ibid., p. 42.

[6]   Ibid., p. 70.

[7]   Ibid., pp. 70–71.

[8]   Ibid., p. 71.

[9]   Recognising the holy as a 'complex category', Otto seeks to relate its non-rational and rational aspects through 'schematization', connecting the unknown (and unknowable) with aspects of rational religion (see ibid., pp. 45–9). According to John Elbert Wilson, schematization occurs when 'the religious mind "schematizes" the noumena in the act of producing the ideas or concepts that give the noumena intelligible expression' (*Introduction to Modern Theology: Trajectories in the German Tradition* (Louisville, Ky, 2007),

of expressing the numinous, including music amongst 'those means by which we express kindred and similar feelings belonging to the "natural" sphere'.[10] As an example of this indirect means, Otto describes 'a song set to music' in which 'the song in its entirety [including the lyrical text and feelings evoked by the music], is therefore music "rationalized"'.[11] With music thus established as an 'indirect means' of expressing the numinous, sublime aspects of Bach's double-choir *Heilig* can be considered.

Bach's *Heilig* as a Sublime Musical Work

In various ways, *Heilig* achieves sublimity according to the aesthetic standards of the mid-eighteenth century.[12] For example, the large number of performers provide the requisite expansiveness for the musical sublime, as established by Georg Frideric Handel.[13] Written for alto solo voice, two choirs and two orchestras, each including three trumpets, timpani, two oboes and strings, the *Heilig* required an awe-inspiring amount of musical components.[14] As Annette Richards states, '[in the *Heilig*], glory, majesty, divinity, and number are evoked by large performing forces'.[15]

Furthermore, in reference to Henry Drew Wyatt's summary of eighteenth-century 'elevated-style devices' used to achieve the sublime, Bach's *Heilig* exhibits all the traits common to 'sublime' works, including:

1. slow tempo (e.g. the *Adagio* section in bars 47–83),
2. dotted rhythms (e.g. the accompaniment figures in bars 54–8, 64–7, 76–83),

---

p. 147). For more on Otto's use of schematization, see Philip C. Almond, *Rudolf Otto: An Introduction to His Philosophical Theology*, Studies in Religion (Chapel Hill, NC, 1984), esp. pp. 34–8, 43–7; on Otto's choice of Kant's terminology for an arguably un-Kantian use of 'schema', see ibid., pp. 97–102.

[10]   Otto, *The Idea of the Holy*, p. 61.

[11]   Ibid., p. 48.

[12]   The seminal study on eighteenth-century views of sublimity in England is Samuel Holt Monk, *The Sublime: A Study of Critical Theories in XVIII-Century England* (New York, 1935). A more recent summary can be found in Emily Brady, *The Sublime in Modern Philosophy: Aesthetics, Ethics and Nature* (Cambridge, 2013), pp. 11–46.

[13]   For studies of Handel's 'sublime' music, see Alexander H. Shapiro, '"Drama of an Infinitely Superior Nature": Handel's Early English Oratorios and the Religious Sublime', *Music and Letters*, 74/2 (1993): 215–45; Ruth Smith, *Handel's Oratorios and Eighteenth-Century Thought* (Cambridge, 1995); Todd Gilman, 'Arne, Handel, the Beautiful, and the Sublime', *Eighteenth-Century Studies* 42/4 (2009): 529–55.

[14]   Reginald Sanders has also observed that the *Heilig*, when performed in St Machaelis Church, Hamburg, in 1776, would have made use of an expanded upper level with two balconies on either side 'that provided an excellent performance venue for Bach's two-chorus work' ('Carl Phillipp Emanuel Bach and Liturgical Music at the Hamburg Principal Churches from 1768 to 1788' (PhD thesis: Yale University, 2001), p. 75).

[15]   Richards, 'An Enduring Moment', p. 158.

3. unison monophonic texture (evident when the 'Choir of the Peoples'
   sing D's in unisons and octaves in bars 64–8, as well as the *tutti* coda in
   bars 225–8, with all voices and instruments together), and
4. stile antico polyphony (seen in the *Alla breve* metre in the fugue beginning
   bar 84).[16]

As Richards has demonstrated, C.P.E. Bach emphasised musical and religious
aspects to 'aspire to a particular sublime mode in the *Heilig* and other works',
such that, in the last decade of his life and beyond, 'the language of Bach criticism
… amounted to a lexicon of the sublime'.[17]

Bach's *Heilig* as a Schema of the Holy and Experience of the *Mysterium Tremendum*

It is also notable that specific musical aspects of the works described by Otto
are also apparent in Bach's *Heilig*. For example, the 'subdued' aspects of J.S.
Bach's 'Incarnatus', Mendelssohn's Psalm 2 setting and Victoria's 'Populus
meus' are evident in the restrained dynamics of the *Heilig*'s passages for the
'Choir of Angels'. Also in these angel passages are 'harmonic eccentricities'
even more strange than in the 'Incarnatus', including a move from F minor
to B major in bars 69–75. Considering the answers of the 'Choir of Peoples',
Heilig's double-choir textural contrasts are very similar to the works by Victoria
and Mendelssohn. Lastly, the concluding fugue of the *Heilig* is similar to the
'Incarnatus' in its use of imitative counterpoint.

Thus, not only does Bach's *Heilig* achieve sublimity by eighteenth-century
standards, his work also displays aspects of sublimity praised by Otto as ways to
represent the holy by 'indirect means', showing the validity of *Heilig* as a musical
simulation for much of the experience of the holy. To consider how closely *Heilig*
corresponds to Otto's experience of the holy, the work will now be analysed with
respect to Otto's full description of the *mysterium tremendum fascinans et augustum*.

The Mysterium

Otto defines the initial aspect of the numinous, the *mysterium*, as 'the wholly
other' – 'that which is quite beyond the sphere of the usual, the intelligible, and
the familiar, which therefore falls quite outside the limits of the "canny", and is

---

[16] See Henry Drew Wyatt, 'Aspects of Sublime Rhetoric in Eighteenth-Century
Music' (PhD thesis: Rutgers University, 2000), p. 226.

[17] Richards, 'An Enduring Moment', p. 151. Richards further explains that 'the
sublime offered Bach's listeners an aesthetic framework for their experience of his music,
and a language with which to describe the profoundly moving effect of its moments of
amazing grandeur as well as those of baffling artistic license' (ibid., pp. 151–2).

contrasted with it, filling the mind with blank wonder and astonishment'.[18] How, then, does C.P.E. Bach's *Heilig* portray the *mysterium*? In Richards's words, *Heilig*'s antiphonal choruses display 'the sublime distance between heaven and earth'.[19] The tranquil 'Choir of Angels' in the opening bars of the chorus are set apart by texture (a *soli* quartet) and dynamic (*piano*) from the answering 'Choir of the Peoples' which sings *tutti* at a *forte* dynamic. Bach's angelic choir is (at least initially), 'beyond the sphere' of the singing peoples.

This distance is accentuated by remote tonal centres emphasised in the angels' passages: the *Ariette* and 'Choir of the Peoples' segments before the fugue involve 'predictable' and 'worldly' harmonic relationships. Bars 1–46, the opening *Ariette*, are solidly in G major. The three brief passages which answer the 'Choir of Angels' demonstrate closely related harmonies to G major: (1) bars 54–8 are in D major; (2) bars 64–8 are in G major (see Example 9.1); (3) bars 76–83 are in C major.

Example 9.1   Bach, *Heilig*, bars 64–8[20]

In contrast, in the 'Choir of Angels' segments, quite distant harmonies are explored. Bars 47–53 begin abruptly in E major, modulate to C-sharp major, and conclude with a plagal cadence. Bars 59–63 shift to B major, ending with

---

[18]   Otto, *The Idea of the Holy*, p. 26.

[19]   Richards, 'An Enduring Moment', p. 161.

[20]   Score excerpts are based on Carl Philipp Emanuel Bach, *Heilig: Mit zwey Chören und einer Ariette zur Einleitung* (Hamburg and Leipzig, 1779), available at <http://pds.lib.harvard.edu/pds/view/2581450> (accessed 16 Mar. 2013), with keyboard reductions from Carl Philipp Emanuel Bach, *Holy is God (Heilig)*, ed. Karl Geiringer, Eng. trans. Henry S. Drinker (St. Louis, Miss., 1956). The critical edition of the score is in preparation: Carl Philipp Emanuel Bach, *The Complete Works* (Los Altos, Calif., 2005–).

an F-sharp chord on a half cadence. Bars 69–75 commence in F minor, and then modulate to B major, which is confirmed with a plagal cadence (see Example 9.2). These harmonies, especially the 'wayward harmony' of F minor, are 'outside the limits of the "canny"', especially for eighteenth-century ears.[21]

Example 9.2   Bach, *Heilig*, bars 69–75

The Tremendum

The next aspect of Otto's encounter with the holy, the *tremendum*, has been described as having not one (as the *mysterium*), but three moments: the first is that of 'religious dread' or 'awe'.[22] The moment of 'overwhelming majesty' follows, which Otto describes as 'the annihilation of self' in which the transcendent becomes the sole and entire reality.[23] Third, the *tremendum* concludes with an

---

[21]   For a full analysis of Bach's wayward harmony, see Richard Kramer, 'The New Modulation of the 1770s: C.P.E. Bach in Theory, Criticism, and Practice', *Journal of the American Musicological Society*, 38/3 (1985): 551–92. Richards argues that Bach's choice of harmonies in these segments displays a sublime rhetoric of 'ellipses' similar to the literary sublime of German eighteenth-century ode poetry. Through connections with contemporary reviews by Carl Friedrich Cramer and Johann Friedrich Reichardt and an essay in the aesthetic treatise of Johann Georg Sulzer, Bach's 'harmonic mortal leaps' between the two choirs are shown to defy musical logic, yet, on some level, make harmonic sense. Richards specifically mentions an essay on the symphony by Johann Abraham Peter Schulz in the *Allgemeine Theorie der schönen Künste* (2 vols, 1771–74, with important later editions, especially 1792) ('An Enduring Moment', pp. 153–5).

[22]   See Otto, *The Idea of the Holy*, p. 14. According to Gooch, 'the principle characteristic of the *tremendum* is its terrifying or dreadful aspect' (*The Numinous and Modernity*, p. 113).

[23]   Otto, *The Idea of the Holy*, p. 21; see Gooch, *The Numinous and Modernity*, p. 115.

Example 9.3   Bach, *Heilig*, bars 76–83

'energic' moment in which the numinous seems to will and move in a way that demands a response from the mortal.[24]

Bach's *Heilig* initially seems quite distinct from this terrifying series of moments. The opening *Ariette* declares the individual's joy in singing praise to God along with angels and peoples. While expressing humility, this opening segment is far from

---

[24]   As Gooch states, this moment includes 'those characteristics of the divine that are expressed in terms of willfulness, dynamism, and overpowering compulsion' (*The Numinous and Modernity*, p. 115).

the experience of *tremendum* that Otto describes. However, the entrances of *tutti* forces after each of the 'Choir of Angels' segments has the potential to take the listener through the three moments of the *tremendum* experience. First, after the sweet *Ariette* and soft angel's chorus, an entrance of the full 'Choir of Peoples' in four-part harmony startles us in bar 54. Second, all human voices enter in bar 64 with a unified *fortissimo* on a sustained D in octaves, blending all human voices into one (see Example 9.1). Third, in bar 76, all human and angel voices blend into four-part harmonies in a declaration that this God is 'der Herr Zebaoth!' (the Lord of Hosts, bars 76–83; see Example 9.3). This passage leads inevitably to an elided cadence at bar 84, where the fugal statement begins. In these three moments, the alto soloist has been gradually enveloped in the texture of angelic and human voices, fulfilling her declaration that angels and peoples are 'joyfully singing … with me'.

Furthermore, the entrance of the timpani, first in bar 64, and then on a pronounced roll in bar 76, emphasise what Markus Rathey has termed 'die Semantik der Pauke' (the semantics of the timpani).[25] The dramatic use of timpani (connoting military associations) may strike the listener with images of a Lord of Hosts that is indeed quite dreadful.

Todd Gooch clarifies, however, that the *tremendum* 'experience of religious dread is *qualitatively* distinct from normal fear'.[26] This distinct fear, according to Otto, appears 'in a form ennobled beyond measure where the soul, held speechless, trembles inwardly to the furthest fibre of its being'.[27] Thus Bach's *Heilig*, both in text and musical affect, seems capable of conveying the *tremendum* to the attentive listener, extending further the correspondence between *Heilig* and Otto's experience of the holy.

The Fascinans

Otto's definition of the *mysterium tremendum* continues with another aspect of religious feeling that, as he asserts, appears at the same time as the *mysterium* and the moments of the *tremendum*. This is the numen's 'fascinating and intoxicating attraction' which Otto terms the *fascinans*.[28] Otto describes this aspect in generous and welcoming terms 'as something that bestows upon man a beatitude beyond compare'.[29] According to Gooch, at this point, 'the numinous comes to be regarded as a positive good'.[30]

---

[25] On the sublime use of timpani without brass in Telemann's *Donnerode* and C.P.E. Bach's late oratorios, see Markus Rathey, 'Carl Philipp Emanuel Bachs *Donnerode*: Zur Politischen Funktion Des "*Erhabenen*" in der zweiten Hälfte des 18. Jahrhunderts', *Archiv für Musikwissenschaft*, 66/4 (2009): 286–305, esp. pp. 290, 301–3.

[26] Gooch, *The Numinous and Modernity*, p. 115.

[27] Otto, *The Idea of the Holy*, p. 17.

[28] Wilson, *Introduction to Modern Theology*, p. 147.

[29] Otto, *The Idea of the Holy*, p. 33.

[30] Gooch, *The Numinous and Modernity*, p. 118.

Example 9.4   Bach, *Heilig*, bars 84–100

In Bach's *Heilig*, this corresponds with the joyous commencement of fugal activity involving all voices on the text 'all the earth is filled with His majesty' (bar 84–100; see Example 9.4). Aesthetically, late eighteenth-century German audiences would certainly have considered this concluding fugue of *Heilig* 'a positive good', recalling great choral fugues by C.P.E.'s father, J.S. Bach, and those introduced more recently on the Continent in performances of Handel's *Messiah*.[31] As David Yearsley has shown, Bach uses counterpoint 'to evoke the

---

[31]   See Richards, 'An Enduring Moment', p. 157. Note that Richards refers to the commencement of the fugue as the moment of 'jubilation'.

endless and uncountable that can only be experienced finally in heaven'.[32] One can see in the imitative texture of the *Heilig* fugue Bach's attempt to evoke a sublime scene of heavenly praise involving multitudes of angels and saints.

The Augustus

Thus far, *Heilig* has progressed from a mysterious experience of distant angelic choirs through three moments of increasing awe into a final fugue evoking the infinite. It seems that Bach's sublime *Heilig* has accurately demonstrated Otto's experience of the holy as *mysterium tremendum fascinans*. However, Otto adds one additional qualification in a later chapter entitled 'The Holy as a Category of Value'. The holy is now qualified as *augustus*, referring to '[the] supreme worth or *value* [of the numen]'.[33] Otto states that the holy is '"august" … in so far as it is recognized as possessing in itself *objective* value that claims our homage'.[34] Otto relates this aspect of the holy to the prophet Isaiah's spontaneous feeling of original guilt and his ensuing confession: 'I am a man of *unclean* lips and dwell among a peoples of unclean lips' (Isaiah 6:5).[35] Otto further comments:

> This self-deprecating feeling-response is marked by an immediate, almost instinctive, spontaneity. … It does not spring from the consciousness of some committed transgression, but rather is an immediate datum given with the feeling of the numen: it proceeds to 'disvalue' together with the self the tribe to which the person belongs, and indeed, together with that, all existence in general. … It is the feeling of absolute 'profaneness'.[36]

Clearly, Otto considers this last 'disvaluing' stage of the *mysterium tremendum* experience significant for a true encounter with the holy.

Does Bach's *Heilig* include this aspect of the encounter, as it does the other three? Does either the text or music contain any sense of profound devaluation of self through recognition of original sin or guilt, experienced in a moment of instinctive realisation? A survey of Bach's *Heilig* text does not reveal any acknowledgement of human guilt. Nor does the musical content seem to pause and reflect upon personal sin or imply a realisation of 'profaneness'. Instead, Bach's *Heilig* represents an approach to the deity full of rational confidence

---

[32]   David Yearsley, 'C.P.E. Bach and the Living Traditions of Learned Counterpoint', in Richards (ed.), *C.P.E. Bach Studies*, pp 173–201 (p. 201).

[33]   Otto, *The Idea of the Holy*, p. 52.

[34]   Ibid.

[35]   Quoted ibid., p. 50: italics original. As Almond summarises, 'theologically expressed, the recognition of the objective value of the *numen* and the corresponding devaluation of self is original sin or original guilt (*Urschuld*)' (*Rudolf Otto*, p. 76).

[36]   Otto, *The Idea of the Holy*, pp. 50–51.

in humankind's position, valuing his musical expressions alongside those of angelic beings.[37]

Complete Text of C.P.E. Bach, Heilig[38]

Herr, wert, daß Scharen der Engel	Lord, who art worthy that angels shall
dir dienen und daß dich der Glaube	serve Thee and that all the faithful shall
der Völker verehrt,	worship Thy name,
ich danke dir, Herr … !	I thank Thee, Lord God … !
Sei mir gepriesen unter ihnen!	I sing Thy praise among Thine angels.
Ich jauchze dir … !	I praise Thee, God … !
Und jauchzend und lobsingen dir	And joyfully singing are angels and
Engel und Völker mit mir,	nations with me,
Engel, Völker jauchzend lobsingen	angels, nations, joyfully sing to Thee
dir mit mir!	with me.
Heilig ist Gott, der Herr Zebaoth!	Holy is God, the Lord God of Hosts!
Alle Lande sind seiner Ehren voll.	All the earth is filled with His majesty.
Herr Gott, dich loben wir,	Lord God, Thy praise we sing,
Herr Gott, wir danken dir.	Lord God, our thanks we bring.

Conclusion

The comparison of C.P.E. Bach's *Heilig* with Otto's description of the experience of the holy has revealed many levels of correspondence, both in details of musical sublimity as well as in the *mysterium tremendum fascinas* experience. However, the lack of the final aspect of the holy brings into question the ability of musical experience to truly simulate the numinous experience or elucidate a transcendent object.

Looking further at Otto's views as recorded in *Das Heilige*, a significant footnote clearly distinguishes the experience of aesthetic sublimity from 'religious feelings'. Otto states:

> We are often prone to resort to this familiar feeling-content [aesthetic sublimity] to fill out the negative concept 'transcendent', explaining frankly God's 'transcendence' by His 'sublimity'. As a figurative analogical description this is perfectly allowable, but it would be an error if we meant it literally and in earnest. Religious feelings are not the same as aesthetic feelings, and 'the sublime' is as

---

[37] Otto critiqued the 'morally robust older [Enlightenment] rationalism' on precisely this point: 'rationalism lacked understanding of what "sin" is' (ibid., p. 53).

[38] Bach, *Holy Is God (Heilig)*.

definitely an aesthetic term as 'the beautiful', however widely different may be the facts denoted by the words.[39]

According to Otto, music, even if considered sublime, is not able to fully explicate a numinous or transcendent object. Although it can sometimes simulate a subjective encounter with the holy, it cannot fully represent the divine being in its essence (especially as seen in Otto's *augustus* qualification). Even if the music allows the listener to ascend to sublime heights of angelic praise, it does not transcend natural, rational experience.

Likewise, C.P.E. Bach's *Heilig* does not represent a complete numinous experience, considered in terms of Otto's understanding of *mysterium tremendum fascinans et augustum*. However, through the work's acknowledged sublimity and correspondence with subjective aspects of Otto's encounter with the holy, *Heilig* does evoke religious ideas and feelings in such a way that allows the listener to schematize an encounter with the transcendent in the natural realm of musical experience. The work takes the listener to the boundary of natural experience and inspires a look beyond.

---

[39]   Otto, *The Idea of the Holy*, p. 41 n.

Chapter 10

Music and World-Making: Haydn's String Quartet in E-Flat Major (op. 33 no. 2)

Férdia J. Stone-Davis[1]

Human beings are border people, living in the between, in the transition from the present to what is coming. To be in truth requires that we confess our exposure to what is not yet true.[2]

As place is sensed, senses are placed; as places make sense, senses make place.[3]

This chapter proceeds from an acknowledgement that human identity emerges in and through time, that self-identity entails self-construction and that, therefore, self-knowledge arises through a process wherein past aspects and events are approached from the standpoint of the 'now', acquiring a certain salience as a result. In this way meaning is assembled, as is identity. Elaborating upon this recognition, the chapter will draw out the idea that as a 'border people', that is, as always 'in between' in Caputo's sense, human beings are spatially as well as temporally situated. That is, meaning is not only constructed through time but in space, emerging from the interrelation between features of an environment and the particular situation, the 'here' of an individual. On this basis, music as a means of world-making will be considered:[4] just as humans are a border people so music is a border or liminal practice, operating by means of thresholds. That is, just as human identity emerges through a relational process, one that requires the constant transcendence of physical and imaginative limits, so music does the same. It

---

[1]   The section of this chapter relating to Haydn and 'home' was presented as part of a response given to Mieke Bal (Amsterdam School for Cultural Analysis) on 'travelling concepts' as part of a featured-thinker day held by the Zentrum für Theorie und Methodik der Kulturwissenschaften, University of Göttingen, Germany.

[2]   John Caputo, *Truth: Philosophy in Transit* (London, 2013), p. 242.

[3]   Steven Feld, 'Waterfalls of Song: An Acoustemology of Place Resounding in Bosavi, Papua New Guinea', in Steven Feld and Keith Basso (eds), *Senses of Place* (Santa Fe, N.Mex., 1997), pp. 90–135 (p. 90).

[4]   This resonates with the 'dwelling perspective' advocated by Tim Ingold and the recognition that the landscape (which is of central concern to him) is constituted as 'an enduring record of – and testimony to – the lives and works of past generations who have dwelt within it, and in so doing, have left there something of themselves' ('The Temporality of the Landscape', *World Archaeology*, 25/2 (1993): 152–74 (p. 152)). Ingold later replaces the dwelling perspective with 'habitation' since he believes the former carries 'a heavy connotation of snug, well-wrapped localism'. I am neither convinced that 'dwelling' has this connotation nor persuaded that, if it does, 'habitation' avoids it.

sensuously constructs time and space, facilitating the production and renewal of relations and enabling different constructions of subjectivity. The chapter consists of four sections: the first outlines what is meant by world-making and why the notion of place is valuable; the second sketches the ways in which music world-makes, creating 'real' and 'virtual' places, and grounds this capacity in its reliance upon thresholds (and the types of relations that these enable); the third considers the connection between self-construction in autobiography, on the one hand, and the music event, on the other, in order to bring attention to key aspects that are at play in a subject's interaction with musical place; the fourth will turn to the final movement of Joseph Haydn's String Quartet in E-flat major (op. 33 no. 2, 1781) in order to outline how the self becomes emplaced within music and how world-making can be said to occur in practice. It will do so by positioning the virtual musical place of the movement in relation to the broader 'region' of tonality in which it is embedded.

World-Making and Place

By 'world-making', I refer to attempts to make sense of the human person, the environment in which she is situated and the relationship between the two.[5] Such attempts necessarily rely on and arise from an interaction between the subject and her environment, which includes the physical world but also other subjects. Within this interaction a sense of feeling at-home in the world is enabled. Such attempts do not arise simply from intellectual effort but emerge more fundamentally, through physical interaction: 'life goes on in an environment, not merely *in* it but because of it, through interaction with it. No creature lives merely under its skin, its subcutaneous organs are means of connection with what lies beyond its bodily frame'.[6] Thus, 'by the time we think about things, or explicitly perceive them as what they are, we have already been immersed in their pragmatic meaning'.[7]

It is by virtue of the dynamic between the subject and her environment that certain objects in the world afford different interpretations and uses in particular situations and to certain individuals or groups: 'perceptual specification is a

---

[5]   Limiting world-making to the human person acknowledges the imaginative character of the response to the environment that distinguishes human action from other forms of animal action.

[6]   John Dewey, *Art as Experience* (New York, 1934), p. 12.

[7]   Shaun Gallagher, 'Philosophical Antecedents of Situated Cognition', in Philip Robbins and Murat Aydede (eds), *The Cambridge Handbook of Situated Cognition* (Cambridge, 2008), pp. 35–51 (p. 39). This resonates with Ingold's understanding of the 'taskscape' which comprises the myriad activities that comprise dwelling ('The Temporality of the Landscape').

reciprocal relationship between the invariants of the environment and the particular capacities of the perceiver'.[8] For this reason, a stick will afford throwing or burning depending upon the mode of engagement that a subject has with the object, which is influenced in turn by the circumstances informing the engagement. Thus, time and space are not neutral frames since they are related in the first instance to the kinds of activity in which the subject is engaged: it is on this basis that ideas of 'quick' and 'slow', 'far' and 'close', are determined.[9]

The interaction between the subject and her environment, that which I am calling the process of world-making, brings into relief the poverty of descriptions of existence that speak simply in temporal and spatial terms, casting them as disinterested. In doing so, it gestures towards the importance of recognising place:

> *Lived bodies belong to places* and help to constitute them. Even if such bodies may be displaced in certain respects, they are never placeless; they are never *only* at discrete positions in world time and space, though they may *also* be at such positions.[10]

In some sense, that is, existence is only partially explained through a mapping of a body onto temporal and spatial co-ordinates and is better accounted for in terms of both the amenability of an environment to a subject as well as the influence that a body exerts on it.

The dynamic nature of place is well articulated by Edward Casey: 'A place is more an *event* than a *thing*' to be assimilated into known categories.[11] That is, places 'not only *are*, they *happen*'.[12] Noticeably, this understanding of place

---

[8]   Eric Clarke, *Ways of Listening: An Ecological Approach to the Perception of Musical Meaning* (Oxford, 2005), p. 44.

[9]   Gallagher, 'Philosophical Antecedents of Situated Cognition', p. 41. This of course stands against conceiving time and space as absolutes, which is typically thought to occur primarily in the course of modernity. Edward Casey explains: 'Beginning with Philoponus in the sixth century A.D. and reaching an apogee in fourteenth-century theology and above all in seventeenth-century physics, place has been assimilated to space. The latter, regarded as infinite extension, has become a cosmic and extra-cosmic Moloch that consumes every corpuscle of place to be found within its greedy reach. ... In the course of the eighteenth and nineteenth centuries place was also made subject to time, regarded as chronometric and universal, indeed as "the formal *a priori* condition of all appearances whatsoever", in Kant's commanding phrase' (*The Fate of Place: A Philosophical History* (Berkeley, Calif., 2008), p. x).

[10]   Edward S. Casey, 'How to Get from Space to Place in a Fairly Short Stretch of Time: Phenomenological Prolegomena', in Feld and Basso (eds), *Senses of Place*, pp. 13–52 (p. 24).

[11]   Ibid., p. 26.

[12]   Ibid., p. 27.

coincides with a conception of music that emphasises its mode of being as event, as temporally performed practice.[13] Moreover, *as event*, place, just as music, is

> deconstructive of oppositions that it brings and holds together within its own ambience. These oppositions include binary pairs of terms that have enjoyed hegemonic power in western epistemology and metaphysics ... subject and object, self and other, formal and substantive, mind and body, inner and outer, perception and imagination (or memory), and nature and culture.[14]

Due to the resonances between Casey's account of place and music understood as event, it is worth summarising the four other aspects of place he identifies. First, places gather. For Casey, this gathering is of 'experiences and histories, languages and thoughts'.[15] Second, in gathering, places hold. They hold together 'a particular configuration' that 'allows for certain things – people, ideas and so forth – to overlap with, and sometimes to occlude, others as they recede or come forward together'.[16] In holding a configuration in place, a 'holding in' and a 'holding out' occurs.[17] That is, place holds in the 'occupants' without which the place would not be (this can be read as those elements comprising a place). Simultaneously, place holds out, 'beckoning to its inhabitants and, assembling them, making them manifest (though not necessarily manifest to each other, or to the same degree)'.[18] Third, the holding that occurs involves a 'configurative complex of things'.[19] Place is created by gathering together and embracing the 'outlines' and 'inlines' of an environment: 'The result is not confusion of container with contained but a literal configuration in which the form of the place ... joins up with the shapes of the things in it'.[20] Fourth, the holding enacts a form of keeping, since when a subject revisits a place she finds it 'more or less securely holding memories'.[21] Importantly, however, keeping does not involve a straightforward retrieval, for place gathers together 'lives and things, each with its own space and time, into one arena of common engagement'[22] and thus holds together many levels of meaning at one time. It is a 'matrix for mergings'

---

[13]   On the importance of considering music as event, see Férdia J. Stone-Davis, 'Music and Liminality: Becoming Sensitized', in Birgit Abels (ed.), *Embracing Restlessness: Cultural Musicology* (Hildesheim, forthcoming).

[14]   Casey, 'How to Get from Space to Place in a Fairly Short Stretch of Time', p. 34; see also Férdia J. Stone-Davis, *Musical Beauty: Negotiating the Boundary between Subject and Object* (Eugene, Oreg., 2011).

[15]   Casey, 'How to Get from Space to Place in a Fairly Short Stretch of Time', pp. 24–5.

[16]   Ibid., p. 25.

[17]   Ibid.

[18]   Ibid.

[19]   Ibid.

[20]   Ibid.

[21]   Ibid.

[22]   Ibid., p. 26.

that most obviously brings together past and present but extends far beyond this in scope, so that 'keeping in memory is a continual re-keeping: hence the many variant versions of the "same" past with which we regale ourselves in remembering'.[23]

Music, World-Making and Place

Casey's concern is with the sense of place afforded by physical geography. However, physical place clearly involves imaginative involvement and engagement. Thus, in what follows I will transfer the world-making about which Casey implicitly talks from its most immediate (geographical) application into the domain of music, where the physical affords another form of world-making. For, taking the interaction between the subject and her environment as the foundation of the world-making process and acknowledging the importance of the physical and the imaginative in the creation of place, music has a particular role to play, since it combines the physical and the imaginative in a way that opens up 'real' and 'virtual' places.

Music can be understood as a border or liminal practice due its reliance upon thresholds, and it is thus that it forms an active component of and force within culture. A threshold (*limen*) is a point at which transition occurs. However, that which is most significant about thresholds is not the moment of crossing but the relation that is brought about at the instant before that crossing, since it is here that binaries such as inside and outside, subject and object, are transcended: they are brought into relation and held in tension. In music, then, different but interrelating thresholds are at work, sensory, processual and relational. The thresholds operate in time but also across time and impact upon a more fundamental threshold between the subject and that which is other than the subject (which can include other subjects as well as the environment), creating an attunement.[24] Although it is difficult, as well as unwise, to unpick the thresholds from one another, since they are mutually reliant, one might distinguish between them within a music event in order to bring certain features to light. Moreover, echoing Casey, who maintains

---

[23] Edward S. Casey, 'Keeping the Past in Mind', in D. Ihde and H.J. Silverman (eds), *Descriptions* (Albany, NY, 1985), pp 36–56 (p. 49).

[24] Elsewhere, I have unpacked thresholds in implicit terms through the moments of 'impact', 'absorption' and 'ekstasis' which are identifiable within the music event. These are not isolated moments but points of interaction that occur throughout the musical process as a result of the self acting as well as being acted upon. 'Impact' refers to the physical effect that sound has upon the human body. 'Absorption' indicates the embodied 'occupation' that can obtain, that is, the housing of the sound within the human body and the housing of the human within sound. 'Ekstasis' refers to the outward facing attention that this involves on the part of the subject. Through these points of interaction, musical experience has the potential to elicit a form of attunement (Stone-Davis, *Musical Beauty*, pp. 161–90).

that subjects are emplaced even when 'between' particular geographical places, although music's mode of being is bound up with thresholds, this does not preclude its association with place, for although a threshold is strictly speaking in between it is still in place. To explain: as an event, a temporally performed practice, music is performed by individuals in contexts and is reliant upon material and cultural conditions, sustaining thresholds and forging and supporting connections in real as well as virtual time and space (undoing oppositions). Although the following discussion employs the division between the real and the virtual, it will become clear that they are intimately related. Indeed, this is another binary that music as threshold holds in tension.

Sensory Thresholds

Sensory thresholds underpin the physical impact music has on subject(s) and object(s), and it is this that underpins world-making in real time and space. Sound is heard and orients the subject within her physical surroundings: 'reflexively turning to look for the source of sound or ducking when you hear something coming from behind would make little sense unless you were aware of sound sources'.[25] However, it is not a simple conception of a sound source that results, for sound imparts information about the environment and the interaction that gives rise to it:

> Because the pattern of frequency components that comprise the vibration of an object and the way that pattern changes over time is determined by the nature of the object and the events that caused it to vibrate, that pattern and the way it changes provide a great deal of information about the object and the interaction that produced the vibration.[26]

Within music practices, sensory thresholds provide another means of orientation: the shaping of sounds allows co-ordination between those making music and extends outwards, making communication with others possible. It is also sensory thresholds that, as we shall see, establish virtual world-making, since they

---

[25]   Casey O'Callaghan and Matthew Nudds, 'Introduction: The Philosophy of Sounds and Auditory Perception', in eid. (eds), *Sounds and Perception: New Philosophical Essays* (Oxford, 2009), pp. 1–25 (p. 12).

[26]   Matthew Nudds, 'Sounds and Space', in O'Callaghan and Nudds (eds), *Sounds and Perception*, pp. 69–96 (p. 71). Thus: 'we can perceive the size of an object dropped into water, that something is rolling, the material composition of an object from the sound of an impact, and the force of an impact. We can distinguish objects with different shapes, and we can tell the length of a rod dropped onto the floor. When something is dropped, we can hear whether it bounced or broke. We are good at recognising natural sounds, such as footsteps, hands clapping, paper tearing, and so on. We can tell that a cup is being filled and when it is full' (ibid., p. 70).

underpin the processual thresholds that occur within music, as sound is shaped and transformed into an imaginative realm of intention with its own 'field of force'.[27]

In short, sensory thresholds show knowledge to be grounded in processes informed by the subject going beyond herself. Here, subjects, objects and the environment are gathered together. Indeed, it is in this manner that place is configured in both outline and inline. That is, just as for Casey a landscape is a 'configuration in which the form of the place', including mountains and gullies, 'joins up with the shapes of the things in it',[28] so in the case of music, the outline is formed by the qualities of the space in which an acoustic encounter occurs, including whether it happens inside or outside, what surfaces and textures are present and what other sounds are in attendance. The inlines are those musical actions that occur within the physical environment. It is the process of this gathering together and configuration that enables the dynamic motion of holding in and holding out, and lays the foundation for musical place.

Processual Thresholds

Processual thresholds arise in the structural and imaginative developments that underpin musical organisation. In real time and space, processual thresholds are bound up with sensory thresholds, since they arise from physical methods of sound production and the structure of its treatment. This includes the interaction between a subject and an instrument which is struck, plucked, bowed, blown or programmed in order to produce sound, the influence of other subjects and instruments upon that sound production, and the environment in which the sounds are made. All of these aspects feed back into ongoing processes, determining parameters such as volume, speed and articulation. A dynamic process is set in motion between the subject, the instrument, the sound and the environment, each informing the other and provoking certain responses such that the subject is caught up in both the physical pattern and its sonic corollary, and is immersed simultaneously in the pattern as it has been and as it will be.[29] Hence, the focused concentration of the practising musician who executes physical actions on an instrument, listens to the resulting sound and how it is moulded by the space in which it is heard, and responds to this in the next physical action, creating a real musical place.

It is the same process that underpins the creation of a virtual musical place in an imaginative time and space, for although music is at a basic level a succession of sounds created through physical action, it is not only this. The production of sounds, organised and transmitted, opens up 'a phenomenal space of tones',[30] one that is understood in relation to (since it is shaped by) physical experience. To

---

[27] Roger Scruton, *The Aesthetics of Music* (Oxford, 1999), p. 17.

[28] Casey, 'How to Get from Space to Place in a Fairly Short Stretch of Time', p. 25.

[29] Stone-Davis, *Musical Beauty*, p. 164.

[30] Scruton, *The Aesthetics of Music*, p. 75; see also Scruton's contribution to this volume.

explain: our experience of music is grounded in our own physicality and 'shares something with our experience of seeing objects move in physical space'.[31] Thus, when the subject inhabits music, she is guided by a momentum that points both forwards and backwards. The subject has a sense of types of movement arising from her own movement, her own embodied experience and, thus, within the musical experience is able to feel 'all the ways it [music] moves, swells, hops, rushes, floats, trips along, drags, soars, and falls'.[32]

Moreover, the entwining of the real and the virtual realms means that the physical production of sound informs imaginative processes. Thus, for example, convention within the western tradition suggests a certain neutrality of middle C (which is of course a construction). This is exemplified by the piano, which moves from middle C to the C above in an 'almost resistance-free switch selection'.[33] However, this is not the case on other instruments. Simon Waters explains:

> The same pitch change on a bassoon, for example, speaks of immense difficulty
> – of a physical system at the upper limits of availability – and the same change
> on a cello generates the pull of the real distance travelled up the fingerboard in
> an equivalent response somewhere in our autonomic nervous system.[34]

It is the resistances built into the physical production of sound and the negotiation of a tone's development that imbues virtual time and space with shape and feel, giving a sense of height, depth and extension. As Roger Scruton notes, the timbre of tones allows perception of them as more or less thick, as having a weight and mass, and clusters of tones can appear as 'open', 'hollow', 'filled' and 'stretched'.[35]

In real musical places, then, the processual thresholds of music are bound up with the gathering and configuration that occur as part of sensory thresholds, since they involve the production of sounds which are shaped by the physical environment in which they are situated. However, in turn, as music, the sounds produced manifest their own outlines and inlines. It is through the patterning of these that virtual world-making occurs and place arises. Music consists of many structural levels, spanning from the outlines supplied by extended configurations of tones, through inlines that are more fractional, including those emerging from gesture and articulation such as the 'sigh' that accompanies a slurred intervallic movement downwards, and the shape of tones (whether they are short or long, light or heavy). It is in this way that tones are given musically expressive contours

---

[31] Mark Johnson, *The Meaning of the Body: Aesthetics of Human Understanding* (Chicago, 2007), p. 249.

[32] Ibid., p. 239.

[33] Simon Waters, 'Touching at a Distance: Resistance, Tactility, Proxemics and the Development of a Hybrid Virtual/Physical Performance System', *Contemporary Music Review*, 32/2–3 (2013): 119–34 (p. 123).

[34] Ibid., pp. 123–4.

[35] Scruton, *The Aesthetics of Music*, p. 78.

that feed into longer configurations. Thus, in both real and imaginative time and space the subject is taken beyond its seemingly discrete existence and is set in relation.

Through this gathering together, another level of holding in and holding out is made possible: the tones are held together in a configuration and extend out to inhabitants of the virtual musical place who are assembled through their participation in it. Elements of the virtual processes of world-making will be the focus of the analysis of the final movement of Haydn's quartet. Here, musical aspects are presented to the subject and understood by her over time. It is only by means of this process that the significance of musical inlines is disclosed.

Relational Thresholds

Music's relational thresholds are found in the interrelationship of discrete existences that are brought about, including objects, people, ideas and actions. Most immediately this occurs in the creation of a real musical place through the relation of the subject to her environment and those subjects and objects most directly within it. However, in the process of real world-making, the social, cultural and political frames, that is, the broader regions that both enable and constrain it, come into view. Casey states: 'moving between places corresponds to an entire *region*, that is, an area concatenated by peregrinations between the places it connects'.[36] The idea that places acquire meaning through their situation within a broader context is supported by Tim Ingold:

> Places do not have locations but histories. Bound together by the itineraries of their inhabitants, places exist not in space but as nodes in a matrix of movement. I shall call this matrix a 'region'. It is the knowledge of the region, and with it the ability to situate one's current position within the historical context of journeys previously made – journeys to, from and around places – that distinguishes the countryman from the stranger. Ordinary wayfinding, then, more closely resembles storytelling than map-using.[37]

It is because places acquire their significance in relation to regions that one can legitimately discover vestiges in music of those social factors that surround it directly and indirectly, including not only circumstances that influence music's production (issues concerning patronage, life events of composers and performers, as well as the demands made by particular performance spaces and the development of particular instruments) but also the social and cultural matrix within which music is embedded, and which it reflects and refracts. It is for this reason that Susan McClary can reasonably make the case that she does about

---

[36]   Casey, 'How to Get from Space to Place in a Fairly Short Stretch of Time', p. 24.

[37]   Tim Ingold, *The Perception of the Environment: Essays on Livelihood, Dwelling and Skill* (London, 2000), p. 219.

Schubert. She suggests that since there was a movement towards representations of the self in music at the time that Schubert was writing, and since, therefore, different constructions of subjectivity are active in both compositional practice and the reception of particular composer's works, Schubert's compositional style can be understood as presenting an alternative form of masculinity from that portrayed by the music of Beethoven.[38] In the analysis of the Haydn quartet, the broader region of tonality will be brought into focus, since it provides a contour for the particular outlines and inlines which the musical place opens up.

At a virtual level, music allows the interaction between the subject and her environment to be honed and/or restructured by modifying the subject's way of being in the world as she goes about her everyday activities. The imaginative time and space of the musical place can entrain and support the subject so that she can achieve more within a particular context, for example, such as the use of music to order the bodies of subjects doing aerobics.[39] It can also reshape and personalise the soundscape within which the subject is immersed, for example, through the use of mobile audio devices, so that 'manageable sites of habitation'[40] or, in my terms, a world-within-a-world, can be created.[41]

---

[38]   According to Susan McClary, 'music *need not* reveal anything personal about the composer (although the discursive decisions a composer makes – such as avoiding certain available options, affiliating with others – always signify)' ('Constructions of Subjectivity in Schubert's Music', in *Reading Music: Selected Essays* (Aldershot, 2007), pp. 169–92 (p. 175)). Clearly, here, we can see the connection between the relational and processual thresholds of music: Schubert 'tends to disdain goal-oriented desire per se for the sake of a sustained image of pleasure and an open, flexible sense of self – both of which are quite alien to the constructions of masculinity then being adopted as natural, and also to the premises of musical form as they were commonly construed at the time' (ibid., p. 187).

[39]   Tia DeNora identifies core components of this process, where music organises bodily activity: 'warm up', 'pre-core', 'core', 'cool down' and 'floor exercises' (*Music in Everyday Life* (Cambridge, 2000), pp. 90–91).

[40]   Michael Bull, *Sounding Out the City: Personal Stereos and the Management of Everyday Life* (Oxford and New York, 2000), p. 2.

[41]   Virtual world-making also happens at a meta-level by means of intellectual reflection, which sets certain frameworks in place which not only throw into relief certain aspects of human beings and the world but in doing so influence and shape understandings and practices of music. For an example of the ways in which understandings of music are underpinned by surrounding philosophies, see Stone-Davis, *Musical Beauty*; Andrew Bowie, *Music Philosophy, and Modernity* (Cambridge, 2007). For an example of how philosophies have an impact on music practices specifically, see Lydia Goehr, *The Imaginary Museum of Musical Works: An Essay in the Philosophy of Music* (Oxford, 1992). This can be seen in two cases significant for the development of music thought and practice in the western trajectory. Anicius Boethius (*c*.480–*c*.525) and Immanuel Kant (1724–1804) have contrasting conceptions of beauty which, in each case, are shaped by prior understandings about the self and the world and convictions about the priority of either one or the other. The notion of beauty is used to negotiate and configure this relationship, and 'beautiful

In sum, the relational thresholds of music indicate the way in which the musical place discloses, since it holds within itself, the experiences, histories and thoughts that mould its existence. This occurs in real terms: each music event involves the application of performance traditions and practices to the production of tones, and bears traces of the society and culture that conditions its appearance, explicitly and implicitly. Virtually, music has the capacity to gather across time as well as in time, enacting a form of keeping. It keeps as it configures, enabling participation within its imaginative movements and allowing the retrieval of this upon return to it, even though this retrieval is in effect a reconfigured memory. Thus, music can powerfully evoke feelings and thoughts, as seen in Tia DeNora's analysis of the complex ongoing involvement that 'Lucy' has with Schubert's *Impromptus*, which is bound up with 'a complex of childhood memories and associations' but is informed by her current context and state of mind.[42] Music can also allow one to feel distanced from feelings and thoughts, as when music heard at a particular time does not bear the same emotional load when later re-heard.

Musical World-Making and Musical Self-Making

As a liminal practice reliant upon sensory, processual and relational thresholds, music is not easily reducible to simple categories of time and space in either real or virtual terms. This is because it involves an interaction between and the hospitability of the musical environment and the subject, entails a process of world-making that combines the physical and the imaginative, and gives rise to what can aptly be described as place. This place is neither static nor bounded since it is fluid, comprising movements that extend outwards.[43]

Thus, to speak of place is to draw attention to the fact that time and space are fundamentally related to the ways in which the subject is in the world. In both real and virtual terms, music has the capacity to create an environment into which the subject steps and explores and in which she dwells. Understanding music as constitutive of real and virtual places, then, is to reflect the amenability of the

---

music' is determined on this basis. (See Stone-Davis, *Musical Beauty*). At this meta-level of world-making, music contributes to by sustaining an existing frame or 'world' of meaning.

[42] DeNora, *Music in Everyday Life*, pp. 41–2. This interaction resonates with Ingold's understanding of landscape: 'through living in it, the landscape becomes a part of us, just as we are a part of it' ('The Temporality of the Landscape', p. 154).

[43] Tim Ingold challenges the idea of place and goes against Edward S. Casey saying: 'Thus to be, I would say, is not to be in place but to be along paths. The path, not the place, is the primary condition of being, or rather of becoming' ('Bindings against Boundaries: Entanglements of Life in an Open World', *Environment and Planning A*, 40 (2008): 1796–1810 (p. 1808)). The idea of musical place navigates between these two emphases, here place is movement.

musical environment to the subject as well as the fact that the musical environment 'extends its own influence back onto this subject'.[44] Just as with other forms of world-making, 'bodies and places are connatural terms. They inter-animate each other'.[45] The subject is constituted in relation, through a process of 'self-transcendence'.

Given that a certain inter-animation occurs between music and the subject, and that in the process the subject world-makes, one might ask how this manifests in practical terms. Before suggesting how, a juxtaposition of 'autobiographical consciousness'[46] and the music event will highlight the mechanism that underpins the subject's capacity to world-make: in both autobiographical self-making and musical self-making, the subject interacts with invariants from the position of the here-and-now. By becoming emplaced, constructions of subjectivity are enabled.

Exploring the philosophical import of autobiographical forms of writing, Garry L. Hagberg points to an entry in Iris Murdoch's diary from 1957: 'Man is a creature who makes pictures of himself, and then comes to resemble the picture.'[47] Elucidating the implications of the autobiographical process for philosophical notions of the self (primarily showing the unsustainability of Cartesianism),[48] Hagberg argues the falsity of the notion of the autobiographer as a narrator who retrieves and re-presents a past from a privileged vantage point. This implies a distinction between 'action' and 'narration'[49] and views the autobiographer as a narrator of fiction: 'The fictional narrator does not enter into the causal and contextual continuum, and not only does he or she not, he or she metaphysically *cannot*, precisely because he or she does not have a causal foothold in the world, thus precluding the very capacity to act.'[50]

As Hagberg makes clear, it is misplaced to hold this position in relation to autobiographical writing since the process enacts the formation of the 'I'. Through

---

[44]   Casey 'How to Get from Space to Place in a Fairly Short Stretch of Time', p. 22.

[45]   Ibid., p. 24.

[46]   Garry L. Hagberg, *Describing Ourselves: Wittgenstein and Autobiographical Consciousness* (Oxford, 2008).

[47]   Iris Murdoch, diary entry, 1957, quoted ibid., p. 202.

[48]   In using the term 'Cartesian', Hagberg refers to 'a cluster of intertwined metaphysically dualistic views in the philosophy of mind and language'. Broadly put, these include the views '(*a*) that the self is most fundamentally a contingently embodied point of consciousness transparently knowable to itself via introspection, (*b*) that its contents are knowable immediately by contrast to all outward mediated knowledge (and that self-knowledge is thus non-evidential), (*c*) that first-person thought and experience is invariably private, thus presenting as a brute first fact of human existence and other-minds problem, and (*d*) that language is contingent and *ex post facto* externalisation of prior private, pre-linguistic, and mentally internal content' (*Describing Ourselves*, pp. 2–3).

[49]   'The autobiographical position, we too easily think, is that of the narrator; the past actions of that pre-narrating self (now recollected and reported) are the actions of the "actor"' (ibid., p. 68).

[50]   Ibid., pp. 70–71.

self-description the subject relates to aspects of her life and makes sense of them from the standpoint of the 'I' that is here-and-now. It is from this perspective that events acquire significance and that 'I' create a picture to which 'I' bear resemblance. It is for this reason, the enactment of the 'I', that aspect-perception stands central to the process of self-description and self-understanding that underpins autobiography:

> Just as we can speak of looking at the flower without seeing it, we can speak of looking at an episode or event in one's life without at first, or for a long time, seeing it, and then at some point coming to see it. This is precisely analogous, in ocular terms, to what Murdoch meant in autobiographical terms, by 're-thinking'. The past is not changed and yet, only seemingly paradoxically, it is. It is being struck by the newly appreciated significance of an event in our past.[51]

That is, it is not objects and events that change but their hue as sets of relations are 'awakened' and a larger 'picture' created.[52] It is in this way that facets of experience attain coherence and that narrative threads appear.

So what of music? It seems that there is some kind of analogy to be made between autobiographical self-making and musical self-making.[53] The music event provides an immersive environment, wherein each participating subject, each 'I', is situated, moving in a stream of occurrences that happens to 'me'. 'I' respond to these as they happen and continue to respond to them through the course of real and virtual movements in which 'I' am caught up. It is on this basis that the significance of aspects and relations evolve, and according to which 'I' anticipate and make sense of further aspects and relations. Thus, in some sense, the musical subject is positioned similarly to the autobiographical subject. Through aspect-perception she finds coherence and draws out 'narrative threads'.[54]

It is on this basis that the idea of narrator (one synonymous with actor since it not only *can* be but *is* implicated in the causal network of the musical place) is relevant

---

[51] Ibid., p. 213.

[52] Ibid., p. 221.

[53] Hagberg suggests that the process of self-constitution through introspection occurs not only in autobiography but in other 'self-representational works of art' such as fiction, poetry, film, theatre, opera and the visual arts. These are enactments of introspection and are 'presented within the stream of life depicted within the artwork' and not within the stream of our own lives, thus enabling us to attend to them from a 'safe, indeed aesthetic, distance' (ibid., p. 102).

[54] To be clear, I am not taking unequivocally from literature and drama. Indeed, as Byron Almén has pointed out, it is because of direct importation from these fields that narrative has been problematically applied to music. Almén cites, for instance, those cases where 'traditional formal, harmonic and generic paradigms' do not apply, and in those instance when music is prefaced with 'attachments' that prepare participants to receive the music in a particular way (Byron Almén, *A Theory of Musical Narrative* (Bloomington and Indianapolis, 2008), p. 3).

to the music event but in a complex way. There is no single narrator, no simple sense of something narrated, and no straightforward sense in which narrative is received, since each participating subject enacts narration, responding physically and imaginatively to musical sounds. In short, there is no simple presentation of events, even when a performer works closely with a score, since each reception of music involves an interpretation in terms of an individual subject's own set of experiences. Narrative threads are multiple, since different aspects are perceptible, depending on perspective, and are generated by immersion in sensory, processual and relational thresholds and the real and virtual places, which at any one time are more or less apparent.

Haydn's Joke

It is in the light of the co-creative character of place, wherein aspects accrue significance by means of a subject's interpretation, and the analogy between autobiographical and musical self-making, where the subject is situated in relation to invariants, that we turn to the final movement of Haydn's String Quartet in E-flat major (op. 33 no. 2). It provides an apt case in point since quartet-writing and quartet-performance were commonly understood at the time to be akin to 'a conversation "among four reasonable people"'.[55] Mary Hunter explains:

> [The metaphor of conversation] had been used for various kinds of chamber music throughout the eighteenth century, but between the 1770s and the early nineteenth century it became particularly attached to the string quartet. And indeed, the quartet as a genre, certainly, if not exclusively in Haydn's hands, was in part 'about' the conversations possible when four people play music together in a given situation; primarily among the four parts (and secondarily among the players of those parts), but also between the players and the audience, and between the composer as represented in the 'work itself' and the listeners.[56]

Understanding the character of quartets as a form of conversation reinforces the idea that place arises from interaction and that meaning emerges in process, varying between subjects according to the investment that each makes to the experience as a whole, and formed by the experiences that each subject brings to bear.

As a result, there are many ways in which one might unpack the real and virtual places enabled by the final movement, and there are many ways in which sensory, processual and relational thresholds can be explored. Present constraints, however, require a narrow scope, and in what follows the sensory thresholds in real terms will be taken as a given, and discussion of the processual and relational

---

[55]   See Mary Hunter, 'The Quartets', in Caryl Clark (ed.), *The Cambridge Companion to Haydn* (Cambridge, 2005), pp. 112–25 (p. 119).

[56]   Ibid.

thresholds will remain gestural. The aim is to give a programmatic account of how world-making in music might be approached in concrete terms, focusing on aspect-perception. Thus, in a sense, the aim of what follows is to show the potential ways through which the subject is gathered into the music and constituted over its course, making sense of the music and being emplaced within it.

In considering how aspects of the final movement might become apparent to the subject it is important to keep in mind that Haydn was working within a western tradition reliant on harmony. Herein, most importantly, one key tends to feature predominantly, generating a sense of home in terms of familiarity, security and centre. It is from this and in relation to it that music evolves. The home key exerts almost a gravitational pull, shaping musical movement. Thus, having established a point of tonal focus, the music 'moves away' and in doing so stretches harmonic boundaries as well as exploring melodic trajectories. It then very often returns home, closing the piece. In this way, tonality organises the musical experience, providing a context in and through which process can be felt and understood.[57] Hence, within a piece that arises within a western tonal scheme at a general level, and within the Haydn movement in particular, the eventual return to home is expected, both harmonically and melodically, by the subject who is familiar with the terrain[58]

Tonality, then, provides a broader region for the creation of the particular musical place opened up by Haydn's final movement, providing a contour in relation to which certain outlines and inlines stand and can be understood. Moreover, it is familiarity with the region that facilitates the process of world-making, enabling and constraining a subject's habitation of a place. Indeed, as Richard Taruskin notes in relation to music: 'absolutely unchallenged "normality" is perhaps the most boring form of discourse. ... It is the existence of norms that allows departures to become meaningful.'[59] In terms of creating a place into which the subject is drawn and inhabits, tonality provides a matrix within which the final Presto movement of Haydn's quartet creates outlines and inlines that play upon expectations and subversion of those expectations, as it develops in relation to

---

[57] See Julian Johnson, *Classical Music: A Beginners Guide* (Oxford, 2009), esp. chs 2, 3; see also Patricia Carpenter. 'Aspects of Musical Space', in Eugene Narmour and Ruth A. Solie (eds), *Explorations in Music, The Arts, and Ideas: Essays in Honour of Leonard B. Meyer* (Stuyvesant, NY, 1988), pp. 341–73.

[58] Richard Taruskin notes that at the time, in addition to 'extroversive' signs (including representations of the 'sights and sounds of the natural world' and 'moods and feelings of the human world', the most basic set of 'introversive' signs consisted in 'the relationship of dominant and tonic – a normative relationship of two triads that marked them as signs of tension and repose, respectively'. 'Each event in the unfolding of the piece, then, carries implications for future unfolding, even as it seems to be a consequence of past unfolding. Thus everything happens within the piece can be construed as a pointer toward some other thing – or better, toward all the other things – taking place within the piece' (*The Oxford History of Western Music* (New York, 2010), vol. 2, pp. 497–588 (p. 539)).

[59] Ibid.

Example 10.1   Haydn, String Quartet in E-flat major (op. 33 no. 2), Presto,
bars 1–8

the musical home.[60] In doing so it brings to the fore different aspects that evolve
over time in conjunction with the subject. This happens at a large-scale structural
level, in relation to melody, rhythm and metre, and is reinforced by the texture of
the movement.[61]

To explain: within the large-scale structure, the movement follows rondo form
(A–B–A–C–A); the musical journey oscillates between the familiarity provided
by the music's home (the movement's 'theme') and travels that lead away from it
(the contrasting 'episodes' of the movement). This dynamic instils a sense of the
inevitability of the main theme's return, one that is disrupted at the movement's

---

[60]   Casey says, analogously, in relation to geographical place: 'A place is not a setting
of indifferent space, homogeneous and isotropic (I prefer to call this characteristically
seventeenth-century view of space as 'site'). Place works on us, and on our memories, by
its very peculiarities and tropisms, its inhomogeneity' ('Keeping the Past in Mind', p. 46).

[61]   Taruskin calls the 'introversive pointing' that occurs both 'horizontally' (that is,
'structurally') and 'vertically' (or 'texturally') the 'warp and woof' of a piece (*The Oxford
History of Western Music*, vol. 2, p. 542).

Example 10.2   Haydn, String Quartet in E-flat major (op. 33 no. 2), Presto,
bars 16–28

end. Thus, a recurring theme is interspersed with contrasting material. The main theme is in the home key of the piece (E-flat major) and is so each time it returns. The texture of the musical layers is light: the first violin carries a motif that launches with an upbeat that propels it forward, its energy swiftly dissipating; the second violin, viola and cello accompany for the most part with staccato crotchets, supporting the forward-directed movement of the motif. Importantly, in order to encourage the subject to perceive the initial material as formative to the development of the movement and to be open to the place that the music opens up, it is repeated twice (see Example 10.1).

In the first episode, the subject is led away from the musical centre to the dominant key (B-flat major). This episode maintains the vital and energetic rhythm of the initial material as well as elements of the melody, but develops them. In this way a feeling of recognition coincides with an acknowledgement of difference and a sense of expectation. This stems from a mixture of the familiar and the unfamiliar: this is highlighted when the musical journey begins to drive towards its home, since an expectation of its return is generated by holding the dominant note (B-flat) in the cello, which emphasises the need for resolution in the form of a return to the musical centre provided by the home key. This state of expectation is reinforced texturally by the second violin and viola which move in a half-tone downward movement over two bars. The first of each set of paired notes are loud in dynamic before becoming quieter, creating an oscillation that mirrors the repetition of material by the first violin and creates a momentary loop before pushing forward. To encourage this sense of movement, the cello remains on the dominant note but no longer sustains it and instead pulses. The first and second violins use the propulsion supplied by the upbeat energy of the main motif, ascending stepwise to a suspenseful but temporary halt that, through its distance from the home key and the harmonic iteration of a dominant seventh, creates a strong pull towards the home chord and reinforces expectation of the theme's return (see Example 10.2).

Following a restatement of the original section, a second journey away from the musical home occurs. The harmony moves to the subdominant key (A-flat major), and a similar sense of expectation is created through a pedal on the dominant note of that key (E-flat). The contrast of this material relies on its exploitation of the driving rhythmic energy of the main theme, the first beat of which no longer rests after the preceding upbeat but carries the momentum forward by means of somewhat lumbering quavers. These quavers are set over longer oscillating movements in the second violin and viola, and the resulting texture is punctuated with sforzando chords that although more static, since longer in duration, bear a latent energy through their weight and force. Eventually, as with the first episode, the cello pedals on the dominant to reinforce expectation of the return to E-flat major.

Returning to the musical home, the material is stated once and then briefly and incompletely iterated again. Where the second half of the opening section is expected a transition occurs, one with a seeming aim to drive towards the end of the movement, an impression given, in the first instance, by the sudden move of the first violin up an octave and subsequent increase in momentum across all parts, which move predominantly in quaver rhythm, and, in the second instance, by gathering together elements that have featured earlier in the movement. Thus, an echo of the angular staccato passage of the first contrasting section appears, as does the forward-driven upbeat momentum, which again leads to a hiatus, on this occasion extended in time by a pause, reinforcing and prolonging a desire for the return to the main theme.

These conventions, within the musical horizons of expectation set up by the piece, which arise from the importance of the harmonic home, are in some sense typical of the tonal region of the period. The more unexpected ones are those that are employed towards the end of the movement. To explain: after the last note of the statement of the theme that follows the final contrasting episode, a pause is signalled in the score and executed in performance, which gives a feeling that the movement is in fact complete, along with the fact that the home key is firmly

Example 10.3   Haydn, String Quartet in E-flat major (op. 33 no. 2), Presto, bars 148–53

in place. However, a circumvention of the movement's closure occurs: the music launches into an adagio section of only four bars. This provides a striking and unexpected contrast, moving away from the buoyancy of what has preceded to a deliberate and slow section. The dynamic is loud and the texture chordal before diminishing to a quiet and sparse downward statement on the first violin. The fading texture alludes back to the initial motif through the diminishing energy it exhibits. Again, there is a sense of finality since the home key chord is settled upon (and another pause reinforces this) but the closure is disrupted by the return of the theme (see Example 10.3).

Although the inevitability of the main musical material has been disturbed, it is within this final restatement of the theme that expectation is dislocated further, providing what has been termed the movement's 'joke'. To elucidate: it is not only the structure of the main musical theme that undergoes a journey, but the melody also. The melody of the main theme is internally balanced, mirroring the harmonic journey of the main theme through the contrasting episodes: the first two bars reside at the musical centre (E-flat major [I]), the second two bars move away from this (B-flat major [V]), the third pair of bars travel yet again (A-flat major [IV]) whilst the fourth stays 'away' before returning home (it moves from a B-flat chord to an E-flat one, which sounds a V/I cadence and provides a return to the home chord and key). It is upon the basis of the internal coherence of the melody, its metric equilibrium and the pull of the musical home that the joke at the end works. An expectation of the melodic process has been set in place at the beginning and reinforced upon each return. Thus, in its final appearance (which texturally is exactly the same as in its first articulation) the insertion of two-bar rests between each of its four constituent parts already subverts expectation, creating a sense of metric instability. However, this subversion is surpassed by the ensuing insertion of a four-bar rest and the closure of the piece with the opening rather than the

Example 10.4   Haydn, String Quartet in E flat major (op. 33 no. 2), Presto,
                  bars 153–72

closing part of the melodic phrase, which is played pianissimo. Thus, although the piece finishes by returning to the music's harmonic home, it remains unfinished since its melodic home has been displaced (see Example 10.4).

In sum: it is through a process of going beyond and being set in relation, which allows the subject to in-dwell a musical process, that aspects of the musical environment become apparent, that the subject is able to make sense of what is presented and that musical place is generated. This occurs through the changing perception of musical aspects across the time span of the piece as the subject gathers the experience into a whole (and is thereby gathered into it), drawing relations between musical configurations and their simultaneous proximity and distance (iterations are interspersed with contrasts and appear as echoes rather than identical repetitions). In this way narrative threads become apparent and the music achieves coherence, hence the centrality of the initial motif, the structure of the phrase and the regularity of its metre, which is only ultimately revealed upon its disruption.[62]

---

[62]   Clearly, even though elements of the musical place are built into the large-scale structure, or outline of the music, it is performance and the shaping of inlines that in part

Of course, the region provided by tonality is just one among many that are held in tension within the musical place opened up by the movement. The relations held together extend beyond tonality, including musical developments more generally, such as the 'region' of Haydn's string quartets as a corpus (which are taken to be formative to the development of the genre),[63] Haydn's use of humour within his string quartets and more generally within his instrumental music.[64] More broadly still, the social, cultural and political frames which inform and mould the musical developments provide further regions. Thus, one can consider the circumstances under which music was commissioned, the sites and functions of music performance, the changing nature of the engagement with audiences as well as the evolution of the distinction between professional and amateur musicians, the role of venues and their effect on music-making and the development of programmed concerts.[65] One can then consider how these factors bear directly on the composition of Haydn's string quartets in general and on the string quartet in E-flat major, in particular.[66]

To conclude, as a 'border people' human beings are always in transition. It is only in and through transition that meaning becomes apparent. As a result, truth is an emergent and evolving property that is experienced within events rather than an unconditional proposition understood in abstraction. The case of the autobiographical consciousness reveals this to be the case, since the subject understands the significance of aspects of her life from the position of the here-and-now. I contend that something analogous occurs within the musical event, which is a border or liminal practice that gathers and holds together relations in both real and virtual time and space: the subject is taken beyond herself and, in the process, aspects of the musical environment within which the subject is situated are revealed in retrospect, accruing significance as the subject makes sense of them, and herself in relation to them, becoming emplaced – something I have made steps towards showing.

---

enables and constrains the subject's interaction with these. Thus, some musical performances will prove more effective than others.

[63]   Cliff Eisen situates Haydn's quartets within the development of string quartets as a genre ('The String Quartet', in Simon P. Keefe (ed.), *The Cambridge History of Eighteenth Century Music* (Cambridge, 2005), pp. 648–60; see also Hunter, 'The Quartets').

[64]   Scott Burnham offers a broad review of 'kinds of material manipulation' that have most often been heard as humorous in music, including 'repetition, contrast, motivic amplification, and the special treatment of returns and endings' ('Haydn and Humour', in Clark (ed.), *The Cambridge Companion to Haydn*, pp. 61–76 (p. 63); see also Hunter, 'The Quartets', pp. 122–4; Taruskin, *The Oxford History of Western Music*, vol. 2, pp. 542–55).

[65]   For a summary of these issues, see Simon McVeigh, 'Performance in the "Long Eighteenth Century": An Overview', in Colin Lawson and Robin Stowell (eds), *The Cambridge History of Musical Performance* (Cambridge, 2012), pp. 473–505.

[66]   For some of the ways in which these factors affected Haydn's quartet output, see Hunter, 'The Quartets'; see also Taruskin's overview of Haydn and his music (*The Oxford History of Western Music*, vol. 2, pp. 497–588).

Chapter 11

Music and Immanence: The 1902 'Klinger: Beethoven Exhibition' and the Vienna Secession

Diane V. Silverthorne

For though Beethoven's name and creations belong to all contemporaneous humanity and every country ... it is Austria which is best entitled to claim him as her own.[1]

Beethoven's compositions have been regarded by many as embodying the idea of music as a universal language.[2] Writing on Beethoven's late style, Martin Cooper described his music and its affect as an 'inarticulate sense of elevation and heightened awareness'. It 'speaks to quite ordinary human sensibilities in ways which are unique'.[3] The Ninth Symphony, in the words of Maynard Solomon, 'forever enlarged the sphere of human experience accessible to the creative imagination'.[4] Associations of similar profundity were attached to Beethoven by his contemporaries and widely circulated in Vienna during his lifetime as the letter written in February 1824 by a 'reverent' circle of influential figures in Vienna and admirers of Beethoven, pleading for performances of his works, reveals.[5] It suggested that Beethoven's 'universal' appeal was due to the fact that he had 'immortalised the emotions of a soul, penetrated and transfigured by the power of faith and super-terrestrial light'.[6] As his *Tagebuch* reflected, in his later years Beethoven determined to sacrifice the pursuit of human worldly happiness for his art. In 1812, he wrote 'you must not be a human being for yourself but only for others. Live only in your art'.[7]

---

[1]   See Alexander Wheelock Thayer, *Life of Beethoven*, ed. E. Forbes, vol. 2 (Princeton, NJ, 1964), p. 897.

[2]   For a consideration of Beethoven as 'the quintessential genius of Western culture' whose 'identity as an exceptional musician appears transcendent', see Tia DeNora, *Beethoven and the Construction of Genius: Musical Politics in Vienna 1792–1803* (Berkeley, Calif. and London, 1995), p. xi; see also David B. Dennis, *Beethoven in German Politics 1870–1969* (New Haven, Conn. and London, 1996), pp. 1–2; Alessandra Comini, *The Changing Image of Beethoven: A Study in Mythmaking* (New York, 1987), pp.17–18.

[3]   Martin Cooper, *Beethoven: The Last Decade* (London, 1970), pp. 3–4.

[4]   Maynard Solomon, *Late Beethoven: Music, Thought, Imagination* (Berkeley and Los Angeles, 2004), p. 1.

[5]   See Thayer, *Life of Beethoven*, vol. 2, p. 897.

[6]   Cited ibid.

[7]   Solomon, *Late Beethoven*, p. 3.

This chapter deals with a particular manifestation of Beethoven and his genius celebrated in a unique event in the annals of the Vienna Secession, the avant-garde artist group led by Gustav Klimt, which broke away from the city's only official exhibiting body (Künstlerhaus) in 1897.[8] The fourteenth exhibition of the Secession, the 'Klinger: Beethoven Exhibition' of 1902, was also named in honour of the Leipzig artist, Max Klinger, who created the central exhibit, the 'Beethoven Monument', a polychrome sculpture.[9] It was staged in the Secession exhibition pavilion designed by the architect Joseph Maria Olbrich as a synthesis of utopian ideals and modern materials in Greek-temple form.[10] In what follows, the path of 'super-terrestrial light' cast by Beethoven's 'celestial presence' is traced, firstly, through a brief account of the mythic status of Beethoven in Vienna and, secondly, through Wagner's writings and ideas, which acted as a cultural catalyst for the artistic productions of the Secession.[11] In particular, the analysis rests on Friedrich Nietzsche's *The Birth of Tragedy out of the Spirit of Music* (1872), which in its first edition was dedicated to the music and ideas of Richard Wagner.[12] In particular, I will consider Nietzsche's concept of *Schein*, which may be translated as 'semblance' or 'appearance'. Nietzsche regarded *Schein* as a manifestation of the 'golden light Apollo', and I will associate this with the artistic productions of the Vienna Secession and in particular the 1902 'Klinger: Beethoven Exhibition'.[13] It is my contention that the aesthetic and metaphysical impulses embodied in Nietzsche's notion of *Schein* were brought together and materially realised in this transcendent event, an art exhibition devoted to a musical figure, not an artist. This event arguably could only have taken place in Vienna at this particular time. As Guido Adler, Hanslick's successor at the University of Vienna, wrote in 1906, Austrian customs and its social structures were inextricably 'interwoven in the works of

---

[8]   For accounts of the unique position of the 'Klinger: Beethoven Exhibition' in the history of the Secession, see Carl E. Schorske, *Fin-de-Siècle Vienna: Politics and Culture* (New York, 1981), pp. 254–63; see also Marian Bisanz-Prakken, 'The Beethoven Exhibition of the Secession and the Younger Viennese Tradition of the Gesamtkunstwerk', in Erika Nielsen (ed.), *Focus on Vienna: Change and Continuity in Literature, Music, Art and Intellectual History*, Houston German Studies 4 (Munich, 1982), pp. 140–49; Jean-Paul Bouillon, *Klimt: Beethoven: The Frieze for the Ninth Symphony* (New York, 1987).

[9]   See Diane V. Silverthorne, 'Wagner's Gesamtkunstwerk', in Tim Shephard and Anne Leonard (eds), *The Routledge Companion to Music and Visual Culture* (New York and Oxford, 2013), pp. 246–53 (p. 251).

[10]   Leslie Topp, *Architecture and Truth in Fin-de-Siècle Vienna* (Cambridge, 2004), pp. 28–62.

[11]   The term 'celestial presence' is used here to reflect Beethoven's affinity for Romantic tropes of 'boundless space' and 'celestial imagery' (see Solomon, *Late Beethoven*, p. 53).

[12]   Friedrich Nietzsche, *The Birth of Tragedy out of the Spirit of Music*, trans. R. Speirs, in *The Birth of Tragedy and Other Writings*, ed. R. Geuss and R. Speirs (Cambridge, 1999), pp. 1–116.

[13]   Ibid., p. 20.

the classical composers of music'.[14] More than any other city in Europe, Vienna was inherently musical, and Beethoven was the most deserving of its musical figures for the accolade of 'genius'.[15]

Beethoven and Vienna

The emblematic figure of Beethoven as both suffering artist and genius, who uniquely in his deafness was deemed able to access 'the music of the spheres', held particular sway in the city of Vienna, his adopted home.[16] The term 'genius' coupled with notions of the sublime, according to DeNora, was used as early as 1893 to describe Beethoven's particular musical talents.[17] Shortly after he took up residence in Vienna, accounts of his musical genius were widely circulated through Schönfeld's 1796 *Jahrbuch*.[18] The composer had 'entered an inner sanctuary ... putting himself in the hands of our immortal Haydn to be initiated into the holy secrets of the art of music'.[19] Within a decade he was recognised as a culturally authoritative figure, his followers actively promoting the view of Beethoven as universally admired. His funeral in 1827, which was attended by many thousands of citizens, was celebrated and recorded in the art of the day.[20] Franz Grillparzer, the notable Austrian dramatist and friend of Beethoven, wrote the oration, quoting passages from Schiller's 'Ode to Joy'.[21] It was delivered at the gates of the cemetery by an actor from the Burghtheatre:

> The harp that is hushed! Let me call him so! For he was an artist, and all that was his, was his through art alone. The thorns of life had wounded him deeply ... so did he seek refuge in thine arms, O though glorious sister and peer of the Good

---

[14] For an account of the symbiotic relationship of music and society in Austria from the seventeenth century onwards, see Nicholas Cook, *The Schenker Project: Culture, Race and Music Theory in Fin-de-Siècle Vienna* (Oxford, 2007), pp. 12–15.

[15] For further views on the idea of Beethoven as genius in *fin-de-siècle* Vienna, see Stefan Zweig, *The World of Yesterday* (London, 1964), p. 162; Michael Steinberg, 'Vienna Trilogy: Vignettes from the City of Music', in Michael Steinberg and Larry Rothe, *For the Love of Music: Invitations to Listening* (Oxford, 2006), pp. 223–30 (p. 224).

[16] For the centrality of this concept in Romantic thought and culture, see Joscelyn Godwin, *Harmonies of Heaven and Earth: The Spiritual Dimensions of Music from Antiquity to the Avant-Garde* (London, 1987); Jamie James, *The Music of the Spheres: Music, Science and the Natural Order of the Universe* (New York, 1995).

[17] DeNora, *Beethoven and the Construction of Genius*, p. 85.

[18] Ibid., p. 87.

[19] Ibid.

[20] For an account of the funeral procession and estimated crowd numbers of between 10,000 and 20,000, see Thayer, *Life of Beethoven*, vol. 2, p. 1054.

[21] Ibid.

and True, balm of wounded hearts, heaven-born Art! He was an artist, and who shall rise to stand beside him?[22]

In this encomium, not one word was spoken of God. Instead Grillparzer summoned the spirit of 'heaven-born art' to bear the spirit of Beethoven, 'wounded by the thorns of life', to his last resting place.

Following his death, these mythic associations were magnified through the lens of Wagner's writings, notably through the wide dissemination of his 1870 essay 'Beethoven'.[23] Wagner championed Beethoven as a peerless musical figure, and the progenitor of Wagner's own music drama as *Gesamtkunstwerk* (total work of art). Wagner's ideas held particular sway in *fin-de-siècle* Vienna in many different manifestations in the visual arts as well as music, where they were creatively reinterpreted in the cause of the unified work of art. The Kunsthistorisches Museum was completed in 1891, the last but certainly not the least of the monumental edifices of Vienna's Ringstrasse. Like Wagner, with whom he shared ideas at the time of their flight from the Dresden revolution, its German architect, Gottfried Semper, strove to 'see beauty as a unity ... not just as a sum or a series'.[24] Semper envisioned, as Mallgrave describes, 'a *Gesamtkunstwerk* in which architectural masses became enlivened and shaped as it were by ornament, colour, and a host of painted and plastic forms'.[25] In Vienna, perhaps more than any other cultural capital in Europe, a close sibling relationship existed between the visual arts, rather than rivalry, with equal status attributed to the applied as to the fine arts, predisposing artists in all fields to Wagner's utopian ideas of the 'The Art-Work of the Future'.[26]

In eighteenth-century philosophical debates about *paragone*, the sentiment *Ut pictura poesis* ('as is poetry, so is painting') had prevailed. Beethoven styled himself as 'tone-poet' (*Tondichter*), an epithet taken up by Wagner, who cast himself in the role of Beethoven's even greater successor. From the mid-nineteenth century onwards, however, Wagner's dissemination of the ideas of Schopenhauer, which attributed a privileged place to music in the hierarchy of the arts as the embodiment of the will, and Wagner's own ideas of the *Gesamtkunstkwerk* contributed to a different orientation and hierarchy, that of

---

[22] Franz Grillparzer, 'Funeral Oration', ibid., pp. 1057–8 (p. 1057).

[23] Richard Wagner, 'Beethoven', trans. W. Ashton-Ellis, in Richard Wagner, *Actors and Singers* (Lincoln, 1995), pp. 57–126.

[24] Gottfried Semper, *Style in the Technical and Techtonic Arts, or Practical Aesthetics*, trans. H.F. Mallgrave and M. Robinson (Los Angeles, 2004), p. 72.

[25] Cited in Harry Francis Mallgrave, 'Introduction', in Gottfried Semper, *The Four Elements of Architecture and Other Writings*, trans. H.F. Mallgrave and W. Hermann (Cambridge, 1989), pp. 1–44 (p. 1).

[26] Richard Wagner, 'The Art-Work of the Future', in *Richard Wagner's Prose Works*, trans. W. Ashton-Ellis, vol. 1 (London, 1895), pp. 69–214. On notions of the *Gesamtkunstwerk* in Viennese culture, see Schorske, *Fin-de-Siècle Vienna*, pp. 63–72.

Ut pictura musica ('as is music, so is painting').[27] As Walter Pater famously declared (1873), 'all art constantly aspires to the condition of music'.[28] This dictum seemed to be the urgent impetus behind the 'Klinger: Beethoven Exhibition'.

Wagner's *Gesamtkunstwerk* acted as a rallying point for a more radical generation of visual artists and was invoked as the paradigm for the modern work of art. The *Gesamtkunstwerk* held out the promise of aesthetic unity, in the place of a sense of chaos and uncertainty which characterised society in Vienna in the immediate years before the fall of the Habsburg Empire, despite its burgeoning prosperity and seeming continuities with the past.[29] Wagner's ideas and the frequent notable performances of the *Ring of the Nibelung* at the Vienna Court Opera seem by implication to confer a halo of light, particularly golden, on the aesthetic productions of the Vienna Secession.[30] The significance of the ring, cast from the stolen gold of the Rhine maidens, symbolising unity and wholeness, on the one hand, and corruption and fragmentation, on the other, is a powerful metaphor for *fin-de-siècle* Vienna itself. As Wagner described, the fault-lines of the *Ring of the Nibelung* rested on the gods' resistance to 'eternal renewal and change of the objective world', a condition that could be ascribed to the Habsburg Empire in its final years.[31] Despite the seemingly settled and unending rule of the Habsburg family, Vienna's modernist writers, artists and composers suggested that something altogether more dissonant and disturbing lay beneath the surface of society's facade.[32]

Given Wagner's powerful support, it is perhaps surprising that Vienna was rather late in publicly commemorating Beethoven's importance to the city. The famous 1880 monument by Kaspar Clemens Zaumbusch was the result of funds raised by Liszt, who was concerned that Bonn, the city of Beethoven's birth had commemorated Beethoven's greatness rather earlier (1845) than Vienna. Beethoven stands 22 feet high, seated and glowering, a monumental superhuman. On one side of the composer, the bound Prometheus suggests suffering artist; on the other side, Nike offers her victory crown to the god-like figure who brought not fire but music to humankind. These figures suggest the opposing poles of struggle and triumph in Beethoven's musical life. Nine putti at the base represent the nine symphonies.

---

[27]   See Simon Shaw-Miller, *Visible Deeds of Music: Art and Music from Wagner to Cage* (New Haven, Conn. and London, 2000), pp. 1–35.

[28]   Walter Pater, *The Renaissance* (Mineola, NY, 2005), p. 90.

[29]   Schorske, *Fin-de-Siècle Vienna*, pp. 68–72.

[30]   For Vienna as a city of 'rings', see Simon Shaw-Miller, *Vienna 1900–1935* (London, 2008), esp. 'Art in Vienna 1900–1935', pp. 24–7.

[31]   See Richard Wagner's letter to August Röckel (1854), cited in Charles Osborne, *The Complete Operas of Richard Wagner* (London, 1990), p. 185.

[32]   For an account of these tensions below the surface, see Schorske, *Fin-de-Siècle Vienna*.

The second monument, the *Heiligenstadt* statue by sculptor Robert Weigl was erected courtesy of the Association of Male Choirs, Austria, in 1901, the year preceding the 'Klinger: Beethoven Exhibition'. Beethoven stands on top of a plinth, surrounded by a half-circle of temple-like neo-classical pillars. The figure is the man, not the god, the familiar Beethoven walking the streets of Vienna, hands clasped behind him, coat flying, caught by the wind, oblivious in his deafness to those around him. These associations, of the loneliness of the human spirit coupled with the other-worldliness which attended the composer, were reinforced by the posthumous publication of Beethoven's *Heiligenstadt Testament* (1802). 'I must live quite alone ... I must live like an outcast', he wrote, and 'my poor hearing haunted me like a ghost'.[33] Addressed to his brothers, fellowmen, and humankind, Beethoven renounced love, admitted defeat in his deafness, and yet affirmed his will to continue. By the turn of the century, the idea of Beethoven was as important in Vienna as was his music.

One further musical figure played a significant part in the embodiment of the living spirit and music of both Beethoven and Wagner in Vienna at this time. Gustav Mahler was appointed to the role of music director of the Vienna Court Opera in 1897, the same year in which Gustav Klimt broke away from the official art exhibiting body to found the Secession. Mahler conducted his first performances of Wagner's music dramas, *Lohengrin* and the *Ring of the Nibelung* in August of that year. They were ecstatically received (apart from in the anti-Semitic press which pursued him with vitriol and satire until he left for New York in 1907). If the ideas and the figure of Beethoven were mythicised in Vienna, then a spiritual shimmer seemed to surround the figure of Mahler in the eyes of his devotees during the Vienna years. He was seen by several of Vienna's music critics as the embodiment of Wagner on earth, 'a total conductor' with 'a sacred mission'.[34]

Mahler's appointment allowed him to put his Nietzschean ideals into practice, fostering cultural regeneration, as McGrath describes, 'through the mystic community of the Dionysian theatre, the rebirth of tragedy from the spirit of music'.[35] Hermann Bahr, theatre director and ardent supporter of new art, particularly the artistic productions of the Secession as the manifestation of Nietzsche's ideas, described Mahler as 'Parsifal', a holy innocent who directed the opera motivated by artistic standards alone. 'Only the boundless innocence of a man completely blind to the world, led by a holy vision, could have succeeded in conducting the Court Opera as if he were in Athens at the time of the great tragedies'.[36] Mahler dominated both the concert and opera

---

[33]   Cited in Solomon, *Late Beethoven*, p. 61.

[34]   For an account of these performances, see Henry-Louis de La Grange, *Gustav Mahler*, vol. 2: *Vienna, the Years of Challenge 1897–1904* (Oxford, 1995), pp. 2, 26–30.

[35]   William J. McGrath, *Dionysian Art and Populist Politics in Austria* (London, 1974), p. 242.

[36]   Cited ibid.

stages in Vienna from 1897, with equally notable performances of Beethoven's symphonies, controversially experimenting with new musical and spatial effects in his interpretation of the Ninth Symphony.[37] His performances of this work were described by one favourable critic as a religious experience and the audience as initiates: 'the hall was packed; the hall had been a temple, the massed audience a flock of devout, the performance a sacred ceremony'.[38] Mahler famously performed an excerpt from Beethoven's Ninth Symphony arranged for wind band on the occasion of the private opening of the 'Klinger: Beethoven Exhibition', thus fulfilling the Secession's aspirations to create an event which aspired to the ideals of Wagner's *Gesamtkunstwerk*: music, sculpture, painting and a singular, designated space devoted to an overriding musical idea.[39] These three musical figures, Beethoven, Wagner and Mahler were inextricably bound up with the realisation of this event.

Tracing the Path of *Schein*: From Wagner to Nietzsche

Wagner's writings connected his own influential ideas in 'The Art-Work of the Future' with Beethoven's music. Beethoven in his turn was inscribed in Wagner's own mythology and his powerful ideas relating to the *Gesamtkunstwerk*. Quoting Schiller and Beethoven's last movement of the Ninth Symphony, Wagner declared:

> This was the word which Beethoven set as crown upon the forehead of his tone-creation; and this word was '*Rejoice!*' With this word he cries to all men: '*This one kiss to all the world*', and *this Word* will be the language of the *Art-work of the Future*.[40]

Wagner's influential essay 'Beethoven' was written in celebration of the 100th anniversary of the composer's birth. Casting Beethoven as 'the great path-breaker in the wilderness of a paradise debased', Beethoven, the man, Wagner argued, had been ill-served by existing analysis and his Ninth Symphony misunderstood.[41] Beethoven's greatness in music was equal to that of Goethe, Schiller and Shakespeare. Like the great poets, Beethoven and his Ninth Symphony emulated the act of creation at the 'vanishing point ... exactly at the spot where creation passes from a conscious to an unconscious act', a transition from the world of realities to the noumenal realm.[42] Beethoven's great gift was to create a musical work, the Ninth Symphony, which no longer obeyed the

---

[37] De La Grange, *Gustav Mahler*, vol. 2, pp. 232–8.
[38] Ibid., p. 233.
[39] Ibid., pp. 508–15.
[40] Wagner, 'The Art-Work of the Future', p. 126: italics original.
[41] Wagner, 'Beethoven', p. 126.
[42] Ibid., p. 63.

laws of time and space. Instead Beethoven took the 'illusive surface' (*Schein*) of the visual world, and by virtue of an ingenious play with semblance 'laid bare *the Idea* (of music) concealed beneath'.[43] The synthesis of these two worlds, 'the light-world' and 'the sound-world', existed on the edge of dreams.[44] Dreams were like music, only entering the world of vision through a form of consciousness elucidated from the mind to the outside world. 'This character (of the dream world) speaks out to us most straightforwardly from the works of the Plastic arts'.[45] Reminding his readers of the significance of the origins of term in the German word for beauty, it seemed that the whole nature of aesthetic pleasure was invested in this transfigured *Schein*. Such beauty, joined to the sublime, in the form of Wagner's music drama would invoke, in the audience, a 'devotional state' (*Andacht*).[46]

The implicit sense of double-consciousness, of Wagnerian ideas overlaid on those of Beethoven, elided Romantic ideals of heroism and spiritual leadership, and of Beethoven and Wagner as modern and exciting (or disturbing, depending on the individual's views at the time).[47] These ideas, given greater momentum by Wagner's 1870 essay, it seemed, held a very present power for the spectators, as well as the designers and artists, involved in the design and construction of the exhibition. In *fin-de-siècle* Vienna, 'Beethoven' was Wagner's Beethoven.

Nietzsche's *The Birth of Tragedy* takes its stepping-off point from Wagner's tribute to Beethoven's Ninth, the greatness of which rested on a synthesis of the rational and irrational forces of poetry and music. In his encomium Nietzsche acknowledged Wagner's 'magnificent celebratory essay on Beethoven'.[48] Nietzsche's thesis was lyrically posited in his argument that great art was characterised by the essential opposing forces of the Apollonian and the Dionysian, representing the rational, on the one hand, and the transgressive and unbounded, on the other. In Attic Greece, the purest distillation of the Apollonian impulse was Greek epic poetry. Through its narrative, epic poetry assembled images of individual persons and events. Poetry was therefore closest to the art of image-creation. 'Quasi-orgiastic forms of music' exemplified the Dionysian impulse.[49]

Nietzsche described these two opposing impulses, the Apollonian as 'art of the Image-maker or sculptor [*Bildner*]' and the Dionysian as 'the imageless art of music'.[50] Nietzsche's project, following Wagner, was to instate a

---

[43]   Ibid., p. 70.

[44]   Ibid., p. 68.

[45]   Ibid., p. 70.

[46]   Ibid., p. 105.

[47]   For an account of the 'rush' experienced on hearing Beethoven's music, see Dennis, *Beethoven in German Politics*, pp. 11–12.

[48]   Nietzsche, *The Birth of Tragedy*, p. 13.

[49]   Raymond Geuss, 'Introduction', in Nietzsche, *The Birth of Tragedy and Other Writings*, pp. vii–xxx (p. xi).

[50]   Nietzsche, *The Birth of Tragedy*, p. 14.

Dionysian interpretation of art in which the 'horror' of untrammelled confusion, represented by the unbounded Dionysian urge, was masked by its other, the Apollonian image of 'intense pleasure, wisdom and beauty'.[51] The Apollonian effect creates the necessary distance to protect from the worst excesses of the Dionysian; the Dionysian impulse 'triumphs over Apollo' in the form of music.[52] The Dionysian was to be found in its most celebratory form in Beethoven's *Ode to Joy*.[53] The unmediated urges of Nietzsche's Dionysian impulse would ideally meet in the embodiment of the artist 'as imitator', an artist 'of both dream and intoxication at once'.[54]

The dream state was evoked firstly as a significant trope in Schopenhauer's *The World as Will and Representation* and later emphasised in Wagner's 'Beethoven'.[55] The dream state becomes, in Nietzsche's *Birth of Tragedy*, the persistent motif of an art formed 'out of the spirit of music': the 'dream-image' (*Gleichnischaft*), or the 'semblance of semblance'.[56] *Schein* 'defined containment (of the Will) in the forms of time and space'.[57] Music was made visible as a *'symbolic dream image'*.[58] As he declared: 'every human being is fully an artist when creating the worlds of dream. The lovely semblance of dream is the father of all the arts of image-making'.[59]

Nietzsche's expanded realm of *Schein* became a transcendent force in the visual arts, acquiring the signification of light by association with the essential Apollonian impulse in art: Apollo, 'the luminious one' (*der Scheinende*), who governs the inner world of fantasy.[60] *Schein* was reflected in the golden light of Apollo and in the glittering, light-reflective surfaces of Secession art. In a passage which seemed to prefigure Klinger's *Beethoven*, Nietzsche suggested that Apollo, the god of dream-representation would be 'as a block of marble, the statue, something very real. [The artist] when he translates this image into marble, is playing with dream.'[61] The surfaces of the *Beethoven* sculpture gleamed with polished marbles, bronze and semi-precious stones.

---

[51] Ibid., p. 17.

[52] Shaw-Miller, *Visible Deeds*, p. 43.

[53] Nietzsche, *The Birth of Tragedy*, p. 18.

[54] Ibid., p. 19.

[55] Arthur Schopenhauer, *The World as Will and Representation*, trans. E.F.J. Payne, vol. 1 (Indiana Hills, Colo., 1958).

[56] Nietzsche, *The Birth of Tragedy*, pp. 19, 26.

[57] Raymond Geuss, 'Glossary', in Nietzsche, *The Birth of Tragedy and Other Writings*, pp. 154–6 (p. 156).

[58] Ibid., p. 30: italics original.

[59] Ibid., p. 16.

[60] Ibid.

[61] Nietzsche, *The Dionysiac World View*, trans. R. Speirs, in Nietzsche, *The Birth of Tragedy and Other Writings*, pp. 119–38 (pp. 119–20).

Schein was, above all, the essential theatrical impulse in art, a term of approbation in Nietzsche's writings.[62] *Schein* in its material embodiment as light and its immanent Apollonian state mediated between the work of art and the spectator in the mysterious spaces of perception and affect. Later, in *The Genealogy of Morals*, Nietzsche affirmed the essential paradox at the core of *Schein*: 'It is no more than a moral prejudice that truth is worth more than semblance [*daß Warheit mehr wert ist als Schein*]'.[63]

The 'Klinger: Beethoven Exhibition', April to June 1902

Myth, or *mythos* as Wagner termed it, was true for all time. The 1902 'Klinger: Beethoven Exhibition' took place in the Secession building, its white walls inspired by the ancient temple at Segesta, and, in the spirit of *mythos*, three stylised gorgon heads embrace the words, 'sculpture', 'painting' and 'architecture' above the entrance, evoking the importance of the unity of the arts. The freedoms promoted by the Secession were enshrined in the emblematic statement in gold relief: 'to every age its art; to art, its freedom'. Its spectacular gold dome was of open-work laurel leaves, another suggestive reference to the Apollonian impulse, with berries in gold and verdigris. It was unseen from the interior of the building, yet illuminated by electricity at night, when it 'shimmered mysteriously'.

Inside the exhibition hall, the stated intent of the Vienna Secession artists was to renew the spiritual in art through the creation of an experience defined as 'temple art' (*Tempelkunst*).[64] Extracts from Klinger's only theoretical text, *Malerei und Zeichnung* (Painting and Drawing, 1899), in the exhibition catalogue acknowledged Wagner's *Gesamtkunstwerk* as the utopian aspiration for the exhibition.[65]

Transcending Life through Art

It is to these spaces I now turn, as the 'Klinger: Beethoven Exhibition' opens in Vienna on a spring morning in April 1902. (It was always spring in *fin-de-siècle* Vienna it seems: the words *Ver Sacrum* – Holy Spring – float in the empty space to

---

[62]   Richard H. Weisberg, 'Der Man Missing Nietzsche: *Hinzugedichtet* Revisited', in Clayton Koelb (ed.), *Nietzsche as Post-Modernist: Essays Pro and Contra* (Albany, NY, 1990), pp. 111–24 (p. 118).

[63]   Cited ibid., p.118.

[64]   Vereinigung bildender Künstler Österreichs [VBKÖ], *XIV Ausstellung der Vereinigung bildender Künstler Österreichs Secession Wien*, 'Klinger: Beethoven Exhibition' catalogue (Vienna, 1902).

[65]   Wagner's *Gesamtkunstwerk* ideas are cited ibid., p. 20; see also Max Klinger, *Painting and Drawing*, trans. F. Elliott (Birmingham, 2004).

the left of the entrance to the Secession building).[66] Readers of this account should imagine for a moment that they are amongst the thousand or so spectators who visited the exhibition every day and followed the route prescribed in the catalogue. Through the first narrow corridor, you catch glimpses of Klinger's 'Beethoven Monument' and its surrounding decorative wall art. Arriving in the 'Klimt room', you gaze upwards at the mysteries of the frieze. Depicted are a progressive series of enigmatic scenes: a knight in shining armour, ancient hags and gorgons, beasts, the mythical monster Typhoön. It is impossible not to follow the impenetrable trajectory of the frieze along three of the four walls. The belt of the eunuch-like figure is encrusted with gold and brilliant blue stones. In the final panel, the hosts of angels and Klimt's embracing lovers draw their inspiration from Beethoven's Ninth Symphony and Schiller's words 'this kiss for the whole world'. Decorated and empty spaces of the frieze construct ideas of silence, sound and duration and the passage of the spectator through space and time. Klimt's repeating, rhythmic forms are suggestive of the abstract, inwardness of musical form transposed to visual leitmotifs.[67]

We are now directed through a dark corridor, into the light of the central hall and the presence of the 'Beethoven Monument', 'the luminous one ... who reveals himself in brilliance'. The heads of white marble putti extend outwards from the surfaces of the bronze throne. The marble figure of Beethoven emanates 'a quiet interplay of force ... a symphony of colours interwoven with light'.[68] Two murals in this central sanctum, *Dawning Day* on the wall facing the monument and *Falling Night* behind, suggest an experience of time suspended. *Falling Night* forms the backdrop to the 'Beethoven Monument' and was designed by Alfred Roller, a founding artist of the Secession, later appointed as stage-designer to the Vienna Court Opera by Gustav Mahler to work on a ground-breaking new production of *Tristan und Isolde*. The mural is dominated by a recurring figural motif drawn from a hieratic engraving of a female goddess from the lid of an ancient Egyptian tomb in Vienna's Kunsthistorisches Museum. The centre of the mosaic is figured with simplified stars. The diffused light from above reflects on the marble, bronze and jewelled surfaces of the monument and catches the details of the murals which gleam with gold, mother of pearl intarsia, coloured glass and metal. Their glittering surfaces and simple, dense colours 'deflect and dilute the impact of reality', an essential impulse of the theatrical in art.[69] The repeating motifs of the mural proclaim an illusory world. As one contemporary critic noted, the audience were brought to a devotional state (*Andacht*) in the presence of Klinger's *Beethoven*.

---

[66]   *Ver Sacrum* was also the title of the Secession art periodical.

[67]   For a musical interpretation of Klimt's 'Beethoven Frieze', see Bouillon, *Klimt: Beethoven*.

[68]   Paul Kühn, *Max Klinger* (Leipzig, 1907), p. 368.

[69]   Geuss, 'Introduction', p. xx.

In conclusion, the imagery of the 1902 'Klinger: Beethoven Exhibition' was little distant from Beethoven's musical world, a part of the mythic Beethoven of Romantic aesthetics, transfigured through time and transported to another space. Starry heavens animated by a numinous power and boundless yet active space were favoured Romantic images, found in great profusion in Beethoven's works. Beethoven's 1820 lied, 'Evening Song Beneath the Starry Heaven' contains words which appear to have inspired the murals in the central hall of the exhibition: 'When the sun sinks down and night descends, so great the soul feels, and from the dust breaks free'.[70] Inside the Secession building, during the 12 weeks of the exhibition, external realities were suspended. The 'temple art' concept of the interior design was created as if for a stage-set. The audience were choreographed through a designated route, the clear intention to prepare them for the experience of Klinger's *Beethoven* through a series of theatrical devices. The audience could see the statue from the Klimt room, but could not approach it until they had completed the first part of their ritualistic passage. The glittering surfaces contribute to ambiguity and the shifting of planes between what is real and what is not, challenging the boundaries between abstraction and representation.

The 'Klinger: Beethoven Exhibition' was characterised as a profoundly important exemplar of the Wagnerian *Gesamtkunstwerk* in Secession art by the Secessionists themselves, synthesising the arts of space and time, art and music, in equal measure. As the exhibition catalogue also suggested, the audience would be 'prepared' for the experience of Klinger's *Beethoven* in the central hall through various theatrical devices that would encourage them to enjoy its 'space and peace'.[71] Certainly, its devotion to aesthetic and spiritual content in order to elevate the experience of the exhibition beyond the quotidian underlined this as an exceptional event.

In this most musical of all cities, the 1902 'Klinger: Beethoven Exhibition' appeared to exemplify the notion of *Schein*, a transcendent experience, endowed with 'the vital quivering of aesthetic beauty, an image of freedom, the promise of reconciliation' and harmony in many ways, both musical and visual.[72] In this more recent definition, Michael Spitzer characterises *Schein* as an attribute of beauty in all art, including music, and most particularly in Beethoven's late work where 'beauty and truth' are thrown into a dialectical dance.[73] These effects were achieved, it is argued here, in many different ways in the Secession exhibition, even without Mahler's musical intervention at the private view. At a tipping point between late Romanticism and early modernism, the artists of the Secession were engaged in making the inexpressible visible.

---

[70]   Solomon, *Late Beethoven*, p. 53.

[71]   VBKÖ, *XIV Ausstellung*, p. 24.

[72]   Michael Spitzer, *Music as Philosophy: Adorno and Beethoven's Late Style* (Bloomington, Ind., 2006), p. 2.

[73]   Ibid.

Chapter 12

'Where nature will speak to them in sacred sounds': Music and Transcendence in Hoffmann's *Kreisleriana*

Thomas J. Mulherin[1]

Should it not always be the case, when music as an independent art is the topic of discussion, that only instrumental music be referred to, i.e. music which, scorning all aid, all admixture of other arts (poetry), purely expresses the peculiar essence that is only recognised in it? It is the most romantic of all arts, one might almost say the only one that is genuinely romantic, since its only subject-matter is infinity. Orpheus's lyre opened the gates of Orcus. Music opens an unknown realm for man, a world that has nothing in common with the external, sensible world that surrounds him, and in which he leaves behind all determinate feelings in order to abandon himself to an inexpressible longing.[2]

Introduction

Of the countless essays written on music in the nineteenth century, few are more famous than E.T.A. Hoffmann's 'Beethovens Instrumentalmusik'.[3] Despite this

---

[1] In addition to its initial presentation at the 'Music and Transcendence' conference, this chapter was also presented at Georgetown University. I would like to thank both audiences, particularly Bruce Ellis Benson, Mary Helen Dupree, Christian Golden, Dana Matthiessen, Terry Pinkard, Yashar Saghai and Linda Wetzel, for helpful feedback. Nick Mulherin and Férdia Stone-Davis provided invaluable assistance in the final stages of writing.

[2] E.T.A. Hoffmann, 'Beethovens Instrumentalmusik', in *Sämtliche Werke*, vol. 2, pt. 1 (Frankfurt am Main, 1985), pp. 52–61 (p. 52); Eng. trans. in id., *Musical Writings*, ed. D. Charlton, trans. M. Clarke (Cambridge, 1989), pp. 96–103. While I have consulted Charlton's edition, translations of Hoffman's works are my own.

[3] Most of 'Beethovens Instrumentalmusik' derives from Hoffmann's 1810 review of the Fifth Symphony for the *Allgemeine musikalische Zeitung*, supplemented with material from his 1813 review of Beethoven's Op. 70 piano trios and a small amount of wholly new content (E.T.A. Hoffmann, 'Ludwig van Beethoven, 5. Sinfonie', in *Schriften zur Musik: Nachlese*, ed. F. Schnapp (Munich, 1963), pp. 34–52; Eng. trans. in *Musical Writings*, pp. 234–51; E.T.A. Hoffmann, 'Beethoven, Zwei Klaviertrios Op. 70', in *Schriften zur Musik*, pp. 118–45; Eng. trans. in *Musical Writings*, pp. 300–325). Despite incorporating this new material, there is little difference in the philosophical content of the original review and the revision (see Fred Lönker, 'Beethovens Instrumentalmusik: Das Erhabene und die unendliche Sehnsucht', in Gunter Saße (ed.), *E.T.A. Hoffmann: Romane und Erzählungen*

fame, the essay's influence has waned in the two centuries since its publication. This is especially true in analytic philosophy of music, where one is hard pressed to find even a passing mention of Hoffmann's work.[4] Such neglect is unsurprising, given the metaphysical character of Hoffmann's writings; proclamations that music reveals 'infinity', 'an unknown realm' and 'the realm of the mighty and immeasurable' sit uneasily with the ontological modesty characteristic of analytic philosophy of music.[5]

In this chapter, I argue that Hoffmann's metaphysical commitments are more modest than a first glance at 'Beethovens Instrumentalmusik' suggests. My argument has two steps. First, I focus on some representative metaphysical interpretations of 'Beethovens Instrumentalmusik', arguing that these readings are vitiated by a reliance on external resources at the expense of the essay's immediate context within Hoffmann's *Kreisleriana*. Second, I ask whether a metaphysical interpretation can be justified within these bounds, concluding that an emphasis on resources internal to Hoffmann's oeuvre moderates his metaphysical commitments significantly. In the final section of the essay I begin to interpret Hoffmann in this new light.

Before commencing, I want to briefly define the terrain of the chapter. I focus strictly on 'Beethovens Instrumentalmusik' and *Kreisleriana*. I neither interpret the entirety of Hoffmann's musical writings nor outline a Hoffmannian philosophy of music, as both tasks would require nothing less than a book. In addition, the term 'music' should be read throughout as short for 'absolute music', understood as music that is independent of any source of extra-musical meaning, such as text, programme, dance, dramatic action or social function.[6] Although this term did not

---

(Stuttgart, 2004), pp. 31–42 (p. 32)); for a dissenting view, see Thomas Wörtche, 'Hoffmanns Erzählungen von der Musik: Einige Distinktionen', *Mitteilungen der E.T.A Hoffmann-Gessellschaft*, 33 (1987): 13–33.

[4]   A survey of the work of some prominent analytic philosophers of music (Peter Kivy, Jenefer Robinson, Jerrold Levinson, Malcolm Budd, Stephen Davies and Roger Scruton) reveals only three references to Hoffmann. Scruton remarks upon the close connection between criticism and analysis in Hoffmann, 'Ludwig van Beethoven, 5. Sinfonie' (see Roger Scruton, *The Aesthetics of Music* (Oxford, 1997), p. 396). Kivy mentions Hoffmann twice, once dismissively and once somewhat more generously (Peter Kivy, *Music Alone: Philosophical Reflections on the Purely Musical Experience* (Ithaca, NY, 1990), pp. 166–7; id., *Authenticities: Philosophical Reflections on Musical Performance* (Ithaca, NY, 1995), p. 211).

[5]   Hoffmann, 'Beethovens Instrumentalmusik', p. 54; Eng. trans., p. 97. For some metaphysical characterisations of Hoffmann's position, see Andrew Bowie, *Music, Philosophy, and Modernity* (Cambridge, 2007), p. 143; Carl Dahlhaus, 'Romantische Musikästhetik und Wiener Klassik', in *Klassische und romantische Musikästhetik* (Laaber, 1988), pp. 86–98 (pp. 86, 94).

[6]   This is the received conception of absolute music, articulated, for example, in Peter Kivy, *Antithetical Arts: On the Ancient Quarrel between Literature and Music* (Oxford, 2009), p. 119.

exist until the middle of the nineteenth century, Hoffmann's characterisation of music as 'scorning all aid, all admixture of other arts' makes it clear that this is the conception of music of interest to him in 'Beethovens Instrumentalmusik'.[7]

Reading 'Beethovens Instrumentalmusik'

While enticing in its unabashed claim of profundity for music, the opening paragraph of 'Beethovens Instrumentalmusik' is nevertheless elusive. Only a few points are clear: (1) that the object of Hoffmann's concern is music, free of any extra-musical adjuncts; (2) that this music reveals something to its auditor; (3) that the affective correlate of this revelation is an 'inexpressible longing'.[8] These claims raise many questions. What is the extension of Hoffmann's concept of music? What are the consequences of its absoluteness? Are there any conditions on the revelation offered? Is this revelation cognitive? What is the ontological status of inexpressible longing – is it aroused by the music and hence subjective, expressed by the music and thus objective or both? Finally, what is 'the realm of the mighty and the immeasurable' that Hoffmann claims is the object of revelation?[9] I focus on this final question, as it is Hoffmann's characterisations of the object of musical revelation that do most to tempt a metaphysical interpretation of his work.

Of course, dubbing the object of musical revelation 'metaphysical' says little, given the breadth of the term's use. Recent literature on Hoffmann's musical aesthetics suggests two general possibilities for specifying Hoffmann's 'unknown realm'. On the one hand, it might be understood religiously. Thus, in Abigail Chantler's recent monograph on Hoffmann, she interprets music's revelation in a broadly Christian fashion.[10] Discussing Hoffmann's conception of music history, she writes:

> It was in accordance with Hoffmann's view of both the sacred vocal music of the Renaissance and the 'new art' evolved by Haydn, Mozart, and Beethoven – both of 'old' and 'new' church music – as music which is not merely an expression of

---

[7] Hoffmann, 'Beethovens Instrumentalmusik', p. 52; Eng. trans., p. 96. The term itself was coined in a programme by Richard Wagner (see 'Bericht über die Aufführung der neunten Symphonie von Beethoven im Jahre 1846 in Dresden (aus meinen Lebenserrinerungen ausgezogen) nebst Programm dazu', in *Gesammelte Schriften und Dichtungen*, vol. 2 (Leipzig, 1887), pp. 50–64 (p. 61)).

[8] Hoffmann, 'Beethovens Instrumentalmusik', p. 52; Eng. trans., p. 92.

[9] Ibid., p. 54; Eng. trans., p. 97.

[10] See Abigail Chantler, *E.T.A. Hoffmann's Musical Aesthetics* (Aldershot, 2006), ch. 1, esp. pp. 10–15. The precise doctrinal content of the religion is unclear and perhaps essentially underdetermined. Chantler sometimes speaks of music as expressing only the 'personal religious-philosophical convictions' of its composers (ibid., pp. 90, 108).

the Christian faith, but the basis for 'art religion', that he attributed to the secular instrumental music of composers of genius equal status as a metaphysical medium, and acknowledged the legitimacy of concert-going as a potentially spiritually elevating experience.[11]

On the other hand, as detailed by Mark Evan Bonds, the unknown realm revealed by absolute music can be interpreted as the 'ideal' of German Idealism; that is, 'a higher form of reality in a spiritual realm':[12]

> Within the idealist aesthetic, then, instrumental music remained an imprecise art, with the essential difference that listeners no longer considered this imprecision in relation to nature, language, or human emotions, but rather in relation to a higher, ideal world – to that 'wondrous realm of the infinite', to use Hoffmann's celebrated phrase.[13]

Depending on how one interprets German Idealism, this view might collapse into Chantler's; as Bonds notes, both the idealists and Hoffmann sometimes expressed themselves in religiously inflected language.[14] However, since it is neither necessary to interpret idealism in this fashion nor to take Hoffmann's own religious language seriously, Bonds's view represents a real alternative to Chantler's.[15]

Such interpretations of Hoffmann are problematic. Specifically, both the Christian and Idealist conceptions of the object of musical revelation are at odds with the position articulated in *Kreisleriana*. Their prominence can be attributed to an attractive but problematic interpretive strategy. Addressing this strategy allows a different interpretation of Hoffmann to emerge.

---

[11]   Ibid., p. 99.

[12]   Mark Evan Bonds, *Music as Thought: Listening to the Symphony in the Age of Beethoven* (Princeton, NJ, 2006), p. 12. This is an instance of what Karl Ameriks refers to as a 'positive interpretation of "idealism"', the contrast being the negative epistemological idealism of (e.g.) Berkeley (see Karl Ameriks, 'Introduction: Interpreting German Idealism', in id. (ed.), *The Cambridge Companion to German Idealism* (Cambridge, 2000), pp. 1–17 (p. 8)).

[13]   Bonds, *Music as Thought*, p. 14.

[14]   Ibid., p. 27.

[15]   On Hoffmann and religion, see n. 37, below. There is, of course, an alternative to any substantive reading of Hoffmann's essay, namely that music reveals nothing whatsoever. On this view, our experience of music is exhausted by its affective aspect (see e.g. Lönker, 'Beethovens Instrumentalmusik', p. 36). I shall not consider this view for two reasons. First, it fails to grapple with the clearly substantive claims of Hoffmann's opening paragraph. Second, it makes Hoffmann less interesting, reducing him to yet another Romantic who sees music's significance in the emotions it arouses.

Interpreting 'Beethovens Instrumentalmusik'

There are two basic strategies for establishing the metaphysical interpretations of Hoffmann adumbrated above. On the one hand, 'Beethovens Instrumentalmusik' can be approached externally, through his intellectual context. Chantler and Bonds both favour this approach, although they differ concerning which figures they take to be important for Hoffmann.[16] For Chantler, Schleiermacher and Wackenroder are the most important; Bonds emphasises German Idealism, focusing on Kant and Hegel.[17] On the other hand, Hoffmann can be interpreted internally, through the rest of his corpus. Thus Carl Dahlhaus interprets 'Beethovens Instrumentalmusik' through Hoffmann's 1814 essay 'Alte und neue Kirchenmusik'.[18] Both approaches are problematic; I begin by considering the external approach.

The external approach

In this discussion, I focus on Chantler's use of Wackenroder to elucidate Hoffmann. I do so for three reasons. First, the affinities between the two writers make this approach extremely tempting. Second, the problems afflicting this interpretation are generalisable to other versions of the external approach. Third, insofar as Chantler follows Dahlhaus and supplements her interpretation with 'Alte und neue Kirchenmusik', focusing on her work provides an easy transition to a discussion of the internal approach.[19]

It is easy to establish a reading of Hoffmann in terms of Wackenroder's *Herzensergießungen eines kunstliebenden Klosterbruders* (1797) and *Phantasien über Kunst, für Freunde der Kunst* (1799), as these works bear undeniable similarities to *Kreisleriana*.[20] Formally, both collections comprise a number of short pieces in disparate genres, including fables,[21] music criticism[22] and short treatises.[23] Additionally, both works employ fictional narrators. The central pieces

---

[16]   Ian Bent offers a third version of this approach (see 'Plato–Beethoven: A Hermeneutics for Nineteenth-Century Music?', in Ian Bent (ed.), *Music Theory in the Age of Romanticism* (Cambridge, 1996), pp. 105–24).

[17]   Chantler, *E.T.A. Hoffmann's Musical Aesthetics*, ch. 1; Bonds, *Music as Thought*, pp. 5–28.

[18]   E.T.A. Hoffman, 'Alte und neue Kirchenmusik', in *Schriften zur Musik*, pp. 209–36; Eng. trans. in *Musical Writings*, pp. 351–76; see Carl Dahlhaus, *Die Idee der absoluten Musik* (Kassel: 1978), ch. 3.

[19]   See Chantler, *E.T.A. Hoffmann's Musical Aesthetics*, ch. 4.

[20]   W.H. Wackenroder, *Werke and Briefe* (Heidelberg, 1967). David Charlton also connects Hoffmann and Wackenroder (Charlton, in Hoffmann, *Musical Writings*, pp. 12–14, 42–6).

[21]   W.H. Wackenroder, 'Ein wunderbares morgenländisches Märchen von einem nackten Heiligen', in *Werke und Briefe*, pp. 197–202.

[22]   Hoffmann, 'Beethovens Instrumentalmusik'.

[23]   Wackenroder, 'Das eigentümliche innere Wesen der Tonkunst', in *Werke und Briefe*, pp. 218–28.

in Wackenroder's collections are written in the voice of the *Kapellmeister* Joseph Berglinger, the majority of the pieces in *Kreisleriana* in that of Hoffmann's own *Kapellmeister*, Johannes Kreisler.[24]

Thematically, both writers believe the realm revealed by music to be superior to the workaday world: for both Berglinger and Kreisler, music offers a vision of a world void of the 'empty, earthly trivialities'[25] and 'worthless banalities that follow and pester human beings … in this miserable life like poisonous pricking vermin'.[26] Moreover, Wackenroder and Hoffmann both emphasise the role of feeling in musical experience. In Wackenroder's most extensive theoretical piece on instrumental music, he insists that music speaks to us strictly through feeling: 'Whoever wants to discover, with the divining rod of investigating reason, that which only allows itself to be felt by his heart [*von innen*], will discover only thoughts about feeling and not feeling itself'.[27] Though Hoffmann demurs from Wackenroder's repudiation of reason, assigning it an important role in 'Beethovens Instrumentalmusik' (more on which below), feeling nonetheless remains a significant part of musical experience. Indeed, Hoffmann indicates that the infinite longing typical of musical experience is a condition of music's 'intimation of the infinite': this is clearest in his description of the experience of Mozart's music, in which an 'endless longing' accompanies our approach toward the ghostly figures revealed thereby.[28]

Despite the suggestiveness of these similarities, the connection between Hoffmann and Wackenroder is underdetermined. As Chantler herself acknowledges, there is no empirical evidence connecting them: Hoffmann never mentions Wackenroder explicitly in *Kreisleriana*, and there is no biographical evidence indicating any

---

[24] W.H. Wackenroder, 'Das merkwürdige musikalische Leben des Tonkünstlers Joseph Berglinger', in *Werke und Briefe*, pp. 111–31; id., 'Fragment aus einem Briefe Joseph Berglingers', in *Werke und Briefe*, pp. 215–17; id., 'Ein Brief Joseph Berglingers', in *Werke und Briefe*, pp. 229–33. On the complexity of authorship in *Kreisleriana*, see Charlton, in Hoffmann, *Musical Writings*, pp. 25–7; Wörtche, 'Hoffmanns Erzählungen von der Musik', pp. 29–30.

[25] Wackenroder, 'Das merkwürdige musikalische Leben', p. 114.

[26] E.T.A. Hoffmann, 'Ombra adorata', in *Sämtliche Werke*, vol. 2, pt. 1, pp. 41–5 (p. 42); Eng. trans. in *Musical Writings*, pp. 88–91 (p. 88). Hoffmann's description of attending a concert here deserves careful comparison with the description in Wackenroder's 'Das merkwürdige musikalische Leben'.

[27] Wackenroder, 'Das eigentümliche innere Wesen der Tonkunst', pp. 221–2. In this essay, Wackenroder backs away from his religious conception of music's revelation, interpreting the object of musical experience as 'a dream vision of every manifold human affect' in a 'mad, pantomimic dance' (ibid., p. 227).

[28] Hoffmann, 'Beethovens Instrumentalmusik', p. 53; Eng. trans., p. 97. On the differences and similarities between the music of Mozart, Haydn and Beethoven in Hoffmann's writings, see Lönker, 'Beethovens Instrumentalmusik', pp. 34–6.

familiarity with Wackenroder on Hoffmann's part.[29] Parallel difficulties confront other attempts at external interpretations of Hoffmann. Thus, Bonds admits that there is only circumstantial evidence suggesting an acquaintance with Hegel's work, and both Chantler and Bent concede that although Hoffmann knew Schleiermacher personally, there is no proof that Hoffmann knew Schleiermacher's hermeneutics.[30]

In response, one might suggest that documentary evidence is not required in this context, that the ideas of Wackenroder, Hegel and Schleiermacher were simply in the air at the time.[31] I do not deny this claim or the possibility that any or all of these thinkers influenced Hoffmann. My point is more modest and concerns the prominence of these thinkers for the interpretation of Hoffmann. There is solid evidence for Hoffmann's reading, both in general and while he was working on *Kreisleriana*.[32] Moreover, as I demonstrate below, *Kreisleriana* provides indications of its own concerning its interpretation. I reserve a discussion of both such directives and Hoffmann's reading list for the following section of this chapter; here I only claim that interpretations of Hoffmann relying upon sources such as those emphasised by Chantler and Bonds should be undertaken after, and in deference to, a careful consideration of the documented sources and the text itself.

The internal approach

As previously mentioned, Chantler bolsters her religious reading of Hoffmann with a discussion of his 'Alte und neue Kirchenmusik'. This tactic suggests an alternative, internal approach to Hoffmann's musical aesthetics, grounded in materials found elsewhere in his work.[33] 'Alte und neue Kirchenmusik' is a particularly promising resource for Chantler, as it suggests that Hoffmann understands music's revelation in religious terms. Here Hoffmann claims that in music 'the intimation of the highest and holiest, the spiritual power, which ignites the vital spark in the entirety of nature, speaks out audibly in tones', concluding that music is essentially 'religious worship'.[34]

---

[29]   Chantler, *E.T.A. Hoffmann's Musical Aesthetics*, pp. ix–x. Charlton believes that the connection can be drawn through Hoffmann's friends Zacharias Werner, an aficionado of the *Frühromantiker*, and Julius Eduard Hitzig, a mutual friend of Werner and Hoffmann (in Hoffmann, *Musical Writings*, p. 42 n. 48). This is suggestive, at best.

[30]   See Bonds, *Music as Thought*, p. 136 n. 30; Bent, 'Plato-Beethoven', pp. 119–24; Chantler, *E.T.A. Hoffmann's Musical Aesthetics*, pp. ix–x, x n. 8.

[31]   I thank Bruce Ellis Benson for insisting on this point.

[32]   Among other resources, we have Hoffmann's letters (E.T.A. Hoffmann, *Briefwechsel*, 3 vols (Munich, 1967–69)) and a list of works that he is known to have read (E.T.A. Hoffmann, *Werke*, 2nd edn, vol. 15 (Berlin, [1927])).

[33]   Chantler, *E.T.A. Hoffmann's Musical Aesthetics*, ch. 4.

[34]   Hoffmann, 'Alte und neue Kirchenmusik', p. 212; Eng. trans., p. 355. Compare Hoffmann's claim that Church music is 'music in the most profound meaning of its specific essence' (ibid., p. 211; Eng. trans., p. 355).

'Alte und neue Kirchenmusik' may represent Hoffmann's considered conception of music. However, there are three reasons not to rely upon it in deciphering 'Beethovens Instrumentalmusik': (1) the material at the core of 'Beethovens Instrumentalmusik' stems from a review drafted in 1809–10, and it was not until July of 1814, well after even the February 1813 completion of 'Beethovens Instrumentalmusik', that he finally wrote 'Alte und neue Kirchenmusik';[35] (2) 'Beethovens Instrumentalmusik' is part of a sequence of writings by the fictional Johannes Kreisler, whose very presence renders problematic the assumption that any given work of Hoffmann's can illuminate this essay;[36] and (3) Chantler's Christian interpretation of Hoffmann is undermined by 'Beethovens Instrumentalmusik' itself. Hoffmann only uses religious language twice in this essay, at one point comparing the 'naive cheerfulness [*kindlichen heitern Gemüts*]' of Haydn's music to prelapsarian innocence and later claiming that music is the only medium capable of revealing the infinite, that 'the dance of the priests of Isis can only be a highly jubilant hymn'.[37]

Of course, none of this implies that all internal approaches to Hoffmann are problematic. In the following section, I argue for an internal approach to 'Beethovens Instrumentalmusik' that relies upon the essay's context in *Kreisleriana*. One result of this reading is that Hoffmann's reference to the priests of Isis is far from accidental.

Grounding 'Beethovens Instrumentalmusik'

Kreisleriana, itself part of Hoffmann's four-volume *Fantasiestücke in Callots Manier* (1814–15), was published in two parts.[38] The first part, which includes 'Beethovens Instrumentalmusik', comprises six pieces and appeared in 1814 in the first volume of the *Fantasiestücke*. The remaining seven pieces of the sequence appeared the following year in the final volume. Together, the two parts of *Kreisleriana* form a *Künstlerroman* chronicling Kreisler's development into

---

[35] For the date of Hoffmann's review of the Fifth Symphony, see Charlton, in Hoffmann, *Musical Writings*, pp. 60, 234. The material on Beethoven's Op. 70 trios dates to 1813 (ibid., pp. 60, 300–301). On 'Alte und Neue Kirchenmusik' and 'Beethovens Instrumentalmusik', see ibid., pp. 351–3, 54.

[36] See n. 24 above on the issue of authorship in *Kreisleriana*. The close connection between Hoffmann's reviews of Beethoven and 'Beethovens Instrumentalmusik' permits an exception to this rule of thumb.

[37] Hoffmann, 'Beethovens Instrumentalmusik', pp. 53, 60; Eng. trans., pp. 97, 102. There is disagreement concerning Hoffmann's religious beliefs. Charlton says that Hoffmann never 'expresses himself in terms implying religious belief' while Kenneth Negus says that Hoffmann was a Christian (see Charlton, in Hoffmann, *Musical Writings*, p. 32; Kenneth Negus, *E.T.A. Hoffmann's Other World: The Romantic Author and His 'New' Mythology* (Philadelphia, 1965), pp. 36–7).

[38] For an extensive discussion of *Kreisleriana*'s publication history, see Charlton, in Hoffmann, *Musical Writings*, pp. 51–5.

a fully fledged composer.[39] This suggests that each piece in the sequence refines positions presented by its antecedents and hence that a proper understanding of 'Beethovens Instrumentalmusik' relies upon its relationship to the prior pieces in the sequence. How do these pieces, particularly 'Ombra adorata' and 'Gedanken über den hohen Wert der Musik', conceive of the unknown realm revealed by music?[40]

In 'Ombra adorata', Hoffmann's description of the world revealed by music is not only decidedly metaphysical, but also religiously inflected.[41] Thus Kreisler says that the ritornello preceding the aria speaks 'in simple yet deeply affecting tones of the longing in which the pious mind soars to heaven', that the following recitative provides a 'heavenly balm' for his ailments and that the aria itself is expressive 'of the state of mind that soars above earthly pain in the blessed hope of soon seeing everything promised to it fulfilled in a higher, better world', providing an experience akin to 'the jubilant exultation of transfigured spirits'.[42] This doctrinally indeterminate Christian character also pervades the essay's opening encomium, in which Kreisler lauds music as 'an utterly miraculous thing' that transports listeners 'from the oppressive torments of earthly existence' into a 'new, transfigured life'.[43] As the passage continues, Kreisler anticipates the opening of 'Beethovens Instrumentalmusik', claiming that music allows its listeners to 'speak the language of that unknown, romantic spirit-realm' and experience an 'infinite, unnameable longing'.[44] The confluence here of the Christian language of 'Ombra adorata' and the more Romantic terminology of 'Beethovens Instrumentalmusik' encourages the thought that the key to Hoffmann's unknown realm is found in this piece.

Although this characteristically Romantic language persists in the following essay, 'Gedanken über den hohen Wert der Musik', it loses its religious inflection.[45] Unlike 'Ombra adorata', it is not a panegyric but a satire written in the voice of Hoffmann's bourgeois contemporaries, for whom music is merely a pleasant

---

[39]   Charlton makes a similar claim, but treats *Kreisleriana* as a *Bildungsroman* instead of a *Künstlerroman* (in Hoffmann, *Musical Writings*, pp. 27–30 (esp. p. 28)). I thank Mary Helen Dupree for impressing the importance of this distinction upon me.

[40]   Since the opening piece of *Kreisleriana*, 'Johannes Kreisler's, des Kappelmeisters musikalische Leiden' (*Sämtliche Werke*, vol. 2, pt. 1, pp. 34–41; Eng. trans. in *Musical Writings*, pp. 81–7), is silent on this matter, I shall set it aside. Note also that the linear conception of the *Künstlerroman* that I assume here can be challenged (see Michael Minden, *The German* Bildungsroman (Cambridge, 1997)).

[41]   Hoffmann, 'Ombra adorata', p. 43; Eng. trans., p. 89.

[42]   Ibid., pp. 43–4; Eng. trans., p. 89.

[43]   Ibid., pp. 41–2; Eng. trans., p. 88.

[44]   Ibid.

[45]   Hoffmann, 'Gedanken über den hohen Wert der Musik', in *Sämtliche Werke*, vol. 2, pt. 1, pp. 45–52; Eng. trans. in *Musical Writings*, 91–6. The sole exception is a reference to the 'divine spark' of genius late in the essay (see ibid., p. 50; Eng. trans., p. 95).

diversion and social lubricant.[46] In it, Kreisler mocks the 'insanity' that grips musicians, who

> think, for instance, that art gives men an intuition of their ideal [*sein höheres Prinzip*], and that it will lead them from the futile hurly-burly of everyday life into the Temple of Isis, where nature will speak to them in sacred sounds, sounds which have never been heard and yet are immediately comprehensible. ... They call it the most romantic of all the arts since its only subject-matter is infinity, the mysterious Sanskrit of nature, enunciated in tones that fill the human breast with infinite yearning, and only through it may they understand the sublime song of – trees, flowers, animals, stones, water![47]

In restricting music's content to 'infinity' and averring to the 'infinite yearning' fostered by musical experience, Kreisler once again anticipates 'Beethovens Instrumentalmusik'. However, insofar as the essay's ironic tone encourages the reader to entertain the views that Kreisler rejects, this essay suggests that the realm revealed by music is not heaven but nature.[48] Which conception of the object of musical revelation is correct? Examining these essays in the light of 'Beethovens Instrumentalmusik' suggests the view that music reveals nature rather than heaven. To establish this, I will show both that the naturalistic view of 'Gedanken' should be taken seriously and that the religious view expressed by Kreisler in 'Ombra adorata' is inadequate. I begin with the latter task.

While it is obvious that 'Gedanken' is intended to be read ironically, matters are not so clear concerning 'Ombra adorata'. When it is read with 'Beethovens Instrumentalmusik' in mind, however, it becomes apparent that 'Ombra adorata', like 'Gedanken', is not to be taken at face value. Consider its opening sentence: 'What an utterly miraculous thing is music; how little can men fathom its deeper mysteries!'[49] This is a clear expression of the Romantic thesis that music lies beyond the ken of reason, a thesis reinforced by the immediacy of the aria's effects upon Kreisler later in the piece. The beginning of the ritornello tears Kreisler from his distraction, and he exclaims: 'How the pain that gnawed at my insides dissolved into wistful longing, which poured heavenly balm into all wounds. – Everything was forgotten and I simply listened, in rapture, to the tones, which consolingly surrounded me, as if descending from another world'.[50] Unfortunately for the metaphysical theorist, both the Romantic thesis of incomprehensibility and the corresponding commitment to immediacy are

---

[46]   Ibid., pp. 47–8; Eng. trans., pp. 92–3.
[47]   Ibid., p. 49; Eng. trans., p. 94.
[48]   To ensure that Kreisler's position is not misunderstood, Hoffmann ends 'Gedanken' by having Kreisler fret that 'much of what has been so honestly meant could well appear as terrible irony' (ibid., p. 51; Eng. trans., p. 95).
[49]   Hoffmann, 'Ombra adorata', p. 41; Eng. trans., p. 88.
[50]   Ibid., p. 43; Eng. trans., p. 89.

belied by the text of 'Beethovens Instrumentalmusik', the fundamental purpose of which is to defend Beethoven against the charge of incomprehensibility.[51]

This defence begins in the middle of the essay, where Kreisler attacks the 'wise judges' of the musical establishment. These critics admit that Beethoven is gifted with a 'very lively imagination', but complain that he does not restrain it, consequently producing musical chaos.[52] Kreisler retorts:

> But what if it is only that the inner coherence of every Beethoven composition escapes *your* weak insight? What if it only lies with *you* that you do not understand the master's language, which is clear to the initiated, if it is only to you that the portal of the innermost sanctum remains closed?[53]

The truth of the matter is that Beethoven, far from lacking control over his material, rules over it 'as its absolute lord', a fact which 'unfolds itself to a very deep investigation of [his] instrumental music'.[54]

Hoffmann's original review makes the case for this claim more thoroughly than 'Beethovens Instrumentalmusik', as the musical literacy of the *Allgemeine musikalische Zeitung*'s readership permitted the use of musical examples in a manner inappropriate for *Kreisleriana*'s lay audience.[55] Nevertheless, the shape of Hoffmann's case is clear enough:

> According to the inner direction of the movements, their working-out, their instrumentation, the way in which they are ordered with regard to one another, everything works toward one point; but it is particularly the inner relationship of the themes to one another which produces that unity, which alone makes the listener capable to maintain *one* mood.[56]

The 'one mood' referred to here is clearly the endless longing mentioned throughout 'Beethovens Instrumentalmusik'. Therefore, Hoffmann is saying that this longing depends upon the listener's recognition of the symphony's coherence. This, in turn, depends upon a 'deep investigation' of the work. Since the wise judges have not undertaken such an investigation, they do not recognise this coherence and, accordingly, do not experience this longing.

---

[51]   Bonds argues that Hoffman's characterisation of contemporary reception of Beethoven is overstated, although he also provides examples of the kind of complaints that Hoffmann might have had in mind (*Music as Thought*, pp. 9, 53).

[52]   Hoffmann, 'Beethovens Instrumentalmusik', pp. 54–5; Eng. trans., p. 98.

[53]   Ibid., p. 55; Eng. trans., p. 98: italics original. This passage was added when Hoffmann revised his original review for *Kreisleriana*.

[54]   Ibid.

[55]   See Hoffmann, 'Ludwig van Beethoven', pp. 37–50; Eng. trans., pp. 239–50.

[56]   Hoffmann, 'Beethovens Instrumentalmusik', p. 57; Eng. trans., p. 100: italics original.

Given the relationship between longing and revelation, this means that Beethoven's critics do not experience music's revelation. In short, an analytic comprehension of Beethoven's music is a necessary condition for disclosing the realm of the mighty and the immeasurable, and the position advanced in the opening paragraph of 'Ombra adorata' becomes unsatisfactory. Far from being unfathomable, music's deepest mysteries must be parsed if the listener is to experience music's revelation. This fits nicely with *Kreisleriana*'s status as a *Künstlerroman*: Kreisler's commitment to the incomprehensibility of music and hence the immediacy of music's effects in 'Ombra adorata' is explicitly overturned by 'Beethovens Instrumentalmusik'.[57]

The claim that the transcendent realm revealed by music is properly characterised in religious terms is suspect for other reasons as well. Most importantly, whenever Hoffmann connects religious imagery and transcendence in *Kreisleriana*, he does so in the context of vocal rather than absolute music. This is true not only in 'Ombra adorata' but also in the opening essay of *Kreisleriana*, where Amalie's singing is described as 'carry[ing] [Kreisler] into heaven' acting as a 'heavenly balm' to soothe the wounds left by Kreisler's day job as a schoolmaster.[58] Combined with Hoffmann's clear restriction of the claims advanced in 'Beethovens Instrumentalmusik' to the domain of absolute music, this consistent association of religious imagery with vocal music casts further doubt on the religious interpretation of the object of musical revelation. What music does with and without the 'admixture of other arts' may well be different.[59]

There are also positive reasons to favour the view expressed in 'Gedanken'. First, the imagery in 'Beethovens Instrumentalmusik' echoes the central figure of 'Gedanken'. In the latter, to experience music's revelation is to enter the Temple of Isis, the Egyptian nature goddess.[60] In 'Beethovens Instrumentalmusik', Kreisler's denial that the Fifth Symphony's meaning can be discursively expressed is framed in his declaration that 'the dance of the priests of Isis can only be a highly jubilant hymn'.[61] This imagery recurs in *Kreisleriana*'s conclusion, where Kreisler's entry into the Temple of Isis marks the completion

---

[57]   This reading might seem to be contradicted by Kreisler's discussion of the Fifth Symphony in the second paragraph of 'Ombra adorata'. Here he says that hearing this symphony could carry him off to 'the realm of the mighty, the unmeasurable', thus suggesting that Kreisler is not the proponent of immediacy that he appears to be. This contradiction is only apparent. The possibility of revelation may be accounted for by positing an untutored capacity for analytic listening in Kreisler, one that only becomes explicit later in his musical development. See Hoffmann, 'Ombra adorata', pp. 42–3; Eng. trans., p. 88.

[58]   Hoffmann, 'Johannes Kreisler's', p. 40; Eng. trans., pp. 87, 86; cf. Hoffmann's introduction to the second part of *Kreisleriana* (*Sämtliche Werke*, vol. 2, pt. 1, pp. 360–61; Eng. trans., pp. 123–4).

[59]   Hoffmann, 'Beethovens Instrumentalmusik', p. 52; Eng. trans., p. 96.

[60]   Hoffmann, 'Gedanken', p. 49; Eng. trans., p. 94.

[61]   Hoffmann, 'Beethovens Instrumentalmusik', p. 60; Eng. trans., p. 102.

of his apprenticeship.[62] This final recurrence is especially significant, as here the reader also learns that to be a composer is to take one's 'recognition and comprehension of the secret music of nature' and 'hold it spellbound in symbols and script'.[63] Far from '[daring] to speak of the things of heaven',[64] music is revealed as 'the universal language of nature, which speaks to us in wonderful echoes, full of mystery'.[65] These connections between the Temple of Isis and musical experience, the temple's position as the terminus of Kreisler's apprenticeship and the idea that music is a language of nature cement the view that nature is the object of music's revelation.

Hoffmann's biography reinforces this preference for the naturalistic conception of his unknown realm. For some readers, the notion that nature is a cipher to be decoded calls to mind the opening pages of Novalis's fragmentary contribution to Romantic *Naturphilosophie*, *Die Lehrlinge zu Sais*.[66] Unlike the philosophical and literary works relied upon by Chantler and Bonds, this text can be connected to *Kreisleriana*: at the end of 'Der Musikfeind', the narrator mentions that he has requested a copy of Novalis's book because Kreisler has compared him to one of the titular novices.[67] Hoffmann also possessed a broad familiarity with *Naturphilosophie*: in addition to Novalis's posthumous novella, Hoffmann is known to have read two of Schelling's three efforts in *Naturphilosophie* (*Ideen zu einer Philosophie der Natur* and *Von der Weltseele*) as well as the work of G.H. Schubert and J.W. Ritter.[68]

---

[62]   Hoffmann, 'Johannes Kreislers Lehrbrief', in *Sämtliche Werke*, vol. 2, pt. 1, pp. 447–55 (p. 454); Eng. trans. in *Musical Writings*, pp. 159–65 (p. 165).

[63]   Ibid., p. 453; Eng. trans., p. 164.

[64]   W.H. Wackenroder, 'Von den verschiedenen Gattungen in jeder Kunst, und insbesondere von verschiedenen Arten der Kirchenmusik', in *Werke und Briefe*, pp. 209–14 (p. 212).

[65]   Hoffmann, 'Johannes Kreislers Lehrbrief', p. 454; Eng. trans., p. 165.

[66]   Novalis, *Die Lehrlinge zu Sais*, in *Werke, Tagebücher, und Briefe Friedrich von Hardenbergs*, ed. Hans-Joachim Mähl and Richard Samuel, vol. 1 (Munich, 1978), pp. 199–236. Novalis deploys the image of a cipher on p. 201.

[67]   E.T.A. Hoffmann, 'Der Musikfeind', in *Sämtliche Werke*, vol. 2, pt. 1, pp. 428–38 (p. 438); Eng. trans. in *Musical Writings*, pp. 144–51 (p. 151). On Hoffmann, Novalis, and *Kreisleriana*, see Negus, *E.T.A. Hoffmann's Other World*, p. 22; Charlton, in Hoffmann, *Musical Writings*, pp. 6–7, 27–30.

[68]   F.W.J. Schelling, *Ideen zu einer Philosophie der Natur* and *Von der Weltseele*, in *Werke*, vol. 1 (Leipzig, 1907), pp. 99–439, 443–679. Hoffmann's familiarity with Schelling is noted in Negus, *E.T.A. Hoffmann's Other World*, p. 20; Charlton, in Hoffmann, *Musical Writings*, p. 32. Concerning Hoffmann and *Naturphilosophie*, see Jürgen Barkhoff, 'Romantische Naturphilosophie', in Detlef Kremer (ed.), *E.T.A. Hoffmann. Leben – Werk – Wirkung*, 2nd expanded edn (Berlin, 2010), pp. 71–5; Charlton, in Hoffmann, *Musical Writings*, pp. 33–5. Barkhoff emphasises Schubert; Charlton also discusses Ritter.

Mediating Music and Nature

I cannot undertake a thorough explication of the claim that music reveals the natural world here: not only is Hoffmann's concept of nature underdetermined, but space does not permit an extensive exegesis of Romantic *Naturphilosophie*. Instead, I consider two possible elaborations of the naturalistic conception of musical revelation as well as some restrictions upon any version of this view.

Any theory that attributes content to music must answer two questions. The first asks how listeners come to experience music as having this meaning. Hoffmann's answer to this question relies upon his account of endless longing as both the condition for music's revelation and the result of the analytic musical understanding modelled in that piece. The second question asks why the musical listener is justified in hearing music as having this meaning. In the present context, this amounts to asking what legitimates hearing nature in music. The easiest way to answer this question is in terms of the mediation of music and nature. Two candidates present themselves: matter and form.

David Charlton suggests the possibility that a shared matter mediates music and nature in the introduction to his translation of *Kreisleriana*: 'The Romantic musician ... not only "reads", but "hears" nature; just as the element of sound (vibration) is essential to nature, so music is its natural Romantic medium of expression.'[69] Charlton's thought is that music reveals nature because it exploits one of nature's essential characteristics.[70]

The primary difficulty with this view is interpretive, as can be seen when it is compared to a passage from 'Johannes Kreislers Lehrbrief'. Here, the narrator, perhaps Hoffmann himself, says:[71]

> Sound dwells in all things, but tones, that is to say melodies, which speak the higher language of the realm of spirits, reside only in the breast of humanity. But doesn't the spirit of music, like the spirit of sound, penetrate the entirety of nature? The mechanically excited sounding body, thus brought to life, articulates its existence [*Dasein*], or, rather, its inner organism steps forward into [human] consciousness. And isn't it as though the spirit of music, excited by the initiated,

---

[69]   Charlton, in Hoffmann, *Musical Writings*, p. 34.

[70]   Charlton traces this view to Ritter's *Fragmente aus dem Nachlasse eines jungen Physikers*; Charlton, in Hoffmann, *Musical Writings*, p. 34. Herder's *Kalligone* is another possible antecedent, see J.G. Herder, *Kalligone*, in *Werke*, ed. H.D. Irmscher, vol. 8 (Frankfurt am Main, 1998), pp. 641–964 (pp. 810–24). Michael N. Forster criticises *Kalligone*'s account of music in 'Hegel and Some (Near-)Contemporaries: Narrow or Broad Expressivism?', in *German Philosophy of Language* (Oxford, 2011), pp. 178–218 (p. 203 n. 29); a more positive response can be found in Bonds, *Music as Thought*, p. 25.

[71]   Concerning the identity of the narrator in this piece, see Charlton, in Hoffmann, *Musical Writings*, pp. 27, 73.

likewise speaks out melodically and harmonically in secret echoes that are only audible to those initiates?[72]

In holding that the musical expression of nature depends upon music's exploitation of sound qua an essential possibility of nature, Charlton's position requires that the matter of music be identical with sound. Hoffmann denies this, claiming that tones 'reside only in the breast of humanity'. While sound is a natural phenomenon, music is an intentional object. Hoffmann is an idealist about music, and the remainder of the passage reinforces this interpretation.[73] While Hoffmann's claim that the 'spirits' of sound and music 'penetrate the entirety of nature' seems to reopen the possibility that music and nature share a common material, this view founders with a closer look at the passage. The spirit of sound emerges whenever a body is struck and begins to vibrate, thereby communicating its essence immediately to listeners. The spirit of music, in contrast, must be activated intentionally and received actively: it emerges only at the behest and in collaboration with the initiated (presumably composers).

Moreover, the view that music and nature are mediated by matter is inconsistent with the rest of 'Beethovens Instrumentalmusik'. As noted above, Hoffmann's primary aim is defending Beethoven against the charge of incoherence, which he does by providing a thematic analysis of the Fifth Symphony. This analysis is in turn the condition of arousing endless longing and therefore music's revelation. In other words, musical experience is, for Hoffmann, a fundamentally cognitive affair. Insofar as the communication of vibrations is passive, views like Charlton's overlook the cognitive aspect of Hoffmann's position. Given how fundamental analysis is to Hoffmann's view, this is a costly way to establish the legitimacy of hearing nature in music.

A more promising possibility is that music and nature are linked not by their matter but by their form. Two passages in 'Beethovens Instrumentalmusik' offer a basis for developing this thought. The first passage asserts the coherence of Beethoven's work:

> Aesthetic dilettantes [*Meßkünstler*] have often complained about the total lack of inner unity and coherence in Shakespeare, while to a deeper gaze a beautiful tree, leaves, petals, and fruit blossom [*treibend erwächst*] from a seed; so it is that the high level of rational awareness [*Besonnenheit*], which is inseparable

---

[72]   Hoffmann, 'Johannes Kreisler's Lehrbrief', pp. 453; Eng. trans., pp. 163–4.
[73]   On the difference between sound and music, see Scruton, *The Aesthetics of Music*, pp. 1–96. Adorno also denies, albeit for different reasons, that music's matter is sound (see Theodor Adorno, *Philosophie der neuen Musik* (Frankfurt am Main, 1975), pp. 38–42).

from true genius and nourished by the study of the art, unfolds itself to a very deep investigation of Beethoven's instrumental music.[74]

The second passage explains this coherence and thus substantiates this assertion:

> How simple – let it be said once again – is the theme that the master has laid at the basis of the whole, but how wonderfully do every secondary theme and transition join themselves to it through their rhythmic character, such that they only serve to unfold, increasingly, the character of the Allegro, which is only intimated by this basic theme.[75]

Combining the imagery from the first passage with the analytic comments in the second yields a conception of musical form modelled on the development of an individual natural organism: just as the development of the organism is governed by a form to be achieved, so the development of musical works is governed by a single theme that mediates all individual events.[76] Although such a model of musical form may apply to the Allegro of Beethoven's Fifth Symphony, it is inadequate as both a general theory of musical form and as an account of Hoffmann.

The former point is straightforward: musical unity does not require, though it may be fostered by, the presence of a single governing theme. Such an account may suffice, as Hoffmann implies, for Beethoven's Fifth Symphony, but it cannot be applied to many other multi-movement works.[77] Moreover, the suggestion that Hoffmann articulates a general concept of musical form misses one of his fundamental innovations. Unlike his predecessors, Hoffmann writes about specific pieces of music rather than music *simpliciter*.[78] As such, a reader should take care in drawing any general conclusions from the analysis presented in 'Beethovens Instrumentalmusik'. (I do not deny that some general claims can be extracted from the essay, such as that endless longing depends upon musical

---

[74] Hoffmann, 'Beethovens Instrumentalmusik', p. 55; Eng. trans., p. 98. The translation of *Meßkünstler* (surveyor) as 'dilettante' is admittedly free. I have chosen it to reflect Hoffmann's belief that those who complain about the incoherence of Beethoven and Shakespeare have only engaged with the surface of their works. Charlton's 'overseer' reflects the fact that these critics represent the musical establishment, but fails to capture the polemical nature of Hoffmann's epithet.

[75] Hoffmann, 'Beethovens Instrumentalmusik', p. 56; Eng. trans., p. 99.

[76] For the background to Hoffmann's organicism, see Chantler, *E.T.A. Hoffmann's Musical Aesthetics*, pp. 67–73; on organicism in music generally, see Ruth Solie, 'The Living Work: Organicism and Musical Analysis', *19th-Century Music*, 4/2 (1980): 147–56.

[77] For intimations of this large-scale unity, see Hoffmann, 'Ludwig van Beethoven', pp. 45–6, 49; Eng. trans., pp. 246, 250.

[78] See Dahlhaus, 'Romantische Musikästhetik und Wiener Klassik', pp. 86–7; Lönker, 'Beethovens Instrumentalmusik', p. 31. Tieck's discussion of Reichardt's *Macbeth* Overture is an exception (see Ludwig Tieck, 'Symphonien', in Wackenroder, *Werke und Briefe*, pp. 249–58).

understanding, and that musical understanding involves grasping the coherence of the musical work; rather, my claim is that nothing Hoffmann says indicates that his explanation of Beethoven's symphony and the corresponding conception of musical form are generalisable to all music.) This failure in generalisation does not require abandoning the thought that form mediates music and nature: it simply means that if music sings the song of nature, it sings this song in different ways. This is a welcome result: in implying that nature itself has no single form, the view resonates nicely with the Romantic *Naturphilosophie* that so interested Hoffmann.[79]

The conception of musical form under consideration is also inconsistent with the pair of passages cited above. Hoffmann's parallel is not between the seed of a tree and a fundamental theme, but rather between the seed and Beethoven's rational awareness (*Besonnenheit*). Hoffmann's deeper investigation of Beethoven's symphony does not reveal that all musical events spring from a fundamental theme in the way that a plant grows from a seed but, rather, that the apparently chaotic events of the symphony are grounded in a controlling intellect. If the musical events of the Allegro or even the entire symphony are related to a fundamental theme, then that is a contingent fact about the work. This does not imply that the connection to nature is lost. Just as nature may embody a plurality of forms, there may well be other ways for music to sing the song of trees, flowers, animals, stones and water.

Conclusion

I have established two things: (1) traditional metaphysical approaches to 'Beethovens Instrumentalmusik' are illegitimate insofar as they rely upon sources whose connection to Hoffmann is unverifiable and license inferences contraindicated by the text of *Kreisleriana*; (2) the unknown world revealed to the understanding listener of Beethoven's Fifth Symphony is best understood as the natural world, the connection to which is established through musical form. Fully elucidating this idea demands more work, but Hoffmann's interest in *Naturphilosophie* provides a natural opening for such reflections. Such development must wait for another occasion, however. Here I simply point to two interesting consequences of my reading of Hoffmann.

First, my interpretation points to a novel and authentically Romantic solution to what Peter Kivy has called 'the problem of absolute music', according to which absolute music's independence from the most obvious sources of value in the arts – that is, narrative, representational or propositional content – makes it difficult to

---

[79]   This is a major theme of Novalis's (see *Die Lehrlinge zu Sais*, ch. 2; Alison Stone, 'Being, Knowledge, and Nature in Novalis', *Journal of the History of Philosophy*, 46/1 (2008): 141–63 (pp. 161–2)).

explain its value.[80] Understanding music as representing nature, as the reading of Hoffmann presented above recommends, solves this problem. But this is not all that can be said on this front in favour of my interpretation of Hoffman. One of *Naturphilosophie*'s goals is articulating a conception of nature that is compatible with human freedom, a conception that allows one to be at home in the world.[81] Given the Kantian understanding of freedom as autonomy and an understanding of music as also developing autonomously – that is, according to the demands imposed by its own fundamental resources – the value of absolute music turns out to lie not merely in its revelation of nature, but in its revelation of a nature that is hospitable to human freedom.

Second, my interpretation of Hoffmann displaces a traditional story about the development of aesthetic theory.[82] According to this story, from antiquity through to the late modern period, aesthetics conceived of art in representational terms and of art's value in cognitive terms. Around 1800, in response to developments such as the advent of absolute music, aesthetics reconceived art and its value in expressive terms. The reading of Hoffmann presented here suggests that this story is too pat: while Hoffmann's musical aesthetics accords a prominent place to emotion in the arousal of endless longing, it does so in service to music's revelation of nature. In other words, Hoffmann's aesthetics of music is cognitive and representational rather than simply expressive.[83] He does not complete a tradition stemming from the idealists or the *Frühromantiker* but, instead, inaugurates a tradition running through Schopenhauer, Nietzsche and Adorno, in which music gives voice to the deep structure of the world. In 'Beethovens Instrumentalmusik', as Mark Evan Bonds has said, 'listening becomes a way of knowing'.[84]

---

[80]   See Peter Kivy, 'Absolute Music and the New Musicology', in *New Essays on Musical Understanding* (Cambridge, 1999), pp. 155–67 (p. 156).

[81]   See e.g. Schelling's rejection of a mechanistic concept of nature in the introduction to *Ideen*, pp. 112–13. This conception of nature is common to the *Frühromantiker* (see Alison Stone, 'Friedrich Schlegel, Romanticism, and the Re-Enchantment of Nature', *Inquiry: An Interdisciplinary Journal of Philosophy*, 48/1 (2005): 3–25; ead., 'German Romantic and Idealist Conceptions of Nature', *International Yearbook of German Idealism*, 6 (2009): 80–101; ead., 'Being, Knowledge, and Nature in Novalis').

[82]   See e.g. Noël Carroll, *Philosophy of Art: A Contemporary Introduction* (London, 1999), pp. 59–61. The conceptualisation of this history in terms of the value imputed to art comes from Paul Guyer, 'Monism and Pluralism in the History of Aesthetics', *Journal of Aesthetics and Art Criticism*, 71/2 (2013): 133–43.

[83]   This is a salutary result for Guyer, whose article is a brief for pluralistic aesthetic theory (see 'Monism and Pluralism in the History of Aesthetics', pp. 133–5). The idea that intuition is a source of knowledge is controversial among Romanticists (see Alison Stone 'The Romantic Absolute', *British Journal for the History of Philosophy*, 19/3 (2011): pp. 497–517; ead., 'Being, Knowledge, and Nature', pp. 143–7).

[84]   Bonds, *Music as Thought*, p. 37.

Chapter 13

Religious Music as Child's Play: Gadamer's Hermeneutics and Instrumental Music

Oane Reitsma

Introduction

Ever since the seventeenth century, with the rise of the 'work' concept in western art music and an increasing focus on the score, it seems that musicians' freedom to play has become more restricted.[1] I use the term 'play' here in the double sense of performing – a musician *plays* an instrument – and playing as a means of passing the time – a relaxed mode of engagement which involves conducting oneself within certain parameters and according to particular rules (the kind of activity in which children and animals engage in). Both forms of play have certain features in common. The player approaches his playing in all seriousness: the focus is directed exclusively at the events within the space in which playing occurs and in which the reality outside that space is temporarily forgotten. The performance or play is constrained by rules that function like the lines of a hopscotch game: they are relevant only in relation to the act of playing. Also, creativity is a key principle within the boundaries of this act. Finally – if one is not performing solo – interaction is important: part and counterpart must arrive at a balanced consonance.

Despite these similarities, the twofold sense of 'play' has been obscured within music-making as a result of the rise of the work concept. This tendency to focus on the score is compounded in the second half of the twentieth century by the notion of *Werktreue*, which implicitly limits the improvisational freedom of the performer, who concentrates fully on the score or the *Urtext* and *Uraufführung* (the first performance of a work in history and therefore called the 'original' performance).[2] Goehr has demonstrated the relation of these views of music to the notion of 'absolute' music, music constituted solely in terms of its own radically immanent forms. In line with this approach to music as autonomous

---

[1] Lydia Goehr describes the development of the work concept in music that had its heyday around 1800 (*The Imaginary Museum of Musical Works: An Essay in the Philosophy of Music*, revd edn (Oxford, 2007), pp. 157–9). Kenneth Hamilton calls the modern concert etiquette stuffy: 'A little less reverence and a bit more entertainment would do us no harm today' (*After the Golden Age: Romantic Pianism and Modern Performance* (Oxford, 2008), p. 31).

[2] For the concept *Werktreue*, see Goehr, *The Imaginary Museum*, pp. 243–86.

sound phenomena, the performance becomes separated from its social and/or religious context. As a result, concert life becomes an independent social event with little or no reference to any external reality, including a transcendent one. This movement culminated in the nineteenth century *Kunstreligion*, in which art itself became the object of worship, sometimes with the artist-genius installed as deity. Although contemporary concert practice is a largely secular performance, there are composers who continue to compose 'religious' music for the concert hall. Messiaen is perhaps the most striking example of such composers in the twentieth century.

The central question posed in this chapter is how religious instrumental music can be understood in a time when both musicians and audiences have less affinity with the traditions from which this music emerges. Specifically, its main concern is with the relationship between religious instrumental music and the modern listener, where listeners include those with a secular worldview, those who regard themselves as holding spiritual beliefs but are not attached to any religion as such, and those who combine aspects from traditional and New Age religions in their spirituality. In short, this chapter will ask how, given that most contemporary listeners are no longer familiar with the traditional religious beliefs to which Messiaen's music, for example, is so indebted,[3] one is able to arrive at new ways of understanding it.[4] It will enquire into the grounds upon which instrumental music (music not connected with the W/word) might be called 'religious'.[5]

It will do so by describing the relationship between religious instrumental music and the secular listener through the concept of 'play' found in Hans-Georg Gadamer (1900–2002). Applying Gadamer's hermeneutics to music, Bruce Ellis Benson connects the act of composing to that of performing through 'improvisation'.[6] Although supportive of his description of the dialogical character of music performance, I have another approach in mind that is suggested by Gadamer's concept of the 'fusion of horizons'.[7]

---

[3]   I take Messiaen as *pars pro toto* for modern religious composers because, in comparison to other modern composers, the religious (or better theological) content of his music is expressed the most strongly.

[4]   Stephen Schloesser shows how Messiaen fused traditional faith with avant-garde and surrealistic twentieth century sounds ('The Charm of Impossibilities: Mystic Surrealism as Contemplative Voluptuousness', in Andrew Shenton (ed.), *Messiaen the Theologian* (Farnham and Burlington, 2010), pp. 163–82).

[5]   I will limit myself to instrumental music because in vocal music the sound often has a reference, namely the text. The relation between form and content is thus different.

[6]   Bruce Ellis Benson, *The Improvisation of Musical Dialogue: A Phenomenology of Music* (Cambridge, 2003).

[7]   The fact that I use the example of the performing musician as the *homo ludens* (playing man) instead of the audience does not undermine my concern with the listener (rather than the composer or performer) as interpreter and is valid in terms of Gadamer's thought, since he does not make any principal distinction between performer and listener in understanding a work of art. The concept *homo ludens* is taken from historian and culture

The first step will be to make Gadamer's hermeneutics and philosophy of art applicable to music. The second will be to reflect on the consequences for religious music: is his metaphor of play a closed system or does it leave room for a 'transcendent player'? The final step will proceed from Gadamer's interpretation of the mimesis concept, which locates religious and secular listening on the same continuum.

Work Concept and *Werktreue*

Since Beethoven, the work concept has been a dominant paradigm in thought about western art music.[8] The musical piece is viewed as an autonomous and independent entity that does not serve any extrinsic purpose in the same way that dance music, liturgical music or music composed in service to one's employer or patron does. As Lydia Goehr has shown, the work concept is closely related to absolute music and its performance practice.[9] The modern concert hall culture, which is closely related to the work concept, serves the music, rather than the other way around. Concert practice thus forms a precursor to the hegemony of the score manifested in the twentieth century. Kenneth Hamilton claims that the programming and performance style, the concert etiquette and the decorum, just like the very strict 'adherence to the letter of the score' is a typically twentieth-century phenomenon due to the influence of the 'recording age' and the ideal of perfection that it propounds.[10]

Actually, however, music in the twentieth-century historical performance movement is also discussed in terms of the work concept and has much in common with the absolute music approach. The goal of historical performances of Bach's *St Matthew Passion* is, after all, to approximate the *Uraufführung*, whatever that means.[11] Originality in music is no longer a matter of the artistic playfulness of the performance, of recreation, but concerns the reproduction of the historical 'original'. The sole focus is on the number of players, tuning and instrumentation current at the time of the music's composition. Any relation to

theorist Johan Huizinga, who presents play as an existential aspect in human life, culture and society. This will be explained further, later in this chapter.

[8]   Goehr, *The Imaginary Museum*, pp. 148, 89, 205–42, 245–53.

[9]   Hamilton shows that, since the late nineteenth century, as far as solo piano performances are concerned, there has been more emphasis on concerts for a large public instead of aristocratic salon performances or private performances for *connoisseurs* (*After the Golden Age*, pp. 16–23).

[10]   Ibid., pp. 17, 21.

[11]   Benson shows that the concept of *Uraufführung* is less unequivocal than it seems: 'Yet, assuming that we are attempting to duplicate something like the sound of a performance that Bach himself would have heard, the question to be asked is: *when*? At the first performance? At subsequent performances during that year? Later in life?' (*The Improvisation of Musical Dialogue*, p. 109).

church, liturgy or religion is ignored. The 'holy' is present here in the music itself as an immanent transcendence; Bach is the creator of this heavenly but also physical and earthly music.[12] It is striking that what is made central is not a sense of doing justice to the specific character of the individual work whose historical context is reconstructed – and from which, logically, a plurality of 'performance-types' might emerge. Rather, it is the attitude toward the work in terms of making performances uniform that is determinative. All types of music in history are treated according to the same principle: an 'objective' attitude of historical distance.[13] Benson concludes that the authenticity movement is an image not so much of the period of the music that is performed as of the restorative tendency of the twentieth century itself.[14] It is striking that the historical approach focuses only on the technical aspects of the music, like ornamentation and tuning, and not on its sociological and religious dimensions. This is a logical consequence of the historical approach, which sees the temporal distance as a gulf and not as a continuing tradition. To return to the iconic example of Bach's *St Matthew Passion*, the concern is with the instrumentation, tuning and number of performers. All liturgical connections are ignored: the musicians do not sing in the name of the community *coram deo* but are viewed as standing over and against the listeners, who are demoted to an audience that in most cases is looking more for an aesthetic experience than a religious one.

This consideration places the problem of religious music within contemporary secular concert practice into the realm of philosophy of music. The work concept and *Werktreue* are aligned directly with absolute music. Philosophically, this type of music is usually approached through formalism: 'Absolute music is pure, objective and self-contained – that is, not subordinated to words (song), to drama (opera), to a literary programme or even to emotional expression.'[15] Form has priority over content, meaning, representation or extrinsic purpose,[16] such that, as the founder of musical formalism Eduard Hanslick argued, 'tonally moving forms' are the sole content and subject of the music.[17] Musical forms, the play of sounds, are the essence of music, referring only to themselves. Through the lens of this paradigm, music connected with an external reality, such as vocal or instrumental religious music, is defined as 'programme' music, and since it arises as the opposite of absolute music (which is determinative and directional for this intellectual paradigm), it has a negative connotation. A more neutral term – but

---

[12] Andy Hamilton emphasises the physical side of music in addition to the cognitive (*Aesthetics and Music* (London and New York, 2007), pp. 6, 115).

[13] Benson, *The Improvisation of Musical Dialogue*, p. 98; Goehr, *The Imaginary Museum*, pp. 8, 244.

[14] Benson, *The Improvisation of Musical Dialogue*, pp. 122–3.

[15] Hamilton, *Aesthetics and Music*, p. 67.

[16] Ibid., p. 71.

[17] Ibid., p. 82; see also Eduard Hanslick, *Vom Musikalisch-Schönen: Ein Beitrag zur Revision der Aestethik der Tonkunst* (Leipzig, 1854), e.g. p. 67.

originating in another paradigm in the philosophy of music – is mimesis,[18] which refers to the imitation or expression of an external entity or reality in music. This obviously connects with religious music because it relates in one way or another to the transcendent.

Since modern concert practice, however, is in large part conceived in terms of absolute music, one cannot simply apply a different intellectual paradigm. Even if people think in terms of content rather than form, the work is still viewed as autonomous, separated from any social or liturgical function. My intention here is thus to make room for religious experience within the movement that begins with the musical form. Gadamer's play metaphor offers a number of access points for doing so.

Religious Music?

Messiaen did not call his music religious in any general sense but referred to it as theological. Indeed, his music is the clearest example of the paradox of religious music in a secular culture. Messiaen's music is approached primarily in terms of its religious content (or by means of the theological programme that stands at its foundation), although there are also more formalistic approaches.[19] Nevertheless, I find Messiaen's oft-heard explanation that the gospel was intended for the world and not for the church to be too much of an internal faith standpoint – and all the more so because the music is played in a secular performance practice that is *de facto* not interested in faith or theology. However, one cannot simply concentrate upon the notion of the religious or theological intention of the composer since most modern and/or secular listeners are more interested in the 'tonally moving forms' than any specifically Catholic content.

One can also attempt an interpretation of music that proceeds from nineteenth-century *Kunstreligion*. But this does not substantiate any religious content since musical sounds are not religious as such. This is because religious music makes use of the same language, grammar and sound as non-religious music.[20] At most,

---

[18] In Platonic philosophy, however, 'mimesis' has a negative connotation, as I explain in n. 51.

[19] A good example of research that starts with the formal characteristics of music is Luke Berryman, 'Messiaen as Explorer in *Livre du Saint Sacrement*', in Shenton (ed.), *Messiaen the Theologian*, pp. 223–39.

[20] Hendrik M. Vroom holds that 'the expression "religious language" is often avoided because the language in which transcendence is discussed consists largely of everyday words applied to God and to the relation between humans and the transcendent. ... The usual meaning of these "normal" words is stretched, as it were, so that they point to the subjects discussed in religion' (*A Spectrum of Worldviews: An Introduction to Philosophy of Religion in a Pluralistic World* (Amsterdam and New York, 2006), pp. 87–8). The same could be said about musical language.

the language-game will vary, but not the language itself.[21] However, the notion of game is key to a further clarification of music's religious dimension, since it is the game, the play, that is central. Thus, I do not just mean the concert or liturgical context. Rather, in taking up Gadamer's play metaphor it is clear that, although there are many aspects involved, the structure of the work of art is primary.[22]

The question sketched above concerning historical performance practice does not arise with Messiaen's music. Although the unicity of each individual instrument, particularly with respect to his organ music, needs adjustment to the timbres of each individual instrument,[23] the concert performance practice of Messiaen's lifetime can nevertheless still be considered close to the concert hall practice of our time in general. This is why I would like to emphasise other aspects of the play metaphor. I began this chapter by noting how the performer's 'freedom to play' has been restricted. However, the more crucial question here is whether certain performance practices which adhere to formalist conceptions of music allow for a transcendent player.[24] To establish whether or not this is the case, we need to answer the question of what determines the religious content in this type of religious music. Is it determined purely by the intention of the composer or the performer, by the structure of the piece, by the context where it is played, or by the experience of the listener? I will suggest that it is primarily the structure of the piece, although Gadamer's play metaphor will show that there are other aspects at play here as well.

Gadamer's Play Metaphor

In *The Relevance of the Beautiful*, Gadamer uses a clear image that summarises his theory:

> The specifically human quality in our play is the self-discipline and order that we impose on our movements when playing, as if particular purposes were involved

---

[21]   I am referring here explicitly to Wittgenstein's language games.

[22]   In addition to the play metaphor, Gadamer also discusses art from the perspective of the concepts of 'symbol' and 'feast' (Hans-Georg Gadamer, *The Relevance of the Beautiful and Other Essays*, trans. N. Walker, ed. R. Bernasconi (Cambridge, 2002)). These will not be discussed as such in this chapter.

[23]   The particularity of the unique situation was discussed by J. Fidom, who emphasised that organs and organ stops have a much more individual character than any other musical instrument. Adjusting the organ music to the sound of one instrument differs fundamentally to adjusting to the timbre of the other instrument, whereas a piano is to a much larger extent a standardised instrument ('Music as Installation Art: Organ Musicology, New Musicology and Situationality' (inaugural lecture: VU University, 2011)).

[24]   This transcendent player is a symbol here of all possible religious content that listeners ascribe to music, varying from a classic personal concept of God to views from modern spirituality not connected with any religious institution.

– just like a child, for example, who counts how often he can bounce the ball on the ground before losing control of it. In this form of nonpurposive activity, it is reason itself that sets the rules. The child is unhappy if he loses control on the tenth bounce and proud of himself if he can keep it going to the thirtieth.[25]

In addition to alluding to Kantian non-purposive efficiency,[26] Gadamer also refers here to the series of aspects that the play metaphor reveals. The player initiates the game: the child bounces the ball. What happens to the ball subsequently determines the course of the game: the child follows the path of the ball with his full attention. During that time, nothing exists outside of the game and the player is simultaneously spectator and participant. Importantly, the rules are set primarily by the child – the ball has to bounce at least 30 times – and these rules become entirely normative and autonomous.

The play metaphor is fundamental to Gadamer's view of art. Basing his view on cultural studies, he sees play as an elementary human motive.[27] It concerns primarily the back-and-forth movement that has no extrinsic purpose,[28] a purposeless activity that recalls the subjective purposiveness of the beautiful in Kant's aesthetics.[29] Reason sets its own rules for the game, and the purposes that are set have no significance beyond the context of the game in which the player plays, with complete and serious 'devotion'.[30] The player knows that he is only playing a game but acts as if he does not. It is not 'serious', but within the rules of the game it is played with an almost 'sacred' seriousness.[31] For Gadamer, it is crucial that the player, in addition to being a player, is also an observer of the game's movement: the child observes the up-and-down movement of the bouncing ball that he himself causes to bounce.

Gadamer emphasises the dynamic interplay between playing and spectating: the player is not only a spectator, but the spectator is also a player. He uses the example of the spectators at a tennis match: everyone joins in the movement.

> Even the onlooker watching the child at play cannot possibly do otherwise. If he really does 'go along with it', that is nothing but a *participatio*, an inner sharing

---

[25] Gadamer, *The Relevance of the Beautiful*, p. 23.

[26] 'Purposiveness without a purpose' (Immanuel Kant, *Critique of the Power Judgement*, trans. and ed. P. Guyer and E. Matthews (Cambridge, 2000), e.g. §15).

[27] Here he is following Johan Huizinga (*Homo Ludens: Proeve eener bepaling van het spel-element der cultuur* (Haarlem, 1938)).

[28] Gadamer, *The Relevance of the Beautiful*, p. 22; Hans-George Gadamer, *Truth and Method*, trans. and ed. J.C. Weinsheimer and D.G. Marshall, 3rd edn (New York and London, 2004), pp. 104–5.

[29] Gadamer, *The Relevance of the Beautiful*, p. 14.

[30] This principle from Huizinga's *Homo ludens* is also applied to Christian liturgy, see e.g. Gerrit J. Hoenderdaal, *Riskant spel: Liturgie in een geseculariseerde wereld* (Zoetermeer, 1977).

[31] Gadamer, *Truth and Method*, pp. 102–3.

in this repetitive movement. This is often very clear in more developed forms of play: for example, we have only to observe on television the spectators at a tennis match cricking their necks. No one can avoid playing along with the game.[32]

With respect to viewing works of art – both the plastic arts and the performing arts – Gadamer states:

> There is constant co-operative activity here. And obviously, it is precisely the identity of the work that invites us to this activity. The activity is not arbitrary, but directed, and all possible realizations are drawn into a specific schema.[33]

Here as well it appears that the structure of the particular work determines the type of play that emerges. 'Here the *primacy of play over the consciousness of the player* is fundamentally acknowledged'.[34] The movement begun by the player determines the progress of the play and demands the entire attention of the players (who are also spectators).

In terms of art, then, the formal characteristics of the work determine the content and meaning of the play. This observation seems to gesture in the direction of formalism. However, the listener and the music are both, with their own horizon, connected with each other. The listener does not listen from the perspective of a distant objective standpoint; rather, the listening experience is determined from the start by an affective relationship whereby one is 'taken hold of'. Being taken hold of arises through the structure of the music, which attracts, deters or moves the listener.

A Play Performed for Others

Before we look further at Gadamer's play metaphor in relation to music, we ought to examine the nature of performing arts more generally. Here one sees that 'play' transforms into 'a play' (something performed for others, for example, on stage). To use Gadamer's terms, one of the four walls of the closed playing space falls away.[35] The child and the ball together form a closed reality. Children play for themselves. But in plays (on stage) and sports, such as tennis, the public is part of the act of play as well. The playing is done for them: something is presented (*dargestellt*) for another. In this instance, according to Gadamer, the spectator completes the meaningful whole of the play, for the player no longer plays for himself alone. This confirms the view described above, that the spectator is also a player.

---

[32] Gadamer, *The Relevance of the Beautiful*, pp. 23–4.
[33] Ibid., p. 27.
[34] Gadamer, *Truth and Method*, p. 105.
[35] Ibid., p. 108.

For Gadamer, prioritising 'a play' over 'play' when talking about art is essential. Central to the arts, after all, is the idea that something is presented;[36] something is shown. However, Gadamer goes further, giving the experience of the spectator priority over the player. It is not the performer of the music who has a better understanding than the listener, but the listener, who is given priority as interpreter.

In Gadamer's view of art, play is always done for someone. In the case of music – and this applies to the arts on stage in general – I would like to suggest that, as a performing art, playing music is playing to a heightened degree because the musician, often with fellow performers, literally performs his play for the listener. The fact that in music the words 'play' and 'to play', just like in a stage play, are not only related to the use of the words '(children's) play' and 'to play' in Gadamer's play metaphor but merge with them reinforces this metaphor, since they are directly applicable to music-making.[37]

Continuing this line of thought within this particular language-game might, however, lead to confusion. Can a performing musician who is a player also be a spectator at the same time? In a certain sense he can, because he views the music in the score. In this way, even before playing the musician is a recipient and listener of the music through the action of the inner ear. Moreover, when he is playing the music, he receives it and also hears it himself. However, even though we saw that the spectator – listener in this case – is in some sense a fellow performer, one can object that the roles of performer and spectator are different. Nonetheless, Gadamer's metaphor is still fruitful since it is concerned with understanding the work of art through a fusion of horizons between the work of art and the interpreter. The role of the performer and listener within modern concert practice is indeed different but, seen from the perspective of the hermeneutical purpose of 'understanding', this is a practical and not principal distinction. Both the listener and the performer listen and interpret from the perspective of their own horizon of understanding and thus come to understand it.

Fusion of Horizons

The play metaphor is a clear example of Gadamer's fundamental principle of the fusion of horizons. This arises from his criticism of Romantic speculative

---

[36] Ibid., pp. 108–10.

[37] Not all languages have corresponding words for 'play' (of children and animals) and the 'playing' (of music, games or sports). My own mother language, Western Frisian, has different words for these activities that are not etymologically related or interchangeable (see e.g. Jan Jelles Hof, 'Bydragen ta de skiednis fen it Fryske Wird: Boartsje', *De Swanneblommen* (1920): 11–15; Douwe A. Tamminga, 'Boartsje en spylje', *Op 'e taelhelling*, 2 (1973): 37–9). Moreover, German only has the word *Spiel*, whereas English has both 'play' and 'game'.

philosophy and the so-called 'historical school'. The latter views the temporal distance between the reader and the historical text as a gulf that must be bridged: every misunderstanding must be prevented in understanding texts or works of art. Thus, Gadamer characterises 'hermeneutics as "the art of avoiding misunderstandings"'.[38] One example of this approach is the historical-critical method found in biblical studies, which attempts, as it were, to crawl inside the skin of the writer in order to understand the text in its historical context, like the twentieth-century historical performance movement did with respect to works of music. In contrast, Gadamer does not see the (historical) distance between the text (or work of art) and the interpreter as an evil that needs to be overcome. His view is that we, as interpreters, do not stand outside history but are part of it. Object and subject are related to each other historically: they are connected, but at the same time they are strange to each other.[39]

Just as in the case of the historical text, we can see the work of art as strange to the interpreter whilst remaining connected in the act of understanding. The child and the ball are connected within the reality that is created by the play itself. At the same time, the ball is capricious and unpredictable. It is an opponent, an alter ego of the child, in the same way that a historical biblical text or work of art constitutes an alter ego for the interpreter who has to make this strange object his own. They are connected and yet are strange to each other, and it is 'tradition' that constitutes the bridge. This filled space (or, in the case of historical distance, filled time) determines how the object is understood. The text or work of art brings its *Wirkungeschichte* with it and the interpreter her own life-world. Neither horizon is a fixed border, but forms the boundary of respective viewpoints. Nonetheless, where these two horizons fuse is where understanding occurs; it is where the point of view changes.[40] The fusion of horizons is always a matter of interaction in which the horizon of the work and the interpreter are narrowed or widened and new horizons are unlocked. Tradition is thus the continuing process of the fusion of horizons.[41]

The fusion of the horizons of subject and object within a new horizon is thus viewed positively. The filled time and filled space see to it that subject and object fuse in continually new ways: there are always new perspectives. As a result, one acquires new insights and the horizon gains in significance and meaning.[42] Gadamer speaks elsewhere of an 'excess' and of the 'immanent transcendence of play'.[43] The unknown is appropriated anew in every situation. Nevertheless, given that secular time involves religious differentiation and fragmentation,

---

[38]   Gadamer follows Schleiermacher's definition of hermeneutics here, see Gadamer, *Truth and Method*, p. 185.

[39]   Ibid., p. 241.

[40]   Ibid., p. 237.

[41]   Ibid., p. 305.

[42]   Ibid., pp. 348–55.

[43]   Gadamer, *The Relevance of the Beautiful*, p. 46.

Gadamer's concept of tradition can be challenged. It is increasingly the case that neither concert-goers nor religious music share religious or even musical traditions. The point of contact at which understanding can occur is not always obvious, as can be seen with respect to the average concert-goer and the reception of explicitly theological music such as Messiaen's. I would rather emphasise 'strangeness' than 'familiarity'. Moreover, since instrumental music is not tangible or visible – music is not physical in the sense of the listener's own existential body – it is arguably even more of an alter ego for the listener. It can indeed be appropriated, which happens afresh in every situation in which the piece is performed. In each new presentation of the piece, the horizons of the listener and the piece fuse[44] and meaning and significance is 'applied' by contemporary performers and audiences within contemporary situations by means of existing instrument(s). The listener has to open himself up to this alter ego, according to Gadamer, although there is no fixed method for arriving at an answer.

We now return to the two central characteristics that I have detected: (1) the listener does indeed have priority over the performer, but (2) it is the structure of the work that is determinative and leads the subject to an answer. That this answer varies constantly is due to the fact that both the context (for example, the character of the individual musical instrument) and the horizon of each individual listener differ.

Religious Music

What is striking about Gadamer's hermeneutics and his philosophy of art in particular is its horizontal orientation. His concept of 'filled time' is defined horizontally. Thus, it displays no single notion of 'higher times'[45] or connectedness with something that transcends it in a temporal sense. The image of a spectacle contained by four walls is viewed only in terms of its horizontal plane. However, all things considered, one might ask, is a space (viewed spatially) not surrounded by six planes? Is there not a floor beneath one's feet and a roof above one's head? The question arises: does Gadamer leave the planes of depth and height

---

[44]   Precisely because the meaning of the piece never comes to completion, Benson prefers to speak about a 'piece of music' instead of a 'work of music', which has the connotation of a 'well-defined meaning' (*The Improvisation of Musical Dialogue*, p. 132).

[45]   I am using the phrase 'higher times' here in Charles Taylor's sense: these 'gathered, assembled, reordered, punctuated profane, ordinary time' through 'kairotic' moments. Such moments are still present in the modern secular age, according to Taylor, but are no longer gathered around 'eternity' (Charles Taylor, *A Secular Age* (Cambridge, Mass. and London, 2007), p. 54). I have discussed these different types of time in connection with various musical structures (Oane Reitsma, 'Some Time for Timelessness', in Wessel Stoker and W.L. van der Merwe (eds), *Looking Beyond: Shifting Views of Transcendence in Philosophy, Theology, the Arts, and Politics*, Currents of Encounter 42 (Amsterdam and New York, 2012), pp. 487–504).

deliberately open? And, regardless of whether or not he does, in relation to our concern with religious music, should we see the surplus that arises in the fusion of horizons between interpreter and art work as radical immanence[46] or might we also see it as religious?[47]

An almost casual remark in *Truth and Method* provides an access point. Gadamer weakens the opposition between sacred and profane by arguing that they are located on the same continuum.[48] Thus, in understanding the musical work, there is no principal distinction between the religious and the secular, just as (as we saw above) there is no principal distinction between listener and performer. The reason for this lies in the method. For Gadamer, 'truth' is not an objective fact that arises through the application of historical and philosophical methods. Rather, it arises each time anew in the act of the fusion of horizons. The truth is found in the method of the fusion of horizons that is always and everywhere different. Although Gadamer does not go any further into this, it is possible to draw the conclusion that the adjective 'religious' in music need not be an objective given that obtains for music as such. Rather, religious experience arises from the life-world of the listener which fuses with the music in the act of hearing. The musical piece (and its *Wirkungsgeschichte*) gives occasion for a religious interpretation. This brings us back to the play metaphor.

In play, the structure of the object – the bouncing ball – has priority over the player. It is the musical structure and texture of the musical piece, then, that indicates an 'opening' to a transcendent player. Transcendence is intrinsically present in the work. The religious understanding emerges from the life-world of the interpreter, but the understanding of the piece of music does not happen simply because of preconceptions held by the interpreter and, thus, not simply on the basis of an a priori religious interpretation of the work. The player initiates the play, but the work then determines how it is experienced. That the experience can vary among different interpreters arises because of their respective horizons. The work takes the leading role in the interconnection of the listener and the music. From the first note, the listening experience is determined by the music, which takes hold of the listener: she does not listen to the music from a distant, objective point of view but is attracted, deterred or moved from the start. This is the way which leads to my earlier statement that the interpretation of the piece

---

[46] I refer here to the four types of transcendence that Stoker differentiated in art: immanent transcendence, radical transcendence, radical immanence and transcendence as alterity (Stoker and van der Merwe, *Looking Beyond*, pp. 5–28; Wessel Stoker and W.L. van der Merwe, *Culture and Transcendence: A Typology of Transcendence* (Leuven, 2012), pp. 5–26 *et passim*).

[47] I will not discuss Gadamer's distinction between aesthetic and religious experience; for that, see Gadamer, 'Aesthetic and Religious Experience', in *The Relevance of the Beautiful*, pp. 140–53.

[48] Gadamer, *Truth and Method*, pp. 143–4.

of music is constructed on the basis of the listener's experience, whereby the unique structure of the work of art is central and has priority.[49]

Mimesis

In Gadamer's hermeneutical philosophy of art, there is still another point of view that can assist in explaining the relation between so-called religious music and the interpreter, namely, the concept of 'mimesis'. It is to this that I now turn and to its relation to formalism. Formalism was developed in a culture of so-called absolute music in which music is not connected with the W/word, in spite of the religious connotations of the word 'absolute'. Mimesis is associated more with that period of history when music was connected with the church and/or social hierarchy. As long as the musician is in service to the church and faith or to a patron, the music composed is often associated with an external reality to which it refers or which is expressed in the music. In the case of religious music, this is primarily a transcendent reality. As soon as the music is given an independent existence in concert life, becoming, even, an (art) religion with its own cult, the immanent world of music becomes normative and nothing external encroaches on it.

Thus far, I have compared the immanent musical world to the immanent reality of play. However, my concern here is with how religious music functions in the secular performance practice of modern concert life, where it does not seem to fit, just as a medieval altar piece fits in a church but does not belong in a museum.[50] Nevertheless, there are instances, as in the case of Messiaen, where religious music is written for performance in concert halls. How is one to account for this? I would like to suggest that whilst absolute music is usually approached through formalism and religious music through mimesis, a synthesis of the two paradigms is productive in understanding absolute music as religious music.

Gadamer rejects the Platonic view of double mimesis whereby the depiction of an external reality is viewed negatively as simply an imitation.[51] Central to Gadamer's concept of mimesis is not imitation but recognition (*Wiedererkenntniss*): whenever players dress up for a play, the primary concern is not to *look* like the people depicted but to *present* them. In this way, more than that which is presented is recognised and transcended: a surplus is revealed.[52] Here play once again comes

---

[49]   I would summarise Gadamer's programme as follows: the musical experience must be constructed on the basis of observation, whereby (1) the structure of the individual work is the starting point and (2) the interpretation occurs on the basis of the particular horizon of the individual.

[50]   Gadamer, *Truth and Method*, p. 76.

[51]   In Plato, an image is an imitation of an observable entity, which in turn is an imitation of an eternal Idea. A 'double mimesis' thus arises, which has a negative connotation because the image is 'only' an imitation.

[52]   Gadamer, *Truth and Method*, pp. 113–14, 141, 145–8.

to the fore since, as noted earlier, play is essentially 'coming-into-being' (*ins-Dasein-treten*), a meaningful whole, when it is performed.[53] At one level, mimesis is indeed copying. However, the new and continually renewed act of creation is more important than simply striving for imitation, which is empty and meaningless: 'Historicizing presentation – e.g., of Music played on old instruments – are not as faithful as they seem. Rather they are an imitation of an imitation and are thus in danger "of standing at a third remove from the truth" (Plato)'.[54]

In *The Relevance of the Beautiful* another level of mimesis becomes apparent: the concept of mimesis as recognition is made clear when Gadamer introduces the example of a *tessera hospitalis*:

> What does the word '*symbol*' mean? Originally it was a technical term in Greek for a token of remembrance. The host presented his guest with the so-called *tessera hospitalis* by breaking some object in two. He kept one half for himself and gave the other half to his guest. If in thirty or fifty years time, a descendant of the guest should ever enter his house, the two pieces could be fitted together again to form a whole in an act of recognition.[55]

Here, the recognition brought about between the host and guest is more than the fitting together of the two pieces. The meaning of the action transcends the simple fact of the restored plate. Gadamer connects his concept of mimesis directly to his view of symbol (which I will not explore any further here). In sum, in his concept of mimesis, Gadamer emphasises representation over pure imitation as such: 'Mimesis here has nothing to do with the mere imitation of something that is already familiar to us. Rather, it implies that something is represented in such a way that it is actually present in sensuous abundance'.[56] The mimetic principle in Gadamer here comes very close to the formalist paradigm.

Fusion of Horizons Once Again

But we should be careful of running with Gadamer's hermeneutics theologically by viewing the inner surplus of the work as religious or spiritual, since '[the work] itself belongs to the World to which it represents itself. A drama really exists only

---

[53] Ibid., p. 116.

[54] Ibid., p. 118.

[55] Gadamer, *The Relevance of the Beautiful*, p. 31. This concept of symbol is also discussed by Vroom, who distinguishes between 'symbol' and 'sign' because there is no structural relationship between the symbol and that to which it refers. With a sign, however, there is always a structural or formal relationship between the signifier and the signified (Vroom, *A Spectrum of Worldviews*, pp. 87–116).

[56] Gadamer, *The Relevance of the Beautiful*, p. 36.

when it is played, and ultimately music must resound.'[57] In other words, the work of art belongs to the immanent sensory world, and one cannot project its resoundings into the world above. The surplus is always connected to the unique sensory form of the work of art and its structure leaves the accidental and the non-essential behind.[58] Intentionally new forms or structures are created in every new piece of art. Emphasising the structure here, Gadamer is not making a distinction between external form and spiritual content. The new 'idea' that is presented converges with the incidental (*okkasionelle*) form. Transcendence is always intrinsically present in the work of art.

Nevertheless, it is my view that the structure of the work can be said to be religious if it fuses in a particular way with the horizon of the interpreter. The religious experience does not seem to arise in Gadamer when he speaks about the play metaphor of the work. But precisely because he looks at the structure of the work and the role of the listener he provides an opening for this. Thus, I am deliberately not situating the religious character of certain concert music in the intention of the composer nor in the *Wirkungsgeschichte* of the work. To do so would be non-sensical, since twenty-first-century listeners no longer necessarily share in the faith world of a composer like Messiaen. Moreover, to situate it elsewhere is to respond to the fact that, particularly in the twenty-first century, a great deal of music can be viewed as religious or spiritual particularly because spirituality is often found outside the frameworks of institutionalised religion. The potential for the aesthetic to be conceived in terms of the religious is thus opened up.

The religious experience of music in the concert hall arises when (1) there is a religious point of contact in the worldview of the listener and (2) the structure of the musical piece provides an occasion for it. The latter involves an infinite number of musical factors since continually new forms and structures must and will be presented. But some pieces of music will lead more easily to religious experience than others, whether through a play between sound and silence, by means of complexity or precisely through simplicity, by means of dissonance or harmony, timbre or rhythm, by means of the unexpected or by means of the predictable and repetition. Thus, the colourful chords of Messiaen's work appeal to the spiritual dimension of the listener differently from the *tintinnabuli* technique of Pärt; the simplicity of Tavener will affect differently from the unexpected in Cage. But the work of the latter will, just like the complexity of Xenakis, be directed more to the immanent world of sound than to religious spirituality. To detect this, however, requires a study on the level of particular works, since (even more strongly, following Gadamer) something is presented not only in the unique structure of every particular work, but in every particular performance of a particular work. If we reason in this way, the very unique structure and particularity of the individual performance should form the starting point.[59] Nevertheless, I believe it is still

---

[57] Gadamer, *Truth and Method*, p. 115.
[58] Ibid., p. 114.
[59] This view can be found in Fidom, 'Music as Installation Art'.

legitimate to begin at the level of the work because the structure is not essentially different in each individual performance. Rather, the structure is precisely one of the few constant factors that connect the different performances of a piece of music.[60]

Just as Gadamer relativizes and nuances the concept of mimesis as simple imitation, I attempt to relativize the formalist approach by viewing it not as a radically immanent approach to 'tonally moving forms' but by allowing these forms to be forms that afford spiritual or even religious experiences that transcend the purely aesthetic. In this way, the dichotomisation of the horizontal and the vertical experience is avoided. Indeed these movements are not at odds with each other. Starting with musical form enables the profane and the sacred to be located on the same continuum. Although the type of experience can vary, there is no principal difference, just as there is no principal difference between religious and secular music. The horizon of the observer – performer or listener – colours the experience.

Conclusion

This chapter began with a consideration of 'freedom' in musical performance practice. But it was not my primary goal to criticise the tendency to focus on the ideal performance of a score. After all, it has been recognised for a long time that freedom and constraint form a unity: rules stimulate creativity.[61] Play is an example of that. The objection to the view entailed by *Werktreue*, however, is that the rules become more than preconditions, such that the improvisational freedom out of which creativity can grow is restricted. But my specific concern within this chapter was the question of whether contemporary performance practice, which I view *de facto* as secular with its emphasis on the radically immanent musical forms, allows room for a transcendent player. The work concept and the *Werktreue* of later historical performance practice each in its own way represents music as absolute. The task was to see whether such music might also express a religious understanding of the absolute.

Gadamer does not seem to deny the question of religiosity; it simply is not an issue for him. This fact legitimises the use of his play metaphor in clarifying the relationship between the religious listener and the work. Following Gadamer's play metaphor, the religious experience emerges from the life-world of the listener.

---

[60] But this does not obtain when we speak about improvisation, which is the starting point for Benson, *The Improvisation of Musical Dialogue*; see also, Jeremy S. Begbie, *Theology, Music and Time* (Cambridge, 2000); Fidom, 'Music as Installation Art'.

[61] The strict contrapuntal rules that lead to the most creative fugues by Bach are a good example in music. In biblical theology, the relationship between law and gospel is a clear example: Jesus radicalizes the law in the Sermon on the Mount, which indicates that rules make room, need further interpretation, and stimulate originality and creativity.

Here, the musical form occasions a religious rather than an aesthetic experience. This makes the idea of absolute music less absolute because it is opened out and room is given to religious transcendence without denying the primacy of the form. This is in line with Gadamer's view of mimesis as original recreation instead of pure reproduction of an historical original.

It is striking how, linguistically, Gadamer's play metaphor converges with discourse about the playing of music. It gives occasion to describe the role of the listener as interpreter, who stands in an existentially strange relation to the body of sound. He is to be described as the *homo ludens* who appropriates the absolute by joining in the (musical) movement of the game. This absolute, however, does not necessarily have to imply radical immanence because new horizons that are unknown until then are opened up in the fusion of horizons. It's all in the game.

Chapter 14

Immanence, Transcendence and Political Song

Christopher Norris

I

The topic of political song and its ontology is one that leads quickly to issues of the kind that have preoccupied contributors to this book, that is to say, issues concerning those aspects of immanence and transcendence that characterise music and our experience of it. Moreover – and for just that reason – it offers a significant challenge to certain deep-laid assumptions concerning the status or mode of existence proper to musical works. Those assumptions have primarily to do with the formal autonomy of such works and hence with their supposed capacity to transcend the order of merely contingent events, whether singing events (for example, in this context, street performances) or events of a more directly political character.

Of course that distinction is one that any writer or performer of political songs would reject straight off as failing to recognise that certain songs in certain situations have a singular capacity to mobilize protest and strengthen resistance to various forms of social injustice that is 'directly political' in every sense of the phrase. Still there is a question as to whether such songs, or the best of them, may be said to possess that galvanizing power not only in virtue of their timeliness and their happening to ride some wave of popular discontent but also on account of certain musical attributes – melodic, harmonic, rhythmic, structural – which place them in a class apart or which define them as veritable classics of the genre. The problem for anyone who makes that claim is that the notion of 'the classic' comes laden with a weight of inherited ideas concerning the markers of canonical status – of literary or musical greatness – and their timeless, transcendent character. It is this way of thinking that political song most pointedly calls into question since its very existence as a popular alternative to 'high-cultural' artforms is premised on its audibly not going along with the various ideologies (of genius, transcendence, organic form, structural complexity and so on) promoted by the guardians of musical good taste. Yet there are other, less ideologically compromised ways of thinking about the classic – among them Frank Kermode's marvellously subtle and nuanced reflections on the topic – that entail no such commitment.[1] For Kermode,

---

[1]   See esp. Frank Kermode, *The Classic* (London, 1975); id., *History and Value* (Oxford, 1988). I discuss this and other aspects of his work in Christopher Norris, 'Remembering Frank Kermode', *Textual Practice*, 25/1 (2011): 1–13.

the classic is most typically a work 'patient of interpretation', or apt to reveal new possibilities of meaning in response to shifting historical-cultural circumstances. On his account it is still a work – not just a 'text' dissolved into its context or reception history – but a work whose very capacity to survive those changes should be taken as evidence of its openness to a range of alternative readings.

I should not wish to say that classic political or protest songs should be thought of in exactly those terms, as sharing with Kermode's prime examples (from Homer and Virgil to Dante and Shakespeare) this quality of holding senses in reserve or this capacity for endless self-renewal in the face of unending historical change. To make such a claim would be doubly mistaken: on the one hand, by ignoring Kermode's emphasis on the subtle, oblique or roundabout ways in which the classic text succeeds in holding out against the ravages of time and change and, on the other, by ignoring the very different range of musical, verbal, social and communal factors that make for the survival of political or protest songs from one specific context to another. For it is precisely their distinctive mark – their claim to an ontological niche quite apart from other, more familiar or tractable genres – that they occupy a different space, one that is more radically open to the reception-changing impact of historical, social and political events. However it seems to me that this constitutes a powerful objection to what I have said so far and will go on to say, only if there is something fundamentally wrong or misconceived about the whole business of theorising in relation to music, literature and the arts. Otherwise the main lesson is that enquiry into ontological issues in the broadly aesthetic sphere had better be ready to adjust its critical focus so as to accommodate the full range of cases that should properly be taken into account by any such enquiry.

My point is that conventions often run very deep and that it actually requires an effort of thought with strong theoretical back-up if we are ever to succeed in breaking or at any rate loosening their hold. Thus it may take something like Derrida's complex modal-logical reflections on the deviant logics of supplementarity, iterability or parergonality – along with his intricate drawing-out of those aporias intrinsic to the 'law of genre' – in order to shift some of our basic assumptions concerning the scope and limits of aesthetic response.[2] Such thinking against the orthodox (canonically invested) grain is strictly prerequisite if any serious question is to be raised with respect to what should or should not qualify as a musical work or an instance of art as distinct from an instance of music put to political or other such non-artistic ends. At any rate we will not get far in any discussion of ontological issues vis-à-vis musical works (or performances) unless, like Derrida, we make a regular practice of challenging those otherwise largely unspoken assumptions that underlie our routine habits of judgement and response. It might even be said that political song is itself such a practice – or exerts such a deconstructive force – by dint of very pointedly calling into question

---

[2]   See Jacques Derrida, 'The Law of Genre', trans. A. Ronell, *Critical Inquiry*, 7/1 (1980): 55–81; id., 'Before the Law', trans. A. Ronell, in *Acts of Literature*, ed. D. Attridge (London, 1992), pp. 181–220.

certain deep-laid values and beliefs concerning the autonomy of musical form, its transcendence of the merely contingent or temporal, and the inviolable unity of words and music as a touchstone of aesthetic worth.

Moreover, those values are further contested by the very existence of a genre (or anti-genre) that so conspicuously flouts the Kantian veto on artworks that have some palpable design on the listener/viewer/reader – some purpose to persuade, arouse or convert – and which therefore conspicuously fail to meet Kant's requirement of aesthetic disinterest.[3] After all it seems pretty much self-evident that any item of purported political song that did manage to satisfy this criterion would *ipso facto* be a bad or ineffectual instance of the kind since incapable of stirring anyone to action or decisively changing their minds. Here again we might usefully recall Derrida's deconstructive reading of Austinian speech-act theory and his convincing demonstration – *pace* opponents like John Searle – that Austin's distinctions, like Kant's before him, are a deal more complex and problematical than his orthodox commentators wish to allow.[4] Just as Kant ends up by unwittingly subverting his own elaborate system of binary pairs – among them 'free' and 'adherent' beauty, aesthetic form and instrumental function, or the artwork itself and its various framing, ornamental or extraneous features – so Austin ends up by providing all manner of problematic instances and arguments that cast doubt on whether he can really hold the line between constative and performative modes of utterance.[5] Where the cases differ is in Kant's deep attachment to the virtues of large-scale system and method – requiring that his doctrine of the faculties be deconstructed in a likewise systematic way – as compared with Austin's gamy readiness to junk the system (or his current version of the system), if it looks like getting in the way of some particularly choice example. It is just such instances of speech-act anomaly ('misfires', as Austin called them) that Searle considers marginal by very definition since they fall short of straightforward performative success while Derrida counts them especially revealing since they demonstrate the inbuilt possibility that speech-acts might always turn out to function or signify in various non-standard, unpredictable or non-speaker-intended ways.

As hardly needs saying this is also the predicament of political songs, destined as they are – if they succeed in catching on – to undergo a history of changing contexts and varied applications which may result in their becoming very largely detached from any meaning or motive plausibly imputed to the original writer, singer or group of performers. In this respect our thinking about political song –

---

[3]   Immanuel Kant, *Critique of Judgement*, trans. J.C. Meredith (Oxford, 1978).

[4]   See John L. Austin, *How To Do Things With Words* (Oxford, 1963); Jacques Derrida, 'Signature Event Context', *Glyph*, 1 (1977): 172–97; id., 'Limited Inc. a b c', *Glyph*, 2 (1977): 162–254; id., 'Afterword: Toward an Ethic of Conversation', in *Limited Inc*, ed. G. Graff (Evanston, Ill., 1979), pp. 111–60; see also John R. Searle, 'Reiterating the Differences: A Reply to Derrida', *Glyph*, 1 (1977): 198–208.

[5]   For Derrida's deconstructive reading of Kant, see 'The Parergon', in *The Truth in Painting*, trans. G. Bennington and I. McLeod (Chicago, 1987), pp. 15–147.

especially with regard to its elusive ontological status – can profit from Derrida's meticulous tracing of the fault-lines that run through Kant's various attempted demarcations between art and non-art or pure and impure modes of aesthetic response, as likewise through the various terms and distinctions by which Austin seeks to hold a normative line between proper and improper, valid and invalid, or 'felicitous' and 'infelicitous' modes of speech-act utterance.[6] Indeed there is something markedly anomalous about the very genre of song, existing as it does across such a range of forms, types, musical-verbal structures, cultural traditions, social contexts, communicative roles, performance locales and so forth, as almost to constitute an anti-genre or a nominal kind identified only by its meeting certain far from precise or exacting criteria.

Thus the minimal requirements would be roughly (1) its being sung or involving the combination of words and music; (2) its relative brevity compared with other, more extended or structurally complex genres such as those of the cantata, oratorio or opera; (3) its predominantly lyrical nature, that is, the focus on expressive elements – again jointly verbal and musical – that give particular songs their distinctive character and (4) the way that it tends to focus attention on the singer, who is often the songwriter, as source and in some sense subjective guarantor of the feelings thereby expressed. Yet of course one could take each of the above desiderata and come up with a song, or several, that failed to satisfy the supposed requirement and thus raised doubts as to whether this is really a genre even in the proposed minimalist sense. (Consider point for point Mendelssohn's *Songs Without Words*, Mahler's symphonic *Song of the Earth*, didactic or primarily political songs [like those of Hanns Eisler or Kurt Weill], or the numerous songs – often parts of some larger dramatic or narrative work – that crucially depend for their meaning and effect on our grasping the disparity between what is expressed and what we are intended to make of it). And if song in general exhibits such a highly elusive ontological character – such extreme resistance to categorization in clear-cut generic terms – then this is even more strikingly the case with regard to political song. For we are here confronted with a genre (or quasi-genre) that goes yet further toward raising large questions with regard to its own status as a verbal-musical kind or as a token of anything – any definite or trans-context specifiable type – that could serve to fix its generic identity.

This is not to suggest that in switching focus from classical song (concert-hall lieder of whatever period or style) to instances of political street-song we are lowering our sights in musical-evaluative terms or electing to consider a sub-genre with no pretensions to high artistic, cultural or aesthetic worth. Hanns Eisler's songs, in particular his settings of Brecht, are equal to the finest of the twentieth or any century if heard without prejudice regarding their strongly marked didactic intent and with an ear to those features typically prized by devotees of the high lieder tradition. Thus they are no less accomplished – dramatically powerful, melodically striking, harmonically resourceful and structurally complex – for

---

[6]   Austin, *How To Do Things With Words*.

the fact of their overt political content or, on occasion, their activist concern to discourage the listener from taking refuge in a purely aesthetic or contemplative mode of response. All the same their very success in so doing comes about through their constant supply of reminders, musical and verbal, that there is a world beyond the concert-hall and that events in that world – like those that befell the twice-over émigré Eisler, driven out first by the Nazis and then by the watchdogs of US anti-communism – cannot be kept at bay by any amount of artistic creativity or degree of formal inventiveness. Indeed it is one of the most distinctive things about Eisler's music, not only his songs but also his larger-scale choral and orchestral works, that it maintains this perpetual sense of a nervous sensitivity to outside events or the impact of extra-musical promptings. This is probably why he seems most at ease, even in large-scale compositions like his epic yet intensely personal *Deutsche Sinfonie*, when writing in a long-breathed melodic style with song-like contours and a strong sense that only by such means can he combine the pressure of subjective feelings with an adequate response to the pressure of (mostly dire) historical or political occurrences.

Political song is the genre that most effectively unites these otherwise conflicting imperatives and which makes it possible for music to express both the passionate force of individual commitment and the historical or socio-political context within which it finds a larger significance. Ontologically speaking, it is that which (in certain cases) has the capacity to maintain its distinctive character while undergoing sometimes drastic changes of context, motivating purpose or performative intent. Songs that started life as protests against British government policy during the miners' strike of 1983 have since done service in a great many other campaigns, sometimes very largely unaltered (except in so far as the shift of context changed their perceived character) and sometimes with verbal modification so as to update their content or enhance their specific relevance. On a larger time-scale, songs that had their origin in the suffering or revolt of black slaves in the American Deep South are nowadays revived – not just recycled – in the name of anti-poverty campaigns, anti-war protests and calls for the re-scheduling or outright cancellation of third world debt. What gives the songs in question this remarkable staying power – beyond some vague appeal to 'the test of time' – is a complex amalgam of musical and verbal features that is likely to elude the best efforts of formal analysis but which is recognisable to anyone who has sung them and registered their continuing impact when performed on any such politically charged occasion. Here again one might aptly recall what Derrida has to say about that minimal trait of 'iterability' that enables speech-acts to function – that is, to retain a certain recognisable (ethically and socially requisite) performative force despite their occurring across a potentially limitless range of contexts and their involving the ever-present possibility of deviant (or devious) motives on the utterer's part.[7] Just as this iterable property of speech-acts is such as to resist any systematic formalisation of the kind attempted by theorists like Searle so likewise

---

[7] Derrida, 'Signature Event Context'.

the 'classic' quality of certain political songs – those that have retained their radical force – is none the less real for its holding out against methods and techniques of analysis trained up on masterworks of the mainstream classical repertoire.

If I placed some queasy scare-quotes around the word 'classic' in that last sentence then it is no doubt a sign of my unease about dragging these songs into the orbit of a high-cultural or academic discourse where they are likely to suffer a gross misprision of their musical, verbal and political character. All the same, as Terry Eagleton has argued, it is just as mistaken for left cultural theorists to let go of the whole kit and caboodle of 'bourgeois' aesthetics – especially its talk of arch-bourgeois values such as beauty, sublimity or aesthetic disinterest – on account of its being so deeply bound up with the hegemonic interests of a once dominant though now declining cultural and socio-political class.[8] The fact that those values have largely been monopolised by that particular power bloc does not mean that they cannot or should not be recovered – won back through a concerted effort – by those among the marginalised and dispossessed who have most to gain from their redefinition in left-activist terms. This is why the label 'classic' may justifiably be used to describe those songs that have shown a special capacity to renew their impact from one situation to the next and have thus come to manifest a singular strength of jointly musical, political and socio-cultural appeal. Indeed, as Kermode very deftly brings out, if there is one perennial feature of the classic then it is the absence of just those reference-fixing indices that would otherwise place certain clearly marked limits on the range of options for anyone seeking authenticity or wishing to remain true to the song's original context and motivation.

Of course 'authenticity' is a notion widely challenged among left cultural theorists – often taking their lead from Adorno – since it is thought to harbour an appeal to supposedly 'timeless' or 'transcendent' values such as those invested in the high tradition of accredited musical or literary masterworks.[9] However, so it is argued, values of this kind even when adduced as the upshot of a lengthy and detailed formal analysis always have a local habitation in the time and place (that is to say, the formative ideological conditions) of their particular socio-politico-cultural setting. Such criticism of the western musical and literary canons has been carried to a high point of technical refinement by various schools of thought – New Musicologists, New Historicists, deconstructionists, cultural materialists, feminists, the more analytically minded postmodernists – well practised in revealing the various sleights of hand by which promoters of a high formalist doctrine manage to occlude what is in fact a highly specific set of class-based or gender-related

---

[8]   Terry Eagleton, *The Ideology of the Aesthetic* (Oxford, 1990).

[9]   Theodor. W. Adorno, *The Jargon of Authenticity* (London, 1973); Lydia Goehr, *The Imaginary Museum of Musical Works: An Essay in the Philosophy of Music*, revd edn (Oxford, 2007); Susan McClary, *The Content of Musical Form* (Berkeley and Los Angeles, 2001).

ideological commitments.[10] From their point of view Kermode could only be selling out when he argues for a stance of mitigated scepticism vis-à-vis the classic, that is, an approach that would balance the claims of intrinsic literary (or musical) worth against the claims of an anti-canonical case for regarding 'the classic' as one of those ideas that have served as a useful means of upholding the cultural and socio-political status quo. If anyone thought to extend Kermode's argument to the case of political song then they would surely invite the charge of misrepresenting what is by its very nature a context-specific, historically located, resolutely non-transcendent mode of expression. That is to say, they would be seen as deludedly seeking to boost its status by hooking it up to an aesthetic ideology that no longer possesses the least credibility even when applied to works in the mainstream classical repertoire.[11]

Such is at any rate the sort of claim nowadays put forward by zealous deconstructors of the western musical canon. This project they pursue partly by engaging those works in a heterodox or counter-canonical way and partly by challenging the discourse of post-Schenkerian music analysis with its deep attachment to (supposedly) conservative notions like organic form, thematic development, harmonic complexity, structural integration, progressive tonality, voice-leading, long-range reconciliation of conflicting key centres and so forth.[12] To think (and to listen) in accordance with these notions is to signal one's complicity – so the argument goes – with a formalist mystique of the unified work of art which mistakes the culturally constructed character of all such aesthetic notions for natural properties somehow inherent in 'the work itself' or else in the musical language (most often that of the high Austro-German line of descent from Bach to Brahms or Wagner) that made such achievements possible.[13] And if this line

---

[10]   Katherine Bergeron and Philip V. Bohlman (eds), *Disciplining Music: Musicology and Its Canons* (Chicago, 1992); Nicholas Cook and Mark Everist (eds), *Re-Thinking Music* (Oxford, 1999); Joseph Kerman, 'How We got into Analysis, and How to Get Out', *Critical Inquiry*, 7/2 (1980): 311–31; id., 'A Few Canonic Variations', *Critical Inquiry*, 10/1 (1983): 107–25; id., *Musicology* (London, 1985); Lawrence Kramer, *Classical Music and Postmodern Knowledge* (Berkeley and Los Angeles, 1995); Judy Lochhead and Joseph Auner (eds), *Postmodern Music / Postmodern Thought* (New York, 2002); Ruth A. Solie (ed.), *Musicology and Difference* (Berkeley, Calif., 1993).

[11]   See e.g. Paul de Man, *Aesthetic Ideology*, ed. A. Warminski (Minneapolis, 1996); Philippe Lacoue-Labarthe and Jean-Luc Nancy, *The Literary Absolute: The Theory of Literature in German Romanticism*, trans. P. Barnard and C. Lester (Albany, NY, 1988); Christopher Norris, *Paul de Man: Deconstruction and the Critique of Aesthetic Ideology* (New York, 1988).

[12]   Heinrich Schenker, *Free Composition*, trans. and ed. E. Oster (New York, 1979). For some representative critiques and revaluations, see Leslie D. Blasius, *Schenker's Argument and the Claims of Music Theory* (Cambridge, 1996); Eugene Narmour, *Beyond Schenkerism: The Need for Alternatives in Music Analysis* (Chicago, 1977); Hedi Siegel (ed.), *Schenker Studies* (Cambridge, 1990); Maury Yeston (ed.), *Readings in Schenker Analysis and Other Approaches* (New Haven, Conn., 1977).

[13]   See nn. 10, 11, 12, above.

of thought has a certain plausibility with regard to the dominant values of 'high' musical culture and their modes of propagation through the arcane discourse of academic musicology then it seems even nearer the mark when applied to any claim for this or that political song as a veritable classic of its kind. After all, what could be plainer as a matter of straightforward response to words and music alike than the fact that such works constitute a standing affront to that whole classical-Romantic aesthetic of timeless, transcendent, ahistorical and hence apolitical values?

It is the latter idea – along with its rootedly nationalist or chauvinist overtones – that finds oblique yet highly effective (since technically geared-up) expression in the various methods of formal analysis bequeathed by German music theorists of the nineteenth century to their present-day academic heirs. Such a notion is maximally remote from the ethos of direct activist engagement that typifies the best, most powerful instances of political song like those that have emerged from various situations of racial oppression, social injustice and class or gender inequality. To this extent the methods of musical analysis as widely practised nowadays are the result of combining a Kantian emphasis on the formal or structural features of the artwork with a marked devaluation of anything describable as programmatic content. However there is no need to adopt this high-formalist or purist approach or go along with the decidedly conservative outlook in philosophical aesthetics which aims to drive a wedge between works of art and the contexts – including the socio-political contexts – of their production and reception.

II

It is perhaps now time to recapitulate the main points of my argument so far in order to firm up the basis for what I have to say in the rest of this chapter. Thus: (1) if the term 'ontology' makes any kind of sense as applied to works of art then it had better be applicable to musical works, in which case (2) it had better be applicable to those works falling under the generic description 'song', and moreover (3) it had best apply convincingly to political song as a litmus-test since this places the maximal strain on received notions of generic character or identity.

Hence the particular problem it poses for any formal ontology of art based on the presumed existence of certain distinctive traits whereby to recognise and specify what counts as a genuine instance of the kind. After all, 'political song' is a pretty elastic label and one that is apt to find itself stretched around some dubious candidate items if taken to denote any relatively short and self-contained vocal work with a text that makes either overt or covert reference to certain themes of a political character. Thus the British national anthem would have to qualify under this definition, although there seems good reason to withhold the title on account of its patently belonging to a genre that endorses rather than challenges the institutional status quo and whose stolid combination of flag-waving words and foursquare music is very much deployed to that end. Yet there are other national anthems – most strikingly those, like 'Amhrán na bhFiann' (Irish Republic) or 'Nkosi Sikelel' iAfrika' (post-Apartheid South Africa, originally ANC) – which, although in very different ways, continue to communicate something of the oppositional spirit or the strength of concerted popular resistance that went into their making and the often strife-torn history of their early performances. Indeed the very fact of this (so to speak) stress-induced and to that extent historically indexed character has a lot to do with their staying power as classics of the genre.

This helps to explain why a classic of the 1983 British miners' strike like 'We are Women, We are Strong' should thereafter have turned up as a highly effective rallying call at numerous sites and in numerous seemingly disparate socio-political contexts over the past quarter-century of popular anti-government protest.[14] It can best be put down to that song's having so perfectly captured the quiet determination, resilience and un-self-conscious heroism not only of the miners' wives and partners but of a great many others whose livelihoods and lives were under threat from government economic and social policy. The case is rather different with those hardy perennials like 'We Shall Not be Moved' where the sentiments expressed, like the melody and harmonies, are so broadly generic – so capable of being adapted to just about any political context – as to offer a kind of Rorschach-blot for those in search of all-purpose emotional uplift. It seems to me that, in order to count as a genuine classic of political song, the piece in question must exhibit something more than this smoothly accommodating power to absorb a great range of otherwise diverse feelings, values, beliefs and commitments. This something more can I think best be specified in ontological terms, even though the terms involved are sure to be somewhat fugitive given that political songs exist very largely in and through their reception history and thus exhibit a peculiar degree of dependence on contextual cues and the vagaries of historically situated listener response. All the same, as I have said, it would be wrong to conclude from this that they fall short of classic status in so far as they fail to meet certain formal standards – at any rate certain widely agreed-upon and clearly specifiable criteria – that alone make it possible for judgement to transcend the shifting tides of social change or cultural fashion.

One might take a lead in thinking about this question from the title of Alain Badiou's essay *Briefings on Existence: A Short Treatise on Transitory Ontology*, as indeed from Badiou's entire project to date.[15] That project has to do with the relationship between being and event or the way that certain unpredictable and yet (as it turns out) epochal or world-changing events – certain breakthrough discoveries whether in mathematics, science, the arts or politics – can lead to a radical transformation in our powers of ontological grasp and hence to a shift in the relationship between currently existing knowledge and objective (recognition-

---

[14] For some highly relevant (and in many ways heartening) socio-historico-political background, see *We are Women, We are Strong* (Sheffield, 1987).

[15] Alain Badiou, *Briefings on Existence: A Short Treatise on Transitory Ontology* (Albany, NY, 2006).

transcendent) truth.[16] What is most remarkable about Badiou's work is its emphasis on truth as always exceeding our utmost powers of cognitive, epistemic or rational grasp and yet as that which constantly exerts a truth-conducive pressure through its absence – its way of creating problems, lacunae, unresolved dilemmas – in our present-best state of understanding. This is not the place for a detailed exposition of Badiou's masterwork *Being and Event*,[17] suffice it to say that he makes this case not only in relation to mathematics (very much Badiou's disciplinary home-ground) but also to the physical sciences, politics and art. More specifically: in each case, it is a matter of truths that are opened up for discovery at a certain stage in the process of knowledge acquisition or cultural-political advance yet which may require a more or less extended process of further working-out at the hands of those faithful exponents – 'militants of truth' – whose office it is to explore their as yet obscure or unrecognisable implications.

However, the main point I wish to make for present purposes is that Badiou offers a distinctive, and distinctly promising, line of enquiry for anyone pondering the ontology of political song and its status vis-à-vis conceptions of art or aesthetic value on the one hand and conceptions of politics or political engagement on the other. Thus on his account there is no choice to be made, as orthodox (Kantian) approaches would have it, between the value-sphere of artistic creativity or inventiveness and the action-oriented practical sphere of incentives to political change. In each case it is a matter of truth-claims – whether claims in respect of an as yet unachieved state of political justice or claims for the integrity of certain as yet unrecognised artistic practices – that exert a potentially transformative pressure on current ideas but which cannot be realised (carried into practice or brought to the point of adequate conceptualisation) under presently existing conditions. Moreover it is with respect to ontology – to the question 'What exists?' as distinct from 'What counts as existing within some given mathematical, scientific, artistic or political conception?' – that those conditions are brought into question or subject to standards of truth that transcend the criteria of presently existing knowledge. Above all, this enables an extension of truth-values beyond the realms of mathematics, science and the factual (for example, historical) disciplines to other areas – such as politics and art – where they have rarely if ever been invoked in so emphatic and rigorously argued a manner.

Thus it is worth thinking some more about Badiou's seemingly oxymoronic or at any rate odd conjunction of terms in the phrase 'transitory ontology'. What it signifies – in short – is a conception of ontological enquiry as none the less objective, rigorous or truth-oriented for the fact that its scope and limits are

---

[16]   See esp. Alain Badiou, *Being and Event*, trans. O. Feltham (London, 2005); id., *Infinite Thought: Truth and the Return to Philosophy*, trans. O. Feltham and J. Clemens (London, 2003); id., *Theoretical Writings*, ed. and trans. R. Brassier and A. Toscano (London, 2004).

[17]   For a detailed introduction, see Christopher Norris, *Badiou's* Being and Event: *A Reader's Guide* (London, 2009).

subject to a constant process of transformation through advances in the range of available forms, techniques, investigative methods, hypotheses, theorems or proof-procedures. Badiou's paradigm case is that of mathematics and, more specifically, post-Cantorian set theory since it is here that thinking can be seen to engage with an order of truths that always necessarily exceeds or transcends any given state of knowledge.[18] It is in consequence of the 'count-as-one' – that is to say, through some schema or selective device for including certain multiples and excluding certain others – that thought is enabled to establish a range of operational concepts and categories within the otherwise featureless domain of 'inconsistent multiplicity'. Most important is Cantor's demonstration that there exist manifold 'sizes', or orders, of infinity, such as those of the integers and the even numbers and moreover – contrary to the verdict of most philosophers and many mathematicians from the ancient Greeks down – that thought is quite capable of working productively (framing hypotheses for proof or refutation) in this paradox-prone region of transfinite set theory.[19] Indeed, it is through the process of 'turning paradox into concept' – a process most strikingly exemplified by Cantor's conceptual breakthrough – that intellectual advances typically come about, whether in mathematics, the physical sciences, politics or art. Hence the main thesis of Badiou's work: that in each case the truth of any given situation (scientific paradigm, political order, artistic stage of advance) will exceed any current state of knowledge even among specialists or expert practitioners and yet be contained within that situation in the form of so far unrecognised problems, dilemmas, paradoxes or elements (multiples) that lack any means of representation in the currently accredited count-as-one.

Politically speaking, this claim works out in a strikingly literal way since it applies to those marginal, stateless or disenfranchised minorities – prototypically, for Badiou, the *sans-papiers* or migrant workers of mainly North African origin – who find themselves excluded from the count-as-one since their lack of official documentation effectively deprives them of civic status or acknowledged social identity.[20] All the same the very fact of their occluded existence on the fringes of a *soi-disant* 'democratic' social order is such as potentially to call that order into question or to constitute a challenge to the self-image projected by its state-sponsored apologists. At certain times – during periods of crisis or rising communal

---

[18] See esp. Alain Badiou, 'Being: Multiple and Void. Plato/Cantor', in *Being and Event*, pp. 21–77; id., 'Theory of the Pure Multiple: Paradoxes and Critical Decision', in *Being and Event*, pp. 38–48; see also id. 'Ontology is Mathematics', in *Theoretical Writing*, pp. 1–93; id., 'The Subtraction of Truth', in *Theoretical Writings*, pp. 95–160.

[19] For a highly accessible introduction to these and other relevant chapters in the history of modern mathematics, see Alain Badiou, *Number and Numbers*, trans. R. MacKay (Cambridge, 2008); see also Michael Potter, *Set Theory and Its Philosophy: A Critical Introduction* (Oxford, 2004).

[20] See e.g. Alain Badiou, *Metapolitics*, trans. J. Barker (London, 2005); id., *Polemics*, trans. S. Corcoran (London, 2006); id., *Century*, trans. A. Toscano (Cambridge, 2007).

tension – those minorities may well turn out to occupy an 'evental site' which then becomes the focus of wider social unrest and potentially the flash-point for some larger-scale challenge to the dominant structures of socio-political power. In the physical sciences, revolutions come about most often at a stage of conceptual crisis in this or that particular region when the anomalies, failed predictions or conflicts of evidence with theory have become simply unignorable and when something – some crucial load-bearing part of the old paradigm – collapses under the strain. In the arts, likewise, such transformations typically occur at times of imminent breakdown: in music, say, with the stretching of resources and extreme intensification of affect that overtook the tonal system in the late nineteenth century, or in literature, with the advent of modernist poetic and fictional genres that signalled a decisive rupture with previous (realist or naturalistic) modes of representation.

Clearly there is much more needed by way of introduction to Badiou's work if the reader is to be in any strong position to assess these claims. However my purpose here is to suggest that his thinking offers some useful guidance for our enquiry into the ontology of political song. More specifically, it may bring us closer to defining the mode of existence of songs whose comparative longevity and power to energise protest across a great range of political movements and causes is such as to merit their being accorded classic status even though – for reasons that I have essayed above – that term seems rather out of place in this context. Badiou's idea of transitory ontology best catches what I have in mind, namely the elusive combination of extreme adaptability or context-sensitivity with the singular power to retain a distinctive musical and verbal-ideational character throughout those (seemingly) protean guises. On his account the marks of a genuine event, as distinct from an episode falsely-so-deemed, are, first, that it make room for the discovery of a truth beyond any present-best state of knowledge and, second, that it henceforth demand the allegiance – the intellectual, scientific or political fidelity – of those committed to its working-out or the following-through of its implications. False claimants may fill up the history books and make the headlines on a regular basis but are none the less false for that, since their occurrence, although unforeseen at the time, is retrospectively explainable as the outcome of various anterior happenings and in-place or ongoing developments. Genuine events may pass largely unnoticed at the time or, like abortive revolutions, go down only in the annals of failure and yet linger on in the memories of those attuned to their so-far unrealised potential and thereby hold in reserve the potential to spark some future transformation.

Badiou offers many such examples, chief among them the Paris Commune of 1871 and Cantor's radical re-thinking of mathematics on the basis of set theory as applied to the multiple orders of infinity.[21] Thus despite the strong resistance to Cantor's ideas put up by many well-placed mathematicians at the time, and despite the Commune's having been suppressed in the most brutal and (apparently) decisive

---

[21]   See nn. 16, 20, above.

way, both can now be seen as events of the first order, since set theory went on to revolutionise mathematical thought while the Commune continues to inspire and motivate successive generations of political activists. This is why I have made the case – an improbable case, so it might be thought – for understanding the ontology of political song in light of Badiou's writings on mathematics and his extension of set-theoretical concepts to other, seemingly remote, contexts of discussion. That case rests partly on the way that he establishes a more-than-analogical relation, through set theory, between the three principal areas – politics, music and poetry – which must enter into any adequate account of what makes a classic instance of the kind. Also it helps to explain how one can speak in ontological terms of an artform – again, if that is the right term – that depends so much on its contexts or occasions of performance and which therefore seems to elude all the terms and conditions typically proposed by critics and philosophers seeking to define what constitutes a veritable classic.

Thus a really effective political song is one that catches the counter-hegemonic spirit of its time and succeeds in communicating that force of resistance to activists in later, politically changed circumstances. By the same token it is one that not only responds to the potential for some future transformative event – whether in the short or the long term – but can itself be heard to constitute such an event on account of its power to express and articulate those pressures of unrest in response to forms of economic, political and social injustice that are building toward a structural crisis point. It is here that Badiou's radical re-thinking of the relationship between art, politics and truth (in his own heterodox yet clearly defined sense of that term) has the greatest power to illuminate our present enquiry into the ontology of political song. At any rate it goes some way toward explaining the anomalous status of a genre that somehow combines an extreme responsiveness to changes in its historically emergent contexts and conditions of existence with a striking capacity to retain its political as well as its musically expressive charge despite and across those changes.

The issue is broached most directly in Badiou's *Handbook of Inaesthetics* where he examines the various kinds of relationship that have characterised art in its dealing with philosophy and politics.[22] Among them may be counted its Brechtian didactic role as a more-or-less compliant vehicle for conveying some preconceived political content (even if with the aid of certain formal innovations); its classical role as a well-crafted product that satisfies purely aesthetic criteria and lays no claim to any truth beyond that of its own artifactual contriving; and its Romantic role in which it aspires to a creative autonomy or self-sufficient power of world-transformative vision that would free art from all such prosaic or quotidian ties. As scarcely needs saying, Badiou has little sympathy with the latter conception, denying as it does his cardinal thesis that philosophy has its own special role in providing a more perspicuous account – a conceptual articulation – of truths that must remain implicit in the work of art. That is, they exist in the

---

[22]   Alain Badiou, *Handbook of Inaesthetics*, trans. A. Toscano (Stanford, Calif., 2005).

'subtractive' mode of that which cannot find direct expression but can none the less be shown to haunt the work as a structural absence or symptomatic silence and thereby to indicate the future possibility of some as yet unknown further stage of advance. Romanticism, with its Shelleyan idea of the artist as unacknowledged legislator, effectively sells art short by ignoring its kinship with the likewise subtractive procedures through which mathematicians 'turn paradox into concept' or physics undergoes periodic revolutions through coming up against recalcitrant data or political transformations are seen – albeit after the event – to have been brought about through the existence of uncounted or unrecognised multiples at evental sites on the margins of the instituted body politic. Classicism fails yet more grievously since it makes a full-scale aesthetic creed of severing any link between art and truth or any pretension on the artist's part to express, convey or communicate truths beyond the technical aspects of their craft.

Then there is the fourth, distinctively modernist conception of art whereby it breaks with all three of those previous modes – didactic, classic and Romantic – and devotes itself instead to a self-reflexive dealing with issues of language, discourse or representation that constantly call its own status into question. It is clear from his writings on (for instance) Mallarmé and Beckett that Badiou is strongly drawn to many works of this kind since for him they constitute one of the ways in which art can create or discover its equivalent to the breakthrough achievements of a formal discipline like set theory. However he also has strong reservations about the tendency of other such works to become overly hermetic, self-absorbed or preoccupied with linguistic or formal-technical devices and developments at the cost of renouncing any involvement with extraneous – that is, political or socio-historical – conditions. After all, this brings them within close range of the turn toward various language-based schools of thought – Wittgensteinian, hermeneutic, post-structuralist, neo-pragmatist – that Badiou regards as a betrayal of philosophy and moreover as lending support to the status quo by reducing all issues of reason and truth to the question of what makes sense by the lights of this or that discourse, language-game, signifying system or horizon of intelligibility.[23] Thus art, like philosophy, had best avoid being too closely linked – 'sutured', in the idiom that Badiou derives from Lacanian psychoanalysis – to any of those conditions (politics among them, but also prevailing ideas of aesthetic value or form) whose function is artistically enabling up to a point but whose effect, if taken beyond that point, is to deprive art of its particular role as an oblique though potentially powerful means of access to truth.

This is one sense of the tern 'inaesthetics' as deployed in the title of Badiou's book: the capacity of certain (rather rare and often under-recognised) artistic practices to question or challenge accepted notions of what properly constitutes art or what counts as aesthetically valid. Another is the sense in which it denotes a strong and principled opposition to any idea that art should occupy a realm of distinctively aesthetic experience removed from all commerce with extra-artistic

---

[23]   Alain Badiou, *Manifesto for Philosophy*, trans. N. Madarasz (Albany, NY, 1999).

interests or imperatives. Badiou's great aim is to specify how art can express or give form to truths that 'inexist' – that lack as yet any adequate means of conceptual articulation – yet which may none the less be signified obliquely by those gaps, anomalies or absences of formal closure that art is best able to reveal through its inventive capacity for testing the limits of established (for example, realist, figurative or conventional) languages and genres.[24] To this extent art has a purchase on truth that may require the mediating offices of philosophy to spell out its implications but which could not possibly have been achieved except by means of its artistic presentation. I have argued here that political song is a test-case for this thesis since it is a genre (or anti-genre) that confronts the existing political order with a downright challenge to all those values political, social, ethical and musical which serve to maintain the preferential self-image of a stable and properly functioning liberal democracy.

III

The starting point of set-theoretical reasoning is the null set – in Badiou's terminology the 'void' – which, despite its foundational character, eludes any ascription of properties or determinate membership conditions. That is to say, it is included in every multiple as a constituent part or strictly indispensable element yet cannot be reckoned as properly belonging to the count-as-one by any of the usual admission criteria.[25] So it is, by far from fanciful analogy, that socially excluded or victimized minorities continue to exist at the margins of the body politic and, through the very fact of this marginal status, to exert a potentially transformative pressure on the forms of state-administered surveillance and control. Nor are the arts by any means excluded from this critical role, since they also have the capacity to function as reminders of that which cannot be expressed or represented in any language, form or genre available to artists working within the dominant socio-cultural conditions of their own time and place. If the phrase 'ontology of political song' makes any kind of sense – if it is not just a bad case of semantic inflation applied to a wholly inappropriate since temporally fleeting and insubstantial (quasi-)artistic cultural phenomenon – then the best means of defending its entitlement to treatment on these terms is by conjoining Badiou's idea of inaesthetics with his notion of transitory ontology. What we are enabled to think without conceptual embarrassment is the standing possibility of works of art (nothing less) that are very much products of their own historical and cultural–political context yet which also have the power to live on – like the classic in other, more-elevated terms of address – and renew their inspirational charge across a wide range of historical, geographical and socio-political situations.

---

[24]   For a full-scale elaboration of these themes across a wide range of subject areas, see Alain Badiou, *Logics of Worlds: Being and Event II*, trans. A. Toscano (London, 2009).
[25]   See nn 16, 18, above.

This is mainly in virtue of Badiou's deploying a 'subtractive' conception of truth whereby, as in the history of set-theoretical advances, progress comes about through locating those absences, lacunae, stress points, anomalies, dilemmas, paradoxes and so forth, that signal the need for some as yet unknown but obscurely prefigured advance. In set theory there is a known method by which such advances can best be explained – that is, how it is that mathematical truth can run ahead of present-best mathematical knowledge and yet exert a knowledge-transformative power on those who are still operating with the old concepts yet who find themselves uneasily responsive to that which finds no place in current understanding. Such is the procedure of 'forcing', devised (or discovered) by the mathematician Paul Cohen who managed to explain its operative conditions in formal – that is, set-theoretical terms.[26] This has been the topic of some highly pertinent commentary by Badiou who takes it to have decisive implications for our grasp of how epochal changes come about in disciplines, fields or histories of thought far afield from mathematics, at least on the commonplace understanding of what mathematics is or does. Whenever there occurs the kind of major transformation that is loosely described, after Kuhn, as a wholesale 'paradigm-shift' then this is sure to involve another instance of the process whereby thought becomes alert to the existence of certain hitherto unrecognised problems, paradoxes or truth-value gaps.

At these points it is only by way of a 'generic' procedure, in Cohen's mathematically defined sense of that term, that knowledge is enabled to transcend its previous limits and achieve a new stage of conceptual advance. Then it becomes possible to explain – always after the truth-event – how and why those limits had remained in place despite their having always potentially been subject to the forcing effect of such unresolved issues at (or beyond) the margins of intelligibility. My main point here has been to argue that political song occupies that same, intrinsically hard-to-specify since at present not fully realised or recognised, ontological domain. That is to say, it gives verbal-musical voice to the standing possibility of a mismatch between that which we are able to know or cognise under currently existing historical, political or socio-cultural conditions and that which may none the less be prefigured – obliquely expressed or latently contained – within those very conditions. Just as knowledge always falls short of truth in mathematics or the physical sciences so likewise our grasp of what can be achieved in the way of political progress falls short of what might counterfactually be achieved if only thought were able to grasp the possibilities for radical change held out by the failings (for example, the democratic deficit) that characterise some given social order. Or again, for those who come later and keep faith with the inaugural truth-event, these may be possibilities that they are able to imagine or conceive yet unable to realise – fully comprehend and carry into practice – by any means presently at their disposal.

Given more space I should want to press further toward an account of just what it is – what specific combination of features melodic, harmonic, rhythmic

---

[26]   Paul J. Cohen, *Set Theory and the Continuum Hypothesis* (New York, 1966).

and of course jointly musical-verbal – that constitutes the classic status or character of some political songs. My own best shot is that it has to do with a quality, analogous to 'forcing' in the set-theoretical domain, whereby such songs are able to communicate – 'connote' would be too weak a term – the idea of an as yet unachieved but achievable state of justice that finds voice in their words and music and which thereby exerts a potentially transformative pressure on existing (conventionally inculcated) notions of the social good. Musically speaking this involves certain distinctive melodic, harmonic and rhythmic patterns that manage to combine a vigorous sense of shared opposition to regnant structures of authority and power with a contrasting sense of the forces currently ranged against them and the outside chance of those structures giving way in response to any such challenge. I say 'contrasting' rather than 'countervailing' because protest songs draw much of their expressive and performative power from this readiness to face the possibility or likelihood of imminent defeat, but also this strong intimation of a will to hold out for the long term despite the current odds. Indeed I would suggest that the crucial difference between political song in the authentic sense of that phrase and political song in the broader, non-qualitative sense that would include, say, 'Rule Britannia' or 'God Save the Queen' has precisely to do with whether or not some particular song is able to express so complex a range of highly charged and powerfully motivating sentiments.

To explain in detail how these feelings are combined in the best, most potent and moving political songs is no doubt a task for literary criticism and music analysis rather than for someone, like myself, making forays into that region where aesthetics overlaps with politics and where both intersect with the elusive domain of musical ontology. We can take a lead from Badiou's conception of being and event as forever bound up in an asymptotic process of discovery – an open-ended dialectic of 'infinite truth' and approximate states of knowledge – that is driven on from one landmark stage to the next by the powers of creative, inventive, paradigm-transformative or progressively oriented thought. This conception in its detailed working-out by Badiou is one that very aptly captures the transitory ontology of political song. It does so through a bringing-together of art, politics and – improbably enough – those formal procedures that he finds most strongly represented in the history of set-theoretical advances from Cantor to the present day. What it enables us to think is a conception of art that would endorse none of those received ideas – least of all Kantian ideas about aesthetic disinterest or beauty as the product of an ideal harmony between the faculties in a state of perfect disengagement from all aesthetically extraneous matters – that have left such a deep imprint even on philosophies of art which expressly disavow them.[27] On the other hand Badiou can be seen to offer equally powerful arguments against the radically nominalist or conventionalist approach of a thinker like Nelson Goodman who would press just as far in the opposite direction – that is, toward a wholesale dissolution of art into the various 'art'-constitutive languages or modes

---

[27]   Kant, *Critique of Judgement*.

of representation that properly (that is, by agreed-upon criteria) serve to define it.[28] Nothing could be further from Badiou's passionate defence of the truth-telling power vested in art, along with his justified suspicion of those – especially the followers of Kant – who consign artistic truth to a realm of autonomous or 'purely' aesthetic values wherein that power would languish unexercised. If any meaning attaches to the phrase 'ontology of political song' then Badiou's is the approach that can best accommodate so potent, resilient and endlessly renewable and yet so protean or context-dependent a genre. In short, as I have argued throughout this chapter, it is that which goes furthest toward explaining the peculiar and (on the face of it) paradoxical combination of immanence and transcendence that marks political song.

---

[28] Nelson Goodman, *Languages of Art: An Approach to a Theory of Symbols* (Indianapolis, 1976).

Chapter 15

Music, Transcendence, and Philosophy

Andrew Bowie

In phenomenological terms any mode of being in the world can be understood in terms of 'transcendence', because the subject, by 'intending' anything in the world, takes itself beyond itself, becomes 'ecstatic', in order to understand, act and so on. Transcendence is here seen as a way beyond certain epistemological conceptions based on the idea of a division between subject and object, in favour of the idea that the subject is always already in the world. In Wagner's *Tristan und Isolde*, however, transcendence involves the extinction of the subject by dissolution into the 'All'. Such dissolution relates to certain kinds of religious ecstasy which also lead to a transcendence of the self through loss of self. Here transcendence is seen in terms of existential responses to mortality and finitude: by renouncing individuation, which is the source of endless lack, the pain of temporal existence is to be escaped, even as the music of *Tristan und Isolde* embodies precisely the idea of endless lack until the harmonic resolution in the final bars. For Kant, in contrast, the transcendent – as opposed to the transcendental, which refers to conditions of possibility of experience – is what is beyond our capacity to know, which exceeds the bounds of experience and involves what he thinks of in terms of 'ideas', such as 'immortality' and 'God'. In this case transcendence relates to the questionable claims of traditional metaphysics concerning the world as a whole: Kant does not reject what these claims were concerned with, seeing them as resulting from a natural tendency of human thought, but he restricts what can be warrantably asserted about the world to what can be an object of perceptual experience. The connection of music to transcendence has been seen in terms of all of these conceptions, all of which in some way point to a moving beyond the subject that music can enable. The massive contrasts between the conceptions, though, are an indication of fundamental philosophical divergences that one can use music to elucidate.

Rather than attempt to judge how each of these conceptions might be criticised or defended, it is more instructive to ask why music is associated with differing forms of transcendence and how this is manifest in differing historical circumstances. Doing this will hopefully offer a frame for the other chapters in this section, which deal with specific manifestations of the issues I am concerned with. I will not, then, give a philosophical account of transcendence in relation, say, to the idea of ineffability and how it may or may not be a meaningful philosophical term. I want instead first to look at why in certain circumstances a focus on a move beyond widely accepted versions of what is rationally intelligible and conceptually articulable becomes philosophically important. The reason for this is that if one were to give a supposedly fully justified philosophical argument for or against the use of terms like 'transcendence' or 'ineffability' in relation to music, it can be claimed that the argument does not capture what is at issue, which is important precisely because it is not conceptual. If art is philosophically important, art's significance need not be thought of in terms of a philosophical account of that importance, but may actually be understood in terms of what art reveals that is not sayable in philosophy. Were that not the case, art would essentially be reducible to philosophy, and so not that philosophically significant at all. The alternative that interests me lies in seeing art as adding dimensions to philosophy, but also in the process changing how we think philosophy should be constituted.

Assertions like these go against the grain of a still dominant philosophical culture which sees itself mainly in terms of the presentation of arguments and rational justifications. Surely, though, what I am doing here is presenting arguments in precisely this manner? The point is, however, that such a culture can fail to appreciate that many ways in which people make sense of the world do not take the form of arguments based on objective appraisals, including of the kind I am making now, but are rather constituted in participation in practices whose sense cannot be separated from that participation. Clearly aspects of such practices are in turn open to observation, description and critical appraisal, but the prior element, without which the practice makes no sense, can be the kind of engagement in a practice which resists reduction to what Robert Brandom calls the 'game of giving and asking for reasons'.[1]

The banal notion that music cannot be captured by words here gains some traction, because it can be linked to a wider concern that philosophy may actually lead to vital sources of understanding and sense-making being obscured by ungroundable assumptions about its essence. Lee Braver talks of Wittgenstein and Heidegger's attention to 'the meanings flowing through our behaviour which evaporate under the light of theoretical reason'.[2] Importantly, such meanings, though they may be said to transcend theoretical reason, do not have to be thought of in relation to any metaphysical or mystical sense of transcendence, being rather what can be obscured by objectifying philosophical assumptions, and these meanings need not be regarded as mysterious. Those engaged in playing music find immediate sense in what they are doing and might be hard put to give a plausible verbal justification of it. This sense is admittedly cultivated in musical training, but it is grounded in something that cannot be wholly trained. The motivations for even bothering to learn to play or appreciate music are always prior to the specific forms musical training may take, and, crucially, can often be damaged or destroyed by such training. The question is, then, how the meanings that are

---

[1] See Robert Brandom, *Articulating Reasons: An Introduction to Inferentialism* (Cambridge, Mass. and London, 2000).

[2] Lee Braver, *Groundless Grounds: A Study of Heidegger and Wittgenstein* (Cambridge, Mass., 2012), p. 27.

involved in such motivations can be expressed and articulated without what is at issue again evaporating in the course of being expressed and articulated.

Stated in such general terms, this question may seem likely to lead to vague claims that are unlikely to impress anyone working in the philosophical mainstream. Philosophy, though, can be concretised in many ways, and these do not have to be in the form of specific theories in epistemology, semantics, metaphysics, or whatever. By tracking the tension between what is manifest to philosophy, and what is not, in specific historical circumstances, one can develop a different mode of investigation of the significance of such issues as the link between transcendence and music. An immediate way of understanding what I mean here is to look at how 'language' has been discussed in much of the analytical tradition. In many disciplines language is seen as inherently involving crucial expressive elements, such as tone and rhythm, which relate to what Schleiermacher called the 'musical element', and which are inseparable from a proper understanding of how meaning actually functions in real situations. Moreover, 'language' is not a term whose scope is adequately captured by the assumption that it is something essentially verbal, because meaning is conveyed by a whole variety of symbolic forms, such as gestures, images and so on. It may be that these all in fact depend on some core aspect of verbal language, such as the inferential commitments in the 'game of giving and asking for reasons' that Brandom sees as the foundation of other aspects of language. However, this is far from being conclusively established, not least because it is not clear just what distinguishes 'linguistic meaning' from other kinds of meaning, let alone whether it has to be the ground of other meanings. Where does new meaning come from if its ground is supposed to be what is conveyed by words? What grounds the meaning of words?

These are obviously questions that are hardly going to be resolved here, or anywhere else, in a hurry. One can take an analytical stance on these issues and see the main task as such a resolution, but the concrete result of this has been a growing gap between philosophy and other disciplines in the humanities, because the scope of the inquiry is so narrowed. If, instead, one takes a broader notion of meaning, which works in terms of that which makes sense of and in a world, non-verbal articulations can influence verbal articulations and vice versa, which suggests that what is at issue cannot be stably located in one symbolic form.

The real question in the present context is, though, quite simply why, if this view can be taken seriously, the analytical tradition excludes so much of such sense-making and expression from what it purports to explain. One obvious indication of such exclusion is the fact that a concern with language as a form of action, rather than just as a means of representation of states of affairs – or whatever is seen as the object of linguistic representation – is quite a late development in analytical philosophy. The key idea here is Heidegger's notion that the essential nature of being is 'hiddenness' rather than 'presence': what we apprehend and understand is always situated in relation to a background which is not apprehended or understood. In Heidegger's terms the real philosophical task is therefore to understand how things become 'unconcealed'. As such the analytical tradition's apparent blindness with respect to so many dimensions of language, to what can elsewhere seem unproblematically manifest, is itself what needs to be understood. This kind of perspective necessarily introduces history into the core of philosophy, rather than seeing it as a secondary mode of reflection in relation to the primary mode of building explanatory theories.

The fact that at a key moment in modernity the nature of language comes to be a central philosophical concern, and at the same time the status of music radically changes, can illuminate what is at issue here.[3] The reasons for the new status of language relate to what we already touched on in Kant: the world comes at this time to be seen as no longer 'ready-made' and so is in some way also constituted by how we relate to and respond to it. Language can be conceived of as predominantly re-presenting what is already there, especially if the world is assumed to be the product of a divine creator, but in the new climate at the end of the eighteenth century, language comes to be regarded as in some sense constituting what is there, as well as being a key expression of the human form of existence.

The thinkers who start to develop this idea, like Rousseau, Hamann and Herder, often relate language closely to music, suggesting that the notional boundary between the two is a fluid one. This opens the way for language to be understood as offering the possibility of transcending the given, making new things manifest, rather than just re-presenting a reality created by a transcendent author. Such possibilities are related to the idea of music as a language that is able to say what words, which are in some respects tied to the given, though they can be poetically recombined in order to get beyond it, cannot say. The origins of a modern conception of literature and poetry arguably lie in the demand for this kind of transcendence of existing linguistic usage. At the same time, the question of how language arises at all is left open. Language cannot be a product of the subject, as the subject relies on it always already existing to make itself intelligible as a subject, and so seems in some sense to be a 'natural' phenomenon to which one is subordinated. At the same time language does not exist without speakers who can invest it with concrete significance and generate sentences that have never been said before. Moreover, language enables us to exercise freedom in key aspects of our lives, unlike nature conceived of as a system of laws. The 'in-between' status of language suggested here is what is crucial to the philosophical significance of why music changes its status with the onset of modernity.

---

[3]   For details, see Andrew Bowie, *Aesthetics and Subjectivity: From Kant to Nietzsche*, 2nd edn (Manchester, 2003); id., *Music, Philosophy, and Modernity* (Cambridge, 2007). Here I just want to outline a model that suggests the implications for philosophical inquiry. It should be clear from the outset that I regard our present situation as still part of modernity. I have no time at all for the notion of postmodernity: the canonical formulation by Lyotard of the idea of the 'postmodern' as the end of 'grand narratives' is self-refuting, as the announcement of such an end is itself a grand narrative.

Any attempt to give a theoretical account of the origin of language faces the situation that the account has to be in language, which seems to make access to the ground of language inherently elusive if one does not accept some kind of theological ground. This led in the later eighteenth century to the idea of music as a proto-semantic form that offers the key to the transition to verbal meaning.[4] The philosophical tension this points to is between the idea of music as only a stage on the way to full linguistic articulation of meaning, which is essentially how Hegel sees music, and of music as something which expresses what is repressed in the constitution of semantic stability in words. Philosophical stances on music's relationship to transcendence depend on which of these two approaches is regarded as more plausible. It is this kind of alternative, though, which the approach I am interested in can begin to question, because putting things in terms of such alternatives can reify the notions of language and music, when they are arguably better conceived as being in a dialectical relationship, in which changes on one side of the relationship alter what is on the other.

If there were a philosophical resolution of the music-language issue which came down in favour of either approach, it could either fall prey to the problem we saw earlier of rendering music relatively insignificant in relation to theoretical claims in philosophy, which would fail to do justice to the core role of music in nearly all human cultures, or it could be open to the danger of having to invoke something mystical, which does too little to do justice to the concrete sense people find in musical practices. Both stances, then, seem to neglect the centrality of the aspect of music as participation in a sense-generating practice which can illuminate and enhance, criticise and subvert ways of being in the world. Think of the way in which great jazz improvisation is directed, in musical terms, against established patterns and expectations which fail to say anything new, and, in social and political terms, against being co-opted into a comfortable sense of culture as a mere ornament of dominant social relations. From bebop onwards there has often been an explicit socio-political aspect to the refusal to stand still musically in jazz, and this further highlights the fact that any consideration of the notion of transcendence has to take account of the historical world in which the question of music and transcendence arises.[5]

The most simple way of thinking about why music is linked to transcendence and to ineffability is in terms of what the content of religion becomes once belief in divine transcendence becomes either a matter just of faith, or a mere dogmatic residue of dead metaphysics. Secularised notions of transcendence necessarily become 'inner-worldly' (Max Weber) in the sense that transcendence must be sought using already existing practices and ways of being. Music is a key focus for this change because its ways of making sense survive the demise of theological content, as the enduring appeal to secular listeners of, say, Bach's B Minor Mass

---

[4] See Downing A. Thomas, *Music and the Origins of Language: Theories from the French Enlightenment* (Cambridge, 1995).

[5] See Christopher Norris's chapter in this volume.

makes clear.[6] The philosophical importance of such phenomena lies in the way in which the sense made by this music is not directly theological, ethical or philosophical, in the manner of a propositionally articulated set of beliefs or a theory, but at the same time involves aspects that are involved in each of these. If philosophy is to do justice to such sense it must find ways of articulating it which embody its specific nature, and this suggests that the scope of philosophical expression needs to be widened.

Indeed, as I have suggested elsewhere,[7] the philosophy of music should arguably be concerned with the philosophy which emerges from music itself, rather than with incorporating music into the existing conceptual repertoire of philosophy. The point in this respect is that participation in music can inherently involve kinds of transcendence which need not be translated into the ways that transcendence has often been characterised in philosophy. As such the phenomenological approach to transcendence I began with still offers viable ways of approaching the issue, because it can develop the concept of transcendence by attention to specific ways of being without reducing them to a theory that grounds those ways in some notionally unified manner.

Bruckner's music would not be what it is without his Catholicism, nor would Coltrane's without his spiritual beliefs, but their music makes profound sense to those who share nothing of those beliefs. The sense made is not something to be reduced to a psychological theory, because what the music does is transform the world of its recipients. It does not just stimulate psychological responses to a notional objective world, nor does it just reflect the psychology of its creator. In Heidegger's terms the music is 'world-disclosive', making accessible what without it would be hidden, in the form of such things as specific articulations of time, changes of mood and intensity, melodic movement, progress towards a notional goal and its interruption or destruction. These fundamental aspects of being, which can only make the sense they do in the specific form in which they occur in the music – the generality and banality of my characterisation make this clear – can transform aspects of a listener's life-experience, creating new ways in which the world manifests itself and in which people locate themselves in that world.[8] They can also create a pressure for those musicians who come after not to ignore the new ways in which such music changes the space of expressive possibilities that relate to the historical circumstances of the musician and the audience. Such pressure need not be felt at an explicit, verbally articulable level and can have to do, for example, with the way in which Coltrane's saxophone sound focuses protest, anguish, lyricism and exhilaration in new ways, so provoking engaged musicians to move beyond the sound they produced before hearing Coltrane.

This sort of immanent transcendence can be connected to religious and other forms, as is suggested by the frequency with which music is associated with

---

[6]   See Oane Reitsma's chapter in the volume.
[7]   Bowie, *Music, Philosophy, and Modernity.*
[8]   See Férdia Stone-Davis's chapter in this volume.

those domains, but it can also be seen as a form in which some kinds of formerly religious content may be shared even by the 'religiously unmusical' (Max Weber). The kind of lifelong commitment to music that is a very common part of many people's existence is not something that is best understood through a rational justification, and involves something like the enactment of faith in religious practice. Explaining it in terms of something else, like Freudian sublimation, gets it the wrong way round by prioritising what can be objectified in a theory over the prior participatory practice. In Heidegger's terms it prioritises 'entities' over 'being'. The practice relies on the kind of meanings generated by immediate engagement with things in the world. These can issue in theories, but they depend on what Heidegger sees in terms of the 'care structure' of human existence. The theories are a derivative form of understanding that rely on a deeper, ineliminable connection with things that can easily be obscured by an objectifying stance. The power of music lies not least in its resistance to wholesale incorporation into what theories can tell us, so reminding us that many of the most important relations to things are not cognitive, and this is part of what leads to discussion of its relation to transcendence.

Somebody once referred to Coltrane's playing as 'musical stream of consciousness'. The fact that different forms of expression can illuminate each other while not being reducible to each other is decisive here. The term 'stream of consciousness' is derived from the modernist novel, and using it in the context of Coltrane's music enables a new series of associations which can illuminate the way in which, in modernity, subjects' awareness shifts towards a more developed realisation of the fluidity and frequent uncontrollability of how we actually exist in and experience the world. Where modernist narrative may convey the dynamic nature of consciousness at the level of shifting images and propositional or proto-propositional thoughts, Coltrane conveys the temporality of shifting affective and other intensities. Schleiermacher talks of music as essentially relating to the 'mobility of self-consciousness'.[9] It is precisely the fact that the sense of music is conveyed by movement, not just by what in it can be characterised in objective terms, that gives rise to the concern with how it relates to what can be articulated in propositions that has dominated a lot of philosophical discussion of music and so led to the emphasis on ineffability and the like.

The point is that listeners, composers and players intuitively grasp the fact that music makes sense by our participation in it, not by our attempting to objectify what that participation consists in, an attempt which tends to lead to the idea of music conveying something mysterious and constitutively unsayable. In *Culture and Value* Wittgenstein suggests the alternative to this when he asserts that the 'simplest explanation' of a musical phrase 'is sometimes a gesture; another might be a dance step, or words which describe a dance'.[10] It is not that we always lack

---

[9] Friedrich Schleiermacher, *Vorlesungen über die Aesthetik* ed C. Lommatzsch (Berlin, 1842), p. 393.

[10] Ludwig Wittgenstein, *Culture and Value* (Oxford, 1980), p. 69.

rational responses to trying to understand music, but the responses have to take a form which is apt to music, and what such aptness consists in depends on the specific circumstances in which the music occurs. When music is detached from theology the significance, for example, of the B Minor Mass for secular listeners comes to have to do with the way in which formerly religious sentiments may be better articulated in music, precisely because they are no longer attached to anything verbal of the kind which introduces considerations of warrantable truth. This does not mean that the content of the music has nothing to do with truth, just that a purely semantic conception of truth does not do justice to the relationship between world-disclosure and propositional truth.[11] Such musical articulations can be and are shared by those who share few verbal claims about the nature of existence, and so enable different kinds of connections between people who otherwise may be at odds with each other. This kind of inner-worldly transcendence also has clear ethical significance, because it offers ways beyond social antagonisms by creating different forms of mutual acknowledgement: the role of jazz in combatting racism, for example, resulted in part from creating connections between different social groups that made it clear how prejudice against the cultural Other is unjustifiable. At the same time it should also be remembered that the capacity of music to create social bonds can be deeply problematic, as the Nazis' use of Beethoven showed. There are no unambiguous aspects to these issues, but that is no reason to neglect the ethical import of music.

Such phenomena are, I think, more significant as a focus of the debate about music and transcendence than the concern to associate music with ineffability and so hang onto its connection to religion conceived of in doctrinal or theological terms. This concern can often result from a representationalist view of language, of the kind adopted by many analytical philosophers, which tries to interpret non-representational forms of expression and sense-making in representational terms and inevitably finds that this does not work. The consequence is a false alternative between denying any meaning to music at all, in the manner of Peter Kivy, or enlisting music for theology in a dogmatic manner, which obscures the ways in which music can avoid the divisions which are inherent in the holding of any explicit doctrinal position, and can create forms of social engagement that transcend religious divisions.

The underlying question here is simply why we should still be concerned with transcendence at all in philosophy and music. One obvious answer is that many directions in contemporary thinking are essentially immanentist, notably in such areas as certain versions of neuroscience and associated materialist and reductionist philosophies. Once again it can be argued that the tendency of some of these approaches to rely on representationalist premises blinds them to the kind of sense that music makes of the world. It is not that such sense need be thought of as disembodied and mysterious: the somatic aspects of rhythm as a means of structuring and enlivening a world should already suggest why. At the

---

[11]   See Mark A. Wrathall, *Heidegger and Unconcealment* (Cambridge, 2011).

same time, I can see no philosophical legitimation for the more emphatic versions of transcendence which seek to associate music with what is essentially a version of dogmatic metaphysics or theology of the kind Kant showed to be philosophically unsustainable. That many people experience music in a theologically imbued manner is undeniable, but this is essentially a matter of faith, which does not allow one to arrive at any viable philosophical response. The question is, therefore, what forms of transcendence can play a defensible role in philosophical reflection, and how this relates to music in modernity.

Richard Rorty sees questions of transcendence as 'private' sense-making, which cannot be made part of the 'public' space of reasons in the way that scientific and legal claims can be. The justification for this view is that religion should be excluded from being a basis for political decisions. Rorty wishes philosophy as a metaphysical project to be replaced by 'literature', a concern with what different vocabularies can do to transform our relations to the world and each other:

> A culture which has substituted literature for both religion and philosophy finds redemption neither in a non-cognitive relation to a non-human person nor in a cognitive relation to propositions, but in non-cognitive relations to other human beings, relations mediated by human artefacts such as books and buildings, paintings and songs. These artefacts provide glimpses of alternative ways of being human.[12]

If one cedes many of the explanatory tasks associated with western metaphysics to the natural sciences – the later Heidegger thinks metaphysics becomes the modern sciences – the focus of philosophy should move towards kinds of sense-making which cannot be achieved in scientific terms. This does not entail abandoning all of the established philosophical agenda – though it questions the analytical emphasis on epistemology, because of its signal failure in relation to the massive success of the scientific knowledge it is supposed to ground – but it does change the way in which that agenda is responded to.

I want to conclude with an example of how such a change can look, which is clearly associated with issues of transcendence, and which suggests how the kind of philosophical direction I am sketching here relates to music. The metaphysical debate over freedom of the will, which arises in its modern form with the empiricism of Locke, and which asks whether there can be freedom in a nature which is wholly deterministic, continues to rage, especially in the light of neuroscientific advances, which are regularly inflated into supposed refutations of the possibility of free-will, usually without any serious reflection on just what is meant by the term. The first thing to note here, as Adorno points out,[13] is that the way the issue of freedom of the will is conceived is itself a historical phenomenon,

---

[12]   Richard Rorty, 'The Decline of Redemptive Truth and the Rise of a Literary Culture' (2000), available at <http://olincenter.uchicago.edu/pdf/rorty.pdf> (accessed 8 Oct. 2013).

[13]   See Andrew Bowie, *Adorno and the Ends of Philosophy* (Cambridge, 2013), ch. 5.

arising, via Locke in particular, at a specific point in the emergence of bourgeois individualism. In its least reflective version the metaphysical idea of freedom of the will involves a special kind of causality in the subject which flicks an on-off switch when a real decision is made. If something else flicks the switch, like 'the brain' – though how the brain knows how to do anything is unclear, given that action is a social category not an attribute of neurones or anything else in the organism – we are supposedly just natural determined mechanisms. The point is that such a picture is essentially empty, telling us nothing about freedom as something which is inseparable from the notion of a meaningful human life. What would change in the unlikely event of there being a decisive demonstration that subjects indeed have this special causality? Would we really think moral life would be transformed? With respect to the other alternative, Adorno maintains, 'in the situation of a complete determinism with no gaps, criteria of good and evil would be just completely meaningless, you couldn't even ask about them'.[14] Why are people so excited by the possibility that there is no such thing as free-will, given that without their already having some real sense of freedom there would be nothing exciting in the issue to begin with? Even thinking about whether free-will exists and drawing consequences from that thinking involves capacities of reflection and criticism which make no sense if everything is actually determined.

The crucial point in the present context, which Schelling articulated when he moved away in the early 1800s from the heroic idealist view of freedom he shared early in his career with Fichte, is that if freedom is to be understood as some kind of transcendence our conception of it must incorporate what it is that freedom transcends. Without a ground that threatens to negate freedom, there would be no motivating force in the notion at all.[15] Schelling imagines a purely 'free' God who exists in the manner of a contented baby, in harmony with itself, who has no need to create the universe and then ponders why such a God would create the world. It is, he contends, only when there is a conflict between one impulse, and another which seeks to transcend it, but therefore requires it as the ground which it moves beyond, that freedom can become real. What Schelling's approach begins to reveal is how the very content of the notion of freedom is inherently historical, generated by its shifting dialectical counterparts, rather than metaphysical, in the sense of pertaining to some fundamental attribute of rational beings.[16] Instead of being some mysterious internal capacity for absolute beginnings, freedom has to do with the fact that the nature of being always involves transcendence of the historical given, and so a tension between a ground, and that which moves beyond it. Such a view can incorporate many of the ways in which freedom has been understood, but

---

[14]   Theodor W. Adorno, *Probleme der Moralphilosophie* (Frankfurt am Main, 1996), p. 218.

[15]   See Andrew Bowie, *Schelling and Modern European Philosophy* (London, 1993), ch. 5.

[16]   For a different, but related Hegelian take on freedom, see Robert Pippin, *Hegel's Practical Philosophy* (Cambridge, 2008).

makes no definitive metaphysical claims. Self-determination, for example, gains its significance in modernity because it is achieved against the ground of Kant's 'heteronomy', acquiescence before the given norms of traditional society whose legitimacy has been put in question by processes of secularisation.

If one looks at the most significant music in modernity, it can be understood precisely in terms of how it plays out this tension of ground and freedom. More importantly, music provides ways of understanding the tensions which circumvent another rerun of the usual philosophical arguments about freedom, by manifesting the way in which the ground-freedom relationship is inherent in our most basic ways of being in the world. It is often remarked that the most significant music is precisely concerned with the negative sides of human existence, with sadness, loss, mortality, transience, pain and longing. If we see these aspects of being as the ground in Schelling's sense, music and other arts can enact and communicate human freedom by making sense of things which may have no other way of being transcended in a secular world. The greatness of Bach's, Beethoven's, Bruckner's and others' music and of the most significant jazz musicians is generated precisely by the extent to which the music confronts negativity and turns it into something whose sense lies in transforming that negativity into a form of expression that temporarily liberates one from it, even as it incorporates the negativity into itself. In more everyday terms, the overcoming of obstacles in making music and moving to a higher level of music-making can offer a better understanding of freedom than some philosophical debates. Such overcoming is based in irreducible experiences of liberation that make no sense if one begins by trying to establish the theoretical justification for talking about freedom at all. The transcendence at issue here is, then, anchored in a thoroughly realistic (though not in the current philosophical sense) sense of the finitude and limitations of embodied human existence. It serves as a reminder that any current or dominant form of human existence can become a ground from which one may need to liberate oneself. In modernity, it seems that art may often provide more effective ways of achieving such transcendence than many forms of philosophy.

Bibliography

Adorno, Theodor. W., *The Jargon of Authenticity* (London: Routledge & Kegan Paul, 1973).

—— *Philosophie der neuen Musik* (Frankfurt am Main: Suhrkamp, 1975).

—— *Probleme der Moralphilosophie* (Frankfurt am Main: Suhrkamp, 1996).

Albrecht, Christian, *Schleiermachers Theorie der Frömmigkeit: Ihr wissenschaftlicher Ort und ihr systematischer Gehalt in den Reden, in der Glaubenslehre und in der Dialektik* (Berlin and New York: De Gruyter, 1994).

Almén, Byron, *A Theory of Musical Narrative* (Bloomington and Indianapolis: Indiana University Press, 2008).

Almond, Philip C., *Rudolf Otto: An Introduction to His Philosophical Theology*, Studies in Religion (Chapel Hill, NC: University of North Carolina Press, 1984).

Ameriks, Karl, 'Introduction: Interpreting German Idealism', in id. (ed.), *The Cambridge Companion to German Idealism* (Cambridge: Cambridge University Press, 2000).

Arndt, Andreas, '"Bedenke, daß alle Poesie schlechthin als Werk der Liebe anzusehen ist": Ethik und Ästhetik bei Schleiermacher', in *Friedrich Schleiermacher als Philosoph* (Berlin: De Gruyter, 2013).

Arndt, Wilhelm, and Bruno Krusch (eds), *Gregorii Turonensis Opera*, Monumenta Germaniae Historica: Scriptores rerum Merovingicarum 1 (Hannover, 1885).

Athanasius, *On the Incarnation of the Word*, in *Selected Works and Letters*, ed. A. Robinson, Nicene and Post-Nicene Fathers, ser. 2: 4 (Buffalo, NY: Christian Literature, 1892).

Austin, John L., *How To Do Things With Words* (Oxford: Oxford University Press, 1963).

Bach, Carl Philipp Emanuel, *The Complete Works* (Los Altos, Calif.: Packard Humanities Institute, 2005–).

—— *Heilig: Mit zwey Chören und einer Ariette zur Einleitung* (Hamburg: Verlage des Autors; Leipzig: Breikopfischen Buchdruckerey, 1779), available at <http://pds.lib.harvard.edu/pds/view/2581450> (accessed 16 Mar. 2013).

—— *Holy is God (Heilig)*, ed. Karl Geiringer (St. Louis, Miss.: Concordia Publishing House, 1956).

Bachmann, Werner, *The Origins of Bowing and the Development of Bowed Instruments up to the Thirteenth Century*, trans. Norma Deane (Oxford: Oxford University Press, 1969).

Badiou, Alain, *Being and Event*, trans. Oliver Feltham (London: Continuum, 2005).

——— *Briefings on Existence: A Short Treatise on Transitory Ontology* (Albany: State University of New York Press, 2006).

——— *Century*, trans. Alberto Toscano (Cambridge: Polity Press, 2007).

——— *Handbook of Inaesthetics*, trans. Alberto Toscano (Stanford, Calif.: Stanford University Press, 2005).

——— *Infinite Thought: Truth and the Return to Philosophy*, trans. Oliver Feltham and Justin Clemens (London: Continuum, 2003).

——— *Logics of Worlds: Being and Event II*, trans. Alberto Toscano (London: Continuum, 2009).

——— *Manifesto for Philosophy*, trans. Norman Madarasz (Albany: State University of New York Press, 1999).

——— *Metapolitics*, trans. Jason Barker (London: Verso, 2005).

——— *Number and Numbers*, trans. Robin MacKay (Cambridge: Polity Press, 2008).

——— *Polemics*, trans. Steve Corcoran (London: Verso, 2006).

——— *Theoretical Writings*, trans. and ed. Ray Brassier and Alberto Toscano (London: Continuum, 2004).

Baines, Anthony, 'Fifteenth-Century Instruments in Tinctoris's *De Inventione et Usu Musicae*', *Galpin Society Journal*, 3 (1950): 19–26.

Balkwill, Laura-Lee, and William Forde Thompson, 'A Cross-Cultural Investigation of the Perception of Emotion in Music: Psychophysical and Cultural Cues', *Music Perception: An Interdisciplinary Journal*, 17/1 (1999): 43–64.

Bamberger, Jeanne, 'How the Conventions of Music Notation Shape Musical Perception and Performance', in Dorothy Miell, Raymond MacDonald and David J. Hargreaves (eds), *Musical Communication* (Oxford: Oxford University Press, 2005).

Barbour, Ian, *Issues in Science and Religion* (Englewood Cliffs, NJ: Prentice-Hall, 1966).

Barkhoff, Jürgen, 'Romantische Naturphilosophie', in Detlef Kremer (ed.), *E.T.A. Hoffmann: Leben – Werk – Wirkung*, 2nd expanded edn (Berlin: De Gruyter, 2010).

Barnes, Jonathan (trans. and ed.), *Early Greek Philosophy* (London: Penguin, 1987).

Barth, Karl, 'Schleiermachers "Weihnachtsfeier"', in *Gesamtausgabe*, vol. 3: *Vorträge und kleinere Arbeiten 1922–1925*, ed. Holger Finze (Zurich: Theologischer Verlag, 1990).

Barth, Ulrich, 'Die Religionstheorie der "Reden": Schleiermachers theologisches Modernisierungsprogramm', in *Aufgeklärter Protestantismus* (Tübingen: Mohr Siebeck, 2004).

Batteux, Charles, *Les Beaux Arts réduits à un même principe* (Paris: Durand, 1746).

Beaumont, Antony, *Busoni the Composer* (London: Faber & Faber, 1985).

Beck, Guy L., *Sonic Theology* (Columbia: University of South Carolina Press, 1993).

Becker, Judith, *Deep Listeners: Music, Emotion and Trancing* (Bloomington and Indianapolis: Indiana University Press, 2004).

Begbie, Jeremy S., *Theology, Music and Time* (Cambridge: Cambridge University Press, 2000).

—— and Steven R. Guthrie, *Resonant Witness: Conservations between Music and Theology* (Grand Rapids, Mich.: Eerdmans, 2011).

Beiser, Frederick C., *The Romantic Imperative: The Concept of Early German Romanticism* (Cambridge, Mass.: Harvard University Press, 2003).

Bellah, Robert N., and Hans Joas (eds), *The Axial Age and Its Consequences* (Cambridge, Mass.: Harvard University Press, 2012).

Benson, Bruce Ellis, *The Improvisation of Musical Dialogue: A Phenomenology of Music* (Cambridge: Cambridge University Press, 2003).

Bent, Ian, 'Plato-Beethoven: A Hermeneutics for Nineteenth-Century Music?', in id. (ed.), *Music Theory in the Age of Romanticism* (Cambridge: Cambridge University Press, 1996).

Bergeron, Katherine, and Philip V. Bohlman (eds), *Disciplining Music: Musicology and Its Canons* (Chicago: University of Chicago Press, 1992).

Berryman, Luke, 'Messiaen as Explorer in *Livre du Saint Sacrement*', in Andrew Shenton (ed.), *Messiaen the Theologian* (Farnham and Burlington: Ashgate, 2010).

Bisanz-Prakken, Marian, 'The Beethoven Exhibition of the Secession and the Younger Viennese Tradition of the Gesamtkunstwerk', in Erika Nielsen (ed.), *Focus on Vienna: Change and Continuity in Literature, Music, Art and Intellectual History*, Houston German Studies 4 (Munich: Wilhelm Fink, 1982).

Blasius, Leslie D., *Schenker's Argument and the Claims of Music Theory* (Cambridge: Cambridge University Press, 1996).

Bloom, Harold, *The Anxiety of Influence* (Oxford: Oxford University Press, 1973).

Blume, Friedrich, *Classic and Romantic Music: A Comprehensive Survey*, trans. M.D. Herter Horton (New York: Norton, 1970).

Boethius, Anicius, *De Institutione Musica* [Fundamentals of Music], trans. Calvin M. Bower, ed. Claude V. Palisca (New Haven, Conn.: Yale University Press, 1989).

Bolland, Jean et al. (eds), *Acta Sanctorum*, 68 vols. (Brussels and Antwerp: Société des Bollandistes, 1643–1940).

Bonds, Mark Evan, *Music as Thought: Listening to the Symphony in the Age of Beethoven* (Princeton, NJ: Princeton University Press, 2006).

Borges, Jorge Luis, *Labyrinths* (London: Penguin, 1970).

Born, Georgina, and David Hesmondhalgh (eds), *Western Music and Its Others: Difference, Representation and Appropriation in Music* (Berkeley: University of California Press, 2000).

Bouillon, Jean-Paul, *Klimt: Beethoven: The Frieze for the Ninth Symphony* (New York: Rizzoli, 1987).

Boulez, Pierre, *Orientations*, trans. Martin Cooper (Cambridge, Mass.: Harvard University Press, 1986).

Bourdieu, Pierre, *Outline of a Theory of Practice*, trans. Richard Nice (Cambridge: Cambridge University Press, 1977).

Bowie, Andrew, *Adorno and the Ends of Philosophy* (Cambridge: Polity, 2013).

—— *Aesthetics and Subjectivity: from Kant to Nietzsche*, 2nd edn (Manchester: Manchester University Press, 2003).

—— *Music, Philosophy, and Modernity* (Cambridge: Cambridge University Press, 2007).

—— *Schelling and Modern European Philosophy* (London: Routledge, 1993).

Bowman, Wayne C., *Philosophical Perspectives on Music* (Oxford: Oxford University Press, 1998).

Brady, Emily, *The Sublime in Modern Philosophy: Aesthetics, Ethics and Nature* (Cambridge: Cambridge University Press, 2013).

Brandom, Robert, *Articulating Reasons: An Introduction to Inferentialism* (Cambridge Mass. and London: Harvard University Press, 2000).

Braver, Lee, *Groundless Grounds: A Study of Heidegger and Wittgenstein* (Cambridge, Mass.: MIT Press, 2012).

Brown, Frank Burch, 'Aesthetics and the Arts in Relation to Natural Theology', in Russell Re Manning (ed.), *The Oxford Handbook of Natural Theology* (Oxford: Oxford University Press, 2013).

Brown, William P., *The Ethos of the Cosmos: The Genesis of Moral Imagination in the Bible* (Grand Rapids, Mich.: Eerdmans, 1999).

Bull, Michael, *Sounding Out the City: Personal Stereos and the Management of Everyday Life* (Oxford and New York: Berg, 2000).

Burnham, Scott, 'Haydn and Humour', in Caryl Clark (ed.), *The Cambridge Companion to Haydn* (Cambridge: Cambridge University Press, 2005).

Burrows, David, 'On Hearing Things: Music, The World and Ourselves', *Musical Quarterly*, 66/2 (1980): 180–91.

Busoni, Ferruccio, 'The Essence and Oneness of Music', in *The Essence of Music and Other Papers*, trans. Rosamond Ley (London: Rockliff, 1957).

—— 'The Realm of Music: An Epilogue to the New Esthetic', in *The Essence of Music and Other Papers*, trans. Rosamond Ley (London: Rockliff, 1957).

—— 'Self-Criticism', in *The Essence of Music and Other Papers*, trans. Rosamond Ley (London: Rockliff, 1957).

—— 'Sketch of a New Esthetic of Music', in *Three Classics in the Aesthetic of Music* (New York: Dover, 1962).

—— 'Young Classicism', in *The Essence of Music and Other Papers*, trans. Rosamond Ley (London: Rockliff, 1957).

Caputo, John D., *Truth: Philosophy in Transit* (London: Penguin, 2013).

—— and Michael J. Scanlon, 'Introduction: Do We Need to Transcend Transcendence?', in eid. (eds), *Transcendence and Beyond: A Postmodern Enquiry* (Bloomington and Indianapolis: Indiana University Press, 2007).

Carpenter, Patricia, 'Aspects of Musical Space', in Eugene Narmour and Ruth A. Solie (eds), *Explorations in Music, the Arts, and Ideas: Essays in Honour of Leonard B. Meyer* (Stuyvesant, NY: Pendragon, 1988).

Carroll, Noël, *Philosophy of Art: A Contemporary Introduction* (London: Routledge, 1999).

Casey, Edward S., *The Fate of Place: A Philosophical History* (Berkeley: University of California Press, 2008).

—— 'How to Get from Space to Place in a Fairly Short Stretch of Time: Phenomenological Prolegomena', in Steven Feld and Keith Basso (eds), *Senses of Place* (Santa Fe, N.Mex.: School of American Research Press, 1997).

—— 'Keeping the Past in Mind', in Don Ihde and Hugh J. Silverman (eds), *Descriptions* (Albany: State University of New York Press, 1985).

Chantler, Abigail, *E.T.A. Hoffmann's Musical Aesthetics* (Aldershot: Ashgate, 2006).

Chessa, Luciano, *Luigi Russolo, Futurist: Noise, Visual Arts and the Occult* (Berkeley and Los Angeles: University of California Press, 2012).

Chrétien, Jean-Louis, *The Call and the Response*, trans. Anne A. Davenport (New York: Fordham University Press, 2004).

—— *Hand to Hand: Listening to the Work of Art*, trans. Stephen E. Lewis (New York: Fordham University Press, 2003).

Clarke, Eric, *Ways of Listening: An Ecological Approach to the Perception of Musical Meaning* (Oxford: Oxford University Press, 2005).

Clifton, Thomas, and Alfred Pike, 'A Phenomenological Analysis of Musical Experience and Other Related Essays', *Journal of Musical Theory*, 14/2 (1970): 237–46.

Cohen, Paul J., *Set Theory and the Continuum Hypothesis* (New York: W.A. Benjamin, 1966).

Cohen, Sara, 'Sounding Out the City: Music and the Sensuous Production of Place', *Transactions of the Institute of British Geographers*, 20/4 (1995): 434–46.

Collingwood, Robin G., *The Principles of Art* (Oxford: Oxford University Press, 1938).

Comini, Alessandra, *The Changing Image of Beethoven: A Study in Mythmaking* (New York: Rizzoli, 1987).

Connor, Steven, 'Edison's Teeth: Touching Hearing', in Veit Erlmann (ed.), *Hearing Cultures: Essays on Sound, Listening and Modernity* (Oxford and New York: Berg, 2004).

Cook, Nicholas, *The Schenker Project: Culture, Race and Music Theory in Fin-de-Siècle Vienna* (Oxford: Oxford University Press, 2007).

—— and Mark Everist (eds), *Re-Thinking Music* (Oxford: Oxfrod University Press, 1999).

Cooper, Martin, *Beethoven: The Last Decade* (London: Oxford University Press, 1970).

Couling, Della, *Ferruccio Busoni: A Musical Ishmael* (Oxford: Scarecrow Press, 2005).

Cowan, Michael, *Cult of the Will: Nervousness and German Modernity* (University Park: Pennsylvania State University Press, 2008).

Csordas, Thomas J., 'Asymptote of the Ineffable: Embodiment, Alterity, and the Theory of Religion', *Current Anthropology*, 45/2 (2004): 163–85.

—— *The Sacred Self: A Cultural Phenomenology of Charismatic Healing* (Berkeley, Los Angeles and London: University of California Press, 1994).

Dahlhaus, Carl, *The Idea of Absolute Music*, trans. Roger Lustig (Chicago: Chicago University Press, 1991).

—— *Die Idee der absoluten Musik* (Kassel: Bärenreiter-Verlag, 1978).

—— 'Romantische Musikästhetik und Wiener Klassik', in *Klassische und romantische Musikästhetik* (Laaber: Laaber-Verlag, 1988).

—— and Norbert Miller, *Europäische Romantik in der Musik*, vol. 2: *Oper und symphonischer Stil 1800–1850: Von E.T.A. Hoffmann zu Richard Wagner* (Stuttgart: Metzler, 2007).

Dastur, Francoise, 'Phenomenology of the Event: Waiting and Surprise', *Hypatia*, 15/4 (2000): 178–89.

Dawkins, Richard, *The God Delusion* (London: Bantam Press, 2006).

De La Grange, Henry-Louis, *Gustav Mahler*, vol. 2: *Vienna, the Years of Challenge (1897–1904)* (Oxford: Oxford University, 1995).

De Man, Paul, *Aesthetic Ideology*, ed. Andrzej Warminski (Minneapolis: University of Minnesota Press, 1996).

Dean, Roger T., and Freya Bailes, 'Toward a Sociobiology of Music', *Music Perception: An Interdisciplinary Journal*, 24/1 (2006): 83–5.

Deleuze, Gilles, *Pure Immanence: Essays on A Life*, trans. Anne Boyman (New York: Urzone, 2001).

Dennis, David B., *Beethoven in German Politics 1870–1969* (New Haven, Conn. and London: Yale University Press, 1996).

DeNora, Tia, *Beethoven and the Construction of Genius: Musical Politics in Vienna 1792–1803* (Berkeley and London: University of California Press, 1995).

—— *Music in Everyday Life* (Cambridge: Cambridge University Press, 2000).

Dent, Edward J., *Ferruccio Busoni: A Biography* (Oxford: Oxford University Press, 1933).

Derrida, Jacques, 'Afterword: Toward an Ethic of Conversation', in *Limited Inc*, ed. Gerald Graff (Evanston, Ill.: Northwestern University Press, 1979).

—— 'Before the Law', trans. Avital Ronell, in *Acts of Literature*, ed. Derek Attridge (London: Routledge, 1992).

—— 'The Law of Genre', trans. Avital Ronell, *Critical Inquiry*, 7/1 (1980): 55–81.

—— 'Limited Inc. a b c', *Glyph*, 2 (1977): 162–254.

—— *Of Grammatology*, trans. Gayatri Chakravorty Spivak (Baltimore: John Hopkins University Press, 1997).

—— 'The Parergon', in *The Truth in Painting*, trans. Geoff Bennington and Ian McLeod (Chicago: University of Chicago Press, 1987).

—— 'Signature Event Context', *Glyph*, 1 (1977): 172–97.

Detering, Heinrich, 'Was ist Kunstreligion? Systematische und historische Bemerkungen', in Albert Meier et al. (eds), *Kunstreligion: Ein ästhetisches Konzept der moderne in seiner historischen Entfaltung*, vol. 1: *Der Ursprung des Konzepts um 1800* (Berlin and New York: De Gruyter, 2011).

Dewey, John, *Art as Experience* (New York: Perigee Books, 1934).

Dierkes, Hans, 'Die problematische Poesie. Schleiermachers Beitrag zur Frühromantik', in K.-V. Selge (ed.), *Internationaler Schleiermacher-Kongreß Berlin 1984* (Berlin: De Gruyter, 1985).

Downey, Greg, 'Listening to Capoeira: Phenomenology, Embodiment and the Materiality of Music', *Ethnomusicology*, 46/3 (2002): 487–509.

Drabble, Margaret, *The Red Queen: A Transcultural Tragicomedy* (Orlando: Harcourt, 2004).

Duff, William, *Critical Observations on the Writings of the Most Celebrated Original Geniuses in Poetry* (London: T. Becket and P.A. de Hont, 1770).

Eagleton, Terry, *The Ideology of the Aesthetic* (Oxford: Blackwell, 1990).

Eisen, Cliff, 'The String Quartet', in Simon P. Keefe (ed.), *The Cambridge History of Eighteenth Century Music* (Cambridge: Cambridge University Press, 2005).

Ekkehard I: Vita Sanctae Wiboradae, trans. and ed. Walter Berschin (St Gallen: Historischer Verein des Kantons St Gallen, 1983).

Ellsiepen, Christof, *Anschauung des Universums und Scientia Intuitiva: Die spinozistische Grundlagen von Schleiermachers frühe Religionstheorie (Berlin: De Gruyter, 2006).*

Emerson, Ralph Waldo, 'Quotation and Originality', in *The Collected Works of Ralph Waldo Emerson*, vol. 8, *Letters and Social Aims*, ed. Ronald A. Bosco, Glen M. Johnson and Joel Myerson (Cambridge, Mass.: Belknap, 2010).

Erne, Thomas, 'Schleiermacher on Music and Religion. The "Sound" of Schleiermacher in Felix Mendelssohn-Bartholdy's Music', in Dietrich Korsch and Amber L. Griffioen (eds), *Interpreting Religion* (Tübingen: Mohr Siebeck, 2011).

Ernst, Carl W., 'Situating Sufism and Yoga', *Journal of the Royal Asiatic Society*, 3rd ser., 15/1 (2005): 15–43.

Feld, Steven, 'Waterfalls of Song: An Acoustemology of Place Resounding in Bosavi, Papua New Guinea', in Steven Feld and Keith Basso (eds), *Senses of Place* (Santa Fe, N.Mex.: School of American Research Press, 1997).

—— and Donald Brenneis, 'Doing Anthropology in Sound', *American Ethnologist*, 31/4 (2004): 461–74.

Fidom, J., 'Music as Installation Art: Organ Musicology, New Musicology and Situationality' (inaugural lecture: VU University, Amsterdam, 2011).

Fillippi, Gian Giuseppe, and Thomas Dahnhardt, 'Ananda Yoga: A Contemporary Crossing Between Sufism and Hinduism', in Vasudha Dalmia, Angelika Malinar and Martin Christof (eds), *Charisma and Canon: Essays on the Religious History of the Indian Subcontinent* (Oxford and New York: Oxford University Press, 2001).

Fleet, Paul, *Ferruccio Busoni: A Phenomenological Approach to His Music and Aesthetics* (Saarbrücken: Lambert Academic Publishing, 2009).

Forkel, Johann Nikolaus, *Über Johann Sebastian Bachs Leben, Kunst und Kunstwerke*, ed. Walther Vetter (Kassel: Bärenreiter, 1970).

Forster, Michael N., 'Hegel and Some (Near-)Contemporaries: Narrow or Broad Expressivism?', in *German Philosophy of Language* (Oxford: Oxford University Press, 2011).

Frank, Manfred, 'Metaphysical Foundations: A Look at Schleiermacher's *Dialectic*', in Jacqueline Mariña (ed.), *The Cambridge Companion to Friedrich Schleiermacher* (Cambridge: Cambridge University Press, 2005).

Fuller, David, 'The Performer as Composer', in Howard Mayer Brown and Stanley Sadie (eds), *Performance Practice*, vol. 2 (Basingstoke: Macmillan, 1989).

Gadamer, Hans-Georg, *The Relevance of the Beautiful and Other Essays*, trans. Nicholas Walker, ed. Robert Bernasconi (Cambridge: Cambridge University Press, 2002).

—— *Truth and Method*, trans. Joel Weinsheimer and Donald G. Marshall (New York and London: Continuum, 2nd revd edn, 1989; 3rd edn, 2004).

Gallagher, Shaun, 'Philosophical Antecedents of Situated Cognition', in Philip Robbins and Murat Aydede (eds), *The Cambridge Handbook of Situated Cognition* (Cambridge: Cambridge University Press, 2008).

Garner, Stanton B. Jr., 'Still Living Flesh: Beckett, Merleau Ponty, and the Phenomenological Body', *Theatre Journal*, 65/4 (1993): 443–60.

Gertz, Martin C. (ed.), *Vitae Sanctorum Danorum*, 2 vols (Copenhagen: G.E.C. Gad, 1908–10).

Geuss, Raymond, 'Glossary', in Friedrich Nietzsche, *The Birth of Tragedy and Other Writings*, ed. Raymond Geuss and Ronald Speirs (Cambridge: Cambridge University Press, 1999).

—— 'Introduction', in Friedrich Nietzsche, *The Birth of Tragedy and Other Writings*, ed. Raymond Geuss and Ronald Speirs (Cambridge: Cambridge University Press, 1999).

Gilman, Todd, 'Arne, Handel, the Beautiful, and the Sublime', *Eighteenth-Century Studies*, 42/4 (2009): 529–55.

Godwin, Joscelyn, *Harmonies of Heaven and Earth: The Spiritual Dimensions of Music from Antiquity to the Avant-Garde* (London: Inner Traditions, 1987).

Goehr, Lydia, *The Imaginary Museum of Musical Works: An Essay in the Philosophy of Music* (Oxford: Oxford University Press, 1992; revd edn, 2007).

Gold, Ann Grodzins, and Daniel Gold, 'Fate of the Householder Nath', *History of Religions*, 24/2 (1984): 113–32.

Gold, Daniel, 'Nath Yogis as Established Alternatives: Householders and Ascetics Today', in Karigoudar Ishwaran (ed.), *Ascetic Culture: Renunciation and Worldly Engagement*, International Studies in Sociology and Social Anthropology 73 (Leiden, Boston, Mass. and Cologne: Brill, 1999).

Gooch, Todd A., *The Numinous and Modernity: An Interpretation of Rudolf Otto's Philosophy of Religion*, Beihefte zur Zeitschrift für die Alttestamentliche Wissenschaft (Berlin and New York: De Gruyter, 2000).

Goodman, Nelson, *Languages of Art: An Approach to a Theory of Symbols* (Oxford: Oxford University Press, 1969; Indianapolis, Ind.: Hackett, 1976).

Grant, M.J., and Férdia J. Stone-Davis (eds), *The Soundtrack of Conflict: The Role of Radio Broadcasting in Wartime and Conflict Situations* (Hildesheim: Georg Olms Verlag, 2013).

Graves, Eben, 'Chaitanya Vaishnava Perspectives on the Bengali Khol', *Journal of Vaishnava Studies*, 17/2 (2009): 103–26.

Grillparzer, Franz, 'Funeral Oration', in Alexander Wheelock Thayer, *Life of Beethoven*, ed. Elliot Forbes, vol. 2 (Princeton, NJ: Princeton University Press, 1964).

Grove, Peter, *Deutungen des Subjekts: Schleiermachers Philosophie der Religion* (Berlin: De Gruyter, 2004).

Guido of Arezzo, *Regule Rithmice, Prologus in Antiphonarium and Epistola ad Michahelem: A Critical Text and Translation*, trans. and ed. Dolores Pesce, Institute of Mediaeval Music Musicological Studies 73 (Ottawa: Institute of Mediaeval Music, 1999).

Guyer, Paul, 'Monism and Pluralism in the History of Aesthetics', *Journal of Aesthetics and Art Criticism*, 71/2 (2013): 133–43.

Hagberg, Garry L., *Describing Ourselves: Wittgenstein and Autobiographical Consciousness* (Oxford: Oxford University Press, 2008).

Hamilton, Andy, *Aesthetics and Music* (London and New York: Continuum, 2007).

Hamilton, Kenneth, *After the Golden Age: Romantic Pianism and Modern Performance* (Oxford: Oxford University Press, 2008).

Hanslick, Eduard, *Vom Musikalisch-Schönen: Ein Beitrag zur Revision der Aestethik der Tonkunst* (Leipzig: Rudolph Weigel, 1854).

Haydn, Joseph, *String Quartet in E Flat Major*, ed. Wilhelm Altmann (Mineola, NY: Dover Publications, 1985).

Hayes, Glen A., 'The Vaishnava Sahajiya Traditions of Medieval Bengal', in Donald S. Lopez Jr. (ed.), *Religions of India in Practice* (Princeton, NJ: Princeton University Press, 1995).

Hegel, Georg Wilhelm Friedrich, *Lectures on the Philosophy of Religions*, ed. Peter C. Hodgson, vol. 1 (Oxford: Oxford University Press, 2007).

—— *Phenomenology of Spirit*, trans. A.V. Miller (Oxford: Clarendon, 1977).

Hein, Norvin, 'Comments: Radha and Erotic Community', in John Stratton Hawley and Donna Marie Wulff (eds), *The Divine Consort: Radha and the Goddesses of India* (Berkeley, Calif.: Graduate Theological Union, 1982).

Helmreich, Stefan, 'An Anthropologist Underwater: Immersive Soundscapes, Submarine Cyborgs, and Transductive Ethnography', *American Ethnologist*, 34/4 (2007): 621–41.

Herbert, James D., *Our Distance from God: Studies of the Divine and the Mundane in Western Art and Music* (Berkley and London: University of California Press, 2008).

Herder, Johann Gottfried, *Werke*, 10 vols (Frankfurt am Main: Deutscher Klassiker Verlag, 1998).

Hiley, David, *Western Plainchant: A Handbook* (Oxford: Oxford University Press, 1993).

Hirschkind, Charles, *The Ethical Soundscape: Cassette Sermons and Islamic Counterpublics* (New York: Columbia University Press, 2006).

'Historia de translatione sanctorum magni Nicolai terra marique miraculis gloriosi, ejusdem avunculi, alterius Nicolai, Theodorique, martyris pretiosi de civitate Mirea in monasterium S. Nicolai de Littore Venetiarum', in *Recueil des Historiens des Croisades, Historiens Occidentaux*, vol. 5 (Paris: Imprimerie royale, 1866).

Hoenderdaal, Gerrit J., *Riskant spel: Liturgie in een geseculariseerde wereld* (Zoetermeer: Boekencentrum, 1977).

Hof, Jan Jelles, 'Bydragen ta de skiednis fen it Fryske Wird: Boartsje', *De Swanneblommen* (1920): 11–15.

Hoffman, E.T.A., *Briefwechsel*, 3 vols (Munich: Winkler Verlag, 1967–69).

—— *Musical Writings*, ed. David Charlton, trans. Martyn Clarke (Cambridge: Cambridge University Press, 1989).

—— *Sämtliche Werke*, 6 vols (Frankfurt am Main: Deutscher Klassiker Verlag, 1985).

—— *Schriften zur Musik: Nachlese*, ed. Friedrich Schnapp (Munich: Winkler Verlag, 1963).

—— *Werke*, 2nd edn, 15 vols (Berlin: Bong & Co., [1927]).

Hofmanstahl, Hugo von, 'The Lord Chandos Letter', in *The Lord Chandos Letter and Other Writings*, ed. Joel Rotenberg (New York: New York Review Books, 2005).

Holdrege, Barbara A., 'From Nama-Avatara to Nama-Samkirtana: Gaudiya Perspectives on the Name', *Journal of Vaisnava Studies*, 17/2 (2009): 3–36.

Huizinga, Johan, *Homo ludens: Proeve eener bepaling van het spel-element der cultuur* (Haarlem: H.D. Tjeenk Willink & Zoon N.V., 1938).

Hunter, Mary, 'The Quartets', in Caryl Clark (ed.), *The Cambridge Companion to Haydn* (Cambridge: Cambridge University Press, 2005).

Ingold, Tim, 'Bindings against Boundaries: Entanglements of Life in an Open World', *Environment and Planning A*, 40 (2008): 1796–1810.

—— *The Perception of the Environment: Essays on Livelihood, Dwelling and Skill* (London: Routledge, 2000).

—— 'The Temporality of the Landscape', *World Archaeology*, 25/2 (1993): 152–74.

Irigaray, Luce, *Between East and West: From Singularity to Community* (New York: Columbia University Press, 2002).

James, Jamie, *The Music of the Spheres: Music, Science and the Natural Order of the Universe* (New York: Springer, 1995).

Joas, Hans, 'The Axial Age Debate as Religious Discourse', in Robert N. Bellah and Hans Joas (eds), *The Axial Age and Its Consequences* (Cambridge, Mass.: Harvard University Press, 2012).

Johnson, Julian, *Classical Music: A Beginners Guide* (Oxford: Oneworld, 2009).

Johnson, Mark, *The Meaning of the Body: Aesthetics of Human Understanding* (Chicago: University of Chicago Press, 2007).

Johnston, Mark, *Saving God: Religion after Idolatry* (Princeton, NJ: Princeton University Press, 2009).

—— *Surviving Death* (Princeton, NJ: Princeton University Press, 2010).

Johnstone, Keith, *Impro: Improvisation and the Theatre* (New York: Theatre Arts Books, 1979).

Justin Martyr, *The First Apology*, in *St Justin Martyr: The First and Second Apologies*, trans. L.W. Barnard (Mahwah, NJ: Paulist Press, 1997).

Kakar, Sudhir, 'Psychoanalysis and Religious Healing: Siblings or Strangers?', *Journal of the American Academy of Religion*, 53/4 (1985): 841–53.

Kant, Immanuel, *Critique of Judgement*, trans. J.C. Meredith (Oxford: Clarendon Press, 1978); trans. Werner S. Pluhar (Indianapolis: Hackett, 1987); *Critique of the Power of Judgment*, trans. and ed. Paul Guyer and Eric Matthews (Cambridge: Cambridge University Press, 2000).

—— *Prolegomena to Any Future Metaphysics that will be able to Come Forward as Science with Selections from the Critique of Pure Reason*, trans. and ed. Gary Hatfield, revd edn (Cambridge: Cambridge University Press, 2004).

Kearns, Cleo McNelly, 'Irigaray's *Between East and West*: Breath, Pranayama, and the Phenomenology of Prayer', in Bruce Ellis Benson and Norman Wirzba (eds), *The Phenomenology of Prayer* (New York: Fordham University Press, 2005).

Keller, Catherine, *Face of the Deep: A Theology of Becoming* (London: Routledge, 2003).

Kerman, Joseph, 'A Few Canonic Variations', *Critical Inquiry*, 10/1 (1983): 107–25.

—— 'How We got into Analysis, and How to get Out', *Critical Inquiry*, 7/2 (1980): 311–31.

—— *Musicology* (London: Fontana, 1985).

Kermode, Frank, *The Classic* (London: Faber, 1975).

—— *History and Value* (Oxford: Clarendon Press, 1988).

Kivy, Peter, 'Absolute Music and the New Musicology', in *New Essays on Musical Understanding* (Cambridge: Cambridge University Press, 1999).

—— *Antithetical Arts: On the Ancient Quarrel between Literature and Music* (Oxford: Oxford University Press, 2009).

—— *Authenticities: Philosophical Reflections on Musical Performance* (Ithaca, NY: Cornell University Press, 1995).

—— *Music Alone: Philosophical Reflections on the Purely Musical Experience* (Ithaca, NY: Cornell University Press, 1990).

Klemm, David, 'Schleiermacher on the Self: Immediate Self-Consciousness as Feeling and as Thinking', in David Klemm and Günter Zöller (eds), *Figuring the Self: Subject, Absolute and Others in Classical German Philosophy* (Albany: State University of New York Press, 1997).

Klinger, Max, *Painting and Drawing*, trans. Fiona Elliott (Birmingham: Ikon Gallery, 2004).

Knyt, Erinn E., 'Ferruccio Busoni and the Absolute in Music: Form, Nature and *Idee*', *Journal of the Royal Musical Association*, 137/1 (2012): 35–69.

—— 'Ferruccio Busoni and the Ontology of the Musical Work: Permutations and Possibilities' (PhD thesis: Stanford University, 2010).

—— '"How I Compose": Ferruccio Busoni's Views about Invention, Quotation, and the Compositional Process', *Journal of Musicology*, 27/2 (2011): 224–64.

Korsch, Dietrich, 'Das Universum im Ohr: Umrisse einer theologischen Musikästhetik', in Dietrich Korsch, Klaus Röhring and Joachim Herten (eds), *Das Universum im Ohr: Variationen zu einer theologischen Musikästhetik* (Leipzig: Evangelischer Verlagsanstalt, 2011).

Kramer, Lawrence, *Classical Music and Postmodern Knowledge* (Berkeley and Los Angeles: University of California Press, 1995).

—— *Music and Poetry: The Nineteenth Century and After* (Berkeley: University of California Press, 1984).

Kramer, Richard, 'The New Modulation of the 1770s: C.P.E. Bach in Theory, Criticism, and Practice', *Journal of the American Musicological Society*, 38/3 (1985): 551–92.

Krell, David Farrell, 'Phenomenology of Memory from Husserl to Merleau Ponty', *Philosophy and Phenomenological Research*, 42/4 (1982): 492–505.

Kühn, Paul, *Max Klinger* (Leipzig: Breitkopf & Hartel, 1907).

Lacoue-Labarthe, Philippe, and Jean-Luc Nancy, *The Literary Absolute: The Theory of Literature in German Romanticism*, trans. Philip Barnard and Cheryl Lester (Albany: State University of New York Press, 1988).

Lanfranc of Bec, *De corpore et sanguine Domini adversus Berengarium Turonensem liber*, Patrologiae cursus completes: Series latina 150, ed. J.P. Migne (Paris, 1844–45).

Langer, Susanne, *Feeling and Form: A Theory of Art Developed from Philosophy in a New Key* (New York: Macmillan, 1953).

Lehnerer, Thomas, *Die Kunsttheorie Friedrich Schleiermachers* (Stuttgart: Klett-Cotta, 1987).

Levinas, Emmanuel, 'God and Philosophy', in *Basic Philosophical Writings*, ed. Adriaan T. Peperzak, Simon Critchley and Robert Bernasconi (Bloomington: Indiana University Press, 1996).

Levinson, Jerrold, 'What a Musical Work Is', in *Music, Art, and Metaphysics: Essays in Philosophical Aesthetics* (Ithaca, NY: Cornell University Press, 1990).

Levitz, Tamara, *Teaching New Classicality: Ferruccio Busoni's Master Class in Composition* (Frankfurt am Main: Peter Lang, 1996).

Levy, Kenneth, *Gregorian Chant and the Carolingians* (Princeton, NJ: Princeton University Press, 1998).

Lindbeck, George A., *The Nature of Doctrine; Religion and Theology in a Postliberal Age* (London: SPCK, 1984).

Lochhead, Judy, and Joseph Auner (eds), *Postmodern Music / Postmodern Thought* (New York: Garland, 2002).

Lombardi, Daniele, *Il suono veloce: Futurismo e futurismi in musica* (Milan: Ricordi LIM, 1996).

Lönker, Fred, 'Beethovens Instrumentalmusik: Das Erhabene und die unendliche Sehnsucht', in Günter Saße (ed.), *E.T.A. Hoffmann: Romane und Erzählungen* (Stuttgart: Reclam Verlag, 2004).

Lowe, Walter, 'Postmodern Theology', in J.B. Webster, Kathryn Tanner and Iain R. Torrance (eds), *The Oxford Handbook of Systematic Theology* (Oxford: Oxford University Press, 2007).

McClary, Susan, 'Constructions of Subjectivity in Schubert's Music', in *Reading Music: Selected Essays* (Aldershot: Ashgate, 2007).

—— *The Content of Musical Form* (Berkeley and Los Angeles: University of California Press, 2001).

McDaniel, June, 'Emotion in Bengali Religious Thought: Substance and Metaphor', in Joel Marks and Roger T. Ames (eds), *Emotions in Asian Thought: A Dialogue in Comparative Philosophy* (Albany: State University of New York Press, 1995).

McGrath, Alister, *The Dawkins Delusion? Atheist Fundamentalism and the Denial of the Divine* (London: SPCK, 2007).

McGrath, William J., *Dionysian Art and Populist Politics in Austria* (London: Yale University Press, 1974).

McKinnon, James, *The Advent Project: The Later Seventh-Century Creation of the Roman Mass Proper* (Berkeley: University of California Press, 2000).

McVeigh, Simon, 'Performance in the "Long Eighteenth Century": An Overview', in Colin Lawson and Robin Stowell (eds), *The Cambridge History of Musical Performance* (Cambridge: Cambridge University Press, 2012).

Mallgrave, Harry Francis, 'Introduction', in Gottfried Semper, *The Four Elements of Architecture and Other Writings*, trans. Harry Francis Mallgrave and Wolfgang Hermann (Cambridge: Cambridge University Press, 1989).

Margolis, Joseph, 'Nothing Can Be Heard But Sound', *Analysis*, 20/4 (1960): 82–7.

Marion, Jean-Luc, 'The Final Appeal of the Subject', in John D. Caputo (ed.), *The Religious* (Oxford: Blackwell, 2002).

——— *The Idol and the Distance: Five Studies*, trans. Thomas A. Carlson (New York: Fordham University Press, 2001).

Marshall, Douglas A., 'Behavior, Belonging and Belief: A Theory of Ritual Practice', *Sociological Theory*, 20/3 (2002): 360–80.

Mattheson, Johann, *Der vollkommene Capellmeister*, trans. Ernest Charles Harris (Ann Arbor, Mich.: UMI Research Press, 1981).

May, Gerhard, *Creatio Ex Nihilo: The Doctrine of 'Creation out of Nothing' in Early Christian Thought*, trans. A.S. Worrall (Edinburgh: T.&T. Clark, 1994).

Mendelssohn Bartholdy, Felix, *Letters of Felix Mendelssohn Bartholdy from 1833–1847*, ed. Paul Mendelssohn Bartholdy and Carl Mendelssohn Bartholdy (London: Longman, Green, Longman, Robert & Green, 1864).

Midgley, Mary, *Are You an Illusion?* (Durham: Acumen, 2014).

Milbank, John, *Being Reconciled: Ontology and Pardon* (London: Routledge, 2003).

——— '"Postmodern Critical Augustinianism": A Short *Summa* in Forty Two Responses to Unasked Questions', *Modern Theology*, 7/3 (1991): 225–37.

——— 'Sublimity: The Modern Transcendent', in Regina M. Schwartz (ed.), *Transcendence: Philosophy, Literature, and Theology Approach the Beyond* (New York: Routledge, 2004).

Milton, John, *Eikonoklastes*, in *Complete Prose Works of John Milton*, vol. 3, *1648–1649*, ed. Merritt Y. Hughes (New Haven, Conn.: Yale University Press, 1962).

Minden, Michael, *The German* Bildungsroman (Cambridge: Cambridge University Press, 1997).

Monelle, Raymond, *The Sense of Music: Semiotic Essays* (Princeton, NJ: Princeton University Press, 2000).

Monk, Samuel Holt, *The Sublime: A Study of Critical Theories in XVIII-Century England* (New York: Modern Language Association of America, 1935).

Morley, James, 'Inspiration and Expiration: Yoga Practice through Merleau-Ponty's Phenomenology of the Body', *Philosophy East and West*, 51/1 (2001): 73–82.

Morris, Leslie, 'The Sound of Memory', *German Quarterly*, 74/4 (2001): 368–78.

Murphy, John P., 'Jazz Improvisation: The Joy of Influence', *Black Perspective in Music*, 18:1/2 (1990): 7–19.

Narmour, Eugene, *Beyond Schenkerism: The Need for Alternatives in Music Analysis* (Chicago: University of Chicago Press, 1977).

Naumann, Barbara, *Musikalisches Ideen-Instrument: Das Musikalische in Poetik und Sprachtheorie der Frühromantik* (Stuttgart: Metzler, 1990).

Negus, Kenneth, *E.T.A. Hoffmann's Other World: The Romantic Author and His 'New' Mythology* (Philadelphia: University of Pennsylvania Press, 1965).

Nietzsche, Friedrich, *Beyond Good and Evil*, trans. Judith Norman (Cambridge: Cambridge University Press, 2002).

—— *The Birth of Tragedy out of the Spirit of Music*, trans. Ronald Speirs, in *The Birth of Tragedy and Other Writings*, ed. Raymond Geuss and Ronald Speirs (Cambridge: Cambridge University Press, 1999).

—— *The Dionysiac World View*, trans. Ronald Speirs, in *The Birth of Tragedy and Other Writings*, ed. Raymond Geuss and Ronald Speirs (Cambridge: Cambridge University Press, 1999).

Norris, Christopher, *Badiou's* Being and Event: *A Reader's Guide* (London: Continuum, 2009).

—— *Paul de Man: Deconstruction and the Critique of Aesthetic Ideology* (New York: Routledge, 1988).

—— 'Remembering Frank Kermode', *Textual Practice*, 25/1 (2011): 1–13.

Novalis, *Die Lehrlinge zu Sais*, in *Werke, Tagebücher, und Briefe Friedrich von Hardenbergs*, ed. Hans-Joachim Mähl and Richard Samuel, 3 vols (Munich: Hanser Verlag, 1978–87).

Nowak, Kurt, *Schleiermacher: Leben, Werk und Wirkung* (Göttingen: Vandenhoeck & Ruprecht, 2002).

—— *Schleiermacher und die Frühromantik: Eine literaturgeschichtliche Studie zum romantischen Religionsverständnis und Menschenbild am Ende des 18. Jahrhunderts in Deutschland* (Göttingen: Vandenhoeck & Ruprecht, 1986).

Nudds, Matthew, 'Sounds and Space', in Casey O'Callaghan and Matthew Nudds (eds), *Sounds and Perception: New Philosophical Essays* (Oxford: Oxford University Press, 2009).

Nuovo, Victor, *Visionary Science: A Translation of Tillich's 'On the Idea of a Theology of Culture' with Interpretive Essay* (Detroit: Wayne State University Press, 1987).

O'Callaghan, Casey, and Matthew Nudds, 'Introduction: The Philosophy of Sounds and Auditory Perception', in eid. (eds), *Sounds and Perception: New Philosophical Essays* (Oxford: Oxford University Press, 2009).

O'Shaughnessy, Brian, 'The Location of Sound', *Mind*, ns 66/264 (1957): 471–90.

Obeyeskere, Gananath, 'The Fire Walkers of Kataragama: The Rise of Bhakti Religiosity in Buddhist Sri Lanka', *Journal of Asian Studies*, 37/3 (1978): 457–76.

Osborne, Charles, *The Complete Operas of Richard Wagner* (London: Da Capo Press, 1990).

Ottenberg, Hans-Günter, *C.P.E. Bach* (Oxford and New York: Oxford University Press, 1987).

Otto, Rudolf, *The Idea of the Holy: An Inquiry into the Non-Rational Factor in the Idea of the Divine and Its Relation to the Rational*, trans. John W. Harvey (London and New York: Oxford University Press, 1923; 2nd edn, 1950).

Page, Christopher, *The Christian West and Its Singers: The First Thousand Years* (New Haven, Conn.: Yale University Press, 2010).

—— 'An English Motet of the 14th Century in Performance: Two Contemporary Images', *Early Music*, 25 (1997): 7–32.

—— *The Owl and the Nightingale: Musical Life and Ideas in France 1100–1300* (London: Dent, 1989).

Panksepp, Jaak, 'The Emotional Sources of "Chills" Induced by Music', *Music Perception: An Interdisciplinary Journal*, 13/2 (1995): 171–207.

Pasnau, Robert, 'What is Sound', *Philosophical Quarterly*, 49/196 (1999): 309–24.

Pater, Walter, *The Renaissance* (Mineola, NY: Dover, 2005).

Peraino, Judith A., 'Listening to the Sirens: Music as Queer Ethical Practice', *Journal of Lesbian and Gay Studies*, 9/4 (2003): 433–70.

Pippin, Robert, *Hegel's Practical Philosophy* (Cambridge: Cambridge University Press, 2008).

Plato, *Symposium*, in *The Collected Dialogues*, ed. Edith Hamilton and Huntington Cairns (Princeton, NJ: Princeton University Press, 1961).

Poland, Lynn, 'The Idea of the Holy and the History of the Sublime', *Journal of Religion*, 72/2 (1992): 175–97.

Potter, Michael, *Set Theory and Its Philosophy: A Critical Introduction* (Oxford: Oxford University Press, 2004).

Proudfoot, Wayne, *Religious Experience* (Berkeley: University of California Press, 1985).

Pseudo-Dionysius, *The Divine Names*, in *The Complete Works*, trans. Colin Luibheid and Paul Rorem (New York: Paulist Press, 1987).

Quine, Willard van Orman, *From a Logical Point of View* (Cambridge, Mass. and London: Harvard University Press, 1980).

Rad, Gerhard von, *Old Testament Theology*, trans. D.M.G. Stalker, 2 vols (New York: Harper & Row, 1962).

Rajchman, John, 'Introduction', in Gilles Deleuze, *Pure Immanence: Essays on A Life*, trans. Anne Boyman (New York: Urzone, 2001).

Raphael, Melissa, *Rudolf Otto and the Concept of Holiness* (Oxford and New York: Clarendon Press, 1997).

Rathey, Markus, 'Carl Philipp Emanuel Bachs *Donnerode*: Zur Politischen Funktion des "*Erhabenen*" in der zweiten Hälfte des 18. Jahrhunderts', *Archiv für Musikwissenschaft*, 66/4 (2009): 286–305.

Re Manning, Russell (ed.), *The Oxford Handbook of Natural Theology* (Oxford: Oxford University Press, 2013).

—— 'The Religious Meaning of Culture: Paul Tillich and Beyond', *International Journal of Systematic Theology*, 15/4 (2013): 437–52.

—— *Theology at the End of Culture: Paul Tillich's Theology of Culture and Art* (Leuven: Peeters Press, 2005).

—— 'Tillich's Theology of Art', in id. (ed.), *The Cambridge Companion to Paul Tillich* (Cambridge: Cambridge University Press, 2009).

Reitsma, Oane, 'Some Time for Timelessness', in Wessel Stoker and W.L. van der Merwe (eds), *Looking Beyond: Shifting Views of Transcendence in Philosophy, Theology, the Arts, and Politics*, Currents of Encounter 42 (Amsterdam and New York: Rodopi, 2012).

Richards, Annette. 'An Enduring Moment: C.P.E. Bach and the Musical Sublime', in ead. (ed.), *C.P.E. Bach Studies* (Cambridge and New York: Cambridge University Press, 2006).

Ridley, Aaron, *Nietzsche on Art* (London: Routledge, 2007).

Rodaway, Paul, *Sensuous Geographies: Body, Sense and Place* (London and New York: Routledge, 1994).

Rorty, Richard, 'The Decline of Redemptive Truth and the Rise of a Literary Culture' (2000), available at <http://olincenter.uchicago.edu/pdf/rorty.pdf> (accessed 8 Oct. 2013).

Sabaneyeff, Leonid, *Modern Russian Composers*, trans. Judah A. Joffe (1927; repr. New York: Da Capo, 1975).

Said, Edward, *Beginnings: Intention and Method* (New York: Columbia University Press, 1985).

Salmen, Walter, 'Social Obligations of the Emancipated Musician in the 19th Century', trans. Herbert Kaufman and Barbara Reisner, in Herbert Kaufman and Barbara Reisner (eds), *The Social Status of the Professional Musician from the Middle Ages to the 19th Century* (New York: Pendragon, 1983).

Salomon, Carol, 'Baul Songs', in Donald S. Lopez Jr. (ed.), *Religions of India in Practice* (Princeton, NJ: Princeton University Press, 1995).

Sanders, Reginald LeMonte, 'Carl Phillipp Emanuel Bach and Liturgical Music at the Hamburg Principal Churches from 1768 to 1788' (PhD thesis: Yale University, 2001).

Schelling, F.W.J., *Werke*, 3 vols (Leipzig: F. Eckhardt, 1907).

Schenker, Heinrich, *Free Composition*, trans. and ed. Ernst Oster (New York: Longman, 1979).

Schleiermacher, Friedrich, *Ästhetik*, ed. Rudolf Odebrecht (Berlin and Leipzig: De Gruyter, 1931); *Ästhetik (1819/25): Über den Begriff der Kunst*, ed. Thomas Lehnerer (Hamburg: Meiner Verlag, 1984).

—— *The Christian Faith* (London and New York: T.&T. Clark, 1999).

—— *Christmas Eve Celebration: A Dialogue*, trans. and ed. Terrence N. Tice (Eugene, Oreg.: Cascade Books, 2010).

—— *Dialektik*, ed. Manfred Frank (Frankfurt am Main: Suhrkamp, 2001).

—— *Lectures on Philosophical Ethics*, ed. Robert B. Louden (Cambridge: Cambridge University Press, 2002).

—— *On Religion: Speeches to Its Cultured Despisers*, trans. and ed. Richard Crouter (Cambridge: Cambridge University Press, 1996).

—— *Vorlesungen über die Aesthetik*, ed. Carl Lommatzsch (Berlin: Reimer, 1842).

—— *Vorlesungen über die Dialektik*, ed. Andreas Arndt, Kritische Gesamtausgabe 2: 10/2 (Berlin: De Gruyter, 2002).

Schloesser, Stephen, 'The Charm of Impossibilities: Mystic Surrealism as Contemplative Voluptuousness', in Andrew Shenton (ed.), *Messiaen the Theologian* (Farnham and Burlington: Ashgate, 2010).

Scholtz, Gunter, 'Schleiermacher', trans. Susan H. Gillespie, in Stefan Lorenz Sorgner and Oliver Fürbeth (eds), *Music in German Philosophy* (Chicago: Chicago University Press, 2010).

—— *Schleiermachers Musikphilosophie* (Göttingen: Vandenhoeck & Ruprecht, 1981).

Schopenhauer, Arthur, *The World as Will and Representation*, trans. E.F.J. Payne, 2 vols (Indiana Hills, Colo.: Falcon's Wing Press, 1958).

Schorske, Carl E., *Fin-de-Siècle Vienna: Politics and Culture* (New York: Vintage, 1981).

Schrag, Calvin O., *God as Otherwise than Being: Towards a Semantics of the Gift* (Evanston, Ill.: Northwestern University Press, 2002).

—— 'Transcendence and Transversality', in John D. Caputo and Michael J. Scanlon (eds), *Transcendence and Beyond: A Postmodern Enquiry* (Bloomington and Indianapolis: Indiana University Press, 2007).

Schryer, Claude, 'Sound Ecology', *Leonardo*, 25/2 (1992): 219–20.

Schüßler, Werner, 'Where Does Religion Come From? Paul Tillich's Concept of *Grundoffenbarung*', in Michel Despland, Jean-Claude Petit and Jean Richard (eds), *Religion et Culture* (Laval: Les Presses de l'Université de Laval, 1987).

Schwartz, Benjamin I., 'The Age of Transcendence', *Daedalus*, 104/2 (1975): 1–7.

Scruton, Roger, *The Aesthetics of Music* (Oxford: Oxford University Press, 1997; 1999).

—— 'Review: Aesthetics and Music, by Andy Hamilton', *Mind*, 117/467 (2008): 702–5.

—— *The Soul of the World* (Princeton, NJ: Princeton University Press, 2014).

—— 'The Space of Music: Review Essay of Dmitri Tymoczko's *A Geometry of Music*', *Reason Papers*, 34/2 (2012): 167–83.

Searle, John R., 'Reiterating the Differences: A Reply to Derrida', *Glyph*, 1 (1977): 198–208.

Seeger, Charles, 'Who Owns Folklore? A Rejoinder', *Western Folklore*, 21/2 (1962): 93–101.

Semper, Gottfried, *The Four Elements of Architecture and Other Writings*, trans. Harry Francis Mallgrave and Wolfgang Hermann (Cambridge: Cambridge University Press, 1989).

—— *Style in the Technical and Tectonic Arts, or Practical Aesthetics*, trans. Harry Francis Mallgrave and Michael Robinson (Los Angeles: Getty, 2004).

Shannon, Jonathan H., 'The Aesthetics of Spiritual Practice and the Creation of Moral and Musical Subjectivities in Aleppo, Syria', *Ethnology*, 43/4 (2004): 381–91.

Shapiro, Alexander H., '"Drama of an Infinitely Superior Nature": Handel's Early English Oratorios and the Religious Sublime', *Music and Letters*, 74/2 (1993): 215–45.

Shaw-Miller, Simon, *Vienna 1900–1935* (London: Cantate, 2008).

—— *Visible Deeds of Music: Art and Music from Wagner to Cage* (New Haven, Conn. and London: Yale University Press, 2002).

Shepherd, John, and Peter Wicke, *Music and Cultural Theory* (Cambridge: Polity, 1997).

Siegel, Hedi (ed.), *Schenker Studies* (Cambridge: Cambridge University Press, 1990).

Siegel, Linda, 'Wackenroder's Musical Essays in "Phantasien über die Kunst"', *Journal of Aesthetics and Art Criticism*, 30/3 (1972): 351–8.

Silverthorne, Diane V., 'Wagner's Gesamtkunstwerk', in Tim Shephard and Anne Leonard (eds), *The Routledge Companion to Music and the Visual Arts* (New York, Oxford: Routledge, 2013).

Sjöberg, Sami, 'Mysticism of Immanence: Lettrism, Sprachkritik, and the Immediate Message', *Partial Answers: Journal of Literature and the History of Ideas*, 11/1 (2013): 53–69.

Slawek, Stephen M., 'Popular Kirtan in Benaras: Some "Great" Aspects of a Little Tradition', *Ethnomusicology*, 32/2 (1988): 77–92.

Smith, Ruth, *Handel's Oratorios and Eighteenth-Century Thought* (Cambridge: Cambridge University Press, 1995).

Solie, Ruth A., 'The Living Work: Organicism and Musical Analysis', *19th-Century Music*, 4/2 (1980): 147–56.

—— (ed.), *Musicology and Difference* (Berkeley: University of California Press, 1993).

Solomon, Maynard, 'Beethoven's Creative Process: A Two-Part Invention', in *Beethoven Essays* (Cambridge, Mass.: Harvard University Press, 1988).

—— *Late Beethoven: Music, Thought, Imagination* (Berkeley and Los Angeles: University of California Press, 2004).

Spitzer, Michael, *Music as Philosophy: Adorno and Beethoven's Late Style* (Bloomington: Indiana University Press, 2006).

Steinberg, Michael P., *Listening to Reason: Culture, Subjectivity, and Nineteenth-Century Music* (Princeton, NJ: Princeton University Press, 2006).

—— 'Vienna Trilogy: Vignettes from the City of Music', in Michael Steinberg and Larry Rothe, *For the Love of Music: Invitations to Listening* (Oxford: Oxford University Press, 2006).

Steiner, George, *Grammars of Creation* (London: Faber & Faber, 2002).

—— *Real Presences: Is There Anything in What We Say?* (Chicago: University of Chicago Press, 1989).

Stoker, Wessel, and W.L. van der Merwe (eds), *Culture and Transcendence: A Typology of Transcendence* (Leuven: Peeters, 2012).

—— and —— (eds), *Looking Beyond: Shifting Views of Transcendence in Philosophy, Theology, the Arts, and Politics*, Currents of Encounter 42 (Amsterdam and New York: Rodopi, 2012).

Stoller, Paul, *The Taste of Ethnographic Things: The Senses in Anthropology* (Philadelphia: University of Pennsylvania Press, 1989).

Stoltzfus, Philip, *Theology as Performance: Music, Aesthetics, and God in Western Thought* (New York and London: T.&T. Clark, 2006).

Stone, Alison, 'Being, Knowledge, and Nature in Novalis', *Journal of the History of Philosophy*, 46/ 1 (2008): 141–63.

—— 'Friedrich Schlegel, Romanticism, and the Re-Enchantment of Nature', *Inquiry: An Interdisciplinary Journal of Philosophy*, 48/1 (2005): 3–25.

—— 'German Romantic and Idealist Conceptions of Nature', *International Yearbook of German Idealism*, 6 (2009): 80–101.

—— 'The Romantic Absolute', *British Journal for the History of Philosophy*, 19/3 (2011): 497–517.

Stone-Davis, Férdia J., 'Music and Liminality: Becoming Sensitized', in Birgit Abels (ed.), *Embracing Restlessness: Cultural Musicology* (Hildesheim: Georg Olms Verlag, forthcoming).

—— *Musical Beauty: Negotiating the Boundary between Subject and Object* (Eugene, Oreg.: Cascade Books, 2011).

Sulzer, Johann Georg, and Heinrich Christoph Koch, *Aesthetics and the Art of Musical Composition in the German Enlightenment: Selected Writings of Johann Georg Sulzer and Heinrich Christoph Koch*, trans. and ed. Nancy Kovaleff Baker and Thomas Street Christensen, Cambridge Studies in Music Theory and Analysis (Cambridge and New York: Cambridge University Press, 1995).

Tamminga, Douwe A., 'Boartsje en spylje', *Op 'e taelhelling* 2 (1973): 37–9.

Taruskin, Richard, *The Oxford History of Western Music*, 5 vols (New York: Oxford University Press, 2010).

—— *Stravinsky and the Russian Traditions: A Biography of the Works Through Mavra*, 2 vols (Berkeley: University of California Press, 1996).

Taylor, Charles, 'Closed World Structures', in Mark A. Wrathall (ed.), *Religion after Metaphysics* (Cambridge: Cambridge University Press, 2003).

—— *A Secular Age* (Cambridge, Mass. and London: Belknap Press of Harvard University Press, 2007).

Thayer, Alexander Wheelock, *Life of Beethoven*, ed. Elliot Forbes, 2 vols (Princeton, NJ: Princeton University Press, 1964).

Thietmar of Merseburg, *Die Chronik des Bischofs Thietmar von Merseburg und ihre Korveier Überarbeitung*, ed. Robert Holtzmann, Monumenta Germaniae Historica: Scriptores rerum Germanicarum, NS 9 (Berlin, 1955).

Thomas, Downing A., *Music and the Origins of Language: Theories from the French Enlightenment* (Cambridge: Cambridge University Press, 1995).

Tice, Terrence N., *Schleiermacher* (Nashville, Tenn.: Abingdon Press, 2006).

Tieck, Ludwig, 'Symphonien', in W.H. Wackenroder, *Werke und Briefe* (Heidelberg: L. Schneider, 1967).

Tilley, Christopher, *Body and Image*, Explorations in Landscape Phenomenology 2 (Walnut Creek, Calif.: Left Coast Press, 2008).

Tillich, Paul, 'Rechtfertigung und Zweifel (1924)', in *Gesammelte Werke*, vol. 8: *Offenbarung und Glaube: Schriften zur Theologie II*, ed. Renate Albrecht (Stuttgart: Evangelisches Verlagswerk, 1970).

—— *The System of the Sciences: According to Objects and Methods*, trans. Paul Wiebe (East Brunswick, NJ: Bucknell University Press, 1981).

—— 'Das Wesen der Bildung und das Bildungsideal (1926)', in *Ergänzungs- und Nachlassbände zu den Gesammelten Werken von Paul Tillich*, vol. 11: *Religion, Kultur, Gesellschaft: Unveröffentlichte Texte aus der deutschen Zeit (1908–1933)*, ed. Erdmann Sturm, Pt 2 (Berlin: De Gruyter, 1999).

—— *What is Religion?*, ed. James Luther Adams (New York: Harper & Row, 1969).

Topp, Leslie, *Architecture and Truth in Fin-de-Siècle Vienna* (Cambridge: Cambridge University Press, 2004).

Treitler, Leo, *With Voice and Pen: Coming to Know Medieval Song and How It was Made* (Oxford: Oxford University Press, 2003).

Tymoczko, Dmitri, *The Geometry of Music Harmony and Counterpoint in the Extended Common Practice* (Oxford: Oxford University Press, 2011).

Vereinigung Bildender Künstler Österreichs [VBKÖ], *XIV Ausstellung der Vereinigung bildender Künstler Österreichs Secession Wien*, 'Klinger: Beethoven Exhibition' catalogue (Vienna: Adolf Holzhausen, 1902).

Vial, Theodore, 'Anschauung and Intuition, Again (Or, "We Remain Bound to the Earth")', in Brent W. Sockness and Wilhelm Gräb (eds), *Schleiermacher, the Study of Religion, and the Future of Theology: A Transatlantic Dialogue* (New York and Berlin: De Gruyter, 2010).

Vroom, Hendrik M., *A Spectrum of Worldviews: An Introduction to Philosophy of Religion in a Pluralistic World* (Amsterdam and New York: Rodopi, 2006).

Wackenroder, Wilhelm Heinrich, *Confessions and Fantasies*, trans. Mary Hurst Schubert (University Park: Pennsylvania State University Press, 1971).

—— *Werke und Briefe* (Heidelberg: L. Schneider, 1967).

—— and Ludwig Tieck, *Outpourings of an Art-Loving Friar*, trans. Edward Mornin (New York: Frederick Ungar, 1975).

Wagner, Richard, 'The Art-Work of the Future', in *Richard Wagner's Prose Works*, trans. William Ashton-Ellis, vol. 1 (London: Kegan Paul, 1895).

—— 'Beethoven', trans. William Ashton-Ellis, in Richard Wagner, *Actors and Singers* (Lincoln: University of Nebraska Press, 1995).

—— *Gesammelte Schriften und Dichtungen*, 10 vols (Leipzig, E.W. Fritzsch, 1887).

Walton, John H., *The Lost World of Genesis One: Ancient Cosmology and the Origins Debate* (Downers Grove, Ill.: IVP Academic, 2009).

—— *Genesis*, NIV Application Commentary (Grand Rapids, Mich.: Zondervan, 2001).

Ward, Graham, 'Review Article: George Steiner's *Real Presences*', *Journal of Literature and Theology*, 4/2 (1990): 226–38.

Waters, Simon, 'Touching at a Distance: Resistance, Tactility, Proxemics and the Development of a Hybrid Virtual/Physical Performance System', *Contemporary Music Review*, 32/2–3 (2013): 119–34.

We are Women, We are Strong (Sheffield: Sheffield Women Against Pit Closures, 1987).

Weisberg, Richard H., 'Der Man Missing Nietzsche: *Hinzugedichtet* Revisited', in Clayton Koelb (ed.), *Nietzsche as Post-Modernist: Essays Pro and Contra* (Albany: State University of New York Press, 1990).

Wellmer, Albrecht, 'On Spirit as Part of Nature', *Constellations*, 16/2 (2009): 213–26.

Williams, Paul, 'Some Mahayana Buddhist Perspectives on the Body', in Sarah Coakley (ed.), *Religion and the Body* (Cambridge: Cambridge University Press, 1997).

Williams, Rowan, and Mike Higton (eds), *Wrestling with Angels: Conversations in Modern Theology* (Grand Rapids, Mich.: Eerdmans, 2007).

Williamson, John, 'The Musical Artwork and Its Materials in the Music and Aesthetics of Busoni', in Michael Talbot (ed.), *The Musical Work: Reality or Invention?* (Liverpool: Liverpool University Press, 2000).

Wilson, John Elbert, *Introduction to Modern Theology: Trajectories in the German Tradition* (Louisville, Ky.: Westminster John Knox Press, 2007).

Wittekind, Folkart, '"… die Musik meiner Religion": Schleiermachers ethische Funktionalisierung der Musik bis zur "Weihnachtsfeier" und seine Kritik der frühromantischen Kunstreligion', in Ulrich Barth, Andreas Arndt and Wilhelm Gräb (eds), *Christentum – Staat – Kultur: Akten des Kongresses der Internationalen Schleiermacher gesellschaft, Berlin, März 2006* (Berlin: De Gruyter, 2008).

—— 'Die Vision der Gesellschaft und die Bedeutung religiöser Kommunikation. Schleiermachers Kritik am Atheismusstreit als Leitmotiv der "Reden"', in Ulrich Barth and Claus-Dieter Osthövener (eds), *200 Jahre 'Reden über die Religion': Akten des 1. Internationalen Kongresses der Schleiermacher Gesellschaft, Halle, 14.–17. März 1999* (Berlin: De Gruyter, 2000).

Wittgenstein, Ludwig, *The Blue and Brown Books* (Oxford: Blackwell, 1958).

—— *Culture and Value* (Oxford: Blackwell, 1980).

—— *Tractatus Logico-Philosophicus* (London: Routledge, 1974).

Wolf, Richard K., 'The Poetics of "Sufi" Practice: Drumming, Dancing and Complex Agency at Mado Lal Husain and Beyond', *American Ethnologist*, 33/2 (2006): 246–68.

Wolfson, Elliot R., 'Weeping, Death and Spiritual Ascent in Sixteenth-Century Jewish Mysticism', in John Corrigan (ed.), *Religion and Emotion: Approaches and Interpretations* (New York: Oxford University Press, 2004).

Wörtche, Thomas, 'Hoffmanns Erzählungen von der Musik: Einige Distinktionen', *Mitteilungen der E.T.A. Hoffmann-Gesellschaft*, 33 (1987): 13–33.

Wrathall, Mark, *Heidegger and Unconcealment: Truth, Language, and History* (Cambridge: Cambridge University Press, 2011).

Wyatt, Henry Drew, 'Aspects of Sublime Rhetoric in Eighteenth-Century Music' (PhD thesis: Rutgers University, 2000).

Yearsley, David, 'C.P.E. Bach and the Living Tradition of Learned Counterpoint', in Annette Richards (ed.), *C.P.E. Bach Studies* (Cambridge and New York: Cambridge University Press, 2006).

Yeston, Maury (ed.), *Readings in Schenker Analysis and Other Approaches* (New Haven, Conn.: Yale University Press, 1977).

Zweig, Stefan, *The World of Yesterday* (London: University of Nebraska Press, 1964).

Index